the japanese film

dedicated to
that little
band of men
who have
tried to
make the
japanese
film industry
what every
film industry
should be:
a directors'
cinema

the Japanese
Film: art and industry
(expanded edition)

by
joseph l. anderson
and
donald richie

with a foreword by
akira kurosawa

princeton university press
princeton, new jersey

First Tuttle Edition, 1959
First Evergreen Edition, 1960
First Princeton Paperback printing, 1982

LCC 81-47985
ISBN 0-691-05351-0
ISBN 0-691-00792-6 pbk.

Printed in the United States of America
by Princeton University Press,
Princeton, New Jersey

9 8 7 6 5 4

table of contents

list of plates

New plates for the 1982 edition are located on pages
429 to 436.

foreword

by AKIRA KUROSAWA

IT IS NOT too much to say, I think, that the Japanese cinema has now come to world-wide attention. For this fact all of us here in the industry are pleased and grateful. Personally, I am proud and happy if it has been partially through work of mine that this interest and attention has been aroused.

Yet, though pleased, happy, and proud, many of us within the industry have come to feel that, while apparently liking what it has seen, the West actually knows all too little of both Japan and the Japanese cinema as they really are.

In 1951, when I received the Venice prize for *Rashomon,* I remarked that I would have been still happier, and the prize would have had more meaning, if I had made and been honored for something showing as much of present-day Japan as *Bicycle Thieves* showed of modern Italy. And to-day I still feel the same at I did then, because Japan produces contemporary-life films of the caliber of the De Sica picture at the same time that it also produces those period-films, exceptional and otherwise, that in large part are all the West has seen and continues to see of Japanese cinema.

For this reason I am pleased to be writing the foreword for this book, the first full study of the Japanese film to appear in any foreign language. For one thing, such a book is needed, if only to correct the foreign impression that the

Japanese film is merely technicolored exoticism. For another, I—as a director—cannot help but share the authors' view that it is, in any country, in any film industry, only the work of a dedicated few that is responsible for whatever of enduring value that country's film art may have.

This has been just as true in Japan as anywhere else. All of us who try to do our best have done so in the face of opposition, and, for me at any rate, it is most pleasant to find these authors dealing so honestly and candidly with all the difficulties that we of the industry have faced over these many years and must still face today.

Finally, as a creator, I am particularly pleased that the authors of this book—unlike the authors of many books on the motion pictures, who often seem to shirk their responsibilities as critics in favor of mere reportage—take a firm stand for what they believe right and good. In the first section of the book, they give an impartial and objective account of the history of the Japanese film; and, in the latter section, they turn their attention, as responsible critics, to the more intangible, but perhaps even more important, aspects of the art and the industry, particularly as these exist today. Since the standards they here reveal are those which we also hold, I consider it both fitting and fortunate that it is they who are introducing the true Japanese cinema to the West.

Tokyo, April, 1959

authors' foreword

TEN YEARS AGO this book would never have been written; there was a need for it but no audience. That there is more of a need now not only reflects the increased excellence of Japanese films during the past decade but also the world-wide interest which this excellence has aroused. One of the last film industries to create a national style, the Japanese is now one of the last to retain it.

A major point this book will attempt to make is that, long before *Rashomon*, the Japanese cinema had attained a level which deserved but did not receive international attention. It was far in advance of many motion-picture industries and could have compared favorably with any in Europe or America. The products of this period went necessarily unnoticed in the West, however, and at this late date will never be seen.

As always, these really fine Japanese films, like the fine films of any country, were made and continue to be made in the teeth of commercial restriction and top-level indifference. They are created *despite* the proven formulas which are so insisted upon in the vast film factories in which they are made; they are never created *because* of them.

And, as in any country, fine films are possible because of the dedication and bravery of a few men: some directors, some producers, some writers, some crew and cast members.

These matters will, we trust, become apparent in the pages that follow, and the reader will find in the history of the Japanese film a definite parallel with the other film industries —repeating yet again the tragedy of the commercial film. There are differences to be sure, but the similarities will seem surprising to those few who may still believe that the Japanese turn out nothing but films of the caliber of those of Kurosawa, Kinoshita, Ozu, or Mizoguchi.

This excellence in the work of a few dedicated persons, however, is such that it alone kept the authors sufficiently inspired during the extended preparations for this book; it is this that makes the Japanese cinema worthy of the closest study, and that renders the world's ignorance of the Japanese film before 1950 one of cinema's most melancholy tragedies.

The authors' interest in Japanese films extends well before the overseas recognition of the Japanese cinema; materials were being gathered for this work as early as 1947, though the book itself was written between 1956 and 1959. The authors' sources include not only documents and written materials relating to the subject, not only talks with persons involved in or concerned with Japanese films, but also their viewing and reviewing of more than five hundred features from every period of the industry's history.

The division of labor was that Anderson did most of the basic research for the book and Richie did most of the final writing. Naturally, these two functions frequently overlapped. The raw material for the historical section of the book was largely provided by the former, while both authors contributed material for the critique which forms the second half of the book. The attitudes, the critical standards, the ideas in the book are shared by both authors. Since both are fundamentally agreed upon the basic worth of the cinema and just what this worth consists of—a judgment which will become apparent to the reader—this volume is a collaboration in the fullest sense of the word.

It could not have been finished, however, without the various assistance which the authors received and without the cooperation extended by individuals both within the industry and not. The authors are particularly grateful to the late Tokutaro Osawa, of the *Eiga Hyoron*, whose interest was invaluable in the verification of obscure facts, in the compilation of research bibliographies, and in all-round encouragement. The authors would also like to thank Mr. Hisamitsu Noguchi, of Towa Film, for his very great assistance during the collection of stills for this volume, and Mr. Kiyoaki Murata for his equally great help in proofreading this book and for many helpful suggestions. To this, Joseph Anderson would particularly like to add his acknowledgment of all the direct and indirect help given

him by his wife, Sadako, and to thank both her and their
daughter, Ehry Jane, for the many sacrifices they made to help make this book possible.

Finally, the authors should like to credit, with thanks, the following sources for the stills here reproduced: Hisamitsu Noguchi for Stills 1–42, 44, 46–47, 50–55, 58–59, 61, 63–69, 71, and 72; Tamon Miki of the Tokyo Museum of Modern Art, 43, 49, and 56; Yasujiro Ozu, 70; Keisuke Kinoshita, 73 and 75; Mikio Naruse, 45 and 48; Akira Kurosawa, 76; Heinosuke Gosho, 107; Akira Iwasaki, 100, 103, and 120; the Kokusai Bunka Shinkokai, 57, 60, and 62; Toho, 74, 78–79, 91, 101–2, 108–9, 112–13, 116, 118, 122, 128–29, 132, 136–37, 139, 141 and 144; Shochiku, 77, 80, 83–84, 87–88, 90, 93, 99, 110, 119, 121, 130, 133, 138, 140, and 142; Daiei, 82, 85, 92, 94, 96–97, 104, 106, 126–27, 131, and 143; Shintoho, 81, 86, 89, 95, 105, and 117; Toei, 98, 111, and 134; and Nikkatsu, 114–15 and 123–24.

Since a number of Japanese words and technical terms have been necessary in this work, the authors have compiled a combination glossary-index, so that the reader may refresh his memory without turning back to the original explanation given in the text itself. In the captions for the photographs, unless otherwise indicated, the actors are identified reading from left to right. Throughout the book, Japanese names have been given in the Western fashion, that is, the family name appearing last.

1959

IT IS NOT often that authors have the opportunity to expand their material and review their ideas twenty-three years after the original publication of their work. It is also unusual that a film history this old should be thought worth republication. While we are happy about both events, we also feel that the primary reason is that no subsequent work has superseded ours. There has been in this near quarter-century further study of the Japanese film but an updated and more comprehensive history has unfortunately not appeared outside Japan.

This revised edition is not the totally new and updated version that would be ideal. It is a photographic reprint of the original work with two new essays and other material. Anderson in his essay expands upon a few of the topics that need reconsideration: a new evaluation of the *benshi*, an overview of the peculiar qualities of the *jidai-geki* megagenre, a discussion of the influences of American Bluebird Photoplays and Shiro Kido on the Japanese cinema, and a historical section that summarizes the rise of television. Richie, in his essay, extensively reviews the artistic achievements of the past two decades and discusses many new talents. Both authors, along the way, correct some minor errors of fact and proportion.

While the treatment of the years 1960–1982 is less complete than that for 1896–1959, a volume nearly as large as the original would have been needed, along with several years for research and adequate reconsideration. This has not been feasible.

In making this new edition possible, we are grateful to all who commented upon and in a few instances corrected our original work over the years. We are very appreciative of the help given us by the Japan Film Library Council in collecting new skills for this edition. We remain always grateful for the help and encouragement given us and our work by the late Nagamasa Kawakita and his wife, Madame Kashiko Kawakita.

Anderson thanks the Japan Foundation for support of research which has been partially incorporated into his essay.

1982

part one

background

1 **slow fade-in:**
1896-1917. THE HISTORY OF
the film in Japan began, as in
many countries, with the Edison
Kinetoscope, a. kind of peep-
show apparatus into which one peered through the top and,
by turning a crank, caused George Eastman's recently per-
fected nitro-cellulose film to move noisily past the eyepiece.
The Kinetoscope had been first shown in New York in
1894, and two years later the Japanese, eager for novelty,
imported several.

The time was ripe for novelty. The victorious conclusion
of the Sino-Japanese War in 1895 had finally proved that
Japan could adjust to the modern civilization which less
than fifty years earlier had arrived knocking at the closed
gates of the country in the person of Commodore Perry.

The long reign of the Emperor Meiji, 1868 to 1912, was
an era of rapid commercial expansion. By 1890 there were
two hundred large steam factories where twenty years earlier
there had been none; steamship tonnage increased from
15,000 to over 1,500,000 tons in the period between 1893 and
1905; and by 1896 things Western were in full fashion though
only three decades before incautious foreigners had been
waylaid and murdered. The lunar calendar had only recently
been relinquished, yet by 1896 interest in the West was so
extreme that derbies or straw boaters were worn with formal
kimono, the big gold pocket-watch was tucked into the obi,
and spectacles, whether needed or not, were esteemed as a
sign of learning.

The Kinetoscope's popularity was cut short by an even
greater novelty when, in 1897, the brothers Lumière sent

over a Cinématographe Lumière and a mixed bill of films
including *Baignade en Mer* and *L'Arrivée d'un Train en Gare.*
The French invention was followed within a few days by
the Edison Vitascope, which offered such spectacles as *The
Death of Mary Queen of Scots* and *Feeding Pigeons.*

In contrast to the one-man Kinetoscope, both these later
machines projected moving pictures on a screen. They
were enormously popular with Japanese, who, like most people, are more given to gregarious than solitary amusements.
The crown prince, later the Emperor Taisho, graced a
Vitascope performance with his presence, and soon thousands
of Japanese were conversant with the manner in which Mary
lost her head and what French ladies wore or did not wear
when bathing.

The novelty was so great that even the relatively high
price of admission failed to keep the crowds away. For the
"special seats" at the Kanda Kinki-kan, a legitimate theater
taken over for Vitascope showings in Tokyo in 1897, an
equivalent of ninety cents was charged, while "upper-class"
and "middle-class" seats were available at forty-five and
twelve cents respectively. General admission was nine cents,
and "students and the military" were admitted at half this
price. Pictures continued to be shown at the same admission
scale for the next decade. Unlike in other countries, the very
first motion pictures in Japan were not the theater of the
poor but rather of the well-to-do who were interested in
the Occident.

The audience got more than its money's worth in terms
of time spent in the theater. There were usually two showings
daily, at two and at seven, and though the actual footage
seen at any one showing seldom took more than a total of
twenty minutes to project, the show itself went on for two
or even three hours. For one thing, just changing the reels
required time since, for the first seven or eight years, some
installations insisted that a crew of ten people was necessary
to run one projector. There was a handle-turner to crank
the film through the machine, a lens-focuser, a reel-rewinding
man, a man to look at the screen and make sure everything
was going well, a man to adjust the carbon arcs, a man to
thread the machine between reels, a general supervisor, a
boy to fan those working around the hot projector, and
several others whose duties were not specified.

Time had to be spent in other ways too. According to a
contemporary eyewitness, during one theater's early showings water was poured on the screen after every reel in order

to cool it off and prevent its catching fire from the hot light
thrown from the projection booth. There were also the clapping boards, the *hyoshigi*, taken over from the Kabuki and the Shimpa theaters, which were banged together to herald each new reel some minutes in advance. And finally there was the greatest time-taker of all—the *benshi*.

The *benshi* was so important to the early films and has played such a major rôle in the history of the films in Japan, his influence continuing even to this day, that an understanding of what he did and why is basic to any understanding of Japanese movies. Essentially, he explained. He was somewhat like the lecturer who used to appear with travel films in the West, introducing the film by telling you what you were going to see and then, as the film progressed, telling you what you were seeing. The Japanese, then as now, were constantly afraid of missing a point, of not understanding everything, and demanded a complete explanation. This the *benshi* gave them, usually expanding his services to the extent of explaining the obvious.

Historically, the antecedents of the *benshi* have a very definite place in Japanese theatrical history. Both the Kabuki and the Bunraku, or doll-drama, have *joruri* or *nagauta*, a form of musical accompaniment or commentary consisting of reciters and musicians who sit upon platforms at the side of the stage, explaining, interpolating, and vocally acting out the play. There are also the traditional theatrical storytellers who still exist in the *yose*, the indigenous form of vaudeville.

The *benshi* came to be used with films in a logical enough manner. Lantern-slide shows had been touring Japan from 1886, and as early as 1893 an Italian had brought something called a "kinematograph show" to Nagasaki. Since this form of entertainment has always needed explanation, someone had to comment during the viewing. The same thing was being done in the West during the 1890's when projected lantern slides were offered with live narration. In France, too, a kind of master-of-ceremonies, called a *compère*, was used at early film showings.

When the movies came, the West dropped its equivalent of the *benshi*, but Japan still felt the need for someone to explain. For one thing, the audience was not sure how the projector worked, and this they had to be told, since the ordinary Japanese, unfailingly curious, is usually interested in machinery. Furthermore, Japan has a theatrical convention of treating the necessary mechanics as a part of the perform-

ance itself, as in the Kabuki, where sets are changed with
the curtain up. This interest in the machine rather than in the content of the film shown was most apparent when one of the early showmen placed his projector at the right side of the stage and the screen at the left. Most of the spectators, if they could see the screen at all, viewed it quite obliquely, but at least they had an excellent view of the projection crew in action.

These early films were usually one-minute scenes of life abroad, and the Japanese, despite their straw boaters, gold watches, and spectacles, were naturally ill-informed as to the countries of which they were now enjoying fugitive glimpses. If there had been no explanation during, say, *The Czar's Arrival in Paris*, the audience would have had no way of knowing that the ruler was the man inside the carriage and not the one in the superior position up on the roof.

From the very first the *benshi* tended to dominate the film and, since the audience liked to be instructed, he would rarely let an opportunity slip by; sometimes, running out of more cogent material, he would fall back on such remarks as: "You will kindly note that the smoke comes from the chimney. Also notice dark clouds are in the sky: rain is coming." After the initial novelty of the early showings and when it seemed that the movies had come to Japan to stay, the *benshi* as a matter of course stayed too.

As his popularity grew so did his importance. In the larger theaters a fanfare would sound before every show—from the simple flute and drum of the earliest film showings a full Western-style orchestra with *samisen* had evolved—and the *benshi* would enter with great dignity to sit on his platform beside the screen. There was applause, and in the tense moments before the film began, the audience would call out the *benshi*'s nickname in the manner of Kabuki audiences shouting to a favored actor. While the names used in the Kabuki are more or less formal, those favored by the movie audience were often "Big Mouth" or "Fish Face," for the spectators plainly felt on fairly intimate terms with their beloved *benshi*.

The more famous had different techniques and sometimes differed widely in interpreting the same film. When dramatic pictures became more common, seeing the same picture with a different *benshi* often gave the effect of an entirely new movie. After 1910, films were sometimes distributed with a "dialogue" script for the *benshi* to use, but he was not re-quired to be particularly faithful to it and quite often was not. The only things that remained the same, no matter the film or the *benshi*, were the characters' names in foreign films. The heroine was almost always Mary, the hero was Jim, and the villain was usually called Robert. Even in historical dramas there would come riding a chivalrous knight in shining armor called Jim.

Eventually the *benshi* rather than the film became the box-office attraction. After the arrival of the story film and the star system, film advertising was showing the *benshi*'s name in larger characters than those used for the title of the film, the stars, or the director. His pay became equivalent to that of the highest paid Japanese film actor, and his position was further secured by the producers and distributors, who liked the *benshi*, saying he saved the cost of printing titles.

In the West, even in these early days, film-makers were searching for more and more pictorial ways of presenting a story, since titles alone could not hold a picture together. In Japan, however, no one searched. If there were breaks in the continuity, the *benshi* could fill in. Thus, from the very beginning, Japanese movies were dependent upon the *benshi* and even later remained subordinate to him.

Even though he has now had his day and no longer exists at all except as a picturesque and rather self-conscious addition to silent films shown on television, the influence of the *benshi* continues. In most foreign films where strange languages are spoken—native dialect in African films or American Indian speech—the dialogue is usually subtitled in Japanese, though in most countries audiences are not given any indication of what is being said, the language being treated merely as local color. And since important plot points are also carried in the original language, the Japanese get the same point twice: once in translation from the Bantu or the Sioux, and then in translation from the original French or English.

Even now, almost a quarter-century after the long-protracted death of the *benshi*, the ghost of this lecturer-explainer-commentator is still around. When *Man of a Thousand Faces* was shown, all of the hand language used by the mutes in the film was subtitled. For Cousteau's *Le Monde du Silence*, the Japanese insisted upon superimposing the names of all the fish, even in the straight lyrical sequences where there was no narration at all. The fact that the titles were so scientific that very few in the audience could even read them disturbed no one. When *The Spirit of Saint Louis* was reaching its climax—an exhausted Lindbergh high over

Paris—attention was called from the hero's plight by subtitles superimposed over the aerial shots: "Place de Concorde," "Notre Dame," "Arc de Triomphe." The spirit of the *benshi* is still very near.

The first motion-picture camera was imported from France in 1897 as a commercial speculation by a Kyoto muslin textile company. Unfortunately, the exposed film was ruined on its trip back to France, where it was being sent for processing as there were as yet no developing facilities in Japan, and it was not until the next year that Japanese audiences were treated to movies actually made in their own country.

These first Japanese-made films were the work of Tsune-kichi Shibata, of Mitsukoshi Department Store's newly formed photographic department. They included street scenes taken in the Ginza, Tokyo's most fashionable shopping district, and shots of geisha from Tokyo's Shimbashi and Kyoto's Gion districts. Shibata also turned to Kabuki and, in a teahouse in the theater district, filmed some scenes from the Kabuki version of the Noh drama *Maple Viewing* (Momiji-gari) starring both Kikugoro V and Danjuro IX. Somewhat later Shibata also filmed sections of yet another Kabuki dance, *Two People at Dojo Temple* (Ni-nin Dojo-ji). Having been made as historical records rather than for immediate showing, these films were not publicly viewed until 1904, after Kikugoro's death. Shibata's street scenes, however, were shown with great success at the Kabuki-za, Tokyo's most important theater.

Following Shibata's successful lead, others began entering the field. Among these was Shiro Asano, of the Konishiroku Photographic Store. At the request of a Shimpa troupe that desired publicity he filmed the climax of one of their current plays, *Scene of the Lightning Robber's Being Arrested* (Ina-zuma Goto Hobaku no Ba). This was first shown in 1899, at the Tokyo Engi-za, a theater which showed Shimpa by day and foreign films by night. It featured the actor Umpei Yokoyama, who is still in the films, now playing grandfather rôles, and proved so successful as an advertisement that it was followed by several more Shimpa excerpts.

With movies having soon achieved a considerable success in Japan, it was not long before they began to attain a more professional status. In 1903 the first permanently constructed full-sized theater to be devoted entirely to films, the Denki-kan, or Electric Theater, was built in Asakusa,

Tokyo's amusement district, several years before America and England broke away from store-front nickelodeons.

The Japanese were looking abroad as well. The Yoshizawa Company, which had initially imported Lumière's Cinématographe and later many of the Méliès films, opened a London office in 1902, and two years later Kenichi Kawaura, owner of the company, took films which his production department had made of the Russo-Japanese War to show at the St. Louis International Exposition. Along with these he also showed films of Japanese scenery, Mt. Fuji, geisha, and the like. After an extensive tour of America, Kawaura visited the Edison and Lubin studios, staying to learn their techniques. When he returned to Japan in 1908 he said that the most important thing he had learned was that to make films one must have a permanent studio. He bought some land in Meguro, a section of Tokyo which was then still country, built himself a villa in emulation of Méliès, and erected a studio in the garden, copying the design of the Edison Bronx studios.

Initially, the business of the Yoshizawa and Yokota companies, the two pioneer Japanese film producers, was making movies for the various Shimpa dramatic companies. In such an arrangement, the dramatic troupe would provide both script and actors. Each of these one-reelers took from four hours to three days to shoot. Occasionally a complete movie was turned out before lunch: having afternoon matinees, the actors were free only in the morning.

There were no real directors, although men who were called directors read the *benshi* dialogue aloud while the actors blocked out their own business. This actually was not so difficult as it sounds because, since the camera position never moved, the actors knew they were perfectly all right so long as they stayed within carefully indicated sight lines. The films themselves were shot in the strictest continuity, and when the end of a roll of film was reached the "director" would call out "Hold it!" and everyone would freeze into position until the camera was reloaded, an operation which took from five to thirty minutes.

One of the things these early productions did was to create their half of the *rensa-geki,* or "chain-drama," which had appeared as early as 1904, first become popular in 1908 when *O-Tomi Stabbed* (Kirare O-Tomi) was given in Tokyo, and later had an entire theater, the Asakusa Opera-kan, devoted to it. This was a stage drama which used film as an adjunct, the novelty and popularity of the movies being

such that a few Shimpa troupes decided to take advantage
of them for purposes other than advertising. This they did
by having the outdoor scenes of the drama filmed and then
inserting them into the stage play. Thus, after an interior
scene was played on the theater's stage, a screen was dis-
closed and an outdoor scene projected. Occasionally the
actors were actually behind the screen, reciting lines in an
attempt to match the lip movement of their images on the
screen, thus creating a somewhat crude dubbing effect.
Later on, if the drama had been popular enough, the indoor
scenes were also filmed. Then everything was spliced together and released as a feature film. This hybrid form
proved quite popular and as late as 1922 could still be seen
in rural areas.

In the meantime, in addition to Kawaura's Yoshizawa
Company and Einosuke Yokota's company, a third, called
M. Pathe, had been formed in 1905 by Shokichi Umeya.
After having been involved in various unprofitable business
ventures, Umeya decided to go to China, where he became
interested in the still-photography business. He was making
money until the local police became interested in his Chinese-
republican revolutionary activities, after which he found
Singapore somewhat more congenial. There he put up a tent
theater and showed films he had purchased from the Singapore Pathé office. When he returned to Japan he brought
back one of these films, a spectacle in full hand-painted
color, and with profits from its exhibition opened up Japan's
third producing company. Without Pathé's permission or
knowledge and despite the fact that Yokota was the actual
importer of Pathé films into Japan, he borrowed name and
reputation, added an M. for distinction, and formed the M.
Pathe Company.

Gathering together as much capital as he could, Umeya
rented the largest drama theaters in Tokyo, devised a technique of complete exploitation, including pretty usherettes,
and went into business in a big way. He charged high
prices—on a scale from twenty to sixty cents the performance
—plowed back all profits into his company, and was very
soon a worthy rival to the two older companies. Even though
a large amount of Umeya's profits were eventually diverted
to support Chinese political exiles living in Japan, among
them a close friend and former student at Japan's Military
Academy, Chiang Kai-shek, he managed to build studios in
the outskirts of Tokyo and turn out such costume spectacles as the 1908 *Dawn at the Soga Brothers' Hunting*

Grounds (Soga Kyodai Kariba no Akebono). Accompanied by a full orchestra and singers as well, this film starred an all-girl Kabuki troupe. Despite the success of this effort, Umeya ran into difficulties when he attempted some experiments in speech synchronization on records. The militantly entrenched *benshi* proved too powerful for him; and, later, when his company tried to make subtitled films that eliminated the need for *benshi* narration, these too failed.

It was difficult to interest an audience in a film that relied entirely on titles, and the art of editing had not yet been developed in Japan, though a 1909 film, *The Cuckoo—New Version* (Shin Hototogisu), directed by Shisetsu Iwafuji, introduced the first use of the flashback in Japan just a year or two after D.W. Griffith had begun his important experiments in technique. Most important of all reasons for the failure of these pictures which tried to advance beyond the primitive was that the audience still came to hear the *benshi* and not to see the film. In fact, the only time when his triumph was incomplete was when the projector broke down. The audience always thought this the fault of the *benshi*, since the responsibility for everything else was so plainly his, and he was forced into abject apologies.

Even famous actors were no competition to the *benshi*. Immediately after the introduction of the movies, a few of Japan's leading stage actors consented to being filmed for the purpose of documentation, but they soon began to show resentment both because of their traditional class-consciousness and because they felt that films were an inferior rival to the stage. In addition, there was the definite antagonism of the various leagues of theater managers who prohibited their actors from appearing in films, thinking that if an actor were to be seen in the movies no one would come to see him on the stage.

The situation was somewhat different in other countries. In America, Adolph Zukor was able to prove that filmed theater, with its "famous players" and its disregard for truly cinematic techniques, could make money and achieve a highbrow reputation. And in France the stagy *film d'art* was already returning the young and growing art to its awkward infancy. In Japan, however, the cinema had not even left the cradle.

Thus there were no such innovations in Japan, though about 1910 there was talk of a widescreen process that would require a screen "running the width of a Kabuki stage...a gigantic projection thirty-six feet across encom-

passing the four compass directions." Such stimulus, however, was scarcely needed. Money was rolling in and the
field of film-making was becoming crowded.

In 1909 the Fukuhodo theater chain in Tokyo was so
successful that in little over a year it had eight well-
constructed reinforced-concrete houses. Soon after, this chain
decided to make its own films and thus formed Japan's fourth
production company.

With the field becoming competitive, Umeya had been
running into financial difficulties and, upon hearing details
of the Motion Picture Patents Company in the United States,
began to think of incorporating the four Japanese companies
into one big million-dollar trust. (The American trust, formed
in 1909, comprised the seven most important American
companies, the U.S. branches of two big French companies,
and one importer. They contracted with Eastman Kodak to
sell raw film stock to their group only and taxed all exhibitors
two dollars per film. Through their exclusive control of the
manufacture of projectors and cameras plus their recourse
to strong-arm men, they tried to monopolize all motion
picture production and restrict all exhibition to their films
only.) When Kawaura of the Yoshizawa Company was approached by Umeya with this project, he was inclined to
relinquish control of his company because he too had been
having his troubles. His Luna Park in Asakusa had just burned
down, as also had two of his Osaka theaters. He sold out to
the new combine for the equivalent of $375,000 and retired
from the film business.

The trust was formed in imitation of its American counterpart and was named the Greater Japan Film Machinery Manufacturing Company, Limited. Unlike the Motion Picture
Patents Company, however, the Japanese company had no
connection with the manufacturing of projectors or cameras,
which were still being imported from abroad, though a few
small machine shops, unconnected with the trust, were turning out projector parts. Einosuke Yokota, founder of one
of the first two film companies and the original importer of
Lumière's Cinématographe, became director and later president of the trust. Kisaburo Kobayashi, owner of the Fukuhodo chain, became head of the business department. In 1912
it became the Nippon Katsudo Shashin (Japan Cinemat-
ograph Company), which was in turn soon shortened to
Nikkatsu, today Japan's oldest motion-picture company.
Umeya, more a revolutionary than a film-maker, left Japan
in 1912 and went to China to join Sun Yat-sen's revolution.

The new company had four studios—the former Yoshizawa, M. Pathe, and Fukuhodo studios in Tokyo, and the
former Yokota studio in Kyoto—as well as seventy permanent
theaters all over the country. It shortly abandoned the three
small studios to build a big new one near Tokyo's Asakusa.
This new Mukojima studio specialized in producing dramas
with contemporary settings, called Shimpa because both
stories and actors were borrowed from the young, popular
stage movement of that name, while the Kyoto studios produced costume drama, soon dubbed Kyuha, or "old school,"
in contrast to Shimpa, meaning "new school."

The Shimpa, itself a theatrical outgrowth of the Meiji
revolt against the old, had been created by the Kabuki's
inability to present plays in contemporary settings. Originally
serving to publicize liberal and anti-feudalistic political aims,
it was essentially a theatrical compromise which, though it
searched, never succeeded in finding a realistic approach. It
retained such institutions as the *oyama* (female impersonators)
and, though begun as revolutionary, soon developed a theatrical style almost as rigid as that of the Kabuki itself. Its
outlook became that of the half-modern Meiji era, just as
the Kabuki's was and is that of the preceding, feudalistic
Tokugawa era.

Before Nikkatsu was organized, the Yokota Company had
produced both a director and a star who, if by comparison
with those yet to come proved of no great intrinsic artistic
value, were at least better than anyone who had yet appeared.
Born in Kyoto in 1878, Shozo Makino, the director, was the
son of a soldier who, like D. W. Griffith's father, had been an
officer in the losing rebel faction of a civil war, the 1877 Kyushu rebellion. Makino, like his father, was deeply affected
by rebel prejudices, particularly against those involving "restoration and Westernization," and though his talent was
perhaps more organizational than artistic, he was the first
man to deserve the name of director in the Western sense
of the word.

The actor was Matsunosuke Onoue, who was born in 1875,
made his first appearance on the stage at the age of six, and
for about fifteen years worked in the provincial theaters of
Okayama. Makino discovered him in a tiny rural playhouse
and took him to the Kyoto theater he was then managing.
From the first he was impressed by Matsunosuke's lightness
and grace. He signed him on at double his previous pay,
paying him about forty dollars a month, and by 1909 had
made him famous in the Kyoto area. Two years before,

Makino had begun making occasional films for the Yokota Company, one-reelers for a directorial fee of fifteen dollars a reel. Because of Matsunosuke's sudden rise to local fame, Makino thought he would be good for films and asked Yokota to give him more directorial work. When Nikkatsu was formed, both Yokota and Makino became a part of the new organization.

Matsunosuke soon became phenomenally popular. He was, in fact, the only actor in the following decade who could be called a star in the modern sense of the word. He and Makino turned out eight features a month and at one time were under orders to make a reel a day. During the 1910's Matsunosuke's name was synonymous with costume pictures, and in these films he was always a wizard or some kind of supernatural hero who overcame all obstacles with magic and the greatest bravado. This was because Makino at that time liked to make trick films, somewhat in the manner of Méliès, the difference being that he discarded the painted backdrops and worked amidst natural settings. From 1909 to 1911 the two made 168 films together.

Makino as a director did very little to help the nascent cinema break with the *benshi* tradition in favor of the pictorial storytelling methods being introduced in the West. Though he was aware of the development of Western film techniques, he kept to the *benshi* illustration concept. He was, however, impressed with the faster pace of Western films and decided to quicken his own. It is perhaps typical of both Makino and his whole approach to the film that rather than increasing the tempo of the actors' playing, he merely had the camera cranked more slowly. In those days, to save film, cameras in Japan were usually cranked at twelve frames a second, rather than at the usual sixteen as in the West. Makino shot his at as low as eight frames a second, and when the films were projected the actors consequently scurried about in an enormous hurry. Much later, after 1920, Makino adopted a few of the new techniques from the West. As a producer, however, he subsequently backed men of talent who contributed much to the development of the costume drama.

Makino's 1913 version of *The Loyal Forty-seven Ronin* (Chushingura) reveals how severely the *benshi* limited the development of Japanese film technique. Griffith's films, for example, were known in Japan by this time, but Makino, the nation's first important director, completely ignored Griffith's editing concepts. His only innovation—actors occasionally playing directly into the camera in the manner of a television announcer—was scarcely even that because a first-person camera technique was far beyond his understanding. Until 1920 he kept his camera running without interruption through an entire sequence and never moved it from its front-on angle of a spectator at a stage play.

Nikkatsu, with a director and a very popular star, now had the field to itself, but not for long. In 1914 Kisaburo Kobayashi, who had brought the Fukuhodo chain into the trust, decided to withdraw. This he did, to form the rival company, Tennenshoku Katsudo Shashin (Natural Color Moving Picture Company), the name of which was soon shortened to Tenkatsu. He planned to make films using Kinemacolor, the English color process developed by Charles Urban and George Albert Smith, first publicly shown in London in 1909.

There had already been some little experimentation with color, many of the Shimpa films having been tinted for mood. Night scenes were colored orange in contradistinction to the bluish tints of the West, and spring scenes came out pink, to emphasize cherry blossoms. Since labor was cheap and delicate hand-painting a highly developed skill in Japan, movies in color—each frame painted individually—were also not unknown. The British process, on the other hand, was designed to photograph scenes in something resembling natural color. Ordinary black-and-white stock was used, and the color effect was obtained by two synchronized color filters rotating in front of both camera and projector. By the rapid alternation of red and green filters, coupled with the corresponding alternation of individual frames photographed with equivalent filters on the camera, a wide variety of colors was possible. To obtain the persistency of vision required for the two primary colors to combine properly, however, it was necessary that the film pass through the machine at twice normal speed—thirty-two frames a second.

Tenkatsu's first film, *Yoshitsune and the Thousand Cherry Trees* (Yoshitsune Sembon Zakura), had some success, but more experimentation was cut short by World War I and the resultant shortage of film. The company soon switched back to black-and-white since, for the same amount of raw stock necessary to make one Kinemacolor film, they could make two or more standard monochrome features.

Meanwhile the average film length had grown longer. Before 1911 few productions were more than one reel long, but as two-, three-, and four-reel pictures arrived from

Europe, the Japanese lengthened theirs too. The Italian two-hour *Quo Vadis* was shown in Japan in 1913, though an early M. Pathe film made sometime between 1909 and 1911 had already exceeded this length by forty-five minutes.

With new lengths came new techniques. In this Tenkatsu was ahead of Nikkatsu. It used close-ups and more cutting, while Nikkatsu retained lengthy long-shot set-ups. The average 1915 Nikkatsu film was about forty minutes long and had only from fifteen to thirty different camera set-ups, while those of Tenkatsu, averaging the same length, contained fifty to seventy shots.

The distribution methods of the companies, however, were much the same. Only three or four prints were made from the negative of the average film and these were shown and reshown until they literally fell apart. The used prints were then cut up and undamaged scenes from several films were spliced together to form a new movie. Japanese pictures were so alike in those days and the actors were so far from the camera that continuity was a small problem. Any big gaps were readily filled in by a clever *benshi*.

Tenkatsu's technical advance might logically have been expected to attract a larger public. But Nikkatsu continued to corner two-thirds of the market, mainly because theater owners were fully satisfied with Nikkatsu contracts. Certainly the Japanese audiences did not too much like what little they had seen of new cinematic methods, even though they had originally embraced the novelty of the moving picture with at least as much enthusiasm as audiences of other nations. In this, however, they were following what has become recognized as a peculiarly Japanese pattern of behavior: first the enthusiastic acceptance of a new idea, then a period of reaction against it, and finally the complete assimilation and transformation of the idea to Japanese patterns. Thus, by 1917 movies were on the verge of becoming a Japanese art form.

2 **establishing shot: 1917-23.** WHILE NIK-katsu was giving the public what it wanted, and therefore most directors, like Makino, were still making simple illustrations for the *benshi*, a number of other people were looking at Japanese films with a less indulgent eye. Most of them knew foreign films, knew what those films were trying to do, and were in a position to compare the Japanese product most unfavorably.

Japan as a modern nation was swiftly maturing and, despite its comparative youth, was beginning to be treated as a responsible adult in the family of nations. The United States had been brought to recognize the special interests of Japan in China, and British and Japanese troops, side by side, had landed at Vladivostok. Inside the country the atmosphere was liberal, even revolutionary. For the first time a commoner was premier and rice riots occurred amid pronounced domestic unrest.

During these years of World War I, new films as well as new ideas were being introduced faster than they could be assimilated. Since European films were unavailable due to the war, American movies were pouring into the country, and the developments made by the American industry were being shown to the curious and receptive Japanese; the most impressive of all, *Intolerance*, made its debut before a gasping audience in 1919.

In the theater world there was the strong influence of the Shingeki, or "new drama," a movement born in the middle 1900's. Opposed to the romanticism of Shimpa and the traditional formalism of the Kabuki, it was directly related to the realist reformation of drama then taking place in the West. Thus Ibsen and Shaw were just as much the godfathers of the Japanese Shingeki as they were of modern European drama.

As early as 1914, Shingeki had made its influence felt in the films when the Nikkatsu Shimpa studios made *Katusha* (Kachusha), based on a Shingeki play adapted from Tolstoy's *Resurrection*. This picture, directed by Kiyomatsu Hoso-yama, used strictly Russian costumes and settings, though the director, afraid to go all the way, also employed *oyama* impersonators instead of actresses for the female rôles.

By the end of the war the Japanese film industry had obviously come to some kind of milestone. From now on everything was going to be different. As with most industrial revolutions, the impetus came from outside the industry, and of those playing a major part in it only one, Eizo Tanaka, was an established film director. All of the others were from outside or, at least, were not directors before that time.

Among the outsiders making the revolution was Norimasa Kaeriyama, born in 1893. Leaving an engineering school before graduating in order to follow his increasing interest in films, he studied all the foreign technical literature he could find and began contributing to an early film magazine. Though he later became known as the man who introduced advanced film technique into Japan, he was really a mechanic at heart, rather like Edwin S. Porter in America except that he interested himself considerably more in aesthetic matters. In 1913 he helped establish the *Film Record*, Japan's first motion picture magazine to take an interest in films as an artistic medium, to which he himself contributed mostly technical articles. Being somewhat ahead of its time, it promptly failed.

After Kaeriyama joined Tenkatsu in 1917, it soon became clear that his ideas on films were quite different from even those this semi-liberal company was used to. He stated his aims in a book, *The Production and Photography of Moving Picture Drama*, and launched a movement to put his theories into practice.

His pictures were dedicated to: the introduction of long-, medium-, and close-shots, together with editing principles; the conversion to realistic acting; and the use of actresses in women's rôles instead of *oyama*. While Kaeriyama was not the first to adopt these innovations in Japan, his insistence on all three as essentials of film-making helped touch off a revolution in the Japanese films. He was also opposed to the *benshi* and in favor of titles, but this was a problem so vast that it had to be approached obliquely.

To emphasize the need for a complete break with the *benshi*-oriented films of the past, Kaeriyama discarded the original Japanese word for motion pictures, *katsudo shashin*, literally "moving photographs," and created the new, more elegant word *eiga*, which could mean "descriptive pictures," "reproduced pictures," "projected pictures," and "attractive pictures," all rolled into one. *Eiga* caught on quickly and soon replaced *katsudo shashin*. The latter word is used today in its original sense only by veteran movie-makers. By others it is reserved as a generic term describing the poorest quality films.

Kaeriyama joined Tenkatsu as head of its import department and his job was to arrange for the purchase of supplies. In those days the table of organization was not nearly so rigid as it is now, and it was not at all surprising for the head of a studio's import department to become a film director as well. But his pictures themselves were surprising. Consequently they met with a great deal of resistance from public and front office, both of whom, for entirely different reasons, loved the *benshi*. The opposition was so strong that Kaeriyama had to pretend he was making pictures for export only.

The majority opinion in those days was that short-length shots, editing, dramatic lighting, and close-ups were for foreigners, and this rather arbitrary division of the film vocabulary along national lines was much encouraged by the *benshi*, who knew that anything foreign, whether titles or actresses, was a definite threat. Thus Kaeriyama's pictures were billed by the publicity department as "films in the American style," and the director's big talking point was that since they were making films for foreigners they should put in things that foreigners liked.

This tendency to place things foreign in one class and things Japanese in another is in many ways a genuine national characteristic. Before the war, and to some extent even now, the kimono industry made two kinds of garments, those intended for domestic use and those destined for export. The latter, distinguished by their bright colors, were alive with embroidered dragons and stalking tigers. This snobbism is still strangely powerful in the film industry. Today some movies are made to please what is believed to be foreign taste, while others, like those directed by Gosho or Ozu, are scarcely ever let out of the country, being considered by the Japanese as "far too Japanese for export."

When Kaeriyama's first pictures appeared, it gradually became clear that they were actually for the Japanese market and thus company opposition occurred. His first, *The Glow of Life* (Sei no Kagayaki), produced by Tenkatsu in 1918 in cooperation with the director's newly formed Motion Picture Art Association, was quite short, only four reels long, and starred Minoru Murata, soon to become famous as a director, and others from the Shingeki as well as Kaeri-yama himself. It was the story of a city boy who falls in love with a country girl while convalescing by the sea. She finds herself with child after the recuperated youth has married a banker's daughter, but her suicide is thwarted by a friend of the hero's.

For this and other of his early films, Kaeriyama used real interiors instead of sets built in a studio. His first picture was made inside the Tokyo YMCA. The actors, as was the custom of the time, wore standard white make-up, similar to that used in the West, and also appeared in more than one rôle in a picture as an economy measure. Each of these early films cost from four to eight hundred dollars to make, with the raw-film stock accounting for half of the amount. Kaeri-yama's use of film was thought quite wasteful, the ratio being four thousand feet finally used to every eight thousand feet shot, which was considered quite high for the period. He not only supervised the photography but also processed the film himself.

In his first film, as in his later *Maid of the Deep Moun-tains* (Miyama no Otome) and *Tale of the White Chrysan-themum* (Shiragiku Monogatari), Kaeriyama attempted to make an integrated use of all the cinematic techniques he knew, and, while the result was sometimes derivative and always eclectic, the films might have had some success had they been released at once. Tenkatsu, however, kept them in the vaults for a year and then only released them in two relatively obscure Tokyo theaters. Kaeriyama himself does not believe that a major reason for Tenkatsu's failure to release his early films lay in secret opposition from the *ben-shi*, though this story was believed readily enough by others. Tenkatsu itself used the rather feeble excuse that it held back release only until the then-rampant labor strikes and general unrest had ended. Of the early films only *Tale of the White Chrysanthemum* received adequate distribution—and not in Japan at that, having been backed by a foreign trader for export to Italy. In a few years, however, having proved his point, Kaeriyama returned his attention to technical matters and today remains the dean of Japanese motion-picture projection engineers.

Kaeriyama was joined in his crusade by Yoshiro Emasa, also a technician, who had originally worked at the old Yoshizawa studios, where he had been the assistant of one of the first Japanese cameramen, Kichizo Chiba. Stimulated by the work of Kaeriyama, Emasa's first picture in the new style was *Song of Sorrow* (Aware no Kyoku), a film about Formosa, scripted, directed, and photographed by himself. It was less of a copy of foreign films than Kaeriyama's had been, though it did boast such foreign attractions as real actresses and subtitles.

At Nikkatsu in the meantime, one of their regular directors, Eizo Tanaka, was becoming enthusiastic about the new methods, trying to argue that they might actually make money. Nikkatsu, with the market almost to itself, was not much interested, and so Tanaka had to compromise, continuing to use exaggerated Shimpa techniques and *oyama*, while managing occasionally to slip in a "new style" film. Tanaka himself was well established as a director of Shimpa pictures, and hence his approach to the film was essentially theatrical. His idol was still Ibsen, as it had been since his early days as an actor, while Kaeriyama's was Griffith. This reveals their difference in approach.

Tanaka's *The Living Corpse* (Ikeru Shikabane), made in 1917, marked the dawn of the new technique so far as Nikkatsu was concerned. Teinosuke Kinugasa, later director of *Gate of Hell* (Jigokumon), played the heroine and looked very much like a woman in his dress, wig, and make-up, except for the fact that since the film was shot in muddy November he wore heavy workmen's boots throughout. This directorial slip, however, did not seem to attract much attention. New techniques or not, the audience had not yet been trained to expect the illusion of complete reality.

With the aesthetics of the film changing so rapidly, it is not surprising that a division within the industry itself should occur, and very soon Nikkatsu found itself faced with a number of rivals. In 1920 the new company named Taisho Katsuei was formed; this name, derived from the bright new designation of the Emperor Taisho's reign, was soon shortened to Taikatsu. Though the company ran into difficulties only two years later and merged with Shochiku, it did its part in creating the new Japanese film. The now-famous novelist Junichiro Tanizaki was hired to do scripts; actors were taken in and given half-year courses in the techniques of "movie realism"; and Thomas Kurihara was brought back from America to direct.

Kurihara got his early training in California, working on Thomas H. Ince's productions. In those days Sessue Hayakawa was beginning his rather amazing career as a Hollywood matinee idol, and his success attracted a number of other Japanese to the American industry, including several who were later to become directors in Japan. One of these was Kurihara; two others were Yutaka Abe and Frank Tokunaga. Both played bit rôles and formed part of Hayakawa's large Hollywood retinue.

When Kurihara returned to Japan he at once became a director, as did Abe when he came back several years later. There was the feeling, then as now, that those who had been abroad were in many ways superior to those who stayed home, and Kurihara, who knew precisely what he wanted to do, gave the impression of complete competence. Having played minor villains in various Hayakawa and William S. Hart films, he knew how American movies were made and also had very strong ideas on the director's having the final say over everyone else. Thus in the days when the Japanese film director usually had very little to do, being a sort of assistant cameraman, Kurihara was an exception and soon imprinted his personality on the film.

His first for Taikatsu was the 1920 *Amateur Club* (Amachua Kurabu), a comedy about drama enthusiasts trying to stage a Kabuki play by the seaside. It was done in direct imitation of Hollywood slapstick but proved a little too happy in spirit for Japanese audiences, who, in any case, considered it too American. In the same year he made *The Lasciviousness of the Viper* (Jasei no In), based on an Akinari Ueda story later to become famous as the basis of Mizoguchi's internationally known *Ugetsu Monogatari*. Here Kaeriyama's revolutionary concepts were for the first time applied to a film with a historical setting, and the audiences found it full enough of Japanese flavor.

Taikatsu, young as it was, about this time found itself threatened by a new and spectacularly successful rival, a rival of whom even Nikkatsu was taking wary notice. This was the Shochiku Cinema Company. Organized by two men who had started their careers as peanut vendors in theaters, Shochiku had been around for some years as a theatrical monopoly owning Kabuki troupes, Shimpa companies, and various theaters. Only lately, however, had it awakened to the commercial possibilities of the film. One of the partners, Matsu-

jiro Shirai, had recently returned from a trip abroad, where
he had seen what the movies were doing overseas; while the other, Takejiro Otani, had noticed the tremendous success of *Intolerance*, playing at an admission scale higher than the best live Japanese drama.

In deciding to enter film production, Shochiku saw that the old-style Japanese movies were on their way out, and so they decided to use only the latest ideas. They sent a man to Hollywood to sign up Hayakawa and entice him home. He was by this time too big for Shochiku's finances; so they turned to the Japanese who surrounded him and eventually hired a number of technicians as well as Henry Kotani, who had been an apprentice at the Lasky Famous Players studio, studying under "Papa" Wycoff, the famed "father of cameramen." They gave Kotani more than the premier was receiving and what remained for years the highest pay in the Japanese film world—seven hundred dollars a month.

They next decided to build a studio and, in searching around Tokyo for the site most resembling the Hollywood studio locale, chose Kamata, on the southern outskirts of the city and adjacent to Tokyo Bay. Since they would have to hire people without experience in the new methods, they subsidized the Shochiku Cinema Institute to train new people and develop new forms of expression. In charge of this project they put Kaoru Osanai, one of the founders of the Shingeki movement, a man who had studied at the Moscow Art Theater, had worked in Max Reinhardt's Berlin theater, and in 1913 had introduced Stanislavsky's acting method to Japan. Osanai had long been interested in films and, in fact, his ideas had done much to influence the pictures of his pupil Eizo Tanaka. Osanai's own theatrical group having failed in 1919, he was very much in the market for just the kind of job that Shochiku was offering.

After all this preparation, Shochiku released a prospectus, or manifesto, which read: "The main purpose of this company will be the production of artistic films resembling the latest and most flourishing styles of the Occidental cinema; it will distribute these both at home and abroad; it will introduce the true state of our national life to foreign countries; and it will assist in international reconciliation both here and abroad." There is little evidence that these noble intentions were in any way realized. The first products seem rather to have been aimed directly at the Japanese market, the initial film being *Island Women* (Shima no Onna) directed by Henry Kotani, in which the Kabuki actor Tsuruzo Nakamura, apparently hired to add class to the production, starred in a realistic performance.

From the very first, the American-style productions of Shochiku, both in their creation and in their distribution, experienced the gravest difficulties. One of the reasons was that though Shochiku was buying talent in enormous quantities, it was doing little to coordinate this talent once it had it.

Yoshinobu Ikeda, a writer of "chain-drama" before he entered the industry in 1921, was one day asked by a Shochiku friend to write a script. He wrote two overnight and took them to the head office, where he was at once put on the payroll. At the office next morning he found that his first job was transliterating his own scripts into the Roman alphabet because Shochiku was trying so closely to copy American methods that all scripts had to be written in letters rather than in Japanese characters. Later he was assigned to study under Henry Kotani, but, like most people at the studio, he discovered that he could understand little or nothing of what the director was saying since Kotani, "to get the American flavor," insisted on directing in English.

In addition, Kotani never showed the script to either cast or crew, keeping the plot a secret and hiring musicians to play mood-music in the American manner instead of relying on the customary reading of the script aloud while the actors emoted. Of these early days he now says: "It was awful. All the action took place in front of a single, stationary camera. No close-ups, and no panning." Yet, at the time, his customary way of directing was, for example, when he wanted fear, to shout: "A lion is coming. Be afraid!"—even though nothing whatever was coming and no lion figured in the plot.

Shochiku itself did little to compensate for the havoc this kind of direction created. Though its earliest directors came either from America or the Shimpa, the Shochiku Institute, which trained most of its actors, relied on neither Shimpa nor American techniques, but modeled itself entirely on the Shingeki.

If the "new methods" did not come to much in Shochiku's initial efforts, it at least had no *oyama* to hamper its efforts since it used actresses from the beginning. One of the earliest to join Shochiku was Sumiko Kurishima, who was to become Japan's favorite female star for the next decade. Born in 1903, she first appeared at the age of six in the Yoshizawa children's film *Peach Boy* (Momotaro). Her first Shochiku movie, *An Electrician and His Wife* (Denko to Sono Tsuma), was banned as being "too sexy," but after this slightly false start she soon climbed to stardom. By 1924 her popularity was unrivaled.

Henry Kotani and the others imported from America were not so fortunate. Within two years after their arrival they had all left Shochiku. The invasion from America, which was over by 1923, had failed not only because the Japanese audience continued to prefer the *benshi* films, but also because subject and treatment of the new-style films were considered "too American," the Japanese crews plainly disliking all of these foreign connections and much preferring to work in a "pure Japanese" style. This anti-foreignism held little political implication, but has always been a definite part of the Japanese film world. Thus after the artistic and commercial failure of both Thomas Kurihara and Henry Kotani, the drive to modernize the Japanese film was in the hands of those inclined to a more original Japanese approach.

Shochiku was not alone in its difficulties with film styles. Even Nikkatsu, with a small unit formed to make films in the new tradition, found that many of its modern efforts were commercial failures, though this was in part due to the fact that Eizo Tanaka, supposedly in charge of this experimental unit, had become seriously ill, a fact which considerably lessened his effectiveness as a leader.

Actually, what saved the Japanese film from slipping back to its former stage was that all the mechanical equipment, all the techniques necessary for making films in the new style, now existed in Japan. Money had been invested and no company, least of all the wealthy Shochiku, was going to admit defeat. Consequently it kept up its box-office returns by making the expected kind of film, but at the same time allowed Osanai's Shochiku Cinema Institute to produce the kind of films it wanted.

Among these were a few, like Kaoru Osanai's and Minoru Murata's *Souls on the Road* (Rojo no Reikon), made in 1921, which were equal to the best from the West. This particular film was composed of two cross-cut stories, one about a prodigal who leaves his father's house and returns penniless with wife and child; the other about two convicts newly released from prison who discover the kindness of common people as they wander on an endless journey.

Osanai and Murata used these two situations not to capture events or ideas in conflict, as had Griffith in *Intolerance*, but to show parallels in feeling among their characters. This interest in the emotional overtones of a situation reveals the

origins of the mood film, a most important Japanese genre,
the emphasis being on projecting an overall mood or atmosphere rather than in directly telling a story. The directors particularly sought to capture the components of what were for them the greatest forces in the world: love within a family and comradeship between men. These they preferred to examine not in the uncommon moments of high emotion, as in a plotted film, but rather during those characteristic moments of an enduring period of hardship.

Based on two stories, one of them Gorki's *The Lower Depths*, and filmed on location during early winter among the mountains in central Japan, *Souls on the Road* placed its characters far apart from the crowded world, in a country of dead landscapes and overcast skies, where the men and women moved almost aimlessly, harshly outlined against the somber mountains and the dark forest.

Shochiku continued to turn out films in the new style. In 1922, Hotei Nomura wrote *Jirocho from Shimizu* (Shimizu no Jirocho) and later directed *The Woman and the Pirates* (Onna to Kaizoku), the first major attempts to introduce new methods into the standard-action costume play, but ones which took much of their inspiration from the American Western. In 1923 Yasujiro Shimazu made one of the best of the early Shochiku films, *The Crossing Watchman of the Mountains* (Yama no Senroban), a naturalistic study based on a Japanese version of a Gerhard Hauptman play.

Shochiku had grown in a very short time into Nikkatsu's most formidable rival, while, at the same time, new film companies were springing up all around. In 1919 the Kokusai Katsuei (International Motion Picture Company), or Kokkatsu, had been established by some foreign traders, and in 1920 the Teikoku Kinema Geijutsu (Imperial Cinema Art Company), or Teikine, was formed. By 1921 Nikkatsu had succeeded in annexing Kokkatsu but, in all, fourteen new companies had been established.

Kokkatsu had made films like the 1921 *Winter Camellia* (Kantsubaki), directed by Masao Inoue, a Shingeki actor, recently returned from America. Yaeko Mizutani, one of Japan's first film actresses and still in the movies, appeared under the provocative title of Fukumen Reijo, the "Masked Miss," in this pathetic tragedy of a watermill owner and his only daughter. It opened at the same time as *Souls on the Road* and was a success largely because of the actress. In general it smelled too strongly of the stage and, by comparison with Osanai's and Murata's film, was quite artificial.

The innovation of actresses had received considerable assistance from the increasing popularity of plays with Western
music. Stage actresses were now supposed to sing and no
oyama could compete with them since male contraltos are
a rare commodity. Moreover, with the increasing use of
naturalistic settings, the *oyama* was soon becoming hopelessly out of place. The killing blow to the female impersonators came when Nikkatsu formed its unit to produce
films in the new style and began to hire actresses.

Shortly after this, in 1922, a dozen of the most powerful
of the *oyama*, headed by Teinosuke Kinugasa, swept out of
the Nikkatsu studios as a protest. For a time it seemed as
though the strike might have some effect since it caught
the company short of actresses, and there was some attempt
to build up new *oyama* stars, but before long even the female
impersonators themselves began to realize that their era was
over. They fully understood that the game was up when they
discovered that their own photographs, like those of geisha,
were being outsold by those of pretty screen actresses. These
publicity pictures were bought in large quantities by youngsters and by some not so young; even now they are a rather
reliable indication of the popularity of a film star. During
this early period Sumiko Kurishima set a record when four
thousand copies of her photograph were sold in a single day.
Film vehicles for her, like the 1924 *Princess-Grass* (Ohime
Gusa), made millions weep, and eventually an entire magazine, the *Kurishima Notebook*, was devoted to her.

Nikkatsu, after it had successfully made the difficult shift
to actresses, began to adjust more rapidly to changing conditions. In 1922, Tanaka—no longer forced to disguise his
innovations—made *The Kyoya Collar Shop* (Kyoya Eri-
mise), a tragedy laid in a small-business setting. Though it
used *oyama*, it presaged what in the later 1920's was to become the "Nikkatsu style," which was expressed largely in
realistic stories of the lower classes, a subject which other
producers rarely touched upon, with the exception of films
like Shochiku's *Souls on the Road*.

Little by little, Nikkatsu gave talent its head, within what
it considered reasonable bounds, and new directors and new
actors were brought into the field. In 1923, Kensaku Suzuki
used night-time photography for the first time in *Human
Suffering* (Ningenku), a film which carefully delineated the
character of the unemployed who turned to robbery, also
paying particular attention to women who had "neither employment nor belongings." Though only four reels in length,

it was made with care and included much advanced dramatic
lighting of the kind just then beginning to appear in the German films. It was the first of a genre which was to grow into the *rumpen-mono,* or, in Marxian terms, films about the "lumpenproletariat."

The year before, another new directing talent had appeared; this was Kenji Mizoguchi. After several below-average attempts, he made *Foggy Harbor* (Kiri no Minato), an atmospheric, pictorially beautiful, somewhat melodramatic yet intimate drama, about a sailor and his girl and her father. Based partially on O'Neill's *Anna Christie,* the action occurred all in one night and ended with the sunrise of the next day. It dispensed entirely with the talents of the *benshi* and required very few subtitles, thus pointing the way to an increasingly cinematic use of the camera.

In most countries the progressive film-makers were trying to avoid using titles, preferring to tell their stories through more pictorial, more cinematic methods. In Japan, however, with its all-powerful *benshi,* the use of titles seemed, by comparison with the ubiquitous narration, very cinematic indeed. Thus, to get rid of the *benshi* it was necessary first to use narrative and dialogue titles. These would make the *benshi* narration and commentary redundant. Then, after titles had been established, film technique could evolve along Western lines in a more pictorial direction and thus eliminate the titles themselves. But obviously the jump from the *benshi* film to the completely pictorially-told film was too big to make without the intermediate step of titles, or at least so the film theorists reasoned.

With films like those of Murata's, Tanaka's, and Mizoguchi's, the Japanese industry seemed finally to have reached its stride. Then suddenly it was completely disorganized by the great 1923 Kanto earthquake.

3 wipe: 1923-27.

TOKYO WAS NOT ONLY THE FILM center, it was also the center of all modern Japanese culture. When the Kanto earthquake leveled both Tokyo and Yokohama one bright September forenoon, the modern Japan which had been growing slowly upon the foundations of the Tokugawa age was substantially destroyed.

The film industry was hit extremely hard. Most of the studios and theaters were gone and so was a great part of the audience. Before the beginning of the following year, however, movies were being shown in tents and makeshift theaters, and before too long films about the earthquake itself were appearing: *The Earth Is Angry* (Daichi wa Okoru), *11:58 A.M.* (Juichi-ji Goju Happun), *The Location of the Flames* (Honoo no Yukue), *The Heart of That Day* (Sono Hi no Kokoro), *The Earth Shakes* (Daichi wa Yuru), and *Among the Ruins* (Haikyo no Naka ni).

Earthquake or no, the movies remained popular, and soon more and more films were imported from abroad to fill a demand the Japanese companies could not satisfy. Many foreign film companies, scenting opportunity, opened offices in Tokyo even before reconstruction had begun. Within the next year films like *The Marriage Circle*, *The Covered Wagon*, and *The Birth of a Nation*, to name but a few, were shown in Japan.

The industry was reorganizing after its violent shaking up, and one of the results was that the work of Norimasa Kaeri-yama, the Shochiku Cinema Institute, Minoru Murata, and Eizo Tanaka was paying off in the emergence of a popularly accepted film technique. One of the reasons that more-advanced films were acceptable at all was that the earth-quake and its resultant confusion had upset the industry to the extent that many of the old concepts were relinquished and completely new methods and ideas were adopted. The atmosphere of the film world after the earthquake was one of great and boundless enthusiasm. Otherwise it would be difficult to account for the fact that within a few years Japan would raise her silent cinema to a level which other countries had taken thirty years to reach.

48
back-
ground

An example of this interest and enthusiasm might be found in Shiro Kido, who, at the age of thirty and just after Sho-chiku had reconstructed its earthquake-damaged Kamata studios, was appointed head, taking the place of Hotei No-mura. Kido, unlike Nomura, who was little interested in anything more than the old Shimpa tragedies, wanted to widen and brighten the scope of all Shochiku films. It was through his encouragement that Yasujiro Shimazu made his early comedies, and later, again through him, that directors like Ozu and Gosho got their start.

Kido made many changes. Among them, he revived Osanai's actors' school and originated the "All Star Revue," a monthly gala in which Shochiku film actors took over the Tokyo Kabuki-za for a special variety show presenting screen favorites to the public. They appeared in short plays and everyone sang, including those who could not. The result was that when the talkies finally arrived, Shochiku had a vocally trained group of actors, even though talking films were quite unforeseen when these revues were begun. Perhaps Kido's main contribution to the Japanese film, how-ever, was the stress he put upon the *gendai-geki*, films about contemporary life. This influence brought about a tremen-dous change of atmosphere in the industry at a time when period-drama dominated the public interest.

It is indicative of Japan's attitude toward itself and its own history that it should make such a rigid division between the *jidai-geki*, the period-drama, and the *gendai-geki*. Just as Japanese painting consists of two schools, Western-style and Japanese-style, just as Japanese music is comprised of com-positions in the Western manner and works in the purely Japanese, rarely combined and never confused, so the Japa-nese film product is commonly thought of as falling into these two main categories. The question of Western influence has not been allowed to complicate this division.

Now, after the earthquake, with the use and modification

of foreign film techniques, something more purely Japanese
was slowly emerging: a style, an attitude toward life, the like
of which post-Restoration Japanese literature had already
created and which the enthusiasm within the industry was
now fostering in the film.

Important in establishing the form of Japanese films about
contemporary life were the pictures directed by Minoru
Murata, who as early as 1913 had had his own Shingeki troupe
and had thus gained an insight into the art of realistic drama
such as few other film directors then possessed. He consistently fought against the star system, refusing to make star
vehicles, and instead looked for talented unknowns. Murata
was particularly noted for his ability to turn foreign ideas
and styles into solid Japanese technique. To a large extent
he relied on foreign films for inspiration, but he never
copied; rather, he always adapted his material to meet local
needs.

His ideas obviously suited him for a place in Kaeriyama's
Motion Picture Art Association, which, in 1918, had just
been formed. A good friend of the association's director,
having attended the same high school, Murata later appeared
in all of Kaeriyama's early films. Joining Shochiku shortly
after it was formed, Murata worked on two pictures before
transferring to the Shochiku Cinema Institute to make *Souls
on the Road*. After the earthquake, however, he experienced
some difficulty making the kind of films he wanted, moving
first to Kokkatsu and later to Nikkatsu.

His 1924 *Seisaku's Wife* (Seisaku no Tsuma) was the
tragedy of a man and wife parted by war. As a boy he had
saved her from a life of prostitution. Married, they had to
struggle against the prejudices of society. When he returns
wounded she is afraid of losing him and blinds him so that
he will need her. A year later Murata made *The Street
Juggler* (Machi no Tejinashi), a film about a juggler and
his beautiful girl friend. The theme, somewhat resembling
Molnar's *Liliom*, had as its burden the idea that the sensitive
can oppose the tyranny of society only in their imaginations
and that sooner or later they must wake to unfriendly reality.

Murata's early films had an intimacy and a concern for
detail which made them unusual. He was not just telling a
story; instead, he was creating an entire world. He called
this style "symbolic photographicism," by which he meant a
realism in which all the characters were lifelike and existed
in "natural situations," yet whose actions and personalities
had symbolic, almost allegorical meanings. They were real,

but at the same time they were more real, more important, larger than real life.

A style like that of Murata's early films, personal and unique though it was, often verges on the sentimental, if only because symbolic figures must be symbolic of something very large or very important if we are going to accept them; his were not. If sentimentality is defined as a superfluous amount of emotion lavished upon an unworthy object, then we are forced to conclude that, not only these early films of Murata's, but also the bulk of Japanese films are sentimental. One of the reasons for this is that Japanese society is so rigidly organized that it tends to discourage any of those larger objects of emotional concern—Lear's madness, Hamlet's indecision—the emotional treatment of which escapes any charge of sentimentality simply by the size and importance of the object itself. Instead, the Japanese personal crisis is often of a nature, and a size, which the West would regard as inconsequential. To build an entire film around one of these personal crises and then to expect a vast outlay of emotion from both actors and audience would strike the West as being sentimental.

There are, naturally, many kinds of sentimentality. The Japanese period-film has always insisted—to an almost morbid degree—upon the respectability of the heroic and yet, at the same time, has maintained an absolutely nihilistic attitude toward society as a whole. The plight of the hero is everything. Anything he does is perfectly proper so long as he lives up to his obligations, is brave, and meets death unflinchingly. The main virtue in this kind of hero is an ethical purity which, among other things, makes these heroes the most priggish to ever grace the screen. All of the complicated plot machinery which moves *The Loyal Forty-seven Ronin* is begun and based upon the failure to observe a minute bit of court etiquette. Death, terror, sorrow, and utter sentimentality follow.

Films about contemporary life face the same problem. Given a limited emotional range, the Japanese can find very few objects worthy of such emotional intensity. The result is an emotionally charged and yet often quite sentimental attitude toward life. In speaking of sentimentality, one Japanese critic has attempted to sum up an attitude by saying that the sentimentality of the silent era's period-film was a sentimentality of nothingness, while the sentimentality of the silent films about contemporary life was at least based upon real feelings. That is, the former were sentimental about

such abstract ideas as warrior purity and bravery while the
latter were sentimental about more vital human emotions.

If Murata's early films were sentimental, they were at least eloquent in expressing his fight for individuality and liberal social ideas, and his opposition to the rigid family system. In this, his attitude was somewhat shared by Kiyohiko Ushihara, who had scripted Murata's *Souls on the Road*.

Having directed *The Mountains Grow Dark* (Yama Kururu) the Shochiku Cinema Institute's second production, and a number of other films in the new-style, Ushihara left Japan in 1926 in the middle of an established career to study for a year with Chaplin in Hollywood. He then came back and made pictures like *Love of Life* (Jinsei no Ai), which earned him the name of "Sentimental Ushihara" became of his fondness for nostalgia and tear-jerking. Though he made many pictures after he left the Shochiku Institute, he never equaled the quality of his earlier films until 1928 when he did *He and Life* (Kare to Jinsei) and *A King on Land* (Riku no Oja). In this latter he continued a genre he had helped create with his *The Poet and the Athlete* (Shijin to Undoka) in 1924, the *supotsu-mono*, or sport film. He continued to direct until 1949, and has now become the industry's leading roving ambassador, serving on the Venice Film Festival jury in 1956 and representing Japan at the yearly meetings of the Fédération Internationale des Archives du Film.

The only Shochiku director to stay behind in Tokyo after the Kamata staff moved to Kyoto after the earthquake was Yasujiro Shimazu, who had been the assistant director for *Souls on the Road* and who, on his own, had made several of the finest early Shochiku films. During this period he made *Father* (Chichi), with Yaeko Mizutani, a film noteworthy in that it marked the obscure beginnings of the *shomin-geki*, the drama about the common people, a movie genre later to become very important and seen in its modern form in films by Gosho, Naruse, and Ozu. Essentially a film about proletarian or lower-middle-class life, about the sometimes humorous, sometimes bitter relations within the family, about the struggle for existence, it is the kind of film many Japanese think of as being about "you and me."

Though various directors treat this common-people genre differently, Shimazu at first used it as a vehicle for light comedy. *Father*, a story about a baseball champion and a simple country girl, was somewhat like American comedies of·the period except that it relied more on character and mood than upon plot and slapstick. The tone of the film, like that of many made later, was light and amusing, but from the very first the director made certain that you were laughing with and not at his characters.

Later Shimazu made such excellent comedies as the 1924 *Sunday* (Nichiyobi) and, a year later, *A Village Teacher* (Mura no Sensei), where, as in later films, the fun was of a reflective and sympathetic nature. The former of these films also helped establish another genre: the salary-man comedy, the humorous story of the trials and tribulations of the white-collar worker, the suburban commuter. In the same year he continued the genre with *Stinker* (Warutaro), and by 1926 the form had become accepted to the extent that others, such as Hotei Nomura with his *Collar Button* (Karabotan), were adding to it.

Comedy, long neglected in pre-1920 Japanese films, was now coming into its own, the form receiving yet further impetus when both Yutaka Abe and Frank Tokunaga returned to Japan. The former had been working in Hollywood—as a butler during long periods of "at liberty" as an actor—and came home just in time to see what Shimazu was doing in the way of comedy. Abe's long American training had given him a profound dislike for the tediousness of the Shimpa style, and shortly after his return he began creating films which brought to the new comedy speed, sharpness in editing, and sophistication.

One of the earliest films he made was the 1926 *The Woman Who Touched the Legs* (Ashi ni Sawatta Onna), a comedy inspired by those of Lubitsch, particularly *The Marriage Circle*. A writer meets a girl on the train and they both stop at the same hotel. While he is taking a bath, she steals his wallet. Later he goes off with her to her hometown and is just beginning to fall in love with her when a detective arrives and arrests her. It develops that she is a well-known thief, but the writer, completely undisillusioned, goes to the station to see them off.

The film won Abe the first *Kinema Jumpo* "Best One" Award, a prize annually given by the magazine which still remains one of Japan's leading film publications. There is nothing quite like it in the West. Japanese critics poll to select the ten best films of the year and their choice has the greatest influence, not only in critical circles but also among the public and within the industry itself. It is an award relatively untouched by commercial considerations and is, therefore, highly respected.

After winning this honor, Abe went on to make *A Mermaid*

on Land (Riku no Ningyo) and later *The Five Women*
around Him (Kare o Meguru Go-nin no Onna), the story of a bachelor and his girl friends: an upper-class young lady, an actress, a geisha, a prostitute, and the daughter of a merchant.

Though Abe continued to reflect his American background, he found ways of adapting his methods to Japan. Frank Tokunaga was not so resourceful. He never made this most necessary of adjustments, and all of his films were close copies of those he had seen or worked on while in America. The Japanese themselves called his movies "pictures without a country" or, more explicitly if less politely, *bata kusai*, meaning "smelling of butter," most dairy products having as yet failed to be incorporated into the Japanese way of life. Tokunaga's American imitations did not draw much of a crowd since the real thing was being steadily imported, and he all but left the industry until, fittingly, he was hired to appear in an American film. He played the mayor of Tobiki in MGM's *The Teahouse of the August Moon*.

One of the results of the new comedy film was the creation of another peculiarly Japanese genre, the "nonsense film." Films like Kurihara's *Amateur Club* had been nonsensical, but the genre did not make a real appearance until fairly late in the 1920's. The ground for the nonsense film had been well prepared in literature by both the vast number of naughtily erotic or purposely frivolous novels which had appeared and by a Japanese talent which, if it could not make full-scale tragedy out of the most minute of personal experiences, could at least create a comedy out of nothing at all. The nonsense films were just that, films which made little or no sense whatever, amusing happenings, one thing tacked onto the other, something ludicrous—though not often slapstick—for its own sake. Later, Gosho, Mizoguchi, and, particularly, Ozu put meaning into these comedies by making them realistic studies with comic overtones, but at this period the characters cavorted and chased each other across the screen with very little regard for plot, characterization, or motive.

Working conditions were often just as chaotic as the pictures themselves. Kogo Noda, who does many of Ozu's scripts, writes of Shochiku in 1928, saying: "Everyone in the script-writing department had to turn out one script a month for his monthly salary. After that, for the second or third script each was paid an extra fee. At the time I had a quota of three nonsense films every month for Torajiro Saito.

Luckily, this kind of picture was so short that I could turn
out quite a few. Just as a painter carries a sketchbook wherever he goes, I carried a notebook with me to write down gag ideas. It was impossible to write this kind of picture at a desk, so I did my best work near the source—in street-cars and tearooms."

Among the others who were working toward the gradual emergence of a genuine Japanese technique was Teinosuke Kinugasa, who, with a Shochiku distribution contract in his pocket, formed the Kinugasa Motion Picture League. Back-ing his own unit almost broke him, and he had so little money for his first production, the impressionist *A Crazy Page* (Kurutta Ippeiji), that his stars—some of them rather big names—had to help paint sets, push the dolly, and make props. He had only eight small lights to work with; so he painted the walls of his small studio silver to make them reflect additional illumination. The picture was shot over a relatively long period, an entire month, and since Kinugasa could not afford accommodations for his actors, they slept on the set or in the front office. The film itself was unlike anything which had been made in Japan up to that time. The story was about a sailor, the cause of his wife's insanity, who becomes a servant in the asylum where she is kept. It was shot partly from the point of view of the insane them-selves, with impressionistic cutting in the Russian and French avant-garde manner.

Impressionism as a film technique was to become important in Japan. As it is continually confused with expressionism as a technique, it is necessary to make some distinction between the two. The aim of expressionism, as defined by one of its followers, is to "present the inner life of humanity rather than its outward appearance." Its spiritual home is the Ger-man theater and it originally rose in opposition to naturalism. It insists upon the unseen, upon the subconscious, the evoca-tive, the symbolic, and is best known as a stage technique in, say, the plays of Capek, O'Casey, and O'Neill. As a device it most influenced stage designers and owes more to them than to directors or authors. As a screen technique much the same is true.

Impressionism, on the other hand, has the aim of repro-ducing the impression made by the object or idea itself and is largely of French origin. The term, as taken from the Monet painting "Impressions," has come to mean anti-romantic, anti-academic art, as found in the paintings of Manet, Monet, Renoir, and Degas, but in its stricter sense the word con-

tinues to designate the re-creation of impressions which the
artist himself has received. Distortions, if they may be called
that and if they occur, take place in the artist's treatment
and not in the materials themselves. This is just as true of
Hemingway's prose as it is the films by Eisenstein or the
young René Clair. Thus impressionism is related to how a
viewer *sees* something, while expressionism is related to the
nature of the thing *viewed*.

In a film like *The Cabinet of Doctor Caligari*—the story of
which *A Crazy Page* somewhat resembles—the difference in
these two approaches is obvious. The force of the German
film arises from the very fact that everything—the painted
sets, the artificial make-up, the style of acting itself—is
controlled by the idea of having the audience view the film
through the eyes of the insane. The object viewed is insanity
and the full force of such a view is guaranteed by removing
the audience to the world of the insane. Teinosuke Kinugasa's early films, on the other hand, though they may occasionally try to create what it feels like to be one of the
characters, are much more concerned with the impression the
creator himself felt when first confronted with his material.
He picks and chooses scenes, the sum total of which is the
impression of the emotion itself. Just as Eisenstein gives us
an impression of a massacre in *Potemkin*'s Odessa steps
sequence, so Kinugasa gives us the impression of an insane
asylum.

Because of its treatment, *A Crazy Page* was released
in theaters specializing in foreign films, but, to everyone's
complete surprise, it was at once a big success. At the Shinjuku Musashino-kan it grossed over a thousand dollars a
week, which was rather good when one remembers that by
this time the admission price of films had fallen to the
equivalent of five cents or under. The money was most
welcome to the near-bankrupt Kinugasa, who had had to
bring the film personally from Kyoto to Tokyo to prevent
its being seized by his creditors.

The last film that Kinugasa made with his own company
was one of the milestones of Japanese cinema. It was *Crossroads* (Jujiro), later shown in Europe as *Shadows of the
Yoshiwara*. The story was about a young man who, thinking
he has killed a rival on the archery grounds, flees wounded
to his elder sister and asks her to help him escape from the
authorities. She meets an official who promises to clear her
brother, but when he tries to seduce her in return for the
promised favor, she kills him. Then, by chance, the brother

sees the girl he loves with the man he thought he had killed.
Weak from loss of blood, he dies from the shock.

Since the hero is unable to distinguish the immediacy of
the present from the events of the near or distant past, the
film, in order to reflect his distracted state, dispenses with
strict chronology and relies upon flashbacks to reveal the
reasons for the duel and to show the myriad memories which
flood the hero's mind. His sister's regard is reflected in scenes
from their childhood; he suddenly thinks of running down
the street wounded again; the doors of the room turn into
targets, and arrows come flying at him. The pain becomes
a visible hallucination when the water he is drinking turns
to scalding steam. Interspersed with these pictures from his
mind are the dark and real images of the room: his sister's
frightened face in the shadows, her cat attracted by his open
wounds.

Though Kinugasa occasionally relied on photographic
superimposition, his basic unit of construction was the short,
simple shot containing one small detail. Just as he sought in
this film to anatomize pain, so he tried to break down every
action into its basic components. Instead of showing a full
person, Kinugasa would often dissect him, using what the
Soviets were calling "analytical montage," showing only such
details as eyes, hands, or bits of clothing. To project the
necessary gloom, Kinugasa worked only at night and had
all the sets, realistic in detail, painted a dark gray. This
drabness was well caught by the low-key photography of
Kohei Sugiyama to create what the director himself called
"a film of grays based on the *sumi-e*," that is, on Japanese
ink painting, which is typified by a few but all-inclusive
strokes.

Kinugasa has said that this film came at a dark time in his
life and consequently expressed his depression. Even after
it was finished, he had to go abroad to find himself. While he
was studying with Sergei Eisenstein in Russia, he ran out
of money and so went to Berlin, taking a complete print of
the film with him. He showed the film to UFA, which did not
much care for it. The critics, however, were enthusiastic.
They particularly praised the starkness and coldness of the
film's atmosphere, noting especially the director's genius in
showing the condensation of the actors' breath as they spoke.
Kinugasa must have met this praise with mixed reactions, for
the truth was that this effect had been both uncontrived
and unnoticed, the film having been made in an unheated
and very cold Kyoto studio. When *Crossroads* was shown

in France the critics there also liked it, remarking on its
editing techniques and its lighting. Kinugasa's use of close-
ups was also compared favorably to that of Carl Dreyer's
in the newly released *La Passion de Jeanne d'Arc*.

Meanwhile Shiro Kido, head of Shochiku's Kamata studios,
was in Europe at the same time as Kinugasa, having come
through Russia with a touring Kabuki troupe. The trip had
been organized by the very popular Kabuki actor Sadanji
Ichikawa, who had been a colleague of Osanai's in the founding of the Shingeki movement and who was very far left in
his political opinions. When plans for the trip were announced, the ultrarightists were furious and threatened to
kill all members of the party including Sadanji, but somehow the party eventually managed to leave Japan safely.
Altogether they performed about sixteen days in both Leningrad and Moscow, and the presence of Stalin dignified their
final appearance.

Kido had originally gone along so that he could introduce
Shochiku films abroad, but after having listened to various
comments, he decided that films about contemporary Japanese life would not go over very well. Both Eisenstein and
Pudovkin told him there was "too much unnecessary footage" in Japanese films, and later Eisenstein wrote that Japan
was "a country that has in its culture an infinite number of
cinematographic traits, strewn everywhere with the sole
exception of—its cinema." He also accused the Japanese film
of being "completely unaware of montage," yet chose to see
in the composition of Japanese *kanji*, or ideographs, the
essential principles of his own montage theories. About all
that Kido got from his Russian trip was a chance to see
Potemkin, which the Japanese authorities had thought too
inflammatory for importation.

Yet, despite Kido's fears and Eisenstein's criticisms, the
Japanese industry was beginning to develop a truly Japanese
film genre. Movies about contemporary Japanese life had
taken a completely new turn and, now, the period-film was
turning into something which was both cinematic and Japanese.

The period-picture had, at its beginning, relied somewhat
on the stage, particularly Kabuki. Whatever its merits as
theater, the Kabuki style was not particularly well adapted
to the film and consequently movie versions tended to be
photographed theater. When in 1917 a new kind of period-
drama, called Shinkokugeki, or "new national drama," appeared, it moved the realism of the contemporary-oriented

Shingeki into the setting of the traditional Kabuki. In sword
fighting, always an important part of the Japanese period-story, it substituted fake blood and the real clanging of real swords for the dance-like duels of the Kabuki. Thus the violence only suggested in Kabuki plays was in Shinkokugeki presented in its most realistic form.

Just after the earthquake the Shinkokugeki troupe had a big success with its version of the classic story *Kunisada Chuji*, and a year later a number of this troupe's biggest hits were made into films. This meeting of the Shinkokugeki technique with the period-film created one of the earliest of the indigenous Japanese film genres to last to this day—the period-drama, or *jidai-geki*.

As noted earlier, the term *jidai-geki* is used in contradistinction to *gendai-geki*, or contemporary stories. The division between the two forms is set with considerable historic accuracy as 1868, the beginning of the reign of the Emperor Meiji, which was also the beginning of modern Japan. Contemporary drama is further subdivided by reign names: any film set in the period 1868–1912 is a *Meiji-mono*; 1912–1926, a *Taisho-mono*. Thus there is no hazy distinction between now and the immediate or distant past, but rather a sharp division between feudal Japan and modern Japan.

The first wide use of the term *jidai-geki* was in connection with the advertising of the 1923 film *Woodcut Artist* (Uki-yoe-shi), which was produced by Shozo Makino, who, having been a somewhat reactionary influence as a director, now found himself something of an avant-garde producer. In 1921 he had withdrawn from Nikkatsu to set up his own small production company, while Matsunosuke, whose name Makino had made practically a synonym for the old-style costume drama, took over as head of the Nikkatsu period-drama production unit at Kyoto and continued to star in the films of Tomiyasu Ikeda, a director who held mostly to the old *benshi* techniques and did not introduce editing principles into Matsunosuke pictures until 1924. Even then Ikeda had a hard time convincing the actor that this was a good thing, for Matsunosuke, now growing old and ill, never fully grasped what the new methods were all about, even in such late films as the 1925 *Mataemon Araki* (Araki Mataemon). He died in 1926, after having had the distinction of being Japan's first film star. At the time of his death, the films in which he had starred numbered over a thousand.

As a producer, Makino had great difficulty once he had left Matsunosuke. He contracted to make films for the

Education Ministry, which had signified an early interest in
films by holding a special motion-picture festival in Tokyo
in 1921, and thus established the Makino Educational Motion
Picture Studios. Despite the high-sounding name, the studio
was actually only one small wooden building, which he had
built himself. When it was finally completed he was so poor
that he had to use his own four children, the eldest of whom
was fourteen, as actors. After Taikatsu failed and joined
Shochiku in 1922, however, many of its more talented people
joined Makino's little company, among them Thomas Kurihara, Tomu Uchida, and Kametaro Inoue. Makino changed
the name again, this time to the Makino Motion Picture
Company, and was soon busy adapting the new ideas which
the talented Taikatsu people had brought with them.

Woodcut Artist was one of their earliest films. It had a
script by the twenty-four-year-old Rokuhei Susukida, an
avid follower of American action dramas, whose subsequent
scripts were largely responsible for the style and structure
of present-day period-drama. He had been interested in
Shingeki before he turned to film writing. In addition, Kurihara, Uchida, and the others were interested in trying out
their new cinematic methods on the new form, which, they
found, fitted perfectly into their theories of tempo and visual
image. The fighting scenes were ideal material, and since
period-drama, whatever else, must be visual, the capturing of
the meaningful visual image became—finally—one of the
principles of Japanese film-making.

From the very first, the new form was popular, the overwhelming public acceptance having several reasons. One of
them was the direct result of the earthquake and its consequent hardships. The public developed a sudden and pronounced taste for escapism. Films about contemporary life
had to reflect contemporary problems, but the sword-fight
film reflected nothing at all, no problems, no thought—just
movement. Another reason was that the public, as in so many
times of stress, was reaching for a hero. This was just what
the new period-film was prepared to offer, and soon hero
and actor were becoming confused in the public mind. By
starring in these new period-films, Ryunosuke Tsukigata,
Utaemon Ichikawa, Kanjuro Arashi, Chiezo Kataoka, Chojiro
Hayashi—later to become even more famous as Kazuo Hasegawa—and the greatest of them all, Tsumasaburo Bando, became the heroes of the public.

All were the creations of Makino, who described his theory
of film-making as: "One, strong plot; two, no unessentials,

and three, continual movement." He was opposed to deep
thinking and complicated editing, but he was also opposed
to the shameless tear-jerking of the Shimpa and the static
quality of the old Kyuha. Above all he wanted to make his
films easy to understand, while at the same time avoiding the
slowness of a Matsunosuke. His 1927 *The Loyal Forty-seven
Ronin* showed what he was trying to do. The acting style
of Shinkokugeki, which in the theater had soon abandoned
the seriousness of Shingeki and turned into a "Shimpa with
swords," proved the final answer to all of his problems.

One of the effects that these new-style period-films had
within the industry itself was to introduce the innovation
of a detailed scenario. Since the secret of the new period-
drama's success lay partially in its violence and extremely
realistic sword-fighting, all of this had to be carefully planned
in advance. This, in turn, had the effect of forcing the film-
makers to consider the script as an independent element.
Since the enthusiasm of the public warranted it, these scripts
began to be published, and today in Japan interest in the
films is such that every year about two hundred scripts of
produced films, both foreign and Japanese, are published
either in magazine or in book form.

In the meantime the industry was still shifting and changing. By 1924 there were four major companies—Nikkatsu,
Shochiku, Teikine, and a fourth company, called Toa—as well
as a number of independents. Then in 1925 the big four
formed a league, the Japan Motion Picture Producers Association, to squeeze out the independents, particularly Makino, and to forestall new competition. They formed a three-
part agreement which said that: one, the raiding of the others'
personnel was prohibited; two, other companies would not
service theaters delinquent in payment to members—the real
meaning of which was that the franchise status quo would be
frozen—and, three, companies would use only Eastman film,
which would be ordered en bloc so as to eliminate profiteer-
ing by brokers. The league also implied that all the minor
companies would be bound by the first two rules even though
they themselves could not belong to the closed association.
This pronouncement naturally worried the independents.
The league had locked them out by threatening to boycott
exhibitors who showed non-association films, and the independents themselves could not hope to produce enough
films to fill weekly bills. Thus they had to bargain for major
distribution on the big four distributors' own terms.

The next year, however, the independents struck back.

Taking a cue from Makino, the period-film stars, with their tremendous popularity, soon saw that they could do much better for themselves if they did it alone. Consequently a number of the more famous formed their own companies. Though most of these companies eventually failed, over thirty such small independents appeared between 1925 and 1930, each centering around an actor who either wanted to be a star or thought he already was, and who usually directed and starred in his own productions.

One of the more interesting of these small companies was that formed by Tsumasaburo Bando, who had been Makino's first new star, appearing in such films as *The Last Days of the Shogunate* (Bakumatsu), and who clearly understood what the new period-film had to offer. During this time many of the smaller companies were so poor that they existed without studio facilities, sometimes renting studio space but more often doing without it. Bando's company, though poor and struggling, at least had its own studio. Its big problem was distribution. Then, one day in 1925, it was approached by Universal, the American film company then the largest foreign distributor in Japan, and asked to help in opening a Japanese production branch. Universal's interest in Japan went back to 1916, when it became the first American company to set up its own distribution system in Japan.

Bando readily accepted the proposal. He needed money, and the Japanese were still inclined to think that American technique and technicians were better. Under their agreement Universal provided four American technicians and over twenty thousand dollars' worth of equipment including six Bell and Howell cameras and eighty lights. The new company, which constituted the only major attempt to introduce foreign capital into the Japanese film industry, was called Dai-Nihon Universal, but by the end of two years it had failed.

The main reason for the failure was a disagreement over the small profits earned because they had no really good writers or directors. One of the bones in this contention was a film-footage arrangement which called for the Japanese producers to be reimbursed on a direct per-foot basis. Hence they overloaded the films with long and meaningless titles— so much cheaper to shoot than live action—which began to intrude themselves even into the wildest swordplay, titles like: "I've got him!" followed by "Take that!" held on the screen for a length of time and followed by "And that!"

Despite such failures, however, the period-film had ob-

viously become the leading element of Japanese cinema.
The next few years produced such a flowering of the form that they have become known as "the golden age" of the period-drama. Here the genre became set to such an extent that the average period-films produced today are little more than simple switches on themes of pictures made during this era.

This "golden age" of thirty years ago was the last time that period-films were more important to the public, the industry, and the critics than films about contemporary life. Subsequently, the best period-films, particularly those made after World War II, were to be the work of men who came only temporarily to the period genre from their customary field of the contemporary-life film.

4 costume and property: 1927-31.

THE DEATH OF EMPEROR TAISHO IN 1926 and the succession of his son, the present emperor, marked the end of the liberal Taisho period and the beginning of the very different Showa period. One of the first indications of the change was a gradual and partial repudiation of the more liberal intellectual and cultural aspects of Western civilization, accompanied by a revival of older Japanese ideologies. Little by little, as politicians lost their power, the army and navy became the really influential forces in the government. Opinion within Japan itself became divided when the farmers began supporting the military against the urban rich. Under military leadership Japan was very shortly to begin its dangerous program of territorial expansion in China.

There were many reasons for this sudden change. For one thing, the depression hit Japan before Europe and America, and in 1927 a serious bank crisis occurred. Also the overpopulation of Japan, a problem since the late Tokugawa period, was becoming serious. Public concern over this question and the failure of emigration to provide any solution led to an emphasis on manufacturing and foreign trade as one way to provide both money and employment. By 1928 Japanese industrial capacity had grown rapidly and Japanese manufactured goods began to flood the world market.

By this time there had already been minor clashes between the Chinese and the Japanese. When the latter temporarily seized control of the railways in Shantung, China boycotted the invaders for over a year, and in the end the Japanese were forced to withdraw their troops though the Chinese background 64 back-ground had to pay the damages. Inside the country there was considerable unrest. Labor unions had been growing and by 1929 there were a total of six hundred associations with membership totaling almost a third of a million. Dissatisfaction reigned and in that year there were well over a thousand strikes and almost two thousand five hundred stop-work disputes, rather startling figures when one considers that violent police suppression was common.

The films reflected this unrest in two ways. The first was pure escape, the search for the nihilistic hero; this need was fully satisfied by the period-drama. The second was the search for a violent solution to Japan's economic ills, and this was met mostly by the so-called "tendency films," those motion pictures which sought to encourage, or fight against, a given social tendency. This term, originating in Europe, soon came to have leftist connotations.

The "golden age" of the period-film was almost entirely the work of two men: Daisuke Ito, one of the most talented pupils of Osanai's original Shochiku Cinema Institute, and Masahiro Makino, the eldest son of Shozo, who learned the business as a boy by appearing in his father's films.

Makino became a director in 1927, when he was only eighteen years old, and from the beginning showed something of his father's feeling for spectacle, though he was much more aware of the resources of the cinema than his father had ever been. In 1928 he made a number of period-films, including *The Race Track at Sozenji* (Sozenji Baba), *Fighting Cocks* (Keai-dori), and *The Street of Masterless Samurai* (Ronin-gai), the latter being a study of decadent society in the Tokugawa era. His 1929 *Beheading Place* (Kubi no Za) indicates the form his films usually took. It was about a *ronin*, or masterless samurai, who, falsely accused of a crime, makes the discovery that people only believe what they want to believe. The hero in all these films was usually a samurai, masterless or not, or sometimes a sort of "chivalrous commoner" who is allowed to carry a sword—or, again, he might be a gambler. The plot usually turns upon his receiving an obligation, usually accidentally, which he must discharge by performing some dangerous or distasteful deed, often in conflict with other duties or obligations. Other plot movers are revenge and the protection of the innocent.

While Makino was content to set the patterns, it was Daisuke Ito who, almost single-handedly, pushed the period-film to its greatest heights. Born in 1898, he was originally inter-

ested in drama, acting in Gorky's *The Lower Depths* before
joining the Shochiku Cinema Institute as a script writer. He became a director in 1924 and two years later joined Nikkatsu, forming a team with the actor Denjiro Okochi. With Ito's help the actor became one of the biggest period stars of all time, answering almost perfectly the public need for the superhero, the nihilistic samurai.

Ito had long been noted for the violent realism of his films or, more particularly, for the amount of blood and horror he managed to show on the screen. His early scripts give some indication of this. In his *Don't Fall in Love* (Nasuna Koi), written for Hotei Nomura around 1922, he had the lovers commit suicide on the second floor so that their blood could drip through the ceiling and down onto the first floor. In his script for Yoshinobu Ikeda's *Going through Darkness* (Yami o Iku) he had the hunchbacked hero throw himself on the funeral pyre of his beloved for a final flaming embrace.

His best films, which began appearing after 1927, continued this love for the spectacular or shocking effect but, more important, began more and more to reflect the director's growing interest in reality. In showing the nihilistic hero it was still necessary to have something for the hero to be nihilistic about, and consequently Ito's films became more and more critical of society as a whole, thus paving the way in the period-film for the left-wing tendency pictures which were to come.

Servant (Gero), made in 1927, may be taken as a direct forerunner of the tendency film. It was a savage exposure of Tokugawa-period feudalism, and it broke with the usual pattern in that it did not center around a morally pure superman. Later in the year he began filming his multipart *A Diary of Chuji's Travels* (Chuji Tabi Nikki), which was followed in 1928 by *Ooka's Trial* (Ooka Seidan), a film which, filled with blood and horror as it was, contained Ito's philosophy of rebellion and his exaltation of the nihilist hero. In contradistinction to almost all prior period-heroes, the heroes of these films neither defended nor ignored the social system, but were instead in full revolt against it. Ito's philosophy was, in part, the philosophy of his time, and the former film was enormously popular, so much so that in 1930 he made a sequel to it, and in 1931 another.

His *Man-Slashing, Horse-Piercing Sword* (Zanjin Zamba Ken), made in 1930, was even more outspoken in its denunciation of the "exploiting classes," social criticism being easily hidden under the armor of the samurai. What was unusual about the film was Ito's treatment, since the story itself was rather typical of the average period-film. A *ronin* is searching for his father's enemy, sustaining himself in his search by stealing from the farmers because he knows they cannot oppose him without arms. Later he agrees to help in their fight against the local government when he discovers that the enemy of his father is actually a government official. The hero's motivation somewhat tended to vitiate the social criticism, but Ito's audience seems to have known what he was doing and, again, he had a success. With its near-symbolic hero leading the people in revolt, the film had scenes resembling Pudovkin's *Storm Over Asia*, a movie which had not yet been seen in Japan. An even closer comparison could be made with Kurosawa's 1954 *Seven Samurai* (Shichi-nin no Samurai), released in America as *The Magnificent Seven*, a film which had the same tendency-like theme.

Though Ito and, to some extent, Makino were making the genre what it was to remain for decades, others too were making period-dramas. Among them were Hiroshi Inagaki, who in 1927 had become a director in Tsumasaburo Bando's short-lived company, and Kinugasa, who, leaving the experiments of *Crossroads* far behind, brought sound and spectacle to the period-drama with an all-talking *The Loyal Forty-seven Ronin*. In main, however, it was Ito who was not only typical of the period and the genre, but who also gave its films their vigor. He continued to make excellent films, including his first talkie, the 1933 *Sazen Tange* (Tange Sazen), which contained much of the spirit of the silent era; but his talent did not long survive the era of sound. From a first-class director he eventually became a purveyor of mere swordplay melodrama, and though several later films have shown flashes of genius, none of them has approached his best earlier work.

It was Ito, however, who originally gave the period-film as it is known today its original impetus. Since his heroes performed against the background of society, it was his trenchant criticism of society which made the period-film a vehicle for criticism and thus partly helped to make possible the tendency film which did much in teaching the Japanese cinema how to think for itself.

The conditions which helped produce the tendency film in Japan were much the same as the conditions which were producing similar films abroad. While the Japanese government had its hands full with other things, a number of leftist tendencies in the country came into full view for the first

time. The depression had pushed into public attention an
entire section of the population hitherto largely ignored, the
lower middle-class and the so-called proletariat. This new
interest was both directed and maneuvered, the aim being a
state of civil chaos from which revolution might arise.

From this came a new kind of Japanese film, a film supposedly very realist in manner, always adamantly contemporary, and nearly always concerned with a specific social
issue. These tendency pictures, though short-lived as a movement, helped make realism in the films all the stronger and
opened the eyes of both maker and audience to such an extent
that Japanese films were never again the same.

One of the reasons that the Japanese film industry fell so
easily into the innovation of the realistic tendency films,
when hitherto it had bristled at the very mention of the
new and untried, was that just before this time the Nikkatsu contemporary-life film had turned toward an extreme
form of romanticism. When tendency films came, Nikkatsu
swung correspondingly far in the opposite direction. Shochiku, on the other hand, whose films were always more
oriented toward the female audience, found little reason to
inject politics into tear-jerkers.

The political implications of the tendency pictures were
quite new to the Japanese film-scene, but in the sense that
the genre merely reflected prevailing social conditions it
was not a complete stranger. In 1925 Kenji Mizoguchi had
used a slice-of-life technique in the four-part omnibus *Street
Sketches* (Gaijo no Suketchi) and his 1926 *A Paper Doll's
Whisper of Spring* (Kami-Ningyo Haru no Sasayaki) had
looked long and searchingly at the lower middle-class.
Murata's *Ashes* (Kaijin), made in 1929, showed a cross
section of Japan divided during the Meiji period as reflected
in a lower-class family, and Gosho's 1927 *Tricky Girl* (Kara-
kuri Musume) was also concerned with the plight of the
poor, though Sergei Eisenstein called it "a melodramatic
farce," adding that it "begins in the manner of Monty Banks
[and] ends in incredible gloom."

From 1929 to 1931 many tendency films appeared. One of
the earliest was Tomu Uchida's *A Living Doll* (Ikeru Ningyo), based on a successful Shingeki play, in turn adapted
from a popular novel about a man who rises in the world
by cheating and is in the end cheated by society. In 1929
Mizoguchi made *Tokyo March* (Tokyo Koshinkyoku) and
Metropolitan Symphony (Tokai Kokyogaku), both of which
had similar plots in which the life of a proletarian family was

contrasted with an upper-class counterpart, the connecting links being love and rivalry between the families. In the latter film he used dynamic montage, borrowed from the ideas of the Russians, to throw sudden contrasts at the audience, the very different proletarian and bourgeois worlds as seen by a working girl and an upper-class daughter. The two heroines were played by Shizue Natsukawa and Takako Irie, two top actresses, public taste having already changed to the extent that the traditional Japanese qualities of Sumiko Kurishima and Yoshiko Kawada had been discarded; the public now preferred something more up-to-date: short hair, Western clothes, rouge, and lipstick.

The genre continued with Shigeyoshi Suzuki's *What Made Her Do It?* (Nani ga Kanojo o so Saseta ka), which was based upon a popular Shingeki play. In this 1930 film, a poor girl, finding society against her, is forced to commit arson. Her story is told in flashbacks with dramatic camera angles used for their introspective quality. She started life poor and there is no escape from her misery. She is branded for life. When this film was shown in Tokyo's Asakusa district, audiences rioted in support of its anti-capitalist sentiments, being excited to the point of loud cries of "Down with Capitalism!" and the like. It became the biggest hit in the history of the silent Japanese cinema, running for many weeks in Tokyo and two months in Osaka. After the tremendous profits brought in by this film, no company could resist the tendency picture despite its political orientation. In the same year there was a spate of such pictures, among them Eichi Koishi's *Challenge* (Chosen) and *A History of Undercurrents during the Meiji Restoration* (Ishin Anryu-shi), the latter with a plot taken from, of all things, Rafael Sabatini's *Scaramouche.*

Tomotaka Tasaka's story of a suffering widow, *Behold This Mother* (Kono Haha o Miyo), also made in 1930, proved just how well adapted the *haha-mono*, mother picture, was for the purposes of these tendency pictures. Even sentimental Kiyohiko Ushihara got into the tendency-film act with *The Great Metropolis: Chapter on Labor* (Daitokai Rodo-hen). In 1931 Yasujiro Shimazu made *ABC Lifeline* (Seikatsusen ABC), which explained the class struggle in the most romantic of terms.

Kinugasa's *Before Dawn* (Reimei Izen), the first picture he made upon returning from Europe, was a period-drama about women sold into prostitution, their misery, and, eventually, their revolt. This film might be said to have closed

the era of the tendency film. The censors from the very first
had frowned upon the movement; some films, like Masahiro Makino's *The Street of Masterless Samurai,* which was voted the *Kinema Jumpo* "Best One" of 1928, had had to be cut quite severely. Others, like Tomu Uchida's projected *The Bluebird* (Aoi Tori)—the story, owing something to Maeterlinck but more to Marx, was about a bluebird whose powers prove the only salvation of the working-class—were summarily halted by the censor, who was quite obviously afraid of hidden symbols.

The Japanese censors were particularly worried about the left extreme of the tendency movement, the Japan Proletarian Motion Picture League, which had been formed in 1929 specifically to make documents of the Communist movement in Japan. This movement coincided with the active propaganda troupes in the Shingeki. Despite the extremely low quality of its products, this organization, nicknamed "Pro Kino" for proletarian cinema, was kept active filming demonstrations, slums, and May Days, though it did not have enough resources to move into the dramatic-film field and was eventually suppressed by the laws governing "public peace."

The Japanese tendency-film movement, the world's largest, had its relatives abroad in the German radical theater of the 1920's which in turn influenced such pictures as the most famous of all tendency films, S. Theodore Dudow's *Kuhle Wampe.* What is surprising, however, is that most of the tendency films in Japan reached the screen with little or no direct inspiration from the lively Russian cinema itself. Both *Potemkin* and *Mother* were refused entry into Japan, so the first revolutionary films seen were *Storm Over Asia* and Mihael Kaufmann's *Spring,* both of which were not shown until the tendency-film period was almost over. Films like Turin's *Turksib,* Dovshenko's *Earth,* and Eisenstein's *The General Line,* from which the Japanese movement could have learned much, were finally seen in Japan in 1931, too late for them to have any but the most general influence. The Japanese government would certainly have forbidden entry to these films if they had come from any other country than Russia and perhaps admitted them now only out of extreme eagerness to placate Soviet suspicion of Japan's Manchurian adventures. Also, as shown in such pictures as Pudovkin's, Mongolians in revolt against the British very nicely served Japan's own propaganda interests.

Just how deeply the Japanese films of this period were

influenced from the outside remains obscure. The tendency
film in Japan does not seem to have been following any specific "line." Rather, its creators were interested in social problems simply because they concerned human beings. Making films as examples of specific political doctrines seems to have been far from their intentions. In part they were following the leftist drift of national thought during the period but, at the same time, were without any real identification with a radical movement. In Japan one often sees a profound indifference to political motives, and it is by no means unknown that those on the left will overnight change to the right, and the other way around. When the Japanese government began censoring and suppressing tendency films, the ease with which both government and film-makers satisfied themselves and each other seems quite typical of this profound lack of political conviction in the Japanese.

The tendency-film movement broke into two parts. One, somewhat singularly, joined the "nonsense picture" and drifted off in the direction of erotic comedy, where it remains to this day. The other shifted its aim ever so slightly and, instead of purposely or accidentally suggesting that their characters were part of the "workers' world," made them members of the "lumpenproletariat," that section of the population which the Communist Manifesto so luridly describes as a "passively rotting mass thrown off by the lowest layers of the old society," that section which would probably become the "bribed tool of reactionary intrigue."

The government was pacified and a long train of films about life in the lower depths shuffled forth, led by the 1931 Yoshinobu Ikeda film *Village Lumpen* (Machi no Rumpen). Later in the year, Mizoguchi contributed *And Yet They Go On* (Shikamo Karera wa Iku), about a mother and daughter who become prostitutes. The oppression of society was implicit in these films but not indicted as in the tendency pictures. This ashcan school of films, incidentally, still limps along and is still collectively known as *rumpen-mono*.

In the same year Mizoguchi also made *The Dawn of the Founding of Manchukuo and Mongolia* (Man-Mo Kenkoku no Reimei). That he could make a propaganda film eulogizing the government's expansionist policies in the same year that he made his sympathetic picture of the pauperized mother and daughter is indicative of the total lack of any usual acceptance of political affiliation. This is true not only of Mizoguchi, but of most Japanese as well. Their historical sense is so refined and their political sense often so primitive that they have undeservedly been called political hypocrites.

Both the tendency film and the *rumpen-mono* merely reflected, and to some extent perhaps fostered, an attitude which, in the late 1920's, was quite international. At that time the Soviet experiment actually seemed to hold some promise, and very few indeed were the countries that did not respond to it in some way. In Japan, however, the influence of the tendency film was eventually unpolitical. What it changed was neither public opinion nor the social structure. Rather, it made use of subject matter which had up to that time been largely neglected, and it led film-makers away from the established clichés of both presentation and thought and into something more truly creative, more personal, and more truly Japanese. The message died stillborn in Japan, but the films it had perhaps inspired offered a new way of looking at the world. And, again, it is perhaps characteristic of the Japanese that the film-makers, quite neglecting the content of the tendency films, should rather foster the form of these films. What they were interested in—as always—was the way in which a new thought, a new technique could be adapted to Japanese standards. Thus, the Japanese cinema became increasingly aware of realism as an artistic technique, realism as a storytelling style. And, as in other countries, no sooner had this basic fact of film art been finally established than sound came in and put the development of film art back half a decade.

5 the talkies, exterior: 1931-39. ONLY in the talkie era did films become really big business in Japan. There had been strong competition within the industry for some time, but with the success of the sound film the rivalry became acute. Companies became larger and larger—or else failed.

Japan, unlike many countries, did not take instantly to the talkies. In fact, they did not become a popular success until several years after their introduction. It was the popularity of subtitled foreign talkies that finally drove the domestic industry into sound production. Even then, most Japanese directors refused to have anything to do with the "new toy," feeling that they had already evolved a perfectly adequate style and that the silent film offered all that was necessary to tell a story. Some, like Ozu, felt that they were finally on the verge of reaching the summit of a new art form and that sound was a most unwelcome interruption.

Shochiku's stumbling entrance into the sound era is perhaps indicative of the industry as a whole. Heinosuke Gosho's recent films had been doing very badly at the box office, and after all the other Shochiku directors had flatly rejected sound, the producers turned to him and delivered an ultimatum. He was thus persuaded to do a two-reel trial talkie and was then talked into turning it into a feature.

Gosho's idea of a good talkie was—and to some extent remains—one containing a large amount of silence. He also felt that there should be some intrinsic reason for sound other than mere commercial expediency. After searching, he found a story which lent itself to his ideas: A writer cannot work because the woman next door, a very modern type, has a jazz band practicing in her house. He protests, they become friendly, and a triangle situation develops involving the writer's wife. *The Neighbor's Wife and Mine* (Madamu to Nyobo) is perhaps unimportant to Gosho's status as a director and certainly plays only a very small part in the general aesthetic of the Japanese film, but it does show the director's attitude toward his craft and even today remains indicative of the early Japanese use of sound at its best.

In shooting the film there were no re-recording or dubbing facilities, so that everything had to be recorded at the same time on the final track. All the background sound, plus the jazz band so important to the plot, had to be recorded during shooting. Day after day both cast and production staff were accompanied by the jazz band wherever they went. For exterior scenes the orchestra would often have to find a place for itself among trees and bushes, blowing and fiddling away under the dialogue. They had the greatest difficulty with long-shots since they had to hide the microphone and also had to somehow skirt the orchestra as well. Finally, to get a sense of inter-cutting within scenes, they used several cameras running simultaneously and later cut together the parts they needed from each set-up. Gosho finally finished the film, and to everyone's surprise it was a brilliant success, winning him the 1931 *Kinema Jumpo* "Best One" award. One Japanese critic, on viewing the film two decades later, said of Gosho: "He remained within cinematic traditions and borrowed none from the stage. . . . He knew from the start that film must always be film and must not attempt to be recorded theater."

Gosho's attitude toward sound was quite different from the attitude being shown in other countries, where stage plays were being photographed and conversation for its own sake was insisted upon. Though it was not too long before Japan was doing precisely the same thing, Gosho had, at any rate, indicated the direction of the truly cinematic sound film.

Although by no means the earliest, Gosho's was the first completely successful Japanese talkie. Ever since 1902, when the Yoshizawa Company made a few sound films using the Kinetophone disc-process, there had been sporadic attempts, but all of them were highly unsuccessful.

In 1914, several companies launched independent efforts, the largest being that of the Nihon Kinetophone Corporation, which like Yoshizawa based its system on a sound-on-disc process. It, like all the others, failed largely because of the inability to synchronize records with film and because of the lack of amplification needed for large theaters.

In 1925, De Forest's Phonofilm, direct from America, was premiered at the Shimbashi Embujo, showing a mixed bill of musical shorts: instrumental, vocal, and dance. The system used electronic amplification, in contrast to the older system of mechanical reproduction, but its appeal was strictly novelty since it was out of synchronization most of the time. The process, despite its imperfections, obviously impressed some-one, however, for shortly afterward the Showa Kinema Company was formed to make films using the Phonofilm process. They built studios in a remodeled theater, but since the building was not soundproofed and since a railway ran close by, they could only shoot between midnight and five-thirty in the morning, when there was no outside traffic. Even then they had to stop for long periods at a time when the various nocturnal food-sellers prowled the neighboring alleys, blowing their horns and ringing their bells.

In 1928 another company, Nihon Toki, was organized to make sound films. They too used records, but instead of recording while the picture was being shot, they dubbed everything after the film was edited. Even then the finished product was by no means perfect.

All of these systems had drawbacks. Records became quickly unsynchronized, while sound-on-film, though matching lip-movements, was execrable. There were several more experiments with records, including three films shot in Kyoto by the Makino Company, which used a Japanese "invention," with even more spectacularly unsuccessful results.

By 1929, however, it had become clear that the talkies were something with which the Japanese industry would sooner or later have to come to terms. The convincer was the Fox Movietone musical short *Marching On*, which was shown at the Musashino-kan in Shinjuku and played to full houses for two months, at a time when a two-week run was considered a smash hit.

Some people were not impressed. The critic Yoshihiko Tanaka wrote: "As advertised, this is all-talking. Too much so, because there is no room for the *benshi* explanation. At first the mere mechanics may impress Japanese audiences, but they will soon tire of something they cannot under-stand." Other critics wrote manifestos against the talkies, saying that costs made profits impossible, that the talkies

were only a fad, and, oddly, that talkies were not an art like
silent films but a science.

In the meantime, neither *benshi* nor musicians, both still
fairly active accouterments of the silent screen, were going
to sit quietly by and wait for the critics to drive the erring
public back into the fold. The Fox talking shorts opened
in May and by August the Musashino-kan musicians were
on strike, later joined by musicians and *benshi* from other
leading theaters. The *benshi* had been thrown into complete
confusion by the coming of sound. At first they kept silent,
hoping that the talking films would go away. Then they
decided to take the offensive and tried to narrate over the
sound. This was difficult because they had no public-address
systems and were forced to shout as loud as they could.
Soon they learned to cut down the volume to let themselves
be heard, and, finally, some *benshi* turned off the sound
altogether, showing the film as though it were silent and, as
always, faithfully narrating. Some even narrated strictly
musical shorts which had only songs.

The *benshi* were not alone in their difficulties. The many
theaters specializing in American films faced a tremendous
problem when, upon paying out a lot of money to install
the necessary equipment, they discovered that audiences,
already tired of novelty, would not come because they could
not understand English. This proved a boon to European
films, still largely silent, but the distributors began to worry.

Business was so bad that many of the first-class theaters
in Tokyo were cutting their admission prices from fifteen
to seven cents. Still the audience would not return. News of
the difficulties reached Hollywood and several American
companies tried importing Japanese talent to put into
musical-revue pictures. *Paramount on Parade,* made in
1930, was shown in a specially made "Japanese version,"
in which a Japanese master of ceremonies was cut in between the various acts. In 1931 Fox tried dubbing *The Man
Who Came Back,* starring Charles Farrell, into Japanese.
After spending much money and arranging for more than
the usual fanfare, they found the picture an unconditional
failure. For one thing, it had been dubbed in the United
States using available Japanese, whose language had become
somewhat old-fashioned, and for another, the people used
were amateurs who knew nothing of acting and who made
no attempt whatever to synchronize Japanese dialogue with
the lip movement.

Dubbing was obviously not the answer for the Japanese.

By 1936 only five foreign films had been dubbed and none of them could be considered successful. The audience simply refused to accept foreigners speaking Japanese. One might add, however, that the sight of Japanese in foreign films using foreign languages is apparently equally as shocking. For example, the tendency of the Japanese audience to be disturbed at the sight of Kaoru Yachigusa using Italian in *Madame Butterfly*. Finally a group of men took the lead in finding a better way of explaining the dialogue to the Japanese audience and eventually decided to use subtitles. The men involved were Tadashi Iijima and Akira Iwasaki, both film critics; Yoshihiko Tamura, now with Daiei's export branch; and Musei Tokugawa, who was the top *benshi* of the day.

Tamura was dispatched to the United States and there did the titles for the first subtitled film to come to Japan, Josef von Sternberg's *Morocco*. After he had finished the Japanese version, which averaged only thirty titles a reel, the film was released in February, 1931, with such fantastic success that delegates of the less forward-looking *benshi* paid visits to the Paramount Tokyo offices and, with no success whatever, tried to get the company to withdraw it.

Before *Morocco*, attempts had been made to provide translation of the dialogue by using a small screen placed beside the main one and on it projecting slides containing the Japanese. This was a most unsuccessful procedure because the operator of the projector never knew English and, having no cues for his titles, would always become confused. This meant that, on occasion, he would run out of slides before the end of the picture or, worse still, would have yet a number to project after the film had ended. The subtitled *Morocco*, however, seemed to answer all problems.

Not all perhaps, for, until the commercial value of sound was fully proved, few theater owners wanted to install the sound equipment necessary when they could have much less expensive all-talkies in the form of the *benshi*. Many theaters had phonographs, mostly because of the tendency which had arisen to connect Japanese features with theme-songs, but sound equipment was quite another thing. Thus, for the best of financial reasons, the Japanese companies stayed away from sound for as long as they could. Another reason was that the cost of making films in Japan had, because of simple sets and cheap labor, been extremely low. The added machinery necessary for making talkies, however, required triple-sized budgets. Other countries, of course, had to pay

the same high price, but their margin of profit had always
been higher, so they could make the switch-over without
too much difficulty. During this era of war-industry investment the Japanese simply did not have the money.

In 1929, Nikkatsu, taking the plunge, used a sound-on-disc
system called Minatoki. They made two features, *The Cap-
tain's Daughter* (Taii no Musume) and Mizoguchi's *Hometown* (Furusato). The dialogue during filming was written
on blackboards in the manner of the Teleprompter or "idiot
board," and the actors were constantly looking off the set
to reassure themselves. Both films were unsuccessful, perhaps
because Nikkatsu greedily raised admission prices fifty percent. The failure had the result of frightening the company
away from sound for some time to come.

Shochiku, profiting from Nikkatsu's example, eventually
decided to try sound-on-film, using a Japanese variable-
density system called Tsuchibashi. By this time there were
at least several dozen sound-on-disc features, all unsuccessful,
and Shochiku realized that it was taking a big risk in entering what was proving a dangerous field. The principle of
novelty, which accounted largely for the success of sound
abroad, was partly missing in Japan, where the audience,
long inured to the *benshi*, took sound quite for granted.
Still, Shochiku took the step, and Gosho's *The Neighbor's
Wife and Mine* was such a triumph that it put the company
on top for years to come. Many small companies, unable
to compete, promptly failed when Shochiku followed up
its lead. In 1932 alone, of the forty-five talkies made (out of
four hundred features for the year), thirty were Shochiku's.

These included quite a number which are still remembered.
Yasujiro Shimazu made his *First Steps Ashore* (Joriku no
Dai-ippo), inspired by Von Sternberg's *The Docks of New
York* and Kinugasa made the first period-drama talkie with
his version of *The Surviving Shinsengumi* (Ikinokota Shinsengumi), a film about a group of swordsmen sent to Kyoto
by the shogunate to counteract royalist moves during the
Meiji Restoration. Becoming more confident in the new
medium, Kinugasa released his version of *The Loyal Forty-
seven Ronin*, which had a top cast led by Kazuo Hasegawa,
Kinuyo Tanaka, and Utaemon Ichikawa, the Kabuki actor.
Not only the sound but also the quick cutting was admired
by many critics, and in the following year he made *Kimpei
from Koina* (Koina no Kimpei) and *Two Stone Lanterns*
(Futatsu no Toro), the latter being considered the top
period-film of 1933.

Despite success, all was not going too smoothly with
Shochiku. Its main problem was the opposition it was running into regarding its rather ruthless policy of "fire the
benshi," who, frantic, were prepared to go to practically any
extremes. By April, 1932, the group formerly belonging to
the Shochiku chain specializing in foreign films had formed
a strong protection group. One of its major questions was
the size of the "retirement allowance" it would demand. This
demand of payment was backed by strong-arm methods.
Just a month before, Shiro Kido had been attacked in his
home by two gangsters who turned out to have been in the
pay of the *benshi*. Kido was unhurt and the gangsters were
arrested, but the attack more than dramatized the delicate
relations existing between employer and former employees.

By 1932, after Shochiku's success in the field, Nikkatsu
recovered enough confidence to make another try at the
talkies. Upon announcement of their intentions, the Nikkatsu
benshi and musicians immediately went on strike. While such
strikes had not too much affected Shochiku, they proved
disastrous to Nikkatsu. With its vested exhibition interests to
consider, this company was always the last to convert to new
ways. Just as it had been the last to drop the *oyama*, it was
now last to turn to sound production. The 1932 strike hit
the company so hard that its studios were closed down and
foreign films were booked to fill out its distribution commit-
ments.

In a mood of despair, Nikkatsu approached the Photo
Chemical Laboratories in Tokyo, sent a cast and crew from
their Kyoto studios, and made *Timely Mediator* (Toki no
Ujigami), directed by Kenji Mizoguchi and starring Koji
Shima. This was the first successful Nikkatsu sound-on-film
talkie. Heartened, they released a minor period-drama and
then, two weeks later, Minoru Murata's *Shanghai* (Shanhai).
Though the latter director was in decline, the result was
even more feeble than was expected. He had simply transferred the North African locale of Josef von Sternberg's
Morocco to China.

Despite the unevenness of these products, Nikkatsu finally
saw the light and began to take sound seriously. After
making its first talkie of genuine value—Tomotaka Tasaka's
Spring and a Girl (Haru to Musume), with a script by
Murata and Kajiro Yamamoto—Nikkatsu and the Photo
Chemical Laboratories parted company. The latter, at first
working with a post-recording sound method even now much
used, decided to produce films on its own. Nikkatsu, having

its own studios, contracted with Western Electric for its sound system.

The American concern was in a position to talk business since, just the year before, it had sent equipment and American technicians over to the small Oriental Company, an independent which had some backing from Paramount. The American engineers, however, had not had enough experience: there was both delay and loss and after only one picture the company failed. Western Electric, with expensive equipment going unused in Japan, was eager to come to terms with almost anyone, and when the contract was finally signed, in 1933, Nikkatsu owned the best-quality recording equipment available at the time, though as usual there was some fuss about a Japanese concern's having to suffer the indignity of paying royalties to a foreign company.

All was not well at Nikkatsu even then. It suffered from bad management at the policy-making level. In 1920 it had ignored new techniques; it continued to refuse to produce its contemporary-life films in Tokyo, the center of modern Japan; in 1930 it had tried to act as though talkies did not exist; it refused to raise the pay of its top stars and directors; and it forced employees to make pictures they did not like. The consequence was that many of its best people—Minoru Murata, Tomotaka Tasaka, Tomu Uchida, Daisuke Ito, Kenji Mizoguchi, and many of its top stars—walked out, deciding they could do better on their own. These withdrawals brought about a second cycle of independent production. Murata organized the Shin-Eiga-Sha (New Motion Picture Company) and rented the Photo Chemical Laboratories' recently constructed studios. Daisuke Ito scripted the first production and Tomotaka Tasaka directed. It was an action picture called *Showa Era Shinsengumi* (Showa Shinsengumi), starring two top ex-Nikkatsu stars, Isamu Kosugi and Koji Shima. Shochiku, always anxious to irritate the rival Nikkatsu, thoughtfully provided wide distribution for the film.

Shochiku too was suffering. In 1931 seven of its best talents, including its three biggest male stars, withdrew to form Fuji Eiga, which soon failed mainly because it had neglected to attract good directors and good business managers. Shochiku retaliated by organizing talent and "new face" contests in an attempt to build up new stars, but by now even its unacknowledged offspring, a newly organized company called Shinko, was having trouble. Formed from the old Teikine with additional secret Shochiku capital, the small

company was now laid low when Sotoji Kimura, one of its
leading directors, gathered about thirty members with him and went on strike for more enlightened production policies. The striking group was waylaid by a group of gangsters and blood flowed. Kimura and most of the others withdrew permanently, leaving behind a number of unfinished pictures, and Shinko was able to recover only by rehiring talent from Shin-Eiga-Sha and Fuji Eiga, both of whose days were numbered.

In 1933, Nikkatsu decided to spread out and began shopping for Tokyo studio sites, approaching various private electric-railway companies because the supply of electricity to studios was an enormous problem and the railway companies often owned blocks of land parallel to their tracks. The Keio Line, a small railway servicing the Tokyo suburbs, suggested the Tamagawa studios of an independent company which had recently failed. The railroad offered free electrical distribution equipment, and the only stage was still practically brand new; Nikkatsu made the purchase. A year later they built more sound stages as well as apartments for their workers, moved in, and began production. The move to Tokyo and the adoption of the Western Electric recording system brought in much needed capital and once more the company stock rose.

Hearing of all this activity at Tamagawa, Shochiku was worried, even though it was still the biggest combine and Nikkatsu was still too much occupied with its *benshi*-musician strike to offer any real competition. Nevertheless, even though Nikkatsu was down, it was still kicking. So Shochiku decided it was time to insure its rival's failure by forming yet a second subsidiary in addition to Shinko. Within the month the new Dai-Ichi Eiga was formed. The nominal head was Masaichi Nagata, some ten years with Nikkatsu and, just a month before, head of the production and scenario department of Nikkatsu's new Tamagawa studios.

Nagata, who had entered Nikkatsu as a studio guide in 1924, was among those who, in a move to break the company's "feudalistic" practices, had forced the long-time president Einosuke Yokota to resign. The new president, Sadatomo Nakatani, began a complete renovation of the company by firing a number of people. In the midst of all this Nagata quit, saying that he did not like this sudden firing of veteran personnel, that he was embarrassed when Nakatani found fault with a narration he had written for a film, and that he also disliked sudden commands to do a picture

"in twenty days and eight thousand feet" without consideration of other factors.

These were the reasons that Nagata gave the newspapers. Nikkatsu told the newspapers a different story, saying that Nagata had resigned because he had heard that the company was investigating the report of his having accepted a bribe. According to Nikkatsu, it was later "proved" that Nagata had taken a twenty-thousand-dollar bribe from Shochiku to sabotage production at Nikkatsu's new Tokyo studios. Amid all this talk about money it was ascertained that a part of the sum needed for forming Dai-Ichi Eiga came from Mrs. Nagata's exclusive English school for children of the Kyoto elite, but just where the rest came from remained undetermined.

Shochiku, very quick to guarantee the new company a ready outlet for its films in the form of a full distribution contract, began to relax, certain that the new Dai-Ichi Eiga would very soon begin to aggravate Nikkatsu. Almost immediately, however, Shochiku had its security snatched away when its supremacy was challenged from an entirely different quarter. The threat came from Toho, a company which had started small but grown rapidly.

The birth of Toho had been inauspicious enough. In 1929 the Photo Chemical Laboratories (shortened to P.C.L.) had been founded by Yasuji Uemura, who had studied photographic chemistry in Germany. Initially his plan was merely to do laboratory work, but two years later the small concern built rental studios for sound production. It raised its capital from various companies, including Meiji Candy, Japan Wireless, and Dai-Nippon Beer. As soon as Shochiku's sound-film success had registered, P.C.L. was approached by Nikkatsu who wanted to use the new sound facilities. P.C.L. agreed, but before long financial agreements were such that the deal was called off. Instead, P.C.L. went into production itself, making a series of musical advertising features for their backers, the candy company and the brewery.

In these 1933 productions P.C.L. introduced the "producer system" as opposed to the previous "director system." This meant that the producer would be responsible for the finished production and that everything would thus be under his command. Each producer would select the scripts for the directors under him and would, in turn, be responsible to a general producer.

The company was also opposed to the current view that big stars and big directors were of prime importance in the

success of a film, much preferring to substitute good stories,
modern technique, and close financial supervision. Thus they
broke with the "feudal" system which assumed that employees and studio were mutually bound to each other for
life, and hired everyone on a one-to-three-year contract. If
those hired did not come through or if business was bad,
they were fired. This was in direct contrast to the "family
system" of Japanese business, particularly movie business,
where actors were kept on even when they had neither
drawing power nor talent.

On the other hand, because of their insistence upon the
excellence of the end product, they saw no trouble in building up new stars and directors, thus for a while dispensing
with the usual practice of a new company's stealing established talent from its older rivals. Instead, hoping to create
new film stars, they drew their talent from vaudeville and
Shingeki, and since they wanted to overcome *benshi* opposition, they gave top-*benshi* Musei Tokugawa starring rôles.

Because their early advertising films had been musicals,
they continued in the same general direction, creating the
popular-song genre which Toho still continues. These are
not actually movies so much as photographed vaudeville
turns, many actually sponsored by record companies anxious
to publicize their songs and artists. Including these popular-
song films, P.C.L. made nine features in 1934, seventeen in
1935, and twenty-five in 1936. Though lacking the capital
to expand, they drew a lot of attention with their "modern"
methods and became one of the two small producing companies destined to be turned into Toho.

The other was the J.O. Company, created by a Kyoto man
named Yoshio Osawa. The second initial in the company
name stood for Osawa and the first for Jenkins, the name
of an American recording system to which Osawa had rights.
His company had its own laboratory, in which he used Agfa
supplies since he was the Japanese agent for the German
company. Though he had not precisely planned to open
his own studio, having unsuccessfully tried to sell the Jenkins
rights to Nikkatsu, he eventually turned to producing advertising films in Kyoto as a way of making money.

These two companies soon came to the attention of the
one man who had just the means of creating a new giant
within the industry. This was Ichizo Kobayashi, who had
made a fortune in real estate along his Osaka-Kobe railroad
line, creating and developing the town of Takarazuka and
forming the famous all-girl "opera" troupe of the same name.

In 1932 he organized the Tokyo Takarazuka Theater Corporation and in 1934 acquired both the Hibiya Theater and the Yuraku-za. Across the street from them, in downtown Tokyo, he built the elaborate Tokyo Takarazuka Theater, better known in the days of the U.S. military occupation as the Ernie Pyle. This cost over a million dollars, and Kobayashi even hoped, without success, to take over nearby Hibiya Park, Tokyo's only centrally located spot of greenery, turning it into an amusement center connected by tunnels to his new theater.

His only rival in the neighborhood was the Nihon Gekijo, completed in 1934 on the pattern of the New York Roxy. Kobayashi, determined on a monopoly, waged an especially fierce price war, and after he had all but bankrupted the Nihon Gekijo, he bought the original owners out and by 1935 was ready to launch his drive for absolute power in the industry.

His formula for success, he said, was family entertainment, low admissions, and theaters convenient to public transportation. In line with these policies he moved into the field of stage presentation, not as a troupe-owner like Shochiku but merely as a promoter. He offered four hours of entertainment at an eighty-cent top as opposed to Shochiku's six hours at $2.50 top, even managing to book some Shochiku troupes because of his lucrative offers. Soon Shochiku was uneasily forced to cut both playing time and admission.

With this success, Kobayashi continued his big-theater philosophy with plans for a series of gigantic houses in all cities. These new buildings were necessary since few theaters existed which could accommodate his enormous Takarazuka troupes, and through them he popularized the idea of buildings containing often three or more theaters, a model which is still followed in Japan.

In 1935, Kobayashi successfully completed the first phase of his plans. He gained control of both P.C.L. and J.O. and, at the same time, obtained exclusive use of the very popular Osaka Mainichi Talkie Newsreels. One of the effects of this arrangement was that P.C.L. could for the first time attract major directors like Kajiro Yamamoto from Nikkatsu and Mikio Naruse from Shochiku. A year later Kobayashi made his second move and formed the Toho Motion Picture Distribution Corporation to distribute films produced by the two studios he controlled.

To establish a major release circuit he would have needed at least eight pictures a month. P.C.L. could be counted upon

for four and J.O., two, so the remaining two would have had
to be either imported from abroad or else obtained from back-
some other Japanese film-producer. To help fill this shortage ground
Kobayashi decided upon a distribution arrangement with
Nikkatsu.

Nikkatsu in the meantime had been having even more
troubles than usual. Its main difficulty was money. Not long
after Nagata's resignation, Kanichi Negishi had been named
head of the Tamagawa studios. He wanted to build concrete
stages to supplant the two wooden ones built under Nakatani. For this money was needed. Managing Director Kyusaku Hori searched everywhere and, it is said, eventually
raised the necessary amount only by resorting to the slightly
irregular if time-honored practice of loaning out the prettier
Nikkatsu actresses as collateral. In this case members of the
board of directors of the Bank of Chiba were the lucky
recipients.

Negishi, a man of literary tastes, was interested in introducing more literary adaptations to the screen, and under him
a number of ex-Nikkatsu people returned, among them Takako Irie, Tomu Uchida, and Tomotaka Tasaka. When Kaizan
Nakazato, author of the popular novel *The Great Bodhisattva
Pass* (Dai-Bosatsu Toge), demanded the equivalent of twenty
thousand dollars for the screen rights, Nikkatsu paid, though
this was the highest amount ever asked for film rights in
Japan and Nikkatsu was in no condition to pay that kind of
money. They made a super-production of it, direction by
Hiroshi Inagaki, and a saturation-booking release. Fortunately for Nikkatsu, it was a huge success and put Kanichi
Negishi's hitherto somewhat tottering regime securely on its
feet.

It was at this time that the newly formed Toho approached
Nikkatsu asking for two films a month. When Kido of Shochiku heard of these impending plans he went up to Nikkatsu's Hori and is supposed to have said: "After you've
worked so hard to build up Nikkatsu, why enter into a deal
where your company will be swallowed up? What do you
say to a tie-in between Nikkatsu and Shinko?" (This latter
company, as everyone knew, was being secretly subsidized
by Shochiku; in fact the president's younger brother was
head of Shinko.) To this Hori is said to have replied: "You're
right about Nikkatsu's weak condition, but then Shinko is
in even worse health. And when two sick people marry, the
children are never healthy." Kido, not to be fooled with,
threatened to join Shinko and Shochiku officially and thus

create some heavy competition. Nonetheless, Toho and Nikkatsu came to terms and celebrated with a big party.

That night, while four hundred employees were drinking to mutual success, Managing Director Hori was thrown into jail. The charges included misuse of stocks and bribery of bank officials. It was widely rumored that Shochiku "spies" had tipped off the police, as the arrest itself seemed almost too well-timed for any other conclusion. Another piece of information which seemed to have some connection was that, just three days before, Masaichi Nagata's Dai-Ichi Eiga had failed, and with it all of Shochiku's hopes of establishing its own tightly controlled distribution system.

Though somewhat irritated by this latter development, Shochiku was not weakened. It was, and for years remained, the most financially sound of the entertainment combines of Japan. Its capital was acquired mainly through the buying of already-established companies, both companies thereby enjoying the savings possible in a really big corporation and increasing their profits accordingly. In 1919, for example, its first big purchase, Teikoku Moving Pictures, gave Shochiku money to grow out of partnership and into a corporation, which it did only a year later, being then worth $1,400,000. Every year it bought more big theaters in more major cities, and by the mid-1930's its holdings were valued at close to $14,000,000.

Though it remained on top after its adventures with Nikkatsu and Toho, Shochiku decided to consolidate its position, and so began a new program of even greater expansion. It constructed new theaters, like the Kokusai Gekijo in Asakusa, designed to compete with Toho's Nihon Gekijo, and built itself new studios at Ofuna, an hour's train ride from Tokyo. It then joined together its stage companies and its film company to form the all-inclusive Shochiku Company, Limited, with capital assets of $16,000,000.

Elsewhere the sound of collapsing empires filled the air. Without Hori, the Toho-Nikkatsu tie-up soon fell through. Shochiku, using plain cash instead of pretty actresses, obtained control of the Chiba Bank loans and finally had its chief rival just where it wanted it. In this way it forced Nikkatsu into its own Producers' Association, a four-company agreement which had as its unwritten aim a complete boycott of Toho.

The move was somewhat overdaring for, though it kept Toho at a distance, it frightened the many smaller independent exhibitors who did not want a Shochiku dictatorship.

It also forced Toho to resort to countermeasures, mainly
raids on talent. By offering liberal contracts and freedom of choice as to work performed, Toho was able to lure away a number of artists, the biggest fish caught in this net being Kazuo Hasegawa, whose departure saddened Shochiku considerably. In time Toho also captured Denjiro Okochi, Takako Irie, and the directors Eisuke Takizawa, Hisatora Kumagai, Sadao Yamanaka, and Mansaku Itami.

Shochiku was furious and told the 1,000 theaters under exhibition contract that if they once showed a Toho film, the penalty for disobedience would be loss of contract. This had the desired effect of leaving Toho with only the seventeen theaters it actually owned.

Toho's retaliation took the form of a newspaper and pamphlet war which very soon reached a most personal level, the heads of Shochiku and Toho serving as centers for attack and counterattack. The deadlock did not last long. Toho's break came when it released a series of extremely popular films, among them Kajiro Yamamoto's *A Husband's Chastity* (Otto no Teiso). The public reaction was such that many theater owners felt that they could not possibly refuse to give Toho a helping hand. In this way Toho secured an ample number of distribution contracts with newly formed theatrical chains.

Shochiku next decided to make the Producers' Association even more formidable. It brought in two new independents, Kyokuto and Zensho, both of which specialized in the cheapest sort of period-drama. This made the Shochiku alliance larger and, theoretically, stronger.

It was at this time that Toho reinforced its position by becoming the Toho Motion Picture Company, Limited, with a capitalization of three and a half million dollars. A year later, in 1938, it added a number of live troupes to its stable, including the Roppa Furukawa Troupe, the Enoken Troupe, the Geijutsu-za, and the Shinkokugeki Troupe, all in addition to the popular Takarazuka Girls' Opera.

Most of this martial activity had been brought about by Toho's luring away of Kazuo Hasegawa. In connection with this there occurred one of those bizarre happenings which often serves to illuminate and typify a conflict. Hasegawa had left Shochiku under a cloud, having quarreled with his ex-teacher, who incidentally held a Shochiku contract, and was forced to leave behind his stage-name of Chojiro Hayashi. Shochiku was aghast at this betrayal, having long considered Hasegawa—who had entered the company at the age of nineteen—something of a permanent fixture as well as its biggest star.

One early evening in the fall of 1937 Hasegawa was leaving the Toho studios on his way to the nearby home of Toho's Yoshio Osawa when he was attacked by a man with a razor who, in an attempt to maim him, cut his left cheek. Hasegawa says it did not hurt very much, but that he was intensely worried since his future was with film work. In about three weeks he had recovered and was back on the Toho lot, but even today, after extensive plastic surgery, some traces of the scar remain and in close-ups the right cheek is generally favored.

In the subsequent trial at the Kyoto District Court it was discovered that the Korean who had attacked Hasegawa was a professional hood, often hired to perform such services. It was also established that he had been paid by the president of the Kyoto Boxing Club, by the labor-gang boss of the Shochiku Kyoto studios, and by an unnamed person employed by Shinko. The papers made the most of it, and Toho felt that, at the very least, it had won a decided moral victory. The incident put exhibitor and public all the more on the Toho side and effectively helped to weaken the Shochiku-organized boycott.

Actually, violence of this sort, while not common, was by no means unheard of. When the Kokko Eiga, a small Nara company, was on the verge of collapse in 1933, the company head kept promising to pay his workers, who consequently labored on and on, receiving nothing. Then one day he appeared, surrounded by a gang, and announced that the company was folding. He gave the workers' representative a small bundle of cash which, when divided, turned out to be less than a week's pay. There was no hope for recourse; violence was threatened; the thugs threatened back and bore the fraudulent employer away to safety; and that was the end of that except for the curious sequel that, years later, the open set for *The Teahouse of the August Moon* was located nearby and MGM in all innocence hired the same gang to control traffic.

Star-stealing frequently resulted in violence, as it had in the Hasegawa case. Often companies who had had stars stolen got even by stealing other stars from rival companies whether they had any need for the stars stolen or not. Quite often, too, the company stolen from was not the company which had originally done the stealing. It was a prestige matter in which the commercial value of the star was not so important

as success in bringing off a coup. As a result of this star-
stealing, many of the places frequented by film stars, es- back-
pecially in Kyoto, became hangouts for gangsters, who often ground
extorted the film people, making them pay for protection.
To counter this, it was the custom of the Kyoto studios to
hire their own thugs. Violence was always possible under
such conditions, and in the Hasegawa case it came out into
the open.

Despite his gashed cheek, Hasegawa's transfer to Toho was
a success for both him and his new employers. And, when
Kinugasa and Masahiro Makino followed his lead, Toho was
definitely on top, at least as far as the period-film was concerned. The company also had a great many new stars to
bring to the attention of the public, including Isuzu Yamada,
Setsuko Hara, Takako Irie, and Hideko Takamine.

Toho began things impressively by breaking with the
tradition of shooting period-films in Kyoto, abandoning its
studios there and moving all production to Tokyo. It also
had an exclusive film contract with the Zenshin-za, the
"Progressive Troupe" of Shingeki actors, as well as full call
on the services of rising young directors like Sadao Yamanaka. Though Nikkatsu still had such top period-film stars as
Chiezo Kataoka and Kanjuro Arashi and such directors as
Hiroshi Inagaki, Toho had the real pick of period-film talent,
and Shochiku was finding competition in this lucrative field
almost impossible.

Another strong factor in Toho's favor was its more or less
virtual control over the small independent companies. Shochiku, to be sure, had had Dai-Ichi, which in 1936 produced
two of Mizoguchi's best films, *Sisters of the Gion* (Gion
Shimai) and *Osaka Elegy* (Naniwa Ereji), but Dai-Ichi had
failed in the same year, leaving Shochiku with only Shinko.
Toho, on the other hand, had gained control of a number
of up-and-coming independent companies. These included
Tokyo Hassei, formed in 1935 and staffed, mainly, with ex-
Shochiku people. Among its talent it boasted a young
director, Shiro Toyoda, from whom much was later to be
heard. Using the studios now owned by Shintoho and with
a brand-new Toho distribution contract, Tokyo Hassei
decided to concentrate on quality pictures, and its very first
film made under this new policy, Toyoda's *Young People*
(Wakai Hito), also happened to be a big commercial hit.

Tokyo Hassei's pictures were so good that they outclassed
many of the Toho products, and the fact that Toho held the
distribution contract did much to strengthen the latter's

position against Shochiku opposition. The smaller company
failed in 1941, due mostly to poor management and a considerable speculative use of its own stock, but it had assisted in more firmly establishing Toho.

Among the other independents who helped reinforce Toho's position was the Nan-o Motion Picture Company, founded in 1939 to produce pictures designed especially for children, and the Kyokuto Motion Picture Company, formed in 1935 to specialize in hour-long silent period-films. Toho, growing by the hour, was becoming omnivorous, and before anyone was too aware what had happened it had engulfed Tokyo Hassei, Nan-o, and Kyokuto.

The decade had seen the fall of old empires and the rise of new. Nikkatsu was soon to disappear, though not for good; Shochiku had suffered; dozens of striving independents had been consumed in one way or another; and mammoth Toho had emerged as the virtual ruler of the Japanese film industry.

6 the talkies, interior: 1931-39 (cont.).

THE COMING OF SOUND AND THE resultant commercial expansion have sometimes been thought of as resulting in the death of the period-drama as a living genre, the end of the "golden age." Actually, however, the coming of sound merely coincided with the decline of the form and was not necessarily related to it. The innovations of the golden age would have become the clichés of succeeding periods even without the assistance of either sound or commercialization. Yet, though dying in the slow and occasionally painful manner that genres have, it managed occasionally to produce works of great strength and integrity.

One who continued in the field was Teinosuke Kinugasa, who in 1932 opened the period-film to sound with his mediocre *The Surviving Shinsengumi* and who, five years later, made *The Summer Battle of Osaka* (Osaka Natsu no Jin), which many consider the last of the living traditional genre. Others consider it important merely as a forerunner of the war-time historical films which attempted large-scale reproductions of past events. Though all of Kinugasa's period-films during this time were extremely popular, largely because the idol Kazuo Hasegawa was his hero, many felt them effeminate, calling them "womanly drama" and blaming this on Kinugasa's *oyama* origins. Actually, Kinugasa represented—and in films like *Gate of Hell* continues to represent—a dying strain. He continues to repeat what has long been a formula. From that time to the present day the best period-films usually represent a big departure from both the content and form of the common genre.

Among those who were experimenting with form in the period-drama were Hiroshi Inagaki, Mansaku Itami, and Sadao Yamanaka, all of whom helped the period-film to adjust to the sound era. Inagaki, still one of the most active of the period-film directors, brought a new vitality to the genre even if he could contribute no new ideas comparable to those of Itami's or Yamanaka's. It has been said that his greatest importance was in his spurring of the latter on to greater heights. Still, in such films as the 1931 *A Sword and the Sumo Ring* (Ippon-gatana Dohyori), he introduced wit, humor, and lyricism. A year later he made *Yataro's Sedge Hat* (Yataro-gasa), bringing to a rather typical story of the repayment of moral obligation what has been called "lyrical sentimentalism." This quality is still visible in his work. Some of the style of the period may still be seen in a work as late as *Musashi Miyamoto* (Miyamoto Musashi), released in America as *Samurai*, which, though completely commercialized, still offers a pale image of what Inagaki and the period-style were in better days.

Mansaku Itami brought new ideas to the period-drama. A boyhood friend of Daisuke Ito's, it was the latter who originally induced Itami to take up scenario writing and who, along with Inagaki, later became an assistant to Ito. He himself first became a director in 1932 when, along with Inagaki, he constructed films for Chiezo Kataoka, who owned the independent Chie Productions. Kataoka had the unfailing ability of being able to project the type of hero needed in the 1930 period-dramas, a hero who was heroic without being a nihilistic superman. He was, in fact, often a simpleton who just happened to do the right thing at the right time. For him Itami wrote satirical and wryly ironic scenarios which perfectly fitted this new period-hero.

Itami's first major work was the 1932 silent film *Peerless Patriot* (Kokushi Muso), the story of two *ronin* and an impostor who takes the place of the rightful master. The situation was developed in a satirical manner, ridiculing many feudal traditions, particularly those which had survived in modern Japan. One of the points of the film was that the impostor could in no way be told from the real lord, and this fact resulted in a questioning of the entire concept of hereditary rule. Itami's best work was perhaps the 1936 *Kakita Akanishi* (Akanishi Kakita), a genuine character study of a samurai who was not a hero in any conventional sense of the word, being instead a very ordinary man, weak in body if strong in spirit. The director's interest was not in

showing costumed duels but in reflecting the social and
political situations of the Edo period since, for Itami, this
era was a living and real part of Japan's past.

Itami also indirectly fought the more absurd conventions
of the genre in such films as the 1934 *Bushido Reference
Book* (Bushido Taikan). Later he became involved with Dr.
Arnold Fanck when they jointly directed the Japanese-Ger-
man coproduction *The New Earth* (Atarashiki Tsuchi),
released abroad under the title *Daughter of the Samurai*.
His light ironic and somewhat liberal touch ran into considerable opposition from the thoroughly Nazified Dr. Fanck.
When Itami became seriously ill in 1938—he died eight years
later—the period-drama which he had done so much to keep
alive had no one to prevent its petrifying into its present
form.

The greatest of the directors who added to the period-
drama during the 1930's was Sadao Yamanaka. Born in
1907 and killed in China in 1938, he has become for many a
figure almost symbolic of the hopes and triumphs of the
period. With Itami he was the first director to escape completely from the clichés of the genre and to break the set
pattern into which it had fallen. He was rewarded with
fame, popularity, and, though active only six years, more
critical awards than any other costume-drama director in
Japanese film history.

The differences between Yamanaka and Itami may be seen
in a comparison of their versions of the same story. In 1935
both made a film about Chuji Kunisada, a popular period-
hero about whom films are often made, one of the best
remembered being Daisuke Ito's 1927 *A Diary of Chuji's
Travels.* Itami's was *Chuji Makes a Name for Himself* (Chuji
Uridasu) and Yamanaka's was simply *Chuji Kunisada.* The
former was oriented toward social criticism and contained
the pictorial lyricism for which Itami was known. He dealt
only with the young Chuji after he had abandoned farming
because of oppressive taxes and a despotic government and
had decided to become a gambler. The hero was the center
of the picture and, though modernized, was quite recogniz-
ably the Chuji of the usual period-film. Yamanaka, on the
other hand, was interested in character, the character of
Chuji and, particularly, of those around him. His Chuji, under
an obligation to a man who hid him from the authorities,
must kill to pay back his moral debt. The plot was used to
create a total atmosphere, to re-create an entire period.
Yamanaka was not specifically concerned with social criti-

cism, but only with human emotional problems and the way
in which they reflected character.

From the very first Yamanaka had been interested in people. His first film, the 1932 silent *Sleeping with a Long Sword* (Dakine no Nagadosu), made after having served a five-year apprenticeship as scenario writer and assistant director at the Makino studios, used an old story, but one which Yamanaka made seem quite new because he was interested in the period-hero, not as an abstract idea, but as a real living person. In the same year he made *The Life of Bangoku* (Bangoku no Issho), a satire which showed Itami's influence but also showed the young director's interest in people, an interest which the Japanese were soon to call "humanistic." The film was about a roving *ronin* searching for truth but always finding lies. What Yamanaka thought most worth showing was the character of *ronin*, the plot itself being lyric and relatively slight.

The character of the jobless samurai, the homeless wandering *ronin*, continued to interest him. In 1934 he made *The Elegant Swordsman* (Furyu Katsujinken), about life in a Tokugawa boarding house where the hero, a man who acts on his dreams, faces the lies of life. The film was about the common people of the period, not the daimyo nor the famous samurai, but the country people, the peasants, artisans, and *ronin*. His films, never cheerful in feeling, grew more and more pessimistic in tone, perhaps as a natural consequence of his continual searching for the truth of human existence. In his 1935 *The Village Tattooed Man* (Machi no Irezumi Mono) the story is about a murderer who, freed because he prevents a jail break, finds that life is not much kinder on the outside. In Yamanaka's later works, from *Ishimatsu of the Forest* (Mori no Ishimatsu) to his last film, *Humanity and Paper Balloons* (Ninjo Kami-fusen), the pessimism continued.

It is perhaps indicative of the Japanese mind that Yamanaka searched only in the past for answers to the pressing problems of the present. His objectives went far beyond mere historical reconstruction, however, since his interest in historical material was governed by a desire to show the emotions of which it was made, not merely its physical shape. His dialogue, far removed from the clichés of the conventional period-drama and yet not too close to actual speech, aimed for the poetic. He was one of the few directors who could focus on the verbal without sacrificing the visual.

He was also one of the few to treat period-stories in

a consistently adult manner. Unlike those who followed him in the postwar era—Mizoguchi, Kurosawa, Yoshimura, all of whom turned to materials untouched by the period-films—Yamanaka worked with the very stuff that the common sword-operas were made of. But to him the Tokugawa age was not the romantic idyll of the juvenile mind; it was an era full of life and human problems. In 1937 this thought was heresy, not only to the popular mind, but also to the militarists, for whom the golden age of *bushido*, "the way of the samurai," was a presage of the new Greater East Asia.

Yamanaka attained his objectives through a heightened realism rather than through Itami's social criticism. His 1937 *Humanity and Paper Balloons* opens with a sequence typical of his approach. One of the tenants of the Edo alley where the film is laid, a former samurai, has committed suicide. His friends lament his death and one, disappointed, says: "But he hung himself like a merchant. Where was the man's spirit of *bushido?* Why didn't he disembowel himself like a real samurai?" And the reply comes: "Because he no longer owned a sword; he sold it the other day for rice."

This was the familiar death-theme opening, typical in the conventional period-drama, but in this film the difference is enormous since, in the conventional product, the hero would have come to a glorious end, taking on twenty opposing swordsmen and only dying himself after accounting for nineteen of them.

That night the dead man's friends find some happiness at his funeral, drunken wakes being the only luxury in their miserable lives. At the wake these people are introduced one by one, and later the film presents vignettes of their daily lives: the goldfish seller, the blind masseur, the noodle seller, the street gambler, and, with particular emphasis, another *ronin* and his wife. This is the celebrated Edo period, the flourishing eighteenth century, but the poor have no part of its prodigal artistic life; they do not partake of the almost insatiable zest for living with which the period is now identified.

Having thus set the mood, the film tells the story of the events following the wake. The *ronin*, like his fellow tenants, searches daily for employment, while his wife endlessly makes paper balloons to sell. This warrior lives not by bravado but by the small change received from the sale of children's toys. One day he accidentally becomes involved in a kidnapping unsuccessfully attempted by a friend. The next morning the neighbors find the wife's balloons blowing about in the courtyard. They look into the couple's room and find they have committed suicide. Once more there is a funeral; once more a brief escape.

This was a very daring film for 1937, the year that Japan took Shanghai, Soochow, and Nanking; when persons suspected of liberal or radical tendencies were being openly arrested in Japan. Yamanaka was himself very shortly drafted into the army, sent to China as a common soldier, and killed in battle a year later.

The contribution of both Yamanaka and Itami was that they approached Japanese history as though it were contemporary, looking for values in it that they looked for in their own lives. This deliberate refusal to admit the validity of the self-glorification of the conventional period-film—which shares its unreality with both Kabuki and Shimpa—was responsible for the fact that today, in the films by Mizoguchi, Kurosawa, and Yoshimura, the attitude of Yamanaka and Itami still exists. One critic, Matsuo Kishi, goes so far as to say: "If there had been no Yamanaka or Itami, there would be no period-film today."

Yamanaka's interest in poetic realism was actually only a part of the new interest in realism which was animating the Japanese film. Not only were these costume films seeking a more valid approach to life; the movies about the contemporary scene too were attempting to reflect reality in a more honest, closer-to-life fashion.

These latter films had come a long way from their Shimpa beginnings. First they had timidly explored the lives of the rich and the influential and then, taking the plunge, had gone to the opposite extreme and created the tendency film. The sentimentality of the Shimpa lingered on, however, and during the 1920's one of the few ways of breaking with it was in the creation of the melodrama. Though it never succeeded in becoming an important genre, melodrama in turn became one of the strongest influences in forming the new realism of the 1930's.

One of the directors who during this period specialized in more or less realistic melodramas was Yasujiro Shimazu. Born in Tokyo in 1897, he entered Osanai's Shochiku Cinema Institute in 1920, but upon graduation decided to write scenarios rather than act. After his pioneering work in the 1920's, his skill increased with the coming of sound and in 1932 he made the third Shochiku talkie, *First Steps Ashore,* following it a year later with *Maiden in the Storm* (Arashi no Naka no Shojo). The latter was the story of an elderly

office worker and his family. He tries to forget his troubles
by drinking, the troubles being a nagging wife and a young daughter who falls in love with a cousin who does not love her. In 1934 he made *The Woman That Night* (Sono Yoru no Onna), about one night in the life of a country girl who has come to Tokyo to become a waitress. Then as now Japanese motion picture companies were searching for foreign words to describe their products and give them class. For the Shimazu films, Shochiku borrowed the English "realism," tacked on a "neo," and thus, a decade before the Italians themselves found the term, were talking about "neorealist" films. Realistic though his films were in part, they also represented the main faults of Japanese realism, then as now: a tendency to overstatement, which creates crude melodrama; over-sentimentality; and a presentation of social problems without the slightest hint as to how they may be solved.

Tomotaka Tasaka was also making melodramas, as was Kenji Mizoguchi. In 1932 the former made the all-dubbed talkie *Spring and a Girl,* and a year later Mizoguchi made both *Gion Festival* (Gion Matsuri), a silent quickie about a love triangle, and *White Threads of the Cascades* (Taki no Shiraito). The latter satisfied the melodramatic needs of the most exacting. It was about an entertainer who works hard to get money for her lover, who is in debt. In a desperate effort to obtain cash she finally murders, is arrested and brought to court, where all the evidence is against her. The judge turns out to be her lover. She is found guilty.

One of the more prolific of the melodrama-makers was young Mikio Naruse, who made *Apart from You* (Kimi to Wakarete) in 1932 and, a year later, *Everynight Dreams* (Yo Goto no Yume), a silent film about a woman who works in order to educate her child. Her husband kills himself after being caught in the act of robbing a safe, and she is forced to become a streetwalker, dreaming every night of escape. In 1935 Naruse won the *Kinema Jumpo* "Best One" award with *Wife! Be Like a Rose!* (Tsuma yo Bara no yo ni), a talkie, later shown in America, which marked his departure from melodrama and the beginning of his work in *shomin-geki,* a cinematic genre that had been growing at the same time as the melodrama.

The *shomin-geki* are films about the life of the common people, particularly the lower middle-class. There had previously been many films devoted to the upper classes, and in the tendency films there was an insistence upon the lives of the proletariat, but now there was, finally, a genre devoted

entirely to the middle class. One of the first directors to
specialize in the genre was Shimazu, who had begun experimenting with the form as early as 1925 in *A Village Teacher*, the story of a very old school teacher and his pupils, all of whom have moved on and out of his life. It was a bit similar to the much better known *Twenty-four Eyes* (Nijushi no Hitomi), made in 1954 by Keisuke Kinoshita, one of Shimazu's many assistants to become a first-rate director.

Before this, Shimazu had made *Sunday*, in 1924, and a few years later, *The Coming of Spring* (Haru Hiraku), both using hitherto ignored plot material; the latter was made without subtitles. Shimazu's careful attitude toward film production is shown in the fact that even in the late 1930's he always carried around with him a small *soroban* or abacus, perhaps as a reminder of his early days, when the director was directly responsible for all expenses, but also because the *soroban* in Japan is the symbol of the mercantile middle class.

One of his best films was the 1934 *Our Neighbor Miss Yae* (Tonari no Yae-chan), the story of a young girl who falls in love with the boy next door. Her elder sister, unhappily married, also falls in love with the same boy and eventually leaves her husband. Their father is suddenly transferred to Korea, and while the family makes preparations for departure they decide that the younger daughter may stay on as a boarder at the boy's house until she graduates from school. Technically the film was a triumph, and in it Shimazu was at his most slice-of-life-like. The plot had its climaxes, but these were never over-emphasized. Everything moved along on a single level. The lack of action was carefully calculated by the director to give the effect of eavesdropping on life itself.

His last important film—he was seriously ill from 1935 until his death ten years later—was the 1939 *A Brother and His Younger Sister* (Ani to Sono Imoto), about a company employee troubled by his wife and sister. The sister is a typist who boards with the nephew of the brother's boss. The brother's objections to the marriage force him to resign from the company.

Naruse's *Wife! Be Like a Rose!* told of a man with a rather cold wife who continually writes poetry. Thus he takes a less cultured mistress. His daughter finds out about it but, through coming to know the latter, begins to see that her mother rather than her father was at fault. Another 1935 film, *The Girl in the Rumor* (Uwasa no Musume), showed the new Naruse style as something of a triumph of technique

over old-fashioned material and also as somewhat opposed to
the melodramatics of the period. *Wife! Be Like a Rose!* had used Shimpa sentiment as its base, while in the latter Naruse was much more interested in showing the feelings of his characters than in a presentation of the milieu in which they live. The people were middle class, but their problems in Naruse films tended to be atypical.

Another director specializing in the *shomin-geki* was Heinosuke Gosho, one of Shimazu's former assistants and the man who is usually given credit for developing the form. As early as 1927 he had shown an interest in the genre in films like *The Lonely Roughneck* (Sabishii Rambo-mono), a tremendous critical and popular success about the romance between a well-bred city girl and a rough country horse-cart driver. This was followed in 1928 by *The Village Bride* (Mura no Hanayome), the story of a beautiful young girl crippled in an accident. The basic theme was the prejudice and littleness of village life. The girl was to be married, but after her accident her parents replace her, at the altar, with her younger sister, a not infrequent occurrence in Japanese rural communities.

Gosho's successful early talkie, *The Neighbor's Wife and Mine*, essentially also *shomin-geki*, is a simple comedy, the plot of which is constructed from the foibles of middle-class life: the young couple's being intimidated into buying by a persistent door-to-door peddler, the husband unable to work on his new play first because of noisy cats outside and then because one of his children clamors to be taken to the toilet. At the end of the film both husband and wife remember their courtship during a walk with the children. They become so caught up in their memories that they quite forget the baby in its carriage. In the final scene they are rushing frantically back over the suburban fields to their little responsibility.

This Gosho film is perhaps indicative of the comic turn the *shomin-geki* took when sound came. Comedy usually comes late in Japan, arising only after the seriousness of the situation has been fully exposed, expanded, and insisted upon. The satirical period-film was two decades in appearing; the comedies in the "American style" came only after American-style "drama"; and the *shomin-geki* comedies appeared only when the audience had been fully acquainted with the troubles of middle-class life.

The *shomin-geki* comedy also had roots in the *nansensu-mono*, the nonsense comedy which has been mentioned earlier.

When the government suppressed the tendency films, not all
directors turned to the *rumpen-mono* for expression, a number taking up the erotic and the nonsense film. After the severities of the tendency films, the audience too tended toward the frivolous.

Naruse had made his first appearance as a director of nonsense sex films such as the 1930 *Record of Newlyweds* (Shinkon-ki), the 1931 *Now Don't Get Excited* (Ne Kofun Shicha Iyayo) and *Fickleness Gets on the Train* (Uwaki wa Kisha ni Notte). Gosho made the 1930 *Bachelors Beware* (Dokushinsha Goyojin), about a lady thief's arriving in a village where she attracts a number of men including a detective. In 1933 Gosho was still active in the genre, making such films as *The Bride Talks in Her Sleep* (Hanayome no Negoto), about a university student who makes trouble for newlyweds who would much prefer being left alone.

Some directors, like Enjiro Saito, continued to specialize in the genre. Representative films had titles like *What Made Her Naked?* (Nani ga Kanojo o Hadaka ni Shita ka) and *Uproar over the Aphrodisiac Dumpling* (Iroke Dango Sodoki). In 1932, having carefully read the synopsis for *City Lights*, Saito made *Chaplin! Why Do You Cry?* (Chappurin yo Naze Naku ka), about a Japanese sandwich man, who dresses like Chaplin, and a flowerseller.

Chaplin, incidentally, is the personification of the Japanese comic ideal. The kind of humor which allows one both to laugh and to weep is particularly admired by the Japanese, and when Chaplin visited the country in 1932 the nation overwhelmed him with attention. The industry had flattered him much earlier making quite a number of direct imitations, long before the Saito film. Even today Chaplin remains something of a national hero. His way of walking is still imitated, usually by sandwich men, appearing complete with cane, derby, and oversize shoes. Packed houses always greet a revival of *The Kid*, one of the early Chaplin films still playing in Japan. Even *Monsieur Verdoux* always makes money.

It was in the nonsense film that the talents of Yasujiro Ozu first came to attention. His 1930 *The Revengeful Spirit of Eros* (Erogami no Onryo) was not unusual—a great deal of meaningless comic action flavored with sex. Unlike Saito, however, Ozu very shortly went on to greater things. Among his early *shomin-geki* comedies were the 1928 *Pumpkin* (Kabocha) and the 1930 *Life of an Office Worker* (Kaishain Seikatsu), both of which were about the life of the white-collar worker, a field which has now become recognized as

Ozu's own. These, like his own *Young Lady* (Ojosan) and Gosho's *Chorus of Tokyo* (Tokyo no Gassho), made in 1931, were somewhat related to the social awareness of the tendency films, but here it was the individual relationships of the situation that were insisted upon.

Ozu's contribution to the genre can perhaps be best seen in the 1932 film, *I Was Born, But...* (Umarete wa Mita Keredo), which without qualification belongs in the great silent comedy tradition but which has an approach very different from, say, that of a Chaplin or a Keaton. Ozu took his humor from everyday life. His films were not built around the business of a comedian but were composed from the unconscious comedy of the average person caught unaware by the camera.

Through the eyes of two brothers, one eight and the other ten, Ozu captures the foibles of adults, the middle class as seen, and seen through, by children. Though the boys love their father dearly, they cannot help seeing that the conduct forced on him by adult society is ridiculous. In the final sequence the son of the father's employer invites his little friends over for home movies. Among the purposely confused footage which follows, neatly containing every known vice of the film amateur, are parts in which the father of the brothers acts the fool for his boss's camera. Embarrassed that others have seen, that others now know what they have always known, the boys run home in shame and later protest by a hunger strike.

Up to this point Ozu has told his story in a visual manner; now he turns to subtitles to make his points. The father explains that the family must have money to live and that this is why he has both to work for the boss and to amuse him. The boys ask: "But why aren't you the boss?" Their father answers: "Because I don't own a company like he does." Then one brother wants to know: "But will Taro [the employer's son] own a company when he grows up and will we have to do the same things for him?" And the other brother asks: "Why? When we make better grades at school than he does and can beat him up any time?" To this the father has no immediate answer.

The next morning the brothers, as is their daily habit, question Taro: "Who is greater, your father or ours?" And because of an oath to the brothers as club leaders Taro must give the standard answer: "Yours." The camera cuts to the final shot of the father going out of his way to help his employer into the company limousine.

Such films were Ozu's speciality. The excesses of the typical nonsense film had taught him the value of lightness, of
underplayed, understated humor; the *shomin-geki* gave his
films their solidity and depth. His later films even further
revealed his fruitful preoccupation with middle-class life.
Passing Fancy (Dekigokoro), made in 1933, was about a
father whose wife has died. He and his son live in a cheap
apartment house but find real comradeship together. The
1934 *Duckweed Story* (Ukigusa Monogatari) was about a
troupe of traveling players. Their leading actor accidentally
meets his own son in a small town and is rejected for his past
misdeeds. Ozu's first talkie was *The Only Son* (Hitori Musu-
ko), made in 1936, which retained the structure of the silent
film and was, in fact, originally conceived as a non-talkie. It
was about a mother working in a spinning mill to send her
son through school in Tokyo. After his graduation the son
becomes a teacher, and she spends all of her savings so that
she can visit him. When he learns she is coming, he borrows
a great deal of money so that he can make her believe that
he is prosperous. This is all there is to the plot. All the rest
is characterization.

Shomin films as a genre were becoming character pieces.
Gosho's 1935 *Bundle of Life* (Jinsei no O-nimotsu) was a
story about parents who sell everything in order to prepare
for their three daughters' marriages, only to realize at the last
moment that they have forgotten to think of the future of
their youngest child, their only son. Though the film was
about the middle class, the interest was mainly in character,
the reaction of the members of a family to an incident. The
quality of the genre was changing, but thanks to the institution of the *shomin-geki* as a form, it was now possible to
evade even further the early clichés of filmed family life.

Another reason for the change within the *shomin-geki* was
governmental interference. In 1937, Hisatora Kumagai made
Many People (Sobo), a story about immigrants crowding
together in Kobe, awaiting transportation to a new world in
South America, each wanting land where he could start his
own farm. Kumagai himself admitted that he had had to make
a compromise. If he had shown everything, he would have
risked being censored. Thus he tried for broad scope without focusing on any particular theme, jumping from one
life to another and hoping to suggest what he could not
show. He was able to resist romanticizing farmers and even
managed to show their poverty in full. Yet he could not allow
himself to be critical of the social system which was respon-

sible for this poverty. Rather, he had to blame the eternal
scapegoat, the over-population of Japan.

The *shomin-geki* took yet another form in the films of Kajiro Yamamoto. His 1938 *Composition Class* (Tsuzurikata Kyoshitsu) was a collection of episodes, the main purpose of each being to show how events shape the lives of the central characters, the unity coming not from the story but from the cumulative effect of the episodes themselves. The main story was about a young girl, outstanding in her composition class, who is finally sold by her family to a geisha house so that they can pay their debts. Starring Hideko Takamine, it was actually a rather slick, obvious type of thing, a hangover from the usual frothy Yamamoto film.

In 1941 he made *Horse* (Uma), which took three years to plan, another year to film, and four different cameramen. Under contract to Toho at the time, Yamamoto had to commute from his far mountain location unit, coming back to Tokyo to film money-making comedies and leaving production in charge of his assistant, Akira Kurosawa. The film told the story of a young girl, again Hideko Takamine, who takes care of a colt until it is two years old, when it is taken away by the army. There was realistic photography and a very careful documentation of horses and horse-breeding. This film greatly influenced the rising Japanese documentary movement and the relation of feature films to reality.

Documentary technique was also used in films like Kumagai's *A Story of Leadership* (Shido Monogatari), which told how an aging locomotive engineer sacrifices for the fatherland. It borrowed a number of ideas from a previous documentary study of locomotive engineers, but attempted to use its material for something more than merely interesting background. In Japan, however, the documentary movement had much less effect on commercial films than, say, in England. The Japanese have always been afraid of the amateur and constantly prefer calling in the specialist; so it is not uncommon for professional actors to appear in actuality films. Thus, in Japan, one sees an attitude toward realism which is rather different from that in the West, where "realistic" has become a term of approbation.

It is singular that the rise of realism should have been coincident with Japan's rise to military power, and that 1936, when the movement was at its height, should also have been the year before Japan began its Chinese adventures in earnest. Even more surprising is that fact that in what was fast becoming a military stronghold, the realism of this period implied a social philosophy implicitly opposed to what was happening in Japan at the moment. Though this opposition was not strong enough to be called a protest, Uchida's *Theater of Life* (Jinsei Gekijo), Ozu's *The Only Son*, and both *Osaka Elegy* and *Sisters of the Gion* by Mizoguchi were actually opposed, if obliquely, to the path Japan was taking.

The former of the Mizoguchi films, *Osaka Elegy*, carried realism to an extreme never before seen in Japan. No longer did reality have to be twisted to prove a point. Here, reality was presented on its own terms. There was a meaning to it which the director did not have to force upon his audience. The viewer could look at a situation and judge for himself. The story concerned a young telephone operator whose life is ruined because of an innocent desire for money. Her boss takes advantage of her; the boss's wife takes it out on the girl's family; while her fiancé, a typically unambitious white-collar worker, stands helplessly by. It sounds melodramatic in description but was actually very quietly told, its realism being only slightly vitiated by Mizoguchi's eternal concern for pictorial beauty and atmosphere.

Having thus treated Osaka, Mizoguchi and his producer, Nagata, of the Dai-Ichi Motion Picture Company, decided to make films about two more cities, Kyoto and Kobe. The latter was never completed because the company failed, but the former was one of the best Japanese films ever made, the one which the critic Tadashi Iijima, among others, considers "the best prewar sound film." The title was *Sisters of the Gion*, the sisters being two geisha from the well-known Gion district of Kyoto. The younger is a *moga*—a derogatory portmanteau of the English "modern girl"—and thus is inclined to ignore the traditions of both her profession in particular and Japanese traditional society in general. The elder possesses all of the virtues of the legendary geisha. Despite the geisha code which authorizes a girl only one patron, the younger sister jumps from one man to another in search of ready cash. She also decides that her sister needs a new patron since the old one has lost all of his money, and so tells him that her sister is no longer available; and all the while she herself is going up the ladder of success from one man to that man's boss. Later, one of the younger's jealous ex-patrons pushes her from a moving automobile, but even when she is lying in the hospital, injured and hence unable to interfere with her sister's life, the elder, the traditional geisha, is too stupid, too encumbered by tradition, to attempt to rejoin her old lover. Completely conditioned by her own code, she will always be afraid of going against custom. The younger sister, injured though she is, has every chance of recovery and there is a strong possibility of her taking up where she left off.

If the director's own sentiments occasionally and by default go to the elder sister, his ending leaves her condemned. The situation is such, however, that the spectator too must make a choice, because, for a Japanese at any rate, the problem suggested by the film is a very vital one and by implication goes far beyond the narrow world of the geisha. Aiding this effect of impartiality, which is the effect of realism itself, was Mizoguchi's striving for actuality and, in doing so, successfully evoking the very special atmosphere of this single tiny section of Japan. To project regional atmosphere is no easy task in a country where smallness and centralization conspire to make differences extremely subtle, yet never have the narrow Gion alleys and the backrooms of its teahouses appeared more inviting. To the Japanese this picture was more than merely slice-of-life. It went beyond documentation and projected the other-world atmosphere of the Gion itself.

Mizoguchi's search for realism continued when he moved to Shinko Kinema with Nagata and in 1936 made *The Gorge between Love and Hate* (Aienkyo), a film about a young girl who, having run off to Tokyo with the son of a hotel owner, has to return home, pregnant. Soon after the child is born she becomes first a waitress and then a traveling performer. She again returns to her hometown, where the hotel owner's son spurns both her and her child. At the end of the film, she is resigned to her lonely itinerant life.

The following year Mizoguchi made *Ah, My Hometown* (Aa Furusato), filmed on location in northern Japan, about the daughter of a man who has failed in business. She is in love, but after a short engagement the young man goes off to study in America.

Another major figure in creating the new realism was Tomu Uchida, who had entered the film world as an actor in Thomas Kurihara's *Amateur Club*, then withdrew to join a theatrical road company, and returned to the industry as Frank Tokunaga's assistant at Nikkatsu. Tokunaga was the man who specialized in making cheap copies of American films, and Uchida did not learn very much under him. He received the best of his training with Minoru Murata and Kenji Mizoguchi, with whom he served as assistant before

1. *Gion Geisha*, 1898. A frame taken from the positive print of the original film.

2. *Maple Viewing*, 1898. A scene from the filmed Kabuki version of the Noh drama. Kikugoro V, Danjuro IX.

3. *Katusha*, 1914, Kiyomatsu Hosoyama. One of the first of many adaptations of Tolstoy's *Resurrection*. Sadajiro Tachibana, Tappatsu Sekino.

4. *The Living Corpse*, 1917, Eizo Tanaka. Another Tolstoy adaptation. Foreign-style dress and female impersonators were both soon dropped. Kaichi Yamamoto, Teinosuke Kinugasa.

5. *The Loyal Forty-seven Ronin*, 1919, Shozo Makino. The most popular Japanese screen vehicle: at least twice a year for almost 50 years. Matsunosuke Onoe (*r*).

6. *Island Women*, 1920, Henry Kotani. One of the signs of cinematic maturity was the use of female actors. Yoshiko Kawada, Tsuruzo Nakamura.

7. *Amateur Club*, 1920, Thomas Kurihara. Among the first American-influenced films: a direct imitation of Hollywood slapstick. Sango Kamiyama (*l*), Ichiro Sugiura (*c*), Tokihiko Okada (*r*).

8. *The Lasciviousness of the Viper*, 1921, Thomas Kurihara. Based on the story later used for Mizoguchi's *Ugetsu Monogatari*. Tokihiko Okada (*l*), Yoko Benizawa (*r*).

9. *Souls on the Road*, 1921, Minoru Murata. The first great Japanese film. Komei Minami (*l*).

10. *Winter Camellia*, 1921, Masao Inoue. The film debut of a great actress. Masao Inoue, Yaeko Mizutani.

11. *The Mountains Grow Dark*, 1921, Kiyohiko Ushihara. One of the earliest realistic melodramas. Harumi Hanayagi, Komei Minami.

12. *The Kyoya Collar Shop*, 1922, Eizo Tanaka. Some films attempted to deal realistically with modern Japan. Takeo Azuma, Kenichi Miyajima, Kaichi Yamamoto, Kasuke Koizumi.

13. *The Women and the Pirates*, 1922, Hotei Nomura. Other films were content to repeat the clichés of the standard period-film. Yoko Umemura (*c*), Yotaro Katsumi (*r*).

14. *Human Suffering*, 1923, Kensaku Suzuki. One of the first films to show the lives of the poor. Kaichi Yamamoto.

15. *Love of Life*, 1923, Kiyohiko Ushihara. A sentimental domestic drama. Chiyoko Mimura, Tamaki Hanagawa, Ukichi Iwata, Yoko Umemura.

16. *Turkeys in a Row*, 1924, Kenji Mizoguchi. The boy on the right later became director of *Rickshaw Man*. Kasuke Koizumi, Hiroshi Inagaki.

17. *The Night Tales of Hommoku*, 1924, Minoru Murata. A Japanese vamp. Yoneko Sakai.

18. *Seisaku's Wife*, 1924, Minoru Murata. A tragedy with expressionistic sequences. Kumeko Urabe.

19. *Father*, 1924, Yasujiro Shimazu. Among the better light comedies. Hiroshi Masakuni. Yaeko Mizutani.

20. *Princess-Grass*, 1924, Yoshinobu Ikeda. One of the first real stars. Mitsuko Takao, Sumiko Kurishima.

21. *Mataemon Araki*, 1925, Shozo Makino. King of the period-film stars. Matsunosuke Onoe.

22. *The Woman Who Touched the Legs*, 1926, Yutaka Abe. The Lubitsch-touch in Japan. Tokihiko Okada, Yoko Umemura.

23. *A Paper Doll's Whisper of Spring*, 1926, Kenji Mizoguchi. The slow emergence of a strong directorial style. Tokihiko Okada, Yoko Umemura.

24. *The Last Days of the Shogunate*, 1926, Shozo Makino The political period-drama. Tsumasaburo Bando.

25. *Lonely Roughneck*, 1927, Heinosuke Gosho. A romance about a city girl and country horse-cart driver. Tokuji Kobayashi, Choko Iida, Jun Arai.

26. *A Diary of Chuji's Travels*, 1927, Daisuke Ito. One of the perennial period heroes

27. *A Mermaid on Land*, 1927, Yutaka Abe. A sentimental romance. Yoko Umemura, Hikaru Yamanouchi.

28. *A Crazy Page*, 1927, Teinosuke Kinugasa. One of Japan's first experimental films. Masao Inoue (c).

29. *The Loyal Forty-seven Ronin*, 1927, Shozo Makino. The all-time favorite. Masahiro Makino, Tomoko Makino, Yoho Ii.

30. *Crossroads*, 1928, Teinosuke Kinugasa. One of the world's film classics. Shown abroad as *Shadows of the Yoshiwara*. Kazuo Hasegawa, Masako Chihaya.

31. *The Street of Masterless Samurai*, 1928, Masahiro Makino. The period hero shows signs of life. Komei **Minami.**

32. *Ooka's Trial*, 1928, Daisuke Ito. The period hero with a modern conscience. Denjiro **Okochi.**

33. *He and Life*, 1929, Kiyohiko Ushihara. The typical sentimental comedy. Kinuyo Tanaka, Denmei Suzuki.

34. *Beheading Place*, 1929, Masahiro Makino. Revenge with a social purpose. Juro Tanizaki, Seizaburo Kawazu.

35. *A Living Doll*, 1929, Tomu Uchida. The cheat cheated: a publicity still for the film. Koji Shima.

36. *What Made Her Do It?* 1930, Shigeyoshi Suzuki. The tendency film makes a big hit. Kaku Hamada, Keiko Takatsu.

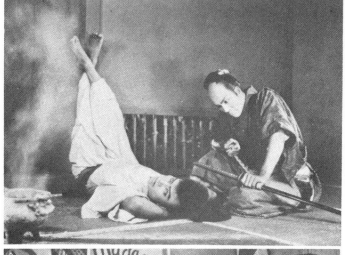

37. *Man-Slashing, Horse-Piercing Sword*, 1930, Daisuke Ito. Social criticism in the period-film. Ryunosuke Tsukikata. Jinichi Amano.

38. *The Neighbor's Wife and Mine*, 1931, Heinosuke Gosho. Japan's first successful talkie. Satoko Date, Atsushi Watanabe, Tokuji Kobayashi.

39. *The Revenge Champion*, 1931, Tomu Uchida. The satirical period hero. Denjiro Okochi, Taeko Sakuma.

40. *Chorus of Tokyo*, 1931, Heinosuke Gosho. The tendency comedy. Tokihiko Okada, Tatsuo Saito.

41. *Young Lady*, 1931, Yasujiro Ozu. The socially-aware nonsense film. Tokihiko Okada, Sumiko Kurishima, Tatsuo Saito.

42. *And Yet They Go On*, 1931, Kenji Mizoguchi. The *lumpenproletariat* on film. Reiji Ichiki (*l*). Yoko Umemura (*r*).

43. *I Was Born, But...* 1932, Yasujiro Ozu. One of the great film comedies. Tatsuo Saito, Tokkankozo, Hideo Sugawara.

44. *The Loyal Forty-seven Ronin,* 1932, Teinosuke Kinugasa. Among the prettier versions of the old favorite. Kotaro Bando, Akiko Chihaya.

45. *Apart from You,* 1932, Mikio Naruse. One of the earlier womens' films. Sumiko Mizukubo.

46. *The Life of Bangoku,* 1932, Sadao Yamanaka. A powerful new director emerges. Isuzu Yamada, Denjiro Okochi.

47. *White Threads of the Cascades,* 1933, Kenji Mizoguchi. The modern melodrama. Takako Irie, Tokihiko Okada.

48. *Three Sisters with Maiden Hearts,* 1934, Mikio Naruse. A woman's problems in a man's world. Ryuko Umezono, Chikako Hosokawa, Masako Tsutsumi.

he himself became a director in 1926. His first important picture was *The Revenge Champion* (Adauchi Senshu), a satirical period-film, and he continued to make farces and satires until he finally found his field in the *shomin-geki*, thereby contributing greatly to the rise of realism in the Japanese films.

One of his best was the 1936 *Theater of Life*, about a merchant who sends his son to a Tokyo university, where he hopes the boy will learn to become a politician. Disgusted by the favoritism practised in the school, the boy quits and marries the daughter of a small restaurant owner. The son returns home by the same train as a local girl who has become a Shimbashi geisha. At the station there is a big reception for her. She is a success, having conquered the capital; he remains unknown and unacclaimed. The film itself was an oblique attack on the distorted values of an overly commercial society.

In the same year, Uchida made *Unending Advance* (Kagirinaki Zenshin), a *shomin-geki* tragedy about an aging office worker facing retirement who finds no pleasure in either looking back over his past life or in looking forward to the future. Based on a magazine serial by director Yasujiro Ozu, it differed from Uchida's usual work in that it reflected the very simple plot lines along which Ozu was experimenting at the time.

A more typical Uchida film was *The Naked Town* (Hadaka no Machi), made in 1937, about a merchant who acts as guarantor for a friend's debt and loses everything when the friend fails to pay. In an attempt to regain some of his losses, the merchant goes to a moneylender. When he is refused, the moneylender's wife takes pity on him, offering him milk to feed his hungry cat. This the cat refuses; it too turns against the unfortunate man. At last, however, he pulls himself together and opens a small street-stall. The first half of the film was very cinematically achieved and became something of a model for further films, for a time being regarded as a standard for literary adaptations. The latter half, however, with its ungrateful cat, sharply betrayed its opening style and was consequently less effective.

Uchida's main contribution to the new realism came in 1939 with the film *Earth* (Tsuchi), which, given the circumstances of its creation, was made possible only by the complete devotion of the director, his actors and technicians, and their firm belief in the potential of realism as a screen style. A documentary in its insistence upon showing only

what actually existed, it very carefully chronicled the seasons
and used only the slightest of stories: a farmer loses his
inherited money and is forced into poverty; driven to despair, he yet manages to find new faith. The film scrupulously
avoided defining the new faith but neither sentimentalized
nor patronized the farmers.

When the Nikkatsu chiefs heard that Uchida wanted to
make *Earth* they were strongly against it. Though Nikkatsu
had been slowly recovering from the losses it had recently
incurred, the company was in no position to make a film as
experimental as this one, the main objection being the expense: since the film was to show the effect of the seasons
on farming life, it would take a year to film. Even if the
head office was opposed, the studio people were behind the
project, and though Nikkatsu had officially decided against
making the film, it continued to be made in secret. Facilities,
money, and film from other productions were slipped to the
Earth production unit. A roll of raw stock from this production, two from that, were smuggled in while Uchida
dashed back to the Tokyo studios every week or so to turn
out money-making films like *A Thousand and One Nights
in Tokyo* (Tokyo Senichi-ya.)

The studio heads, never too close to what was going on
under them, were slow in noticing all this activity, but
eventually became suspicious and finally alarmed. When the
finished film was presented to them they were vastly annoyed
but finally agreed to release it only as a sort of gesture of
good will toward their obviously devoted employees. To
their intense surprise the film was a great success. It won
the *Kinema Jumpo* "Best One" award for the year and earned
an absolutely unprecedented return on investment since no
costs were ever credited to the unit, the film having been
made entirely with "borrowed" resources.

Uchida not only contributed to the new realism, he also
indicated in his early works that literary adaptations need not
be hopelessly literary and that plays and stories could, with
proper treatment, be turned into cinema. Both *The Theater
of Life* and *The Naked Town* had come from literary originals, and the latter became a landmark in the *junbungaku*
film movement, which was to continue until 1941 and
the coming of war. *Junbungaku* means "pure literature,"
but the way the term is used in Japan would seem to indicate
that it is an antonym for popular literature or, more specifically, literature of action, tales of adventure, sex stories, and
so forth. As early as 1908, adaptations of both novels and

plays had filled the Japanese screen, but it was the maturing
of the film in the 1930's that turned certain directors toward the better kinds of Japanese literature.

Film companies accepted the movement because if directors wanted to be highbrow they were at least working with pre-tested material that had already found something of an established audience. Also, the companies could rely on adaptations to hold off the censors, the argument being that the story was already known through the book and that the film was therefore not responsible for the ideology contained.

Though placated from time to time, the censors were none too pleased with these developments, particularly since it was mainly contemporary literature that was being searched for film material. They frowned upon the entire trend because of its supposed leftist origins, though actually one could trace its beginnings well back to a time when there was little danger of any such influence. As far back as the mid-1920's when Minoru Murata was at Nikkatsu, serious Japanese literature had served as the basis for such films as his *The Night Tales of Hommoku* (Hommoku Yawa), taken from a Junichiro Tanizaki original.

The movement appeared in force in 1935 with Yasujiro Shimazu's *O-Koto and Sasuke* (O-Koto to Sasuke), based on a Tanizaki novel, and Gosho's silent film adaptation of Kawabata's *Dancing Girl from Izu* (Izu no Odoriko). A year later Gosho made *Everything That Lives* (Ikitoshi Ikerumono), a talkie based on a Yuzo Yamamoto novel, and in 1940, *Wooden Head* (Mokuseki), taken from a novel by Seiichi Funabashi.

The man who really gave the movement its form, and much of its vitality, was Shiro Toyoda, whose 1937 *Young People* was one of the best of the adaptations. It was also the most popular of these literary-cycle films, and its excellence made it Toyoda's first really important picture. Based on a novel by Yojiro Ishizaka, it was the story of the love affair between a school teacher and one of his students. The girl had never known her father, and the film presented her search for a substitute. Despite its literary origin, the film was highly pictorial in style and also managed to avoid all of the pitfalls usually encountered in reproducing novelistic dialogue.

The following year Toyoda made two more adaptations. One was *Crybaby Apprentice* (Nakimushi Kozo), based on a famous novel by Fumiko Hayashi. After a little boy's father has died, the mother wants to marry again, and so the boy is passed from relative to relative, the story being told

in a series of relatively unrelated sketches. The other was
Nightingale (Uguisu), taken from an Einosuke Ito novel
about life in a rural police station. Again there were various
sketches in which the realism of the film quite matched that
of the novel. There was not much conflict and very little
action, but Toyoda's interest in characterization, which was
to become his strength as a leading postwar director, was
already much in evidence.

Another director who began with adaptations was Kimisaburo Yoshimura. His 1939 *Warm Current* (Danryu), the
story of a hospital superintendent and the two women in his
life, based on a novel by Kunio Kishida, brought him his
first fame as a director. Another newcomer, Minoru Shibuya,
came into attention through adaptations. One of his best, the
1939 *Mother and Child* (Haha to Ko), was taken from a novel
by Tsuneko Yada. This story of a young daughter, her
businessman father, and his mistress was slightly overloaded
with sentiment and burdened with the confused social criticism apparent in some of the director's postwar work, but
was nonetheless representative of the period.

A typical product of the trend was Tomotaka Tasaka's *A
Pebble by the Wayside* (Robo no Ishi), made in 1938 and
taken from a Yuzo Yamamoto novel. The story, which takes
place around 1902, was about a young boy brought up
entirely by his mother since his drunken father is never home.
An intelligent teacher wants to send him to middle school,
but instead the father apprentices him to a clothing store to
which he is in debt. The mother dies and the boy is forced
to quit work when his father insults the store owner. Later
the boy goes to Tokyo, but only to continue his hardships.
First he is forced to do a maid's job at a boarding house and
later is used by an old woman to steal at funerals. Finally he
is rescued by the teacher, whom he meets in Tokyo. Though
the film itself was perhaps overly emotional and at times
seems too much like a Japanese *Oliver Twist*, Tasaka himself
thinks it was the best picture he ever made. Certainly in the
boy, Akihiko Katayama, the son of Koji Shima, then a star
and now a director, Tasaka had all a director could have
asked for in a child actor.

A number of films about children were made during this
period, partially because many of the films were adaptations
of novels and because Japanese literature contains more than
its share of stories about children. Kajiro Yamamoto's *Composition Class* and Toyoda's *Crybaby Apprentice* were about
children, but perhaps the most important director of chil-

dren's films was Hiroshi Shimizu, who, though active since 1924, had never produced any noteworthy films until he made the 1937 *Children in the Wind* (Kaze no Naka no Kodomotachi), about two brothers in primary school whose father is arrested for forgery. The younger goes to live with his uncle and the boys eventually and accidentally discover the evidence to clear their father.

Shimizu's success lay in that he did not make films merely about children; he wanted to capture the child's point of view, and hence many of his films were shot on location, the idea being that he could get a more natural reaction if he directed children in their own surroundings. In 1939 he made *Four Seasons of Children* (Kodomo no Shiki), about some children who, when their father dies, go to live with their grandparents. In this film he did not ignore adults as he had earlier, but the weakest moments of the film are when adults appear. It was excellent in showing the over-indulgent and absolutely blind love for children which is so much a part of Japan, but, while showing it, and engaging in it himself, Shimizu did not hesitate to criticize it. His touch was not as psychological as, say, that of Jean Benoit-Levy in a film like *La Maternelle*, but was rather much closer to the children themselves, and there was a quality about his films which a director like, say, Jean Vigo would have much admired.

It is perhaps ironic that this opening of the world of childhood should have occurred just at the time when Japan itself was again closing up for a state of protracted war. As it was, the happenings from 1941 on put an end to all such peaceful pursuits as making films about children or the middle class or creating film adaptations of *junbungaku*. War did not mean the end of realism but more of a change of direction, as the Japanese cinema again experienced an upheaval, this one so extensive that its films were never again the same.

7 shooting script:
1939-45. THE WAR WITH China was not unexpected. The Japanese, long looking toward the continent and seeking a weak, disunited China, had seen the chance to force its leadership of the new Asia upon the larger country. A pretext occurred in the middle of 1937 when Japanese troops at Lukouchiao clashed with Chinese. This led directly to the seizure of Peking and Tientsin. A war had begun, though, for technical reasons of international law, there was no formal declaration.

The motion-picture industry was caught unprepared, as it had never developed a war genre. The minor Japanese participation in World War I and the earlier conflicts with Russia and China had occurred before the film was capable of reflecting social issues. There had been only some slight precedent for war pictures in Shochiku's big production of 1925, *Fatherland* (Sokoku), which used three thousand extras and four airplanes, but now the presence of actual war was something that the industry could not ignore.

Tomotaka Tasaka's *Five Scouts* (Go-nin no Sekkohei), made in 1939, was the first important Japanese war film and remained the pattern for several subsequent efforts. Seen today, it is a totally unexpected experience because it is without the ultranationalism of much of the militarists' propaganda and lacks even the warrior heroism of the period-drama. It has no counterpart among the wartime films of Germany, Russia, Britain, or the United States, and if one searches for its closest kin, one must go back to films of the pacifist era which were banned in Japan, back to Milestone's *All Quiet on the Western Front* and Pabst's *Westfront 1918*.

The story is very simple. In northern China a company commander calls on five men to reconnoiter. On their way back they are attacked and only four return. While his comrades mourn, the fifth comes back late, having been separated in the confusion. Soon the order comes to move out for the general attack, and this time they know that there will be no false alarms. Death for some is certain. These Japanese soldiers are without any sense of mission, divine or otherwise. They are neither for nor against war; they are simply caught in the middle of hostilities. When the five on patrol are attacked, they see nothing. All they experience is the terrifying effect of the enemy's fire—which the audience too experiences through some of the most horrific sounds ever presented. In turn, the soldiers shoot back into this impersonal void. The enemy is like a fire or a flood. One does not hate the destructive forces of nature, one only struggles against their power to destroy.

There is a unity in the film which had seldom been seen in Tasaka's prior work. His direction is composed of the little things of which soldiers' lives are made. They are bored. They search for the flowers they knew at home. They try to discover something that suggests the floor mats of the Japanese house. Tasaka investigates the personality of each soldier, and the acting suggests that the director worked for weeks to get one of those fine ensemble performances which many think possible only in a closely-knit stage troupe. The picture is admirable not only for its technique but also for its essentially humanistic outlook. It is not at all like the Nazi *Hitlerjunge Quex*, which one may admire for its style but despise for its philosophy. It was made by those who opposed most of what the military stood for but were reluctant to go against what they considered an unavoidable, if inevitably disastrous, flow of events. In a nation where obligation rather than feeling or reason rules the social order, it was not necessary to hide horror or present a rationale for war. It was only necessary to show the people what was required of them.

Tasaka, himself no chauvinist, did just this. The new realism which had been growing in Japanese films during the previous decade he continued in films like *Five Scouts*, and if this film did indirectly and almost unwittingly give comfort to the militarists, it also showed something more than the face of war—it showed something that is common to humanity.

He followed it in 1939 with *Mud and Soldiers* (Tsuchi to Heitai), where again the slice-of-life technique was applied

to the war film. Again there was an over-all lack of dramatic
situation, but here the tension was dissipated, one's attention
being diverted from one situation to another. The company
moves out. A corporal and a private get lost. Soldiers hope
for rest but orders come to move on. There is no fixed battle
line and the soldiers straggle about almost like wandering
samurai. They move along an endless road—the major visual
theme—marching eternally down the road, never seeming to
reach a permanent objective. Though shot on location in
China and using extensive newsreel footage, this picture
as a whole lacks the impact of the studio-made *Five Scouts*,
perhaps because production conditions put Tasaka too close
to his subject this time. Yet in this film too, though not so
plainly, one can see the continuation of the prewar interest
in human values, the realism so painfully discovered, so lately
achieved, which very soon would be obscured by seven
years of total war.

In 1940, Kimisaburo Yoshimura's *The Story of Tank Commander Nishizumi* (Nishizumi Senshacho-den) again reflected
the prewar humanistic ideal. It showed its hero being friendly
with enemy civilians, giving aid to a Chinese woman and
child, and even fraternizing with his men. It was Shochiku's biggest money-maker of the year and next to *Five
Scouts* is usually thought of as being the greatest Japanese
war film.

Such quality, however, was by no means typical of all
these films. As there had previously been no fully developed
war genre, films like these by Tasaka and Yoshimura were
really little more than the earlier realism dressed in uniform.
The industry as a whole was slow in adapting to the military
pattern. Realizing this, the government was quick to make
plans for a wartime regimentation of the movies. In 1937
and 1938 the Home Ministry laid down an increasingly
stringent code of instructions for the industry:

Do not distort military orders. Do not make light of
military matters. Do not exaggerate horror in scenes dealing
with war. Avoid scenes of close fighting. Do nothing to lower
the morale or destroy the fighting spirit of conscripted men
and their families. Avoid scenes of corruption and excessive
merriment. Eliminate tendencies toward individualism as expressed in American and European pictures. Develop the
Japanese national philosophy, especially the beauty of the
peculiarly indigenous family system and the spirit of complete sacrifice for the nation. Because young men and wom-
en, especially modern women, are being Occidentalized,

re-educate the people through films toward true Japanese
emotions. Banish insincere thoughts and words from the
screen; deepen the respect toward fathers and elder brothers.
Films were soon regimented in other ways as well. Playing
time was limited to three hours per show, admission tax was
raised one hundred percent, the additional manufacture of
projection equipment was prohibited, and no one was allowed
to build new theaters or repair old ones. Later, night-time
photography was prohibited for fear of signaling the enemy.

All this had been more or less politely phrased—the government "requested." In April, 1939, however, the first of
the new motion-picture laws were established. Patterned in
part after the Nazi Spitzenorganisation der Filmwirtschaft
which supervised German production, distribution, and exhibition, they were at first fairly mild. As the war progressed,
however, the government became progressively stricter,
and in 1940 ruled: National movies of healthy entertainment
value with themes showing persons ready to serve are hoped
for. Comedians and vaudeville satirists will be restricted if
they overdo their comedy. Slice-of-life films, films describing individual happiness, films treating the lives of the rich,
scenes of women smoking, drinking in cafes, etc., the use of
foreign words, and films dealing with sexual frivolity are all
prohibited. Films showing industrial and food production,
particularly the life in farming villages, should be presented.
Scripts will be censored before production and will be rewritten until they fully satisfy the Censorship Office of the
Home Ministry.

Subsequent laws were largely patterned after those written
by Goebbels. Law: one day of every month will be set aside
as free admission day for families with sons inducted into
military service. Law: in every movie theater and studio one
minute of meditation by everyone will be held at high noon
every day with prayers for those in military service. But as
in so many things, the letter of the law and the actual conditions were at opposite poles.

Thus, despite all the laws and regulations and the government's desire for "positive" propaganda, ultranationalism was
not a real factor in films until after Pearl Harbor. In 1940
the Cabinet created its own Office of Public Information and
soon moved government control from the negative phase of
merely preventing the filming of undesirable subjects to the
more positive position of pushing definite propaganda themes.
Films which were made along government propaganda lines
used what were called "national-policy themes." They had

begun to appear in 1938, but such efforts were largely voluntary on the part of the film-makers. Three years later the themes themselves were inescapable, and the national-policy films soon developed the war picture as a genre.

One of the earliest was the 1940 *Flaming Sky* (Moyuru Ozora), directed by Yutaka Abe, who, along with Kajiro Yamamoto, was the leader in developing the new ultra-nationalistic war genre. About military pilots, it was the first to have extensive aerial footage and to show planes in action, in the manner of foreign aviation pictures. Toho had been making airplane pictures with models for several years, but this was the first time they had used the real thing. Abe's 1942 *South Seas Bouquet* (Nankai no Hanataba) was another airplane film, about the flyers who paved the way for the invasion of the southern islands.

Eiichi Koishi's *Soaring Passion* (Maiagaru Jonetsu), made in 1941, continued the war-in-the-air theme with the story of a young farm boy who wants to be a pilot. It was filmed in a semi-documentary manner with the use of genuine locales and nonactors in minor rôles. In 1943, Kunio Watanabe made *Toward the Decisive Battle in the Sky* (Kessen no Ozora e), about air cadets. It rather resembled American pictures in its handling of theme and was considered one of the better films of the year. It also contained Setsuko Hara, fast becoming ubiquitous as a war-film heroine. In the same year Shochiku decided to do for the Army Air Corps what this picture had done for the Navy Air Corps and brought out *Flying South in His Plane* (Aiki Minami e Tobu). Later in the year Shochiku sponsored Tomotaka Tasaka's *Navy* (Kaigun), a big production about the naval flyers who participated in the Pearl Harbor attack.

The military services demanded absolute control of content in anything that touched upon their activities during the war and thus helped make films like Tetsu Taguchi's *Generals, Staff, and Soldiers* (Shogun to Sambo to Hei), shot near the North China front in 1942 and patterned somewhat after Karl Ritter's *Unternehmen Michael*, which told a war story from the several levels of command. In the same year Tadashi Imai made *The Suicide Troops of the Watchtower* (Boro no Kesshitai), which was largely in the tradition of the American action film but was much influenced by Japanese wartime documentary techniques. It was made with the cooperation of the Chosen [Korea] Motion Picture Company and used Korean actors in many important rôles, being the story of a newly-arrived border guard's adjustment to his new life. The climax of the picture was a big attack by bandits, but there was no indication that these "bandits" were really a guerilla army fighting for an independent Korea.

Some films were even more obviously aimed at the home audience. Také Sado's 1941 *Chocolate and Soldiers* (Chokoreto to Heitai), a mobilized *shomin-geki,* was about a village clerk who is drafted, leaving a wife and son behind. He is sent to China; scenes of the horror of war, mud, marching, fighting. Wherever he goes he picks up chocolate wrappers and sends them to his son; sends last wrappers on night before suicide attack; son wins prize with wrappers; chocolate company takes interest in the boy and father's sacrifice; sends boy to school. Takeo Murata's *Prayer to Mother Earth* (Daichi ni Inoru), made in the same year, saw the war in China from the female point of view since it was about military nurses.

Perhaps most representative of the national-policy films were those by Kajiro Yamamoto, who had started his career in Minoru Murata's theatrical troupe and worked at Nikkatsu since 1920, as actor, scenarist, assistant, and finally director. The war brought him a chance to do his best work, and in 1942 he brought out what the critics decided was the top film of the year, *The War at Sea from Hawaii to Malaya* (Hawai-Marei Oki Kaisen). Sponsored to commemorate the first year of the war against the United States, this was an extension of the documentary approach the director had used in *Horse* but with a great difference in materials. Its purpose was to dramatize "the Navy Spirit as culminated at Pearl Harbor," and in it Yamamoto carefully re-created the years of preparation for the attack. It also marked the greatest use of special effects and miniature work ever seen in a Japanese film up to that time. So effective were these studio shots that after the war Occupation authorities mistook some of them for the real thing. It was gigantic in every sense of the word and cost over $380,000 to make, when the average first-class film was budgeted for $40,000. Released on the first anniversary of Pearl Harbor, it soon made its investment back, and Yamamoto went on to films like *General Kato's Falcon Fighters* (Kato Hayabusa Sentotai), the big success of the first half of 1944. Here he did for the army what he had done two years before for the navy. Scripting both films himself, this one was about an airplane pursuit unit flying and fighting from Canton to Malaya, Burma, and Thailand. In the same year he again favored the navy with

Torpedo Squadrons Move Out (Raigekitai Shutsudo), about three young officers who sink an enemy flagship; it was designed to recruit men for human-torpedo work.

Despite their many similarities to the Western propaganda film, the national-policy films were in many respects markedly different. There was, for example, no appeal to the Deity, or deities, for one's own protection during fighting. One, rather, went forward wanting to die. Even such semi-religious ceremonies as bowing to the rising sun were so formalized as to have had almost no religious significance. There were no speeches to the effect that "God is on our side"; in fact, there was little or no talk about the righteousness of the cause at all. The simple fact that Japan required their services was quite enough motivation for her soldiers.

In studying the better Japanese propaganda films, Ruth Benedict came to a number of highly interesting conclusions: The wide usage of average men and women, neither rich nor heroic types, made for good audience identification. These films had great propaganda "courage" in not glorifying or glossing over the horror of war; the soldiers do not march home triumphant, but die in battle. There was little of the John Wayne type of super-heroism, and the use of both good and bad Japanese soldiers gave a more "objective" picture of reality. The plots posed problems and then answered them forthrightly, the heroes dealing head-on with the situations, and not being saved by luck. There was a careful use of symbolism, and the villains tended, though not always, to be Westernized Orientals rather than enemy nationals.

Whatever their demerits, these pictures were obviously good for propaganda purposes and rather far removed from the film caricatures which we know most World War II pictures elsewhere to have been. After studying a number of Japanese wartime films for their propaganda potential during the war, Frank Capra is supposed to have said: "We can't beat this kind of thing. We can make films like these maybe once in a decade...."

Not content with merely calling the war to the attention of the masses, however, the national-policy films continued to the point of producing another genre, one early developed in the West but until now ignored in Japan, the spy picture, a form which was now reinforced by the fanaticism and extreme measures of Japan's anti-espionage campaign of the late 1930's. One of the earliest was Hiroyuki Yamamoto's *Fifth Column Fear* (Daigoretsu no Kyofu), which revolved around the discovery of fifth columnists and their activities through the deciphering of code messages. Perhaps more typical was Kimisaburo Yoshimura's *The Spy Isn't Dead Yet* (Kancho Mada Shisezu). It was about a spy from Chunking who comes to Japan and is used by a master American spy who also employs a Filipino spy. The Chunking spy realizes he is being exploited but is shortly killed by the American, whereupon the Filipino commits suicide. The near-allegorical overtones are sustained by the fact that the American spy is captured by the Japanese on December 7, 1941. The emphasis, however, was mainly upon the technique of spying, the Japanese audience, as always, being interested in the mechanics of what they were seeing. Actually the film was not too effective as propaganda for it left one too much in sympathy with the Chinese, who, after all, was working against Japan. In fact the film was sharply criticized for its failure to show the Japanese as security-conscious, some of the Japanese characters in the film seeming "almost pro-spy." Yoshimura apparently mended his ways because in 1943 the secret police as a part of their "Prevent Espionage" campaign sponsored his *On the Eve of War* (Kaisen no Zenya).

Such campaigns had been fairly rampant since 1937, and many and curious are the tales told by tourists coming to Japan during that period, usually ending with a secret-police agent in the same bath. Among the more fantastic spy pictures was Shuzo Fukuda's 1938 *Invisible Invader* (Sugata-naki Shinnyusha), which was designed to make the populace suspicious of any and all foreigners in Japan, because "they wander about with their true intentions unknown," a category which included tourists, technicians, businessmen, students, and missionaries.

Later, after the war was well under way, the foreign spies were given specific identities, usually American or British. Yet, oddly, these films rarely made any attempt to use foreigners in the non-Japanese rôles, the parts being usually filled by Japanese actors. There was also very little attempt made to preserve the language distinction. The foreigners all spoke Japanese, even to each other. The same dramatic convention exists in American pictures too, of course, though a heavy foreign accent usually tries to disguise the English. In Japan, however, this was unnecessary. The audience was merely told that these well-known Japanese actors were playing foreign spies and, as a consequence, its disbelief was obediently suspended, as also was its faith in realism.

From this came yet another element of the national-policy films: their encouragement of feeling against the United

States and Britain. In this, Japanese propaganda films came nearer to those of the West than heretofore, a hate-the-enemy campaign being one of the prerequisites of the form. Here too, however, the Japanese wartime film somewhat differed from that of America or England. The Japanese films were mostly historical, and thus the immediacy of dislike, which was the strongest element of the American anti-Japanese movie, was missing. Farley Granger with his tongue cut out, James Cagney pitted against a *sumo* champion—these were powerful and immediate images. For this the Japanese substituted the idea of the historical slights resulting in Japan's taking arms.

The Pirates' Flag Is Blasted Away (Kaizokuki Futtobu), for example, was the Japanese view of the Satsuma clan's fights against the British in the immediate pre-Meiji era. Daisuke Ito's *International Smuggling Gang* (Kokusai Mitsuyudan), made a year later in 1944, was set in the period when Yokohama had just been opened. Perkins, head of the British consulate, runs an opium-smuggling ring through which he hopes to subdue Japan as, said the film, the British had already weakened and subdued China. In 1942 Daisuke Ito had made *Kurama Tengu Appears in Yokohama* (Kurama Tengu Yokohama ni Arawaru), about a group of *ronin* breaking up an international smuggling gang during the early days of the port. Opium was taken up again in Masahiro Makino's 1943 *The Opium War* (Ahen Senso), about how the British stupefy the Chinese with vast quantities of the drug and then start to divide the country.

Some of the films treated comparatively modern history. In 1943 Masanori Igayama, a specialist in naval pictures, made *If We Go to Sea* (Umi Yukaba), about how Japan struggled against international naval disarmament conferences, Britain and the United States wanting to limit Japan so she will be weak and unable to resist attack. A year later Tadashi Imai made *The Angry Sea* (Ikari no Umi), which shows how the United States and Great Britain plotted against Japan at the London Naval Disarmament Conference. A panorama was offered in Shigeo Tanaka's 1942 *The Day England Fell* (Eikoku Kuzururu no Hi), the story of the British "imperialistic and anti-Oriental attitudes" in Hongkong from the opening of the Pacific War to the occupation by the Japanese. In 1943, Teinosuke Kinugasa made *Forward! Flag of Independence* (Susume Dokuritsu-ki), which told how a young Indian prince helps his Japanese comrades smash a British spy ring, thus both helping Japan's crusade and achieving India's inde-

pendence. One of the few virulent hate-the-enemy films was
Daiei's *You're Being Aimed At* (Anata wa Nerawarete Iru), which seems to be the first bacteriological-warfare picture, concerned as it was with American agents trying to spread a deadly disease in Japan.

What was missing from these Japanese films was the element of caricature which, however dishonestly, managed to frighten a good many Westerners, and which American hate-the-enemy films always insisted upon. It was easy to make a comparatively unknown people like the Japanese into squat lustful yellow dwarfs, but the Japanese, even if they had felt inclined, could scarcely have made the Westerner a figure of terror. Almost all Japanese had seen at least several foreigners and, more important, had learned to accept many foreign ways themselves. The prewar influence of America, in particular, had been tremendous, and so while the Japanese knew all about Americans, or at least thought they did, the Americans knew little or nothing about the Japanese. One of the results was the Fu-man-chu type of Japanese, while the Japanese themselves had no recourse to such caricatures other than to attribute to foreigners the basest of motives and foulest of deeds.

Unlike in the West, the greatest propaganda effort in Japan was spent in actively mobilizing the home front. Toward this end the national-policy pictures spared not a single film genre. The light comedy, the film about children, the slice-of-life film, the movie about mother—everything was used. No genre escaped being used for ultranationalistic propaganda, nor did any director. Here the main theme was the "spirit of sacrifice," the necessity of following the prescribed pattern of behavior regardless of difficulties. Individual success, love, or amusement were not to be sought. Filial piety, fidelity, and patriotism were to be emphasized; patience and resignation were to be cultivated.

The entire attitude was shown in a manifesto in the influential *Chuo Koron* magazine of October, 1940: "Dramatic art must forget the old individualistic and class attitudes and must begin to realize that it has a cultural rôle to perform in the total program of our new national consciousness. Actors are no longer to serve a class but the nation and they must act as persons who are part of the whole national entity. They must have the determination to make the cultural wealth of [their art] available to every group in the population. For this reason, the concentration of culture in the big cities should be eliminated."

As early as 1939, Tasaka's *Airplane Drone* (Bakuon) had set the pattern for "home front" films. It was about a public-contribution campaign to buy airplanes. The mayor's son is a pilot, and the story concerns the village's preparations to greet him as he flies over in his airplane. More a document than a piece of propaganda, it was a closely-observed study of village life and there was even a little satire on rural bureaucracy.

One of the first things the wartime Japanese had to learn from the films was the necessity of sacrificing inclination to duty. Minoru Shibuya's 1941 *Cherry Country* (Sakura no Kuni), shot in Peking and the surrounding area, had this as its theme. A Japanese student leaves Peking University to become a propaganda officer for a political society. His girl wants to marry him, but her mother arranges a marriage with a man who already has an illegitimate child. She meets the hero and tells him how unhappy she is. He tells her it is her duty to marry the man and then leaves her to go back to work. Shiro Toyoda's *A Record of My Love* (Waga Ai no Ki), made in the same year, managed to combine the duty theme with a happy ending. Based on a true story, the film was about a nurse who falls in love with a permanently disabled soldier. She marries him, planning to support him by working. This film was used in a national drive to have unmarried working women marry disabled soldiers and thus assume the expenses normally the government's responsibility.

The *shomin-geki* also went to war. Yasujiro Shimazu's 1944 film, *The Daily Battle* (Nichijo no Tatakai), was about a college English teacher who becomes head of a wartime neighborhood association and is later sent to Southeast Asia as an interpreter. It was considered one of the best films of the year, being thought definitive in showing the "little people" during the war.

There were also many reminders that in the past the home front had held strong. Keisuke Kinoshita's *Army* (Rikugun) was about a family who for three generations had sent sons to the Imperial Army, attention being focused on the second generation and its eldest son. *The Last Days of Edo* (Edo Saigo no Hi), a 1941 film by Hiroshi Inagaki, was about the riots in Tokyo when the shogun evacuated Edo Castle and the Emperor Meiji took his place. The film naturally failed to catch the real atmosphere of the period since it failed to include the vast number of people with divided loyalties. Instead, the hero swiftly converts all the rebels to the emperor's side.

In 1940 Tomu Uchida planned a three-part film, *History*
(Rekishi), in honor of the 2,600th anniversary of the legendary founding of Japan, about the Aizu fief's refusing to obey the orders of the Emperor Meiji. In the end the hero becomes a businessman and his friend becomes a policeman who is later drafted for civil-war duty. The film was an enormous failure, and Nikkatsu refused to put up the backing for the remaining two parts, much to Uchida's disappointment.

The women came in for praise in Toyoda's 1940 *Ioko Okumura* (Okumura Ioko), the story of a heroic woman of the Meiji era and her total virtue. She finally goes to Korea as an "educator." Along the same line was Satsuo Yamamoto's 1943 *Hot Wind* (Neppu), which was a part of the "increase industrial production" cycle. It had Setsuko Hara again heroic in a steel foundry. Akira Kurosawa contributed to the cycle with his second picture, *Most Beautifully* (Ichiban Utsukushiku), the story of girl workers in a military optical-instrument factory. In the same year, 1944, Masahiro Makino made *An Unsinkable Warship Sunk* (Fuchinkan Gekichin), about life in an aerial-torpedo factory. A torpedo was traced from manufacture to final destination. At the same time Miyoji Ieki's *Torrent* (Gekiryu) was doing much the same for increased production in the coal mines.

The "be prepared" type of film was also seen. The 1943 *Enemy Air Attack* (Tekki Kushu) was all about civilian defense, and Kinoshita's *Jubilation Street* (Kanko no Machi), made a year later, was a largely unsuccessful attempt to publicize the "evacuate the cities" drive. It was about the happenings on one particular street, in the fashion of King Vidor's version of Elmer Rice's *Street Scene*. If the people did evacuate, preferably to other countries, Shiro Toyoda's 1940 *Ohinata Village* (Ohinata Mura) showed them how happy they would be.

The national-policy program even found a way to use the period-drama, cliché-ridden, without ideals, and near nihilistic as it was. This they did by creating from it a genre they called the "historical film," the duties of which were to dramatize the greatness of Japan's past. Despite the anthropologists who during and after the war insisted that the period-film was a harbinger and virulent carrier of militarism, the Japanese militarists themselves considered the genre a very weak propaganda instrument and thus demanded the formation of the historical film.

The last of the prewar-type period spectaculars was seen in Inagaki's 1941 *Festival across the Sea* (Umi o Wataru Sairei), about festivals in various port towns. This was succeeded in the following year by one of the most important of the new genre of historical films, Tomu Uchida's *Suneemon Tori* (Tori Suneemon). Based on a novel by Eiji Yoshikawa and sponsored by the Office of Public Information, it stressed how important it was for commoners, in contrast to samurai, to become soldiers, and emphasized that soldiers must faithfully perform their duties regardless of the outcome. In general the film was a failure, though the government made much of it as "a turn from the entertainment-oriented [period-film] to the national-policy-oriented historical film." Uchida's earlier *History* had perhaps provided the origin of the historical film concept, but it had been even less successful.

A contemporary critic described the differences between the common period-drama and the historical film by saying that while both dealt with stories in historical settings, the period-drama aimed primarily at telling a dramatic story with history merely as background. The historical film, on the other hand, found that drama was the raw material of history and never allowed plot to assume more importance than actual fact. The distinction now seems a merely academic one since history in the historical films was just as falsified as it was in the period-drama. In the former, as a matter of fact, it was frequently rewritten in the interests of "national policy."

When the militarists began utilizing the Tokugawa era, some directors, partly as a reaction to this pushing of historical films, turned to making pictures about the Meiji era, which had long been the refuge of the period-drama directors when the officials were out after their genre. The *Meiji-mono* was later to shelter again a number of distinguished filmmakers when the Occupation officials, for reasons entirely different from those of the militarists, frowned upon both the period-drama and the wartime historical-film.

Kenji Mizoguchi, backing away from official decrees, was among the first to find a haven in the Meiji era with his 1939 *The Story of the Last Chrysanthemums* (Zangiku Monogatari) and continued this interest right through the war. Although supposedly the biography of the Kabuki actor Kikunosuke Onoe, it was essentially a sentimental tragedy distinguished by its rare insight into the Kabuki world with its traditions and inner-relationships, including the heroine's

sacrifice so that the hero can become great. This was followed
in 1940 by *Woman of Osaka* (Naniwa Onna), about the Bunraku, or puppet drama. Again a woman suffers for a man's art, and this time an actual Bunraku troupe was used, with many of the members figuring in various rôles. The following year Mizoguchi made *The Life of an Artist* (Geido Ichidai Otoko), another tragedy, which in 1944 he followed with yet another Meiji film centered on a Kabuki actor, *Three Generations of Danjuro* (Danjuro San-dai).

Mizoguchi was not alone in the *Meiji-mono* field. Hiroshi Inagaki's *The Life of Matsu the Untamed* (Muho Matsu no Issho), made in 1943, was considered the best film of the year and the finest of the wartime films with a Meiji setting. As such, it was considerably better than his 1958 remake which won the Venice prize under the title of *Rickshaw Man*. About Matsu's going to extremes to pay an obligation, the inference was that he, though lowborn, rough, and something of an outcast, was doing much more than ordinary respectable people would.

Many of the pictures of this Meiji cycle were naturally made by former period-drama specialists such as Makino, Takizawa, and Inagaki, but soon "modern" specialists like Naruse and Shimazu entered the field as well. Even newcomer Akira Kurosawa turned to the period-film. His first picture, the 1943 *Sanshiro Sugata* (Sugata Sanshiro), was a Meiji piece about the originator of judo. It starred period-drama stars but was very different from most of the Meiji films in that it showed very little of the Shimpa influence. The Meiji films, as a rule, tended to identify the period with the "good old days," while Kurosawa was, from the first, interested mainly in the contemporary aspects of past history. The Office of Public Information liked the film because it showed the "spirit of judo" and this was right in line with their policy of aggrandizing things Japanese. Its success was such that in the same year Kurosawa wrote a script that did the same thing for *sumo*. This became Santaro Marune's *The Critical Moment* (Dohyosai).

What with both the historical film and the *Meiji-mono*, the period-film as a genre soon all but disappeared. Hiroshi Inagaki has said that after 1941 it lost its true feeling and soon separated into three different parts: the historical film, the classical adaptation, and the simple costume picture. He himself worked on one of the last true period-films, a multipart *Musashi Miyamoto*. Inagaki is forever remaking his past successes, and this was very much like the color version he

was to make fifteen years later, which won such foreign
praise under the title *Samurai*.

Just as the makers of the period-drama had revolted to
the extent of finding sanctuary in the Meiji period, so the
makers of the films about contemporary life discovered
themselves often in violent disagreement with national policy,
which though openly endorsed by the government and hence
by the country itself, met with some opposition from within the industry. In large part this opposition was not based
on political dislike of the objectives of militant Japan—though
in certain cases this was a factor—but more on a reluctance
and inability to adapt national policy to a personal style, and a
natural fury at being told by non-film people how to make
a film. The opposition appeared in the form of films which
touched on national policy as lightly as possible or else either
ignored or even actively opposed it.

Two of the lighter national-policy films appeared in 1942.
Tasaka's *Mother-and-Child Grass* (Hahako-gusa) belonged
to the sacrificing-mother genre but at least was believable.
Tears were not milked and there was excellent location work
in a small town at the foot of Mt. Fuji. Ozu's *There Was a
Father* (Chichi Ariki) was about a father's devotion to his
son, how the son grows up and marries the daughter of his
father's friend, thus continuing the family strain. It was
similar in plot to his earlier *The Only Son* and was a realistic
portrayal of people's life during the early part of the war.
The emphasis was on Japanese manhood and its obligations
to family and society, but the tone was far removed from
most wartime films with this theme.

In 1943, Keisuke Kinoshita made *The Blossoming Port*
(Hana Saku Minato). About two very sharp confidence men
who deceive an island people into backing a fake ship-build-
ing company, it showed the simple virtues of the islanders
making honest men of the swindlers and creating a real ship
company to help the war effort. Based on a play sponsored
by the Office of Public Information, it was very light and
genuinely gay at a time when even forced, cheap comedy
was scarce. The film's social satire, in addition, did not present national policy in too favorable a light, despite the
picture's official origins. The appearance of this picture, and
Kurosawa's *Sanshiro Sugata*, gave some hope for the future
prospects of the Japanese film. Both opened new horizons
and offered an escape from the dead-end toward which the
wartime films seemed headed. In 1943, though the war was
still on, the direction of the postwar Japanese cinema had

already been determined by the appearance of these two new
talents.

Other film-makers simply ignored national policy. Shiro Toyoda's 1940 *Spring on Lepers' Island* (Kojima no Haru), based on a female doctor's story of her life in an isolated leper colony, was a cry for humanism in an age marching toward militarism. In 1942, Kimisaburo Yoshimura made *South Wind* (Minami no Kaze), a picture about a man of good looks and no talent who will do anything for money, which heavily criticized society for its "money is everything" philosophy.

After Ozu was discharged from military service in 1941, he made *The Toda Brother and His Sisters* (Toda-ke no Kyodai), about a mother and younger daughter who live with the eldest son after the father dies. The son's wife makes life most uncomfortable, so they go to China to live with the second son. In this film, made with an almost silent-film technique, Ozu continued his own development uninfluenced by the happenings around him. Many other directors were taking a stand, for or against, but Ozu ignored the issue. This very close delineation of various Japanese attitudes toward motherhood as an institution made it the first Ozu film to become a box-office hit.

There was some direct opposition to national policy. Heinosuke Gosho, for example, protested by turning all military scripts submitted to him into simple love stories. The military summarily rejected the stories but did not punish him because his health was poor. In 1940, when he made an adaptation of the novel *Wooden Head*, he initially outlined it to Shochiku as a mother film with a national-policy touch. Instead he turned out a rather involved psychological study of an unmarried woman doctor who adopts an illegitimate child in order to keep the father's name clear. She leads a generally frustrated life and forbids the child later to have any friends. In 1942 Gosho did the same thing with *New Snow* (Shinsetsu), which was intended to be a national-policy picture until the director turned it into a romantic melodrama which only accidentally happened to occur during wartime. Kinoshita too was doing his bit against the war effort and in 1943 made *The Living Sugoroku* (Ikite Iru Sugoroku), a light comedy attacking superstition, in this case the belief that the heir to a certain family's name will always die. His rationalist, represented by a professor at a medical school, ended by questioning all unfounded beliefs.

Of all three major companies, Shochiku made the fewest

national-policy films. The reasons were several. First, Shochiku with its long-standing tradition thought that women's films and stories about the daily life of city people made the most money. Second, it had a shortage of executive personnel. Kido was out busy helping organize film activities in occupied lands; hence there was little leadership and no one at all to direct a change in production policies. Finally, Shochiku personnel were not so friendly toward the propaganda officials as were people in the other companies. As a result of these factors, Shochiku's financial position slipped somewhat upon the increased audience demand for war stories.

In 1942 the company ran into real trouble with the military because of its failure to make a sufficient number of national-policy films. The government was quite prepared to destroy Shochiku unless they brought forth a version of *The Loyal Forty-seven Ronin* which stressed the military's conception of *bushido,* and so it was that Kenji Mizoguchi volunteered, to save the company, and made his unsuccessful *The Loyal Forty-seven Ronin of the Genroku Era* (Genroku Chushingura).

Not only the films themselves but also the entire industry had organized for war. During the late 1930's, film companies had become fewer in number but larger in size. Now, due to "national economic factors," the government decided to push consolidation further in order to make the industry easier to control. In mid-1941 it approached the ten major film companies then operating (Nikkatsu, Shochiku, Toho, Shinko, Daito, Tokyo Hassei, Nan-o, Takarazuka, Otaguro, and Koa) and told them they must form themselves into two companies. Each of the two companies was to make just two films a month. The decrease in production would be met by increasing the number of prints of each film from sixteen to fifty. All makers of shorts and educational films, at that time over two hundred in number, would be formed into a single company to produce four films a month, fifty prints of each. A separate company was to handle all distribution.

To encourage consolidation, the Office of Public Information told company representatives that since raw film stock was a war material, it would not be available to the industry unless the studios made the kind of pictures the state required. A line-up for mergers was then suggested. Shochiku was to take Shinko and Koa. Toho was to take all the other independents. Nikkatsu assets would be divided between the remaining two, with Shochiku emerging stronger than Toho.

The announcement of plans to consolidate the industry caused much maneuvering as certain persons saw a chance for great advancement or demotion. Masaichi Nagata claims that the two-film-companies plan was designed by Kido to consolidate his personal power and Shochiku's strength. Certain members of the industry opposed this original government plan, and Nagata found himself elected head of a counter-measures committee. It was thought that as a Kyoto man he could take a more argumentative attitude than the Tokyo people, who came into daily contact with the Office of Public Information. Nagata gladly accepted, for, under the original two-company plan, the Shinko Kyoto studios, which he headed, would be closed and he would be out of a job.

Nagata, instead of opposing the plan too strongly, as his friends had expected, came up with a new plan. This was to form three companies instead of two: the first would be made of Shochiku and Koa; the second of Toho, Otaguro, Tokyo Hassei, Nan-o, and Takarazuka; and the third of Nikkatsu, Shinko, and Daito. He also suggested that each of the three make two films a month, these six productions to have thirty prints each made for distribution. The plan came as a surprise to everyone. They had been bogged down talking endlessly about what company should join which and suddenly in came Nagata with a brand-new idea. The Office of Public Information quickly saw that this new third company, composed of firms with weak management, would have no established executive staff to oppose government policy. The office would have major control and the new third company would be really "semi-official." Nagata's plan was accepted, and almost everyone was happy.

One of the few who was not was Kyusaku Hori, head of Nikkatsu, who objected to the formation of this third company because it would have meant including the large chain of Nikkatsu theaters and not receiving equivalent credit for these assets since the merger was in terms of production facilities. He therefore proposed that only Nikkatsu production and distribution should join the third company. Nikkatsu exhibition would maintain its own identity. In attempting to defend his own company, Hori thus earned the displeasure of the higher powers, and when it came time to join the assets of Nikkatsu, Shinko, and Daito, his concern was purposely undervalued, while Shinko was padded to the extent that it became the dominant company in the combine. This, of course, was outright dishonesty since Shinko had never been a top company equal to Nikkatsu. One of the results, however, was that Shinko's new head found his company now with the real power in the new organization, and he himself consequently in top position. The company head was, of course, Masaichi Nagata. In a very short time a name was found for the new company. It was called the Dai-Nihon Eiga, the Greater Japan Motion Picture Company, or, as it was soon called, Daiei. Subsequently, because the board could not decide on a president, Managing Director Nagata willingly took on the extra duties.

Nikkatsu was not completely sold out. Hori was allowed to keep Nikkatsu as a theater-holding company. This left the new Daiei with plenty of studios but without any theaters except those few brought in by Shinko and Daito. It found itself in financial difficulties from the start. Shochiku had already tied up the women's audience, and Toho was appealing to the urban audience. This left only the farmers and the children to the new Daiei. Its first films did not make too much money and it had to depend on capital funds loaned by the Nagase Company, a concern specializing in selling raw film stock to the industry. The first Daiei film that made any money was Gosho's *New Snow,* and the film must have come as a shock to the government, which had formerly been so certain of the "semi-official" position of the new company.

There was another shock in 1942 when Nagata was suddenly arrested by the police and his rising star was, for the time being, stopped in mid-flight. The Home Ministry, traditional rival of the Information Office, had had the warrant issued. It accused Nagata of having bribed the Information Office to have his three-company plan accepted. This rumor had been current for some time, but the fact that the government decided to do something about it surprised everyone. Nagata, however, denied the charge and was released in fifty days, to the sorrow of others in the industry.

In his memoirs, Kido confirms the rivalry between himself and Nagata, saying that the latter was in chronic fear of being subordinate to somebody and had especially disliked being under Kido. He continues with: "It was mostly fate, not talent, that made Nagata big." Kido himself here confirms his preference for a consolidation plan that would have made only two big companies. His reasons were that they would have had to center around Shochiku and Toho—thus increasing Shochiku's power. To him it was simply a question of dividing the market two ways or three. Naturally he preferred two.

The industry itself was affected in more ways than one.
Due to the cut in production, every studio was overloaded with personnel. Rather than redirect all this labor, however, most were kept on doing nothing. Script writers were maintained on duty, and very soon the supply of scripts greatly exceeded the need. This allowed, at least theoretically, a more careful selection of scenarios. There was also a shortage of raw film stock and this affected even the highest priority productions, those films shown abroad in occupied territories as propaganda. Initially, feature length was limited to one hundred minutes, but this was soon cut to ninety. At the same time, to stretch bookings, showings were limited to two a day, four on Sundays. And, in fact, the audience needed stretching. By the end of 1943, all men over twenty were being drafted, and students were required to work part-time in war industries. The Education Ministry prohibited film-study groups in universities as a "waste of time," and students were no longer allowed to enter theaters freely—they must put their time to better use.

Distribution was vastly affected. Under the new film laws each of the three companies was to turn out only two features a month, whereas before consolidation the industry had been averaging twenty-five. All distribution was put in the hands of one company with two exhibition circuits. Each program was to consist of exactly one feature, one "cultural film," and one newsreel. A theater could play only those features assigned to its circuit, and double-features were outlawed. All of the theaters in Japan—2,350 as of 1942 —were put on one of the two circuits except those few then specializing in foreign films. These were confined to imports of a single company and, American films having been banned in 1941, only German or Italian films were allowed. Rental rates were inflexibly fixed. Forty percent of the gross was for film rental, thirty-five for general expenditures, fifteen for building expenses or rental, and the remaining ten percent was profit. The rental money was divided into eighty percent for the feature, ten for the cultural film, and ten for the newsreel.

By 1944 all the big first-class theaters had to close, there being a new ban on "high-class" entertainment, which included all live drama. In June the air raids began, though there was not too much damage because the American planes had to travel such a distance to bomb. By November, however, the raids were more or less continuous and almost half the theaters were closed.

The rural areas had long been neglected by commercial interests, being usually serviced by traveling projection units which used ancient, often hand-cranked machinery and showed only the poorest and oldest silent films, with occasional free shows sponsored by newspapers as a service to their subscribers. To get the national-policy message to the rural areas required a special effort. One of the difficulties was that sixteen millimeter was in a very early stage of development in Japan. During the war, however, the traveling projection shows were organized into the Japan Traveling Culture Association, and by 1942 there were 157 mobile thirty-five-millimeter units and 162 sixteen-millimeter.

The need for direct propaganda and the government's enforcement of a law requiring the showing of a short, one- to three-reel documentary as a substitute for the second half of the newly-forbidden double-feature created for the first time in Japan a real need for non-dramatic films.

The documentary in Japan, despite its early beginnings in the newsreels of the Russo-Japanese War and the shots of pretty geisha, had never developed into the vital form it had become in other countries. The war with China, however, created a demand for newsreels and war documentaries, and this resulted in Toho's setting up its own documentary department and opening a number of small theaters specializing in news and shorts. National policy appeared in these documentaries long before it was discernible in regular features. As early as 1934 a Yokohama company made the feature-length *Japan Advancing to the North* (Hokushin Nihon), and in 1936 the Japanese-sponsored Manchurian Film Company made *Forbidden Jehol* (Hikyo Nekka), directed by Mitsuzo Akutagawa. Shigeru Miki and Fumio Kamei made *Shanghai* in 1938, which was much influenced by Russian montage, Kamei having been a student at the USSR Institute of Cinematography; this film contrasted the lives of rich foreigners and poor Chinese, much to the detriment of the former. Later Toho made *Nanking* (Nankin) and *Peking* (Pekin) along the same lines.

From 1939 there was an extraordinarily large number of Chinese documentary subjects: *The New Continent* (Shin-tairiku), *Advance on Canton* (Kanton Shingunsho), and many others. There were also a number on rural Japanese subjects, *People Who Make Charcoal* (Sumi Yaku Hitobito) and *The Village Without a Doctor* (Isha no Nai Mura) among them. All of these films were more influenced by the German *kulturfilm* than by the British school of documentary. There was a pseudo-scientific, pseudo-artistic approach which occasionally invalidated the subject and which one still sees in many contemporary Japanese documentaries.

Japan's entry into World War II gave both documentaries and newsreels a big impetus. The very fact that their showing during the war years was compulsory automatically created an audience, captive though it was. By the middle of 1942, feature-length documentaries recording Japan's triumphs began to appear, films like *Malayan War Record* (Marei Senki), based on footage shot by military cameramen, and *Divine Soldiers of the Sky* (Sora no Shimpei), a story of parachute troops in action, movies which made the war more real to those on the home front than any dramatic film could.

While World War II did not substantially affect the industries of France or the United States, it had a real effect upon the Japanese far beyond that of making it documentary-conscious. The industry had been mobilized for war to an extent undreamed of in the Allied countries and one of the results was that the industry had become ingrown without having attained full maturity.

The Japanese film had come a long way, but it still had a long way to go. The question that many within the industry itself were asking was whether the war, in itself a detriment to any attaining of artistic maturity, might not at least have the effect of making the immature industry look outside Japan, thus broadening its view if not deepening its insight.

8 background projection: 1939-45

(cont.). THE PRESSURE OF THE military, whatever adverse effect it also had, was in fact responsible for the industry's being forced to take a more international view. If Japan, as was hoped, was to become the leading nation of Asia, then it clearly must know something of its future dependents and, even more clearly, must teach them all about itself. The result, both ways, was propaganda.

The Japanese began a series of coproductions with foreign countries; units were sent to foreign countries for location shooting; the Japanese encouraged the film industries of the countries they were occupying and showed, in Japan, films made by these industries. Political coproductions officially began in 1936, just after both Japan and Germany had signed their Anti-Communist Pact. Eager Japan, soon to be a member of the three-way Axis, was all for making a joint film, and Germany saw that it could thus introduce its new partner in Europe. They decided to make a film showing the "unity of the Nazi group-spirit and the racial spirit of the Japanese as opposed to the weak spirit of the democracies," which would praise the Japanese family system and particularly stress the "volcano-like sacrificing spirit of Japan."

The volcanic image was particularly appropriate because in the script which one of the directors, Arnold Fanck, finally wrote, Mt. Aso in Kyushu figured prominently, along with other Japanese sights such as views of Nikko and the neon-lit Ginza at night. Actually, the choice of directors was a bit singular. Fanck, to be sure, was connected with mountains, having made *Der Heilige Berg*, but he seemed scarcely the

man for a film about Japanese self-sacrifice. The Japanese
choice was even more odd. Mansaku Itami, a specialist in the period-film, was made to undertake this modern story mainly because the picture was to be produced by the J.O. Studios and Itami was their top director.

The film was *The New Earth*, and from the very first the codirectors failed to hit it off. Fanck, having written a script about a Japanese hero's conversion from democracy back to belief in the Japanese family system, was not about to compromise, and Itami, alarmed at what he considered the many misinterpretations of Japanese life, hesitated to lend himself to what he thought was falsehood. The result was that two versions of the film were made, differing in content and inference. The Japanese critics were particularly hard on it, one finding that though Fanck had spent a year "study-ing" Japan, the finished film was "a flimsy piece of work not nearly so penetratingly realistic as the director thought...at times imaginative but without any real insight into Japanese ways." In 1941 the critic Tsutomu Sawamura said that it was "no more than an attempt to form essentially alien [to Japan] Nazi propaganda out of Japanese raw materials."

Despite the film's signal lack of success, since it was con-sidered a failure from all points of view, a sequel was at-tempted, this time with director Wolfgang Berger. It was called *The Oath of the People* (Kokumin no Chikai), and its failure was, if possible, even more total.

After the expensive fiascos of *The New Earth* and *The Oath of the People*, the Japanese were more wary of co-productions with the West. They turned instead to the other nations of Asia, with whom they had at least something in common. In particular, they were interested in their nearest neighbor and colony, Korea, There had been a long history of political contact, most of it unfriendly, between Japan and Korea until 1910, when the latter was "united" to Japan and thenceforward considered a younger brother.

The first films shown in Korea were sponsored in 1903 by an American-owned cigarette company, which offered ad-mission in exchange for a sufficient quantity of package wrappers. The pioneer Yoshizawa Company soon sent over a traveling projection unit, and after 1909, when the first permanent movie theater was built, film business in Korea expanded as Japanese capital moved in. Very soon Matsu-nosuke was as well known in Korea as he was at home and even Korean *benshi* had managed to entrench themselves.

The first Korean production appeared in 1919, a chain-

drama filmed by a Japanese cameraman, but the first real
dramatic film was not made until 1921 when Yun Paek-nam, a novelist and pioneer in the Korean Shingeki movement, became interested in the movies. The first big production studio, the Chosen Cinema Company, located in Pusan, was formed by Japanese in 1922, with a capital of ninety thousand dollars—much more than any present-day Korean film company has. It soon failed, however, since the small domestic market could not support a company of this size. After the failure, one of the more popular actors, Ra Ung-kyu, got hold of some of the equipment and began making Korean copies of Japanese films—which were themselves often copies of American films. In due time he became more original, eventually making *Arirang,* titled after a popular Korean folk song. This marked the birth of a truly Korean style.

The Korean industry continued, however, to be Japanese dominated. They considerably influenced the Korean product and continued to send over production units. In 1925, Japan's first serial, Nikkatsu's *Queen of the World* (Sekai no Jo-o), was partially filmed in Korea, and ten years later the country was still being used for location work, one of the better productions being Shinko's *Dancer of the Peninsula* (Hanto no Maihime), a film biography about and starring the leading Korean folk-dancer, Ch'oe Sung-hi. Yet the domestic audience was so small that by the time of the coming of sound there were only 140 permanent theaters in the whole country.

Coproductions between the two nations did not begin in a big way until after the China Incident. One of the first was the 1937 *Journey* (Ryoko), which was directed by Yi Kyu-hwan, formerly an assistant director in Japanese studios, and was produced in cooperation with Shinko Kinema. The story, about wandering Korean peasants, was typical of the "double entendre for independence" films made by the Koreans under the Japanese. For instance, to the latter the film was the story of pioneering Koreans moving into new lands under Japanese leadership; to the Koreans, however, it was the story of their people being forced off their ancestral lands into the wilderness. Thus in this and other pictures Korean film-makers gave a political meaning to their work which was seldom detected by the usually sharp eyes of the Japanese police.

By 1941 more elaborate coproductions were common. One of them was the Japanese-titled *You and I* (Kimi to Boku), made under Shochiku supervision and directed by Tomotaka

Tasaka. It had "Asian brotherhood" as its theme and told the story of three girls. The parts were taken by three top stars, Japan's Kuniko Miyake, Korea's Moon Ye-bong, and Man-churia's Li Hsiang-lan. An all-star Japanese and Korean cast was included in Shiro Toyoda's 1943 *Young Figure* (Wakai Sugata), which was designed to publicize and create enthu-siasm for a new law which conscripted Koreans into the Japanese armed forces and was backed by all three of Japan's major companies and the newly formed Chosen Motion Picture Company.

This new Korean company had been formed in 1942 when the motion-picture-industry-consolidation law of Japan united many small Korean companies into one big concern, which was capitalized at $800,000. The Japanese were in complete control, but Koreans occupied many important managerial positions. For the first time Korean films were produced under fully adequate production conditions, and despite the fact that the company was Japanese controlled, the films themselves—feature, news, and cultural pictures—were all Korean, or at least as Korean as they could be.

Japan influenced the Korean industry in more ways than one. Most of the Koreans active in films had been trained in Japan, usually as actors or assistant directors, and used tech-niques borrowed from Japan. Even the new talents which have emerged after World War II have a Japanese back-ground. As a result of this, or perhaps in spite of it, next to Japan, the Koreans, among all the nations of Asia, have gone the furthest in developing the motion picture as an art.

Actually, the Japanese influenced the Manchurian cinema much more than the Korean, influenced it to the extent that it never developed into anything national but remained a sickly hybrid. From time to time the Korean cinema showed independence in many ways, even producing tendency films in the 1930's; but the Manchurian industry, formed and fostered by the occupying army, was really the Japanese industry transplanted to a Chinese setting.

Movies were first shown in Manchuria in 1910. They were largely the products of French Pathé and were shown mainly to the Russians living in Harbin. It was over a decade before the first local films were made, when the Japanese-controlled South Manchuria Railway Company set up a film unit in 1923 to make publicity films to attract settlers and tourists to the country. Thereafter, Japan used Manchuria for location work. In the early 1920's Yasujiro Shimazu made both *Firm Handshake* (Kataki Akushu) and *The Cry of Blood* (Chi no

Sakebi) in Manchuria. Both were thrillers based on foreign
sources requiring wide-open spaces not found in Japan. In 1928, Hotei Nomura made *The Cry of the Nation* (Minzoku no Sakebi), and in 1932, Mizoguchi, shooting all over Manchuria and Mongolia, made *The Dawn of the Foundation of Manchukuo and Mongolia.* A year later Uchida made *Asia Calling* (Sakebu Ajia), the first Japanese talkie to be made on foreign location.

After the war in China had begun, the Japanese felt the need for stronger propaganda in Manchuria and other parts of China. In 1938, under the sponsorship of the army, Manei, the Manchurian Motion Picture Association, was established with a capitalization of two million dollars. Financed by the Manchurian government and the South Manchuria Railway and staffed by both Manchurians and Japanese, the company built studios in Hsinking, and production was begun as soon as the Japanese crew heads could teach the Manchurian employees the various techniques necessary to achieve the initial aim of pushing Chinese and American films off the market. Production itself was divided into Chinese-and-Japanese-language pictures.

Despite the enormous population of Manchuria, there were only around eighty permanent theaters in 1938, though traveling exhibition units were rather highly organized. By 1942, however, the Japanese influence had been such that there were two hundred theaters and the Manchurian company was helping to fill them with from seventeen to twenty-four features a year. These films were also sent to Japan, but since they were mostly written and directed by Manchurians, the Japanese audiences did not like them, saying that the quality was poor and that the pace was too slow. What established the company commercially was not the films it made but the star it created. Li Hsiang-lan, later to become world-famous as Shirley Yamaguchi, was sensationally popular from the first and it was, apparently, her presence that drew both Manchurians and Japanese into the theaters.

Other parts of China, in contradistinction to Manchuria, already had their own industry long before the Japanese came; the first Chinese film companies had been opened in Shanghai in 1909, and the motion-picture industry thereafter centered around the big international cities of Hongkong and Shanghai until 1925, when the first films were shot in Peking.

In 1918, after the war, a book-dealer, Pao Ch'ing-chia, returned from America and opened up a film studio, and it

was only then that the Chinese industry got a real start. In
a few years Mei Lan-fang's Peking opera troupe was being
photographed frequently and soon production consisted
largely of adaptations from this very popular entertainment. In 1931 the Chinese made their first talkie, *Clear
Sky after the Rain* (Yu Kuo T'ien Ch'ing), using the Japanese Minatoki equipment. Though Shanghai production was
about one hundred pictures a year, the coming of sound
and the resultant expense cut annual production to forty and
the outbreak of war in 1937 brought it down even further
to thirty.

By this time the Japanese were taking over the existing
industry, the policy being to establish companies in every
occupied area. Very soon after the war began, the Towa
Company, main distributor of European pictures in Japan,
formed a production unit under Shigeyoshi Suzuki to go to
Peking to shoot *The Road to Peace in the Orient* (Toyo
Heiwa no Michi). The interiors were shot in a rental studio
and the Chinese actors featured in the film were recruited
by newspaper advertisements. Later the Manchuria Motion
Picture Association opened a Peking office to distribute its
own and Japanese pictures, thus creating for the first time
a major outlet in China for Japanese films.

In 1939 the Chinese Motion Picture Company was established in Nanking with the participation of Shiro Kido
of Shochiku. In the same year, using capital put up by the
major Japanese producing companies and equipment manufacturers, the North China Motion Picture Company was established at Peking. The facilities of this Peking company,
together with the larger Manchurian studios, later became
the two main motion-picture installations of Communist
China.

Though the Japanese had a captive audience in those
sections of China they occupied, they were not without
opposition. Studios in Hongkong and Chungking produced a
greater and greater amount of anti-Japanese pictures, a number of Chinese movie people having fled to the latter city.
The Communists also turned out a few films, though they
did not make wartime anti-Japanese theatrical features as did
the Nationalist Government. This competition did not much
worry the Japanese. Upon moving into an area, their invariable program was to prohibit British and American films
and then move Japanese pictures into those theaters specializing in foreign movies. The sheer number of Japanese in
China during the war also assured large audiences for Japa-

nese films. In Shanghai alone there were a hundred thousand
Japanese, mostly civilians.

Those theaters which booked vernacular pictures were, of course, forced to show only those made by Japanese-backed companies. One difficulty was that films made in one Chinese dialect could not be understood by Chinese of other areas. Later, when they moved into Hongkong, the Japanese took over the seventy small producing companies which formed the center of anti-Japanese movie production and organized them into the Hongkong Motion Picture Association. In the same way they had taken over the small independents in Shanghai and vicinity to form the China United Producers Company, the first offering of which was a Chinese *Madame Butterfly* (Hu Tieh Fu-jen).

The Japanese had been using Chinese locales for some time. As early as 1923, Yasujiro Shimazu had made one of his innumerable thrillers, *Market of Human Flesh* (Jinniku no Ichi) there, and in 1925 Nikkatsu's *Day of the Rough Waves* (Namiaraki Hi) had a two-month location in Shanghai. A year later Minoru Murata went to Shanghai to make the first Chinese-Japanese coproduction, *The Spirit of the Man from Kyushu* (Shinshu Danji no Iki), and in 1926 Genjiro Mie's *O-Ryo from Siberia* (Shiberiya no O-Ryo) was released. From 1937 onward the Japanese filmed a great deal in China.

Particularly important were the national-policy pictures with Chinese settings. One of the earliest was the 1939 film, *Song of the White Orchid* (Byakuran no Uta), directed by Kunio Watanabe and starring Kazuo Hasegawa and Yoshiko (Shirley) Yamaguchi. The story was about the love between a beautiful Manchurian girl and a Japanese immigrant. The boy must marry a Japanese in the interests of his country, but despite the rather expected plot, the characters were lifelike and the stereotypes which the story would seem to suggest were avoided.

The two stars repeated their success in Osamu Fushimizu's 1940 film *China Night* (Shina no Yoru), which was set in Shanghai and was about the love between a Chinese war orphan and a Japanese naval officer. Japanese soldiers and sailors threaten her until he steps in to discipline them. Three different endings were made for the film. The Japanese ending showed the officer turning the Chinese girl's fear and hatred of the Japanese into love and respect. Eventually they marry. The hero is called to battle and shot by the Chinese. Upon hearing of his death, the girl commits suicide. In the Chinese ending, however, the couple after marriage simply settle down, virile Japan happily bedded with weak effeminate China. For Southeast Asia there was yet another ending. News of his death proves false: he is really battling with the Chinese Communists and arrives just in time to save the heroine from her own hand. The meaning was obvious: Japan was really rescuing China from, among other things, the perils of Communism. The two were to live in peaceful coprosperity ever after. The success of this film was such that Shochiku a year later released *Suchow Night* (Soshu no Yoru). And soon there was a *Peking Night* (Pekin no Yoru) as well.

Shirley Yamaguchi, star of *China Night* and still using her Chinese name of Li Hsiang-lan (Ri Ko-ran in Japanese), dominated this propaganda genre. She was in Kenkichi Hara's 1942 film, *Fighting Street* (Tatakai no Machi), a story about a Japanese student of Chinese literature who falls in love with a Chinese actress; and a year before she had been in Kunio Watanabe's *Vow in the Desert* (Nessa no Chikai). In the latter, a Japanese civil engineer, Kazuo Hasegawa, falls in love with a Chinese girl, but their idyll is interrupted by a Communist attack. Hasegawa, on his death bed, converts several of the Communists to "pan-Asianism." Another of Miss Yamaguchi's films was *Sayon's Bell* (Sayon no Kane), made in 1943 by Hiroshi Shimizu. This film, a coproduction of the Manchurian company and Shochiku, aimed at introducing the customs of Formosa into Japan, the vehicle being the love life of a young Formosan girl. The Japanese, both producers and audience, failed to understand the customs involved and the film was not a success.

Formosa, Japan's first colony, acquired in 1895 after the Sino-Japanese War, never took to Japanese films. Though the island was Japan's first overseas market, traveling exhibition units being active from 1905, films sent there met with such a discouraging reception that until the outbreak of the Pacific War the market was left largely undeveloped. A major reason was that the Japanese industry wanted to send films subtitled in Chinese, while the Japanese government insisted that Japanese be used. This, they thought, would provide an incentive for the people to learn Japanese as well as punish those who did not want to. The answer, however, was obvious: the Formosans unable to understand Japanese simply went to Chinese films.

Following the pattern established in Manchuria and China, the Japanese also set out to exploit the Southeast Asian film market as well. Soon after occupying French Indo-China and

signing a treaty of friendship with Thailand in 1940, they
formed the South Seas Motion Picture Association, with
Shochiku, Toho, Towa and the China Motion Picture Company contributing capital and personnel. Shiro Kido, who
was the leading light in almost all of these occupation film
activities, was head of the organization.

In Indo-China, before the Japanese came there was some
amateur production activity but no real film industry as the
French colonial authorities discouraged it. With no competition the new company was soon presenting a Japanese newsreel with French commentary and distributing many top
Japanese pictures with French subtitles.

After the outbreak of the Pacific War, the South Seas Association was organized into the Japan Motion Picture Company Overseas Bureau with the area office in Singapore and
a mission to produce propaganda films in the occupied territories. The Japanese had introduced motion pictures to
Thailand, showing their Russo-Japanese War footage there
around 1906. The Thais themselves had no industry whatever until 1936 when two studios were opened, one backed
by the government, the other by the air force. The Thais
had taken to the film and in 1942 there were eighty-five
theaters in the country, showing American talkies and domestically produced silents. The foreign films were shown without subtitles usually, and it was common for the projectionist
to turn down the sound while a Siamese *benshi* or sometimes
a whole troupe of actors provided dialogue, trying to synchronize their words with the lip movements on the screen.

The first Japanese feature film was not exhibited there
until after the Japanese were fairly well in control. As always
the occupiers had gone around changing all the theater
names, substituting a good Japanese name for a Thai, French,
or English name. In a number of instances the Japanese,
running out of Japanese productions and taking advantage
of the Thai's American orientation, would show prints of
American films which they had seized, first very carefully
censoring them.

Burma had its own industry. Just before the war about
fifteen very small production companies turned out from
forty to sixty features a year, most of them very long, in the
Indian fashion, and half of them silent. The first Burmese
talkie was a 1935 coproduction with Japan called *Daughter
of Japan* (Nihon no Musume), which was about a Tokyo-
to-Rangoon nonstop airplane flight.

In Malaya the Japanese themselves filmed a number of

pictures, including *All-out Attack on Singapore* (Shingaporu Sokogeki), made in 1943 and directed by Koji Shima. It was the first picture about the Pacific War filmed on location and was largely a dramatic version of an earlier documentary, *Malayan War Record*. In the same year Masato Koga made *The Tiger of Malaya* (Marei no Tora), which was generally inferior to the former and made largely as a by-product of the Koji Shima picture.

Further south, in Java there were already a few small film-producing companies when the Japanese arrived, all of them making musical revues in the Indonesian language. During the following occupation the studios were seized by the Japanese, who had big plans for the small Javanese industry. But two hours after the ship bringing film equipment and technicians left Nagasaki bound for Djakarta it was sunk by an American submarine. It was not until the end of 1942 that the Japanese-backed Java Motion Picture Company was organized to produce news and culture films as well as dramatic features using local talent.

Professional films in Java and the rest of Indonesia began after 1927 when a German made a few local-color dramas for export. Later some resident Chinese hired an American cameraman and established the first film company. When the Japanese came they subsidized Indonesian feature production and at the same time encouraged the Indonesian modern theater as a movement which would help establish "national consciousness." As the local film industry grew, however, it absorbed all of the new modern theater talent, with the result that the modern theater was severely handicapped in Indonesia, while an active film industry continues the work initiated by the Japanese.

The Japanese influence in Indonesia remains in many other ways. One of the most direct influences is Eitaro Hinatsu, a former Japanese film director, who remained in Indonesia after the war and became a citizen, founding the important Kino Drama Atelier. Another director, Fumindo Kurata, learned the language and set up a school during the war to teach motion-picture techniques to the Indonesians. A total of six films were made under his direction.

Though Japan's film activities abroad during this period were largely in the nature of propaganda and personal aggrandizement, one might argue that, as a by-product of this political interest in other Asian countries, the Japanese were responsible for giving a number of these countries their first really professional work in the films. By engaging in various

coproductions the Japanese were able to train local technicians in the craft of making films of the highest technical
quality while, at the same time, serving their own propaganda interests. In the 1944 Philippine coproduction *Fire
on That Flag!* (Ano Hata o Ute), for example, Toho cooperated with five of the largest Philippine studios in a story
about the Japanese army's fight for Philippine independence,
the flag of the title referring to the Stars and Stripes. Though
Japanese crews took many of the key staff positions on this
and other films, Philippine actors and technicians were used
in what was the largest motion-picture undertaking in the
Philippines to that date.

This rôle of teacher and mentor, though one which Japan
relished, was not the real aim of its film activities abroad.
Technique was taught, but major control was always in the
hands of the Japanese, except in such established colonies as
Korea and, to a lesser extent, Manchuria. Initially, the Japanese announced that their policy toward the industries of
other countries was that of "an older brother to one slightly
younger," but controls were quickly tightened, and by 1943
their dealings with the small film industries of Asia were
"basically the feelings of a wise parent toward his immature
child." Still, for whatever reasons, the Japanese were responsible for accelerating the rise of the Asian film industry as a
whole, and without Japan's occupation of these countries the
production level would not be as high as it is now. In a
military-campaign history studded with horrors it is a
pleasure to be able to discover this one small constructive
effort.

**9 new sequence:
1945-49.** AFTER WORLD WAR II
most of the major cities of Japan
had been destroyed and hundreds
of thousands of persons had been
killed. Cities like Sendai and Hiroshima were almost ob-
literated, while Tokyo was in sections a vast scorched plain
with only chimneys and a few solitary buildings left standing. Over half of all the theaters in Japan had been destroyed
or severely damaged, and immediately after the surrender
announcement by the Emperor those remaining were closed,
only to open a week later when the government decided that
any theater able to get a film program together might again
resume operations.

Though theaters had been destroyed, the studios themselves had been almost undamaged and so production,
although slowed down, never came to a complete halt. After
the announcement of surrender, a number of unfinished films
were abandoned because of their military or "national policy"
slants, but a few which had no political content were rushed
to completion.

The first to be released after the end of the war was the
Gosho film *The Girls of Izu* (Izu no Musumetachi), a little
comedy completed just before the Occupation troops arrived.
The first postwar hit, however, was Shochiku's *Breeze* (Soyo-
kaze), in which a young singer, Michiko Namiki, sang a new
song, *"Ringo no Uta,"* or "The Apple Song," which, with its
facilely optimistic lyrics, soon became a success of fantastic
proportions. The Japanese, afraid to sing their old songs, became quickly attached to this simple popular tune, seeking in
it the first glimmering of light in the postwar darkness.

Yet in the few months between the surrender and the end of 1945 only ten features were made, an alltime production low for the Japanese feature industry. Production quality was also at its lowest. There were no light bulbs, the electric supply was unsteady, the film stock was poor and the cameras worn out. There were not even any nails to hold the scenery together. It was not unusual for the production unit to break off early in the day and everybody—crew, director, and stars—go to the country to search for food.

The biggest production problem of the period was concerned with scripts, with the worry about what kind of films would be favored by the Occupation, or SCAP, as General MacArthur's headquarters were called by the Allies. There was a long time to wait because it took months for the Americans to formulate a policy. Thus during this period the common cry of *"Taiyo machi!"* or "Wait for the sun to come out!" heard on location when the sky turned cloudy, was changed to *"Shinchugun machi!"* or "Wait for the Occupation Army to make up its mind!"

Finally, in October, the Occupation abolished the wartime censorship organization and, two months later, did away with many previous controls such as the law which had restricted distribution to one company and two theater circuits. After this it allowed foreign pictures already in Japan, but heretofore banned by the Japanese authorities, to be shown, while several Japanese companies received tacit permission to release Japanese films which had been banned in wartime.

Since the fall of 1945, the film world had been under the direct eye of SCAP, and soon liaison people were scurrying between Occupation authorities. There was no sudden change, however, from militarist regulations to those of MacArthur. It was much more like a slow dissolve from one to the other, old wartime regulations remaining in force in the teeth of the coming democratization until SCAP decided on policy. In November, SCAP announced a list of prohibited subjects. These included: anything infused with militarism, revenge, nationalism, or anti-foreignism; distortion of history; approval of religious or racial discrimination; favoring or approving feudal loyalty or treating human life lightly; direct or indirect approval of suicide; approval of the oppression or degradation of wives; admiration of cruelty or unjust violence; anti-democratic opinion; exploitation of children; and opposition to the Potsdam Declaration or any SCAP order.

SCAP also issued its first film order, which, in part, said: "In order to secure the objectives of the Occupation so that

Japan will never in the future disturb the peace of the world, so that the freedom of religion, speech, and assembly will be encouraged and that Japanese militarism and military nationalism will be abolished, it is demanded that motion pictures of the following types will be made." There followed a list of themes which the Japanese industry was to incorporate into its product. It was to show how all Japanese from every walk of life were endeavoring to construct a peaceful nation; how soldiers and repatriates were being rehabilitated into civilian life; how the Japanese in industry and farming were resolving the problems of postwar life; how labor unions were peacefully organized; how the hitherto bureaucratic government was cast off and true governmental responsibility adopted; how the free discussion of government problems was encouraged; how every human being and every class of society was respected; how individual rights were respected; and how historical personages too struggled for government representation of the people and for freedom.

By December, scap had reviewed all of the 554 films handled by the wartime motion-picture monopoly and had decided that, of these, 225 would have to be prohibited because of feudal and/or anti-democratic content. Prints of the latter category were ordered turned over to scap. Among them were Kinoshita's *The Blossoming Port*, Kurosawa's *Sanshiro Sugata*, Tasaka's *Five Scouts*, and Inagaki's *Musashi Miyamoto*. The exact disposal of all these films after they were in scap's hands is none too clear. Apparently most of them were destroyed. During the spring of 1946, from April 22 to May 2 to be precise, a colonel of Eighth Army headquarters supervised their burning. One of the dry beds of the Tamagawa River was thought appropriate for this act. The negatives were to have been kept by scap for reference, but it appears that many negatives were burned along with their release prints.

Scap was never certain, however, that it had actually received all the prints of any given film and consequently policed the more populated centers to prevent the showing of these prohibited pictures. In rural areas, however, and especially with the traveling projection units, the remaining copies of wartime movies continued to be shown, not as a sabotage effort but merely because the rural operators were completely unaware of scap orders and because they had no other films to show.

In the meantime the Civil Censorship Division of scap,

charged with the duty of supervising the content of Japanese
motion pictures, had been created. This division gave way in March, 1946, to a unit within the Civil Information and Education Section (CI&E) which viewed all completed films and without whose seal of approval no film could be released. The initial Occupation policy called also for pre-censorship of scripts, and it is claimed by certain critics that CI&E caused many parts of submitted scripts to be rewritten merely because they showed Japanese customs which, although perfectly natural in the situation, disturbed CI&E, which thought them undemocratic. The custom of bowing, for instance, was particularly disliked. Script writers soon found that they could not write about what people would ordinarily do in a given situation but about what they should do if they were "democratized."

In addition to exercising "political censorship," CI&E had a very strict moral viewpoint and frequently ordered cut certain suggestive shots from classic European pictures even though these films had been shown intact before the war. The head of the motion-picture unit, incidentally, was a former John Ford assistant director and is said to be currently running a *sukiyaki* restaurant in Los Angeles.

Among the casualties of the Occupation policies was Kon Ichikawa's clever puppet version of the Kabuki *A Girl at Dojo Temple* (Musume Dojoji), which was banned not for its content but simply because its script had not been submitted for censorship prior to production. Ichikawa still considers this film to have been his masterpiece.

Other directors managed to get around the Occupation officials. Kenji Mizoguchi wanted to make a period-film about the artist Utamaro, SCAP at the time was much opposed to period-films, finding in them the seeds of feudalism and undemocratic thought. Mizoguchi himself finally called on the Occupation authorities and gave any number of cogent reasons for making the film. The common man loved Utamaro, he was a great cultural object, really sort of a pre-Occupation democrat. At the same time Mizoguchi hinted at a desire to make a modern film about female emancipation. Pleased with at least the latter project, SCAP finally gave its approval, and thus Mizoguchi created his *Utamaro and His Five Women* (Utamaro o Meguru Go-nin no Onna), one of the first postwar period-films.

The Occupation film policy naturally irritated a great many people and made SCAP few friends. There was also the suspicion abroad that when the Japanese industry opened the

door to democracy, Communism had come in too. Shiro
Kido, of Shochiku, writing in 1955 with all the blessings of
hindsight and the resentment of having been branded a "war
criminal," claimed that the Occupation controls instituted
after the war were Communist inspired and that some of the
personnel in CI&E Section, including the biggest of wigs,
were Communist. He claimed CI&E was responsible for Communist labor unrest in the industry, and to prove his point
he cited the fact that CI&E relied on the officers of the Japan
Motion Picture and Drama Employees Union to draw up a
list of the industry's "war criminals." In his autobiography
he goes on to name names and cast aspersions, saying: "If I
was to be banished by the order of someone as insignificant
as [Akira] Iwasaki [a film critic who headed the committee
to name war criminals], it is then a glorious thing to have
been banished and, by taking the total responsibility, kept
others free."

The hunting of "war criminals" kept the Occupation
rather busy for a time. As early as 1946, the Japanese government, under pressure from SCAP, had requested the All-
Japan Motion Picture Employees Union to draw up a list
of such criminals in the industry, but since this union was
soon amalgamated with the larger Japan Motion Picture and
Drama Employees Union, the full task fell upon the latter.
That the list was drawn up by Communists seems very likely
since the union itself was communist, but, given the various
categories of war criminals as defined by SCAP, candidates
for each class were rather obvious.

The list broke down into three kinds of criminals, labeled
classes A, B, and C. The first, and most important category,
included all those to be removed "permanently" from the industry. Among its names were those of governmental officials
connected with the Home Ministry; the Office of Public
Information heads; both Takejiro Otani and Shiro Kido, of
Shochiku; Yoshio Osawa, the former head of Toho; Kyusaku Hori, head of Nikkatsu; Kan Kikuchi and Masaichi
Nagata, of Daiei; and the heads of other wartime companies.
In all, the category included twenty-three names. The B-class
criminals comprised those to be removed from the industry
for a fixed period of time. Among them were Nagamasa
Kawakita, former vice-president of the China Motion Picture
Company, now head of Towa and recently decorated by
the French government, coproducer of such films as *The
New Earth* and *The Saga of Anatahan;* Iwao Mori, now
production head of Toho; the director Hisatora Kumagai; and

others, totalling ten people. Finally, C class included those
who were to perform a complete "self-examination" of their own past actions. There were a number of directors including Kajiro Yamamoto, Kimisaburo Yoshimura, Koji Shima, Yasushi Sasaki, and Kunio Watanabe. This is perhaps the most interesting of the lists because it contains the names of several directors who were subsequently considered "leftist."

When the list was finally completed it was found that it was too large, and an industry committee, with a truly Japanese gesture, proposed reducing the number. They finally cut it down to thirty-one persons in all three categories. This time people like Hori, Kikuchi, and Otani were dropped, although Kido, Osawa, and Nagata were included. The latter two were "rehabilitated" early, in 1948, but other purgees had to wait until 1950. It is commonly said that Kido's rancor at being labeled a "war criminal" stems at least in part from the fact that he was still kept out of the industry after his rival Nagata was fully reinstated and busy with big plans and bigger ideas.

The Japanese talent for the volte-face may be seen in the fact that very soon after the surrender it was the same men who had been producing Japan's wartime military pictures who were now among the loudest of the tub-thumpers for democracy. These boosters for even further democratization, in particular wartime film leaders from Toho, very much resembled the fanatic samurai of Choshu who in the 1860's had shouted "Honor the Emperor! Expel the barbarians!" until it became apparent that they were helpless against modern weapons, and thereupon, changing their tune with fluent facility, they became leaders in Westernization, creating a Western-style peasant army and readily holding off the samurai armies from Edo.

Toho had been on top all during the war. Its general position had become the best in the industry. Having jumped on board the national-policy bandwagon at the beginning and cleaned up on military pictures when the subject was popular, it jumped off again at a propitious time and, as the war dragged on, sought to satisfy the public's appetite for sheer escapism. Though this had brought them into censorship difficulties at the time, it also put them in the best possible position to line up with the Occupation authorities after the war. Thus, with the advent of peace, Toho was the healthiest of any of the companies and was naturally very well pleased with itself. Pride, however, was but a preliminary to the fall, and the crash that toppling Toho made shook the industry as it had not been shaken since the 1923 earth-quake.

Toho's trouble was labor, in particular labor unions. There had been labor trouble in the industry—the strikes of the *oyama* and *benshi*, for example, and various work stoppages in studios—but organized labor unions with real power were almost unknown in Japan before the Occupation, whether in the movie world or elsewhere. With the end of the war, however, the formation of unions within the movie industry began even before December, 1945, when the Diet at SCAP's bidding passed the Trade Union Law, patterned after the U.S. National Labor Relations Act of 1935. By the end of the preceding September, within a month after the war was over, employees had begun organizing along industrial lines within their respective companies. Most unions joined the All-Japan Motion Picture Employees Union, which was soon absorbed into the more activist and political Japan Motion Picture and Drama Employees Union, a combine that sought to organize all the performing artists into one big union.

Shochiku's studio union formed fastest. It at once demanded a cost-of-living wage increase and immediately won it. A few days afterwards, Toho and Daiei unions were formed, both demanding what the Shochiku union had gained and, in addition, a voice in management. Though the spectacular success of the Shochiku union was what triggered the organization of unions elsewhere, it should be noted at the beginning that this success was not, as was claimed, based so much upon "effective unionizing" as upon Shochiku's old paternal "always the biggest bonus in the industry" philosophy, keeping the workers reasonably happy having been a long-standing Shochiku principle.

Though the Toho union got what it wanted in 1945, it wanted and needed more the next spring, but turned down the company's proposed cost-of-living increase as too small. Thereupon Toho had its first strike, which was ended after fifteen days by a compromise plan which was largely in the union's favor. In September, 1946, due to the serious inflation, the Toho union again applied for pay increases. Though the company agreed to union demands, it was decided by the Communist-led Congress of Industrial Unions that a test of strike tactics was in order and that the Japan Motion Picture and Drama Employees Union should do the testing. The union picked up the previous demands it had agreed to abandon and again submitted them to the company, which refused. Thus began the second Toho strike.

It was set for October 15, but, six days before, some Toho employees in the film exchanges decided to remain at work and so formed a new Toho union, the so-called Second Toho Employees Union. Despite several such reversals, however, the big exercise in strike techniques came off on schedule in the three major companies only a few days after it had been announced. The Daiei and Shochiku strikes were soon settled, largely in the companies' favor after union officials decided to concentrate their experiments in the Toho sector. Thus, the Toho strike took more time, not ending until December. The settlement conditions were that the union shop should be recognized by the company in return for the union's acknowledgment of management's right to control company policies; union members were to be consulted in planning production; the company was to hire freely, but all firing and disciplinary problems would be handled through the union; there was to be a substantial cost-of-living wage increase; and an eight-hour day was to be established.

Despite earnest objections from some board members, the head of Toho, Yoshio Osawa, agreed to reorganize Toho management so that the union would be represented, but not have a voice, on all policy-making levels. On the heels of this decision came the stirring news that Osawa was a "war criminal." The board was paralyzed. While waiting for the MP's to arrive, it made up its mind and resigned simply so that it would not be in the office when the forces of law and order arrived. This naturally played directly into the union's hands because the replacements were largely newcomers to the movie industry and the union representatives ruled the management committees.

From the first the union's influence was felt. The management had decided that Toho should turn out twenty-four features for the year 1947. Under the new scheme the union imposed its plan of producing only thirteen, but big ones, with bigger crews. One of the results of this was that the budget for every Toho production was doubled or tripled over that of pictures made by other companies, and, since the then current limitations of the market were severe and it was impossible for grosses to rise in proportion to large budgets, the company suffered severe losses.

The union had things pretty much its own way. One of its tactics at joint-management committee meetings was to delay and extend the meetings through the night so that the company people would be so tired that they could not effectively oppose the unions. It is alleged that such meetings were the direct cause of the death of Katamaru Tanabe, the newly elected president who resigned because of ill health after only eight months in office and died soon afterwards.

There was, however, some opposition to the union. Though a union of some kind was clearly needed to establish workers' rights and secure compensation from the severe postwar inflation, quite a few people did not agree with the methods of the Toho union. The stars and directors who were at first enthusiastic began to realize that with their high salaries it was difficult to identify themselves realistically with the working class. The assumption that the intelligentsia and the workers had everything in common was simply not true, and once the immediate postwar enthusiasm had worn off, this fact became quite apparent. It also became more and more apparent that the legitimate grievances of Toho employees were being subordinated to the union's desire for a proving ground for tactics to be used in a coming general strike, a kind of Spanish Civil War preceding the larger hostilities ahead.

For these reasons many joined the rival Second Toho Employees Union and even more banded together to form yet a third. This new union was formed around a so-called "Flag of Ten" faction, named after ten top Toho stars who found themselves in disagreement with the main union's policies. The stars were Denjiro Okochi, Kazuo Hasegawa, Yataro Kurokawa, Susumu Fujita, Setsuko Hara, Hideko Takamine, Hisako Yamano, Ranko Hanai, Takako Irie, and Isuzu Yamada. Altogether, about 450 people entered this third union. They formed a back-to-work movement, but the main union would not let them in the studio. The company, anxious to take advantage of their willingness to work, called them the Toho Second Production Branch and gave them the unused, former Tokyo Hassei studios, planning for them to make a picture a month.

At the same time, in part through dislike of the activities of the Japan Motion Picture and Drama Employees Union and in part through a realization that a union actually had little to offer in the individualized motion picture industry, professional societies confined to exclusive groups of studio talents began to be organized. In 1947 the Japan Motion Picture Technicians Association and the Scenario Writers Association were formed. Two years later, the Japan Motion Picture Directors Association was founded.

As soon as the Toho second strike was settled, in December, 1946, the main studios began a schedule of two

pictures a month, but the heads of both the main and the new
continually found fault with each other, largely over the inaptitude of the inexperienced Toho management. In the spring of 1947, the second studio broke away from its parent and became Shintoho, literally "new Toho." This was theoretically a separate company, but at first the parent put up all the money. Shintoho's first film also marked Kon Ichikawa's debut as a director. It was a hodgepodge called *A Thousand and One Nights with Toho* (Toho Senichi-ya), and it was not until 1948 that they had anything like a smash hit, this time with Ichikawa's melodrama, *Three Hundred and Sixty-five Nights* (Sambyaku-rokujugo-ya).

The parent company, after president Tanabe's enforced illness had caused him to resign shortly before his death, selected Tetsuzo Watanabe as replacement. As his first act Watanabe, a law professor at Tokyo University specializing in labor law and reputedly a strong opponent of Communism, threw down a plan to make twenty-four films a year at budgets equal to those of other companies. Later Toho handed dismissal notices to 270 studio people and 930 other employees all over the country on the grounds that its being forced to retain its wartime employees as well as hire back its old workers who had entered military service had greatly overstaffed the company. The main union, taken aback especially because its militants were among those to be sacked, agreed to double the yearly production if the dismissals were dropped. In answer to this, Toho pointed out that in 1947, with twelve hundred employees, it made only thirteen features, while Shochiku, with the same number of workers, made forty-two. The company also maintained that, coupled with losses due to over-budgeting, this labor superfluity would ruin Toho in half a year. The union made the rebuttal, which had at least some basis in fact, that all the losses were due solely to the new management's inexperience. Then it set about finding a more practical way to fight the company.

Thus began the third Toho strike. This was different from the earlier two in that a new technique was used, the "production control method" which the railway workers had found so effective. Those workers had taken over control of the train stations and, refusing to sell tickets, had allowed all the passengers to pass the wickets free. During the 1946–47 period several film-exhibition unions had used the same technique with great success, admitting free into the theaters anyone who wanted to come.

The same day that negotiations about the dismissal fell

through, the union seized the camera storeroom while those dismissed stayed on the job. Then it brought on the big artillery. In came the fellow-traveling "Defend Japanese Culture Committee," the Young Communists League, the North Korean Peoples League, and members from the Party's militant cells—in all several thousand people. Company management was pushed out of the way while production continued and barricades were thrown up to keep hostile parties outside the studio walls. The union, taking advantage of the Occupation purge of war criminals, knew that the management underlings would be afraid to act in the absence of their seniors and that it would be quite a while before a new chain of command was established. Thus they formed their own managerial committees to run the studio facilities they had seized.

The next step was management's announcement of a month-long suspension of production, but with pay all around; this move fittingly enough taking place on May Day, 1948. The union remained in the studios all day and all night, holding dance parties, singing labor songs, and marching around the lot. At the beginning of June, however, production did not continue and wage payments were stopped when Toho management learned that it was not the American custom to pay wages to striking workers. This introduced a new problem since the strikers now had no way to live. A few found work outside, some forming traveling play groups and touring the countryside. These union members agreed to give from twenty to forty percent of their monthly income to the union to help support those not being paid.

The strike dragged on and on. In July a number of people, tired of continual fighting, formed another faction, the Toho Democratic Club, which particularly opposed the Communist control of the union. Though it began with a membership of only twenty-two, it soon grew to such a size that a more auspicious name was needed, so they chose to call themselves the Toho Employees Union, wearing blue badges to distinguish each other and to set themselves off from the red-badge wearers of the main union. Then they began a back-to-work movement. The "red" union members were waiting for them. They formed strong barricades at all entrances and brought out fire hoses, barbed wire, and the big wind-fans used to create storm effects. Altogether the striking union mobilized over a thousand people.

Seeing that violence was close, directors, scenario writers, and art directors, all of whom had no direct leadership in either faction, tried to mediate, sending parties to various responsible people in order to "explain" the situation. Eisuke Takizawa, Shiro Toyoda, and Senkichi Taniguchi went to talk to Shochiku; Tadashi Imai and Satsuo Yamamoto went to Daiei; and Akira Kurosawa went to the Tokyo District Court. In general these directors were more sympathetic to the union than to the management because they were aware of the company's frequent poor treatment of their crews. They particularly wanted to explain the union's position and, if possible, avert violence.

The company, its patience now gone, was not waiting for any peaceful talkative mediations. Instead it sought a court order giving the management permission to enter its own studios. The court ordered that the studios be put under court control and that both union and management be allowed to enter. In return, the union was not to be allowed to interfere with production plans. The union refused to comply with the court order, and conditions became even more strained. A member of the blue group, carried away by enthusiasm, got into the studio, climbed the sixty-foot chimney of the film laboratory building, and waged a one-man demonstration for thirty-four hours until he was forced down by the laboratory's being set afire, allegedly on purpose, by the red faction.

During the morning of August 19, the Tokyo police chief came to the barricade and read orders telling the union to get out. A few minutes later two thousand fully armed policemen arrived. Later a company of cavalry, seven armored cars and tanks, and three airplanes were sent from the U.S. Eighth Army. As one union actress later said: "The only thing that didn't come was a battleship." The union, behind its barricades, greeted the enemy with the usual flags, yells, and songs and, somewhat unexpectedly, also with poetry recitations, the poems having been composed for the occasion.

One poem said that the youth, sorrow, and happiness of the writer were all in the studio: "I've worked here fifteen years/Even when it was a small, small place." It went on and then concluded with: "And you, what kind of a factory will you enter next?" Another stated flatly that "If Toho Culture comes to an end,/It will be the last of the Japanese Film." It continued: "I'll tell my children:/Somehow father tried to protect Japanese Culture/But strength was not enough./Oh, please forgive your negligent father."

Even in the face of such eloquence the police remained

unmoved. Tanks were lined up outside the gate, ready to
break through, and operations were directed by a U.S. Army major-general circling in an airplane overhead. Sensing defeat, the union agreed to negotiate. It finally agreed to let the police and the management in if its right to negotiate for the workers were not taken from it. While it was taking down the barricades a parade suddenly came from inside and marched into full view.

A contingent of actresses were in the fore putting on a crying act. Among them were Setsuko Wakayama, Chieko Nakakita, and Yoshiko Kuga. Later came Heinosuke Gosho in the lead followed by a cluster of unfurled red flags with everyone singing the *Internationale* in a most defiant manner. There were also placards carrying the slogan: "Protect Japanese Culture." The marchers kept shouting tearfully: "Japanese Culture Goodbye." This display turned out to be a mere formality, however. After 195 days the great Toho strike had ended and, with it, the experiment in strike tactics.

As soon as the Toho people were back at work the management again announced its intention of firing 220 superfluous workers, but on second thought decided to fire only the Communists. At the same time there was a fast shuffle in union control and the new heads proposed that it purge its own left-wing adventurist element. Management agreed and 175 workers were sacked, including a fourth of the personnel of Toho's small educational-film unit. It was soon pointed out that this self purge was engineered by certain Communists who saw a chance to get rid of certain comrades with whom they had been having factional fights.

During 1948, Toho had produced only four films and now, in bad financial straits, decided to abandon its own production and become a rental studio for independent productions, but maintaining distribution facilities to handle the films of Shintoho and the small units who would use its studios.

The new Shintoho was not at all happy about this. With few facilities and not very many employees, it had to grind out films as fast as they could and many complained at their company's being used as a tool by Toho. They said they had originally left so that they would have freedom in making films and now they had to make so many that there was no time for quality. For the time being, however, the new company had to continue to use Toho as a distribution outlet, but it also began to set itself up as a fully independent studio. It financed its own pictures and everyone, from producer to star, was to work on a general profit-sharing basis.

With Toho closed during 1949, Shintoho moved forward
and by the end of the year was on the way to becoming the leading movie company of Japan. When Toho production resumed, however, it began favoring its own films over those of Shintoho and consequently the latter decided to open its own distribution set-up. This meant that Toho did not have enough films and Shintoho did not have enough theaters. The result was that Daiei and Shochiku profited.

Toho's fall from leadership had been swift and spectacular. In only three years it had slipped from first to last place. Both strikes and Shintoho had taken their toll, and the Toho officials were desperately attempting to recoup both their losses and their reputation. They had more top directors than any other company, but they did not have too many stars, a great number having gone over to Shintoho. Among other things, they tried "new face" contests, with the result that, out of four thousand applicants, they signed up Toshiro Mifune and many others who became stars.

They also brought suit against Shintoho, trying to get control of eight films which that company was trying to distribute by itself, claiming that all eight were made with money advanced by Toho. This ended in a victory for the new company because theater owners, fearing they might be without films over the busy New Year's season, deserted the Toho exhibition circuit and signed up with Shintoho. The fight continued. Shintoho's president, Shosaburo Saisho, said: "The trouble goes back to when our company was set up and Toho financing was promised. We never received enough money and the pictures we gave them were not exploited properly. Consequently we lost money." Toho's response was that any film needs a careful exploitation plan. It was Shintoho's duty to provide this and they did not. Toho also claimed that a balanced production and release program was needed but that Shintoho made movies "almost at random."

One of the results of the squabble was that both companies suffered. Shintoho needed at least one good experienced director and after long and delicate negotiations failed to get Heinosuke Gosho. Then Kazuo Hasegawa left Shintoho to form his own company, and in his wake went many other stars who had been given better offers by Daiei or Shochiku.

Not that these other major companies had had an easy time in the postwar era. Shochiku found that paternalism was not enough and therefore had to meet union demands. Thanks to this concession, it found that it also had to better working conditions, employees particularly desiring a formal

setting of work hours instead of just working on and on
without extra compensation until a job was finished.

Daiei's strike had been the shortest of any, ending after only two weeks, but it also had troubles. As youngest of the prewar companies, it owned no chain of theaters and, since it was organized at a time when distribution was in the hands of a monopoly, had no chance to line up contracted theaters. In addition, Daiei had been faithful to the military until the end and thus had no pictures to show after the conclusion of the war, almost all of its products being condemned by the Occupation. Daiei therefore tried various maneuvers. Now very much in favor of a two-company industry, it approached Toho with a distribution tie-up scheme, but Shochiku objected so strenuously that the project had to be dropped. With no big stars on its payroll, the company went in for sensational films: kissing scenes, adultery, and eroticism. Although it had contracts with most of the top costume-picture stars, Daiei's hands were tied so far as period-films went. The Occupation frowned on them, and so the Kyoto branch, which had specialized in just this sort of film, was virtually closed.

The companies were at least united in confronting a common foe: foreign films were again being shown in Japan. After six years of no American pictures whatever the interested public was treated first in 1946 to *Call of the Yukon,* a Republic effort, and then to *Tarzan and the Green Goddess.* Later, when the Central Motion Picture Exchange, a joint operation of American film companies was set up, the Japanese were given *Madame Curie* as an opener. This last was a tremendous success despite the fact that it played at an admission price the equivalent of sixty cents when the current highest admission was about twenty and the average daily wage was less than a dollar.

One of the reasons for the high admission prices was that the Central Exchange demanded a flat fifty percent of the money collected at the box office though the previous Japanese custom had usually been thirty-five percent. Fortunately the demand for American films was so great that the exhibitors could show them and still make a considerable profit. Having thus learned something more than democracy from their occupiers, the Japanese companies soon followed suit in applying the rate to all major showings. Admission prices rose always higher, despite legal ceilings, until they reached a level well over one hundred times that of prewar ticket prices, though the purchasing power of yen had at the same

time greatly declined. In addition the tax on theater admission was shortly raised from the wartime one hundred percent to one hundred and fifty, the highest in the world.

With foreign films now more dominant than they had ever
been in the previous thirty years (but never greater in numbers nor receipts than Japanese pictures), theaters had to be
found to show them, and a mighty boom among exhibitors
began. Just after the war, most of the theaters, despite the
fact that many had no seats and that the light came in
through holes in ceilings and roofs, did a thriving business.
Later, putting money in theaters became one of the most
popular investments for black-market profiteers. The existing
theaters were so overcrowded that a very quick return on investments was practically insured even though construction
costs were so high that only the newly rich could afford to
build. Yet, even so, theaters went on going up at a great
rate. In October, 1945, there were 845 theaters in operation; at the beginning of 1946 there were 1,137.

With the end of the war—which to the Japanese of that
period really meant the end of a way of life—the coming of
the Occupation, the resultant restrictions, and the related
difficulties within the industry, one might think that the films
of the period would have, at best, merely reflected the confusion of the era. That they reflected something much more
is another proof of the often amazing resiliency of the Japanese people and of their ability to fashion something uniquely
Japanese from the most diverse of foreign ideas. The early
postwar period produced no great films, but from it came a
number of extremely interesting film experiments as well as
the maturing of the new talent which was to make the Japanese cinema what it is today.

SCAP control being what it was, the period-film genre was
almost completely forbidden. Out of the sixty-seven films
released in 1946 only seven were period, all of them having
been made before the end of the war, and in the following
year there were only eight period-films out of a total of
ninety-seven. Even these films, having to pass the Occupation
censors, often had their plots and meanings completely
changed. The only serious casualty arising from the Occupation attitude was Kurosawa's *The Men Who Tread on the
Tiger's Tail* (Tora no O o Fumu Otokotachi), which had
been banned by the wartime militarists only to remain banned
by the peacetime occupiers because they believed this parody
of the Kabuki *Kanjincho* was "feudal."

Actually, the Occupation suppression of the period-film

was only incidental to its difficulties since the genre was in such poor condition anyway that it scarcely had the strength to put up a fight against American censorship. During the late 1930's it lost most of its vigor, and during the ensuing war these films became almost entirely worthless, partly because the "historical drama" was being pushed as a substitute. Therefore, the Occupation merely contributed to the degeneration of the form, and what the CI&E officials were so busily building into a large and dangerous carrier of virulent feudal ideas was actually lying quite expired at their feet.

Since the stories themselves were popular, however, a few film-makers attempted to disguise them and use them again. Thus some of the period-hero types were given business suits instead of armor, pistols instead of swords, and put to work as detectives since the Occupation did not mind modern murder-thrillers at all.

Another way of avoiding the Occupation and still using Japanese history was to move back to the Meiji era, a practice that Mizoguchi as well as others had found profitable in avoiding the dicta of the wartime militarists, and one which had long been a favorite device of escape whenever authority became too concerned with period-drama. The same thing happened in the Kabuki when the ruling Tokugawas prohibited dramas dealing with contemporary events: the dramatists merely moved the setting back a few hundred years and disguised a few names. Likewise, under the Occupation, even Teinosuke Kinugasa's 1946 romp, *Lord for a Night* (Aru Yo no Tono-sama), played in a high-comedy style uncommon to Japanese films, had to be given a Meiji setting despite its ridicule of feudal mores.

Yet another way of evading Occupation censorship was to copy approved foreign sources, and just after the war there was something of a rash of foreign-inspired films. Gorky's *The Inspector General* was given a Tokugawa setting in *The Beaten Lord* (Nagurareta O-Tono-sama), in which the impostor was shown working for democracy. Several of Frank Capra's films, seen in Japan before the war, were literally remade. Kiyohiko Ushihara's *A Popular Man in Town* (Machi no Ninkimono) took direct inspiration from *Meet John Doe*, and Naruse's *The Descendants of Taro Urashima* (Urashima Taro no Koei) was indebted to *Mr. Smith Goes to Washington*. Both were rather confused attempts to be democratic.

More often than not, however, what the Occupation said

went, and innovations from abroad were greeted with open arms, Western, specifically American, ideas and customs becoming wildly popular. An example was the practice of kissing, long regarded by the Japanese as an act reserved solely for the privacy of the bedroom, if not indeed as something of an occult art. Now, however, it proved one of the most popular of the Occupation's many cultural importations, and in no time at all the movies were wild to try it.

Daiei planned "the first kiss scene in any Japanese film," to be included in Yasuki Chiba's *A Certain Night's Kiss* (Aru Yo no Seppun), but, though Chiba was considered a pioneer in "frank love stories" and hence was chosen for this possibly dangerous assignment, he lost his nerve at the last minute and shot the scene so that the kiss was obscured by an open umbrella. At the same time Shochiku was rushing to complete Yasushi Sasaki's *Twenty-Year-Old Youth* (Hatachi no Seishun). Its kiss was considerably more visible and since both films opened on the same day, May 23, 1946, the two companies had to share the honors.

The appearance of the kiss caused much discussion in film circles. Heretofore, particularly after the military came to power, all kisses had been cut from foreign films, to the great peril of the continuity, and there had been no opportunity for an intelligent evaluation. Now, however, that a real Japanese kiss had finally been seen on the screen, thanks to Shochiku, everyone could and did talk about it. They talked about whether showing such things was "Japanese or not"; whether it was "merely commercially" or "artistically" motivated; whether a filmed kiss had any sexual meaning; whether it was hygienic. No resolution was reached, however, and even today opinion varies on the subject.

It is still common for kisses to be faked, the act being taken from an angle where the spectator cannot tell that the principals are merely touching cheeks. Sometimes both parties put gauze over their lips and retouch with make-up so that, though the lips seem in contact, they are actually separate, thus preserving health, virginity, and what have you. One of the most ingenious of the postwar kisses occurred in a Daiei film named *Brilliant Revenge* (Kenrantaru Fukushu), which, apparently for the purposes of including a kiss, inserted a scene showing Tolstoy's *Resurrection* being performed on the stage. In this play within a film there could be nothing objectionable since the Japanese involved were playing foreigners and everyone knew that foreigners kiss in public.

Naturally all of these films, no matter how brilliantly the

kiss was staged, aimed at sensationalism, a position which
their makers strongly defended by saying that their products
were really examples of freedom and democracy in action.
During this entire period all companies readily and willingly
confused license with freedom and answered those who raised
moral objections by flatly stating that opposition to such
films was feudal and anti-democratic. Some even went so far
as to say that this kind of sensationalism *was* democracy and
that democracy *was* license.

At the same time more serious work was also being produced in an attempt to assimilate the teachings of the Occupation. Since the Americans insisted upon the emancipation
of women the films faithfully projected the idea of the "new
woman." Shochiku, with its orientation toward female audiences, embarked on a whole series of such pictures. Mizoguchi made his previously promised *Women's Victory* (Josei
no Shori), about professional women in the law courts; Kosho Nomura made *Her Statement* (Kanojo no Hatsugen);
Masahiro Makino made *A Woman Kept Waiting* (Machiboke
no Onna); and Keisuke Sasaki turned out *Girl Pupils and
Teachers* (Joseito to Kyoshi), which emphasized the "new
education." All of these, and many others, were the fruit of
1946.

During the next year the new ideas had been more fully
assimilated and better films on the same subject were the
result. Mizoguchi made *The Love of Actress Sumako* (Joyu
Sumako no Koi), the biography of Sumako Matsui, who
committed suicide in 1918 but was, in a sense, one of Japan's
first emancipated women, having achieved fame by playing
Ibsen heroines in Shingeki. Teinosuke Kinugasa, taking the
same subject, made *Actress* (Joyu), which turned out to be
the better film. In Minoru Shibuya's *Passion Fire* (Joen), a
married couple thinks of divorce but, upon considering that
it would destroy their family, gradually reconsider and, with
the other woman's help, fall in love again. In Kinoshita's
Marriage (Kekkon) the young girl opposes her family, wins
the right to make up her own mind, and marries the man she
wants.

Kinoshita, along with Kurosawa certainly one of the
brightest new talents to emerge from the war, also made the
first picture showing that democracy meant something more
than mere license and sensationalism. His *A Morning with
the Osone Family* (Osone-ke no Asa), released early in 1946,
was about a family during the war whose sons are either
drafted or arrested for their political crimes. Their militarist

uncle disowns them, but with the coming of peace the family is brought together again, the "morning" of the title referring to the new life for the family occasioned by the end of the war.

Another serious film was Kurosawa's *No Regrets for My Youth* (Waga Seishun ni Kuinashi), made in 1946, which had academic freedom for its subject. During the 1930's a democratic-minded teacher is silenced by the military. One of his students, jailed for forming an anti-war movement, dies in prison after being denounced as a spy. His girl friend, who is also the daughter of the teacher, suffers great hardships and goes to work on a farm. After the war she refuses to return to her home, saying that she has grown to love the rural life and now has "no regrets for my youth."

More and more, Japanese postwar society began to be shown in the films. Kimisaburo Yoshimura's 1947 *A Ball at the Anjo House* (Anjo-ke no Butokai) told the story of an aristocratic family who, having lost both fortune and peer status, is forced to close down the family mansion. On the last night a party is held by both family and servants, the occasion serving as a detailed investigation of the thoughts and reactions of the individual members of the household concerning the past and the postwar situation. The same year, Gosho made *Once More* (Ima Hitotabi no), which, treated the changes in intellectual life in Japan and the intellectuals' postwar search for "isms."

In early 1948, Mizoguchi looked at another segment of society in his *Women of the Night* (Yoru no Onnatachi), filmed on location at Osaka, about the life of the streetwalker. In the same year, Ozu made *A Hen in the Wind* (Kaze no Naka no Mendori), which was about a woman forced into prostitution because her child is ill. When her husband is repatriated he is shocked and reprimands her until he comes to realize that, given postwar conditions, she had no choice.

Other films, instead of merely presenting a social condition, called for positive action. Early in 1946, Kurosawa, Kajiro Yamamoto, and Hideo Sekigawa jointly directed *Those Who Make Tomorrow* (Asu o Tsukuru Hitobito), a film which was frankly propaganda for the Toho union's organization campaign and which showed what happened when the members of the Japan Motion Picture and Drama Employees Union took over a film company. The story was about two sisters, one a script-girl, the other a review dancer. The father opposes unions, being a white-collar worker himself, but eventually sees the light, grasps a flag, and heads a strikers'

parade. After the eventual outcome of the Toho strikes, the
film was regarded as being most unfortunate.

Though the early Occupation apparently fully approved this film, it took pains in 1948 over Kimisaburo Yoshimura's *The Day Our Lives Shine* (Waga Shogai no Kagayakeru Hi), cutting out some footage and reprimanding the director. The reason was that the film, essentially a gang "thriller" about black-market money dealers and morphine-peddling gangs, seemed to suggest to hypersensitive eyes that Japan was being turned into a "dollar colony." Tadashi Imai's *An Enemy of the People* (Minshu no Teki), made two years before, right after the surrender, though a much more dangerous film, calling as it did for pro-Communist political action, had passed the Occupation censors unscathed, mainly because it was anti-Zaibatsu and heaped scorn and ridicule on the emperor system.

Less obvious in its political orientation was Toho's *War and Peace* (Senso to Heiwa), directed by Satsuo Yamamoto and Fumio Kamei in 1947. A technically excellent reflection of postwar life, it showed the vast sacrifices made by the common people, attention centering on two returned soldiers and their wives. Later both directors were purged by Toho and became the leading lights of independent companies organized by left-wingers.

Much more important to the Japanese film were the departures made by the new talent which had grown up during the war and which was now expressing itself in a way novel and yet still valid in postwar Japan. The novelty of the new experiments in style is perhaps best shown in the work of the three young directors who began to realize their talent directly after the war: Akira Kurosawa, Keisuke Kinoshita, and Kimisaburo Yoshimura.

Kurosawa's *Wonderful Sunday* (Subarashiki Nichiyobi), made in 1947, was about two young lovers with only twenty-five cents between them who on a rainy Sunday amid the ruins of a bombed-out street realize all of their dreams. Based on an idea taken from an early D.W. Griffith film, carefully written with an eye to character, it was an essay on postwar conditions and manners but completely free from sentimentality. There was a strength and optimism, a joyous acceptance of life as it is, that is rare enough in life and even rarer on film.

In 1946, Kinoshita began his experiments with music in the style of René Clair with *The Girl I Loved* (Waga Koi Seshi Otome), a light romance entirely free from the sensationalism of the "kiss films" and the other romantic essays of the period. The story of a young orphan girl loved by an only son but loving someone else was told with lightness, grace, and a complete absence of the heavy depression and groping for the tragic note that was so common at the time.

Yoshimura brought satire back into the film in his 1947 *The Fellows Who Ate the Elephant* (Zo o Kutta Renchu), which was about five hungry men who, after eating a zoo's elephant, dead from natural causes, get into an enormous amount of difficulty with bureaucratic authorities. Satire, rarely seen in any of the Japanese arts, here emerged as a comic vehicle with pathetic overtones and opened the way for more to come.

These comparative youngsters, and others like them, were to be of the greatest influence in forming the present-day style of Japanese film-making. Yet, of the many new directors to appear since 1946, only a few have made real names for themselves—usually in the early postwar period, while the older talents were readjusting to new situations.

Out of the turmoil of the postwar era one would expect new talents to emerge and so they did but not for the obvious reasons as in Italy and France. The structure of the Japanese film industry is such that over ninety-five percent of its directors rise gradually from the ranks of assistant directors. Therefore, as long as the industry continues production on an assembly line basis it keeps turning out people who reach their majority and almost automatically achieve directorial status, quite independent of their actual worth as directors.

After the war there was a great deal of enthusiasm, a visible quickening of spirit, an opening of new horizons, which caused some to compare the Japanese industry to the Italian. Yet the renaissance of the Japanese film, so confidently expected immediately after the war, was some time in coming.

10 adaptation and atmosphere:

1949-54. THE LAST REALLY IMportant directors to emerge were Kurosawa and Kinoshita, both of whom made their debuts almost fifteen years ago. Before them, during the 1938–39 era, both Imai and Yoshimura had appeared. In 1932, Yamanaka and Itami, both dead before the postwar era was really under way, had been the new talents. Before them, during the 1929–30 period it was Toyoda and Naruse and, yet earlier, during 1926–27, Gosho and Ozu had appeared. These men, along with the late Kenji Mizoguchi, represent the best of the Japanese film and have been responsible for its excellence. A brief resume of their achievements will go a long way toward defining the best in the Japanese film as of today.

Both Gosho and Ozu worked toward a simplicity in style: they evolved the *shomin-geki*, the only genre genuinely descriptive of contemporary Japanese life, and they sought a higher realism, which led to the elimination of plot for its own sake and to the development of the discursive, chronicle style, the simple recording of events, that has now become a definite part of the Japanese film.

Toyoda and Naruse evidenced a new concern for character, being anxious to replace the standard stereotypes with fully conceived and lifelike characterizations. Yamanaka and Itami did much the same thing for the period-drama, moving away from formula and substituting originality for the conventional. Imai and Yoshimura shifted from the political right wing to the left and introduced a stylistic virtuosity into the film; while Kinoshita and Kurosawa stood for the new postwar humanism, at the same time showing an interest in integrating the elements of foreign film-style into the Japanese film through experiments in technique.

Since that time, though many new directors have appeared, there has been no considerable change of direction within the Japanese film. It remains today much as it was at the end of the war, the only difference being that considerably more technical assurance has been achieved and personal styles have been further developed. Within the last ten years, however, new talent of lesser stature has been appearing.

Among the first to emerge after the postwar confusion were Fumio Kamei and Hideo Sekigawa. Both had entered P.C.L. in the early 1930's and later worked in the prewar Toho documentary branch when it was a veritable nest of revolutionaries. Both also found that demands on them as Party members could be made to coincide with those of the Japanese militarists in making propaganda documentaries with an anti-Western, anti-Chinese-Nationalist slant. Both revealed competence in direction but too often got lost in polemic. Now they are doing little more than potboiling, although Sekigawa has the exceptional *Listen to the Roar of the Ocean* (Kike Wadatsumi no Koe) to his credit. Both represent the Japanese cinema at its most extreme left.

Kamei, a graduate of the Leningrad Motion Picture Institute, was one of the leaders in bringing Russian "socialist realism" techniques to Japan. He first achieved fame or, perhaps better, notoriety by making an anti-war short during the Chinese War. This was angrily banned by the army (which had put up the money for the picture), and Kamei was subsequently severely persecuted by the Japanese police.

His feature work began after the war when he codirected with Satsuo Yamamoto the 1947 *War and Peace*. Earlier, in 1945, he had made the documentary *A Japanese Tragedy* (Nihon no Higeki), but this film was banned by the Occupation because of its out-and-out Communist line. Kamei's highest achievement was his 1949 film *A Woman's Life* (Onna no Issho), the story of a woman working in a printing plant and enduring terrible hardships during pregnancy because of the feudal family system and society's indifference. In it he took advantage of the popular opposition to feudal survivals and injected what he had learned politically in Russia. The film enjoyed wide showing, but this brief moment was to be Kamei's last. Today he is out of feature production, back again working in documentaries.

Sekigawa was the more talented of the two. He codirected

a number of productions, including Kurosawa's *Those Who Make Tomorrow*, before making *A Second Life* (Daini no Jinsei) by himself. This story about children represents a genre in which he continues to specialize today, after an interim of virulent anti-American films.

Another postwar talent was Senkichi Taniguchi, who entered P.C.L. from a Shingeki troupe in 1933 and was subsequently assistant to Yasujiro Shimazu and Kajiro Yamamoto. His first film, *Jakoman and Tetsu* (Jakoman to Tetsu), using a Kurosawa script about rough frontier life in a Hokkaido herring-fishing village, revealed Taniguchi's earliest style in quickly-paced action-dramas, a genre new to Japan, where even well-made melodrama all too often borders on the hysterically illogical. His second film, *To the End of the Silver-Capped Mountains* (Ginrei no Hate), had a scenario by both Kajiro Yamamoto and Kurosawa and made excellent use of its out-of-doors location in the Japan Alps. Its pace and sweep reminded one of the better American action pictures, though there was a complete adaptation to a Japanese setting.

Taniguchi followed these two rather good films with many others but gradually cheapened his effects to the extent that today he is undistinguishable from most other makers of Japanese action-drama. This is, in a way, a serious loss since no other director has been able to equal Taniguchi's early skill in producing genuinely thrilling melodrama.

Complimentary to Taniguchi among the postwar directorical talent would be Kon Ichikawa. If the former brought to the Japanese film the swift pace of the American action-film, the latter found the better American film comedies of interest and brought their rapid-fire sophisticated humor to Japan. The best films of these two men were influenced but in no way dominated by American models, the triumph of these two directors being their success in adapting the originals to Japanese forms. Their failure was in their inability to sustain their innovations.

Ichikawa also came up through Toho, having gotten his start in the 1930's at the J.O. cartoon studios in Kyoto. After the war he directed puppet films until leaving for Shintoho with the first dissenting faction of Toho. There, due to a shortage of directorial talent, he was given a job. It took a while for his talent to develop, but for a few years after 1950 his comedy style was at its height.

A jump like that made by Ichikawa, from cartoonist's board to director's megaphone in a single bound, is indicative

of the way in which the industry itself relaxed after the war.
Due to the weakening of the rigid family-system within the industry, directly after the war it became more and more common for directors to appear who had had no period of assistant-director apprenticeship in their backgrounds. Thus it was that in the postwar era even actors found it possible to become directors.

Perhaps the most talented of these was Shin Saburi, a matinee idol during the 1930's and one of Shochiku's biggest stars. Although he originally showed but little talent as an actor, this proved due merely to his inexperience, and as he made more films he developed a genuine skill. His 1950 *Reprieve* (Shikko Yuyo) revealed him to have first-class directorial talent. The story, about a lawyer who is so busy trying to get ahead that he neglects his wife, showed Saburi's talent in handling actors, extracting from them exceptionally fine performances; more than anything else, this reflected his own twenty-year experience as a film actor.

This success was followed by two 1951 films, *Twenty Years in a Storm* (Fusetsu Niju-nen), a very fine study of the changes in Japanese society during recent decades, and *Ah, Youth* (Aa Seishun), an excellent picture of postwar student life concerned as it was with poverty, politics, and romance. After his 1952 *Wail* (Dokoku), another fine character study, this time of the middle-aged intellectual, played by Saburi himself, who wants to accept the new and cannot, Saburi slumped badly and to date has never again succeeded in realizing his particular cinematic talent—the ability to draw from his actors a performance of emotional intensity which is almost foreign to Japanese acting styles.

Parallel to Saburi's rise as a director in 1950 was So Yamamura's debut in 1953 with his *The Crab-Canning Ship* (Kanikosen). This film, later shown at Cannes, was about a group of laborers and farmers recruited to work on the slave-like cannery-factory boats during the depression of the late 1920's. Based on Takiji Kobayashi's popular proletarian novel of the same name, it told the story of an oppression so bad that finally the workers seize control of the vessel, only to be finally suppressed by a boarding party from a Japanese warship. Though this film was exceptionally revolutionary in spirit and content, Yamamura himself, despite a left-wing philosophy, is something of a "political searcher" with no consistent line to propagandize. Stylistically he is less important than Saburi, drawing his effects from other films rather than from life itself. The mutiny in the 1953 film

not only resembled that in *Potemkin*, but also many of Eisenstein's dynamic images and cutting techniques were
borrowed directly, including the idea of the "mass hero."

The only woman to become a director is actress Kinuyo
Tanaka, the heroine of so many of the *shomin-geki*. After
thirty years of acting in the films, she made her debut as a
director in 1953 in *Love Letter* (Koibumi), a film which
revealed a genuine lyrical talent.

Standing alone among the new directorial talent is Kaneto
Shindo, a script writer who became a director in 1951. He
entered the films in 1934, coming straight off the farm to
become a laboratory apprentice. By the beginning of the
Pacific War he had gotten as far as the script department.
After the war he formed an alliance with Kimisaburo Yoshimura, writing the scripts for almost all of that director's
pictures, continuing even after he himself had become a
director. Shindo's style is one of the most distinctive, full of
flashes of insight, the like of which is very rare in Japanese
cinema. His first film, the 1951 *Story of a Beloved Wife*
(Aisai Monogatari), was particularly praised for its brilliant
contribution to postwar realism and for opening up a new
genre concerned with the characterization of wives as individuals. At the same time it was heavily criticized for its
sentimentality since, concurrent with Shindo's real distinction as a director, he reveals an equally real predilection for
the extremes of pathos.

The reasons for the relative failure of all this newer directorial talent are many and varied. One would certainly be
the hostility which the Japanese industry always shows new
talent except in times of desperation, as was the case during
the war. These young directors were never given the
freedom necessary to realize their talent. Another, and more
important, reason, however, was that any director not willing to retreat into the past had to come to terms with the
present, and Japan's postwar present was so confused and
unsettled as to almost deny analysis. Postwar conditions in
other countries were equally bad—witness, for example, the
chaos of Germany and Italy—but in Japan so much depends
on "the well-ordered society where everything and everyone
has and knows his own place" that only a relatively few directors managed to create meaningful films. These almost all
took the form of observations on postwar life, and if they suggested no remedy, they at least cogently stated the problems.

The interest in the postwar mess was earlier evidenced in
such films as Kinoshita's *A Morning with the Osone Family*,

Yoshimura's *A Ball at the Anjo House,* and Mizoguchi's
Women of the Night, but the fullest flavor of the era was
not expressed in its highest form until Kurosawa's mature
films appeared. *Drunken Angel* (Yoidore Tenshi), which
won the *Kinema Jumpo* "Best One" Award for 1948, though
ostensibly about petty black-marketeers, was a beautifully
made and often near-allegorical melodrama about Japan in
her darkest hour. The story centers on a gambler, Toshiro
Mifune, who has been told that he has tuberculosis. Ignorant-
ly believing that the disease is incurable, he proceeds to throw
his life away until taken in hand by the "drunken angel" of
the title, a doctor, played by Takashi Shimura, who goes out
of his way to help people. Both Mifune and Shimura are
shown as postwar products in this film. The former was once
a real power, now completely uprooted, as also is the alcoholic
doctor who tries to save him, the picture focusing on
Mifune's attempted spiritual and physical recovery. The film
develops not through a plotted story but through scenes of
lightning-like swiftness, each raising the tone to greater emotional intensity.

In 1949, Kurosawa used the same general technique, and
again used disease as a symbol, in *The Silent Duel* (Shizuka-
naru Ketto), a film about a young army doctor, again Mifune, who accidentally contracts venereal disease through
open cuts on his hands. When he returns after the war, his
shame causes him to leave the girl who has waited for six
years. Though not one of Kurosawa's best, this film was made
worthwhile by its excellent acting and character description.

His second film in 1949 was *Stray Dog* (Nora-inu), which,
though primarily designed as a commentary on postwar Japanese life, emerged as also probably the best detective picture
ever made in Japan. The story was very simple, being a
recounting of young detective Mifune's search for his re-
volver, stolen from him on a crowded bus. His search takes
him through all strata of society, Japanese low-life being
particularly well represented. One reel, entirely without dialogue, was devoted exclusively to a complete pictorialization
of the detective's search among the homeless. In style very
similar to the very best American crime pictures, a genre of
which Kurosawa has long been very fond, it contained a
great deal of the wildness often associated with the director's
early work. The social milieu was an active part of the film
rather than just exotic background and the story was told at
a breakneck pace which was perfect for the material.

In his next film, the 1950 *Scandal* (Shubun), rather than

picturing all of postwar society, Kurosawa narrowed his
scope and concentrated on just one of postwar Japan's many evils—the corruption of popular culture. The story was about the editor of a blackmailing magazine—similar in some ways to the subsequent American *Confidential*—who will stop at nothing to get or make his story. In this case a painter and a popular singer who met innocently and accidentally at a hot-spring resort are exploited. Kurosawa's concentration on this single episode, brilliant though it was, also narrowed the reference of the film itself and made it more of a simple melodrama and hence less of an achievement.

Kurosawa was not alone in observing the postwar scene. Yotoyoshi Oda's *Lady from Hell* (Jigoku no Kifujin), which had a Kurosawa script, was also about black-marketeers, political corruption, blackmailing journalism, and the social and financial fall of the nobility. Likewise Hideo Oba's *Homecoming* (Kikyo), made a year later in 1950 and based on the Jiro Osaragi novel, showed Japanese postwar corruption, this time through the eyes of a Japanese naval officer exiled to Malaya in the early 1930's who returns after the war. The film was considered a most successful adaptation and became something of a minor landmark in the postwar *junbungaku* film-adaptation movement.

Minoru Shibuya was another young postwar director who, in his 1952 *The Moderns* (Gendaijin), showed the corruption in public life. An innocent young man, extremely well played by Ryo Ikebe, becomes involved in a bribery scandal and is dragged down from his high ideals. As in all of his films, Shibuya's irregularities in direction were confusing. Parts of the film were brilliantly directed, with perfect camerawork, effective control of the actors, and a precise sense of timing. Other sections, however, were almost amateur in their ineffectiveness.

In 1952, Kurosawa, again looking long and steadily at the postwar scene, made one of his finest films, *Living* (Ikiru) —known as *Doomed* in America—which the *Quarterly of Film, Radio, and Television* has called "one of the greatest films of our time." In it Kurosawa explored almost every potentiality of the film medium in illustrating his relatively simple story. A minor bureaucrat, upon learning that he has only six months to live, realizes that he has done nothing during his life which offers him the slightest hope of personal immortality. So in his last half-year he searches for the meaning of life, finding the solution in pushing a playground project through the local bureaucracy. In this film Kuro-

sawa's humanism was at its height. This discursive film is
long and varied; it winds and unwinds; it shifts from mood
to mood, from present to past, from silence to a deafening
roar—and all in the most unabashed and absorbing fashion.
Its greatest success may be in its revitalization of film technique. It, together with Kinoshita's *A Japanese Tragedy*
(Nihon no Higeki) and *Carmen's Pure Love* (Karumen
Junjosu), shows that when it wants to, Japanese film technique can be among the most dynamic in the world. The
film's fault is perhaps that Kurosawa's genius flows unchecked
and that sometimes he carries things too far.

Another experimental approach to postwar Japan was Kinoshita's 1953 *A Japanese Tragedy*, a *haha-mono* or "mother
film," but one of the very finest. Just after the war, a widow
makes every kind of sacrifice to bring up her daughter and
son, only to have them gradually reject her as they grow up.
Set in Atami, Japan's Miami, to accent the over-commercialization of Japanese life, the story continues with the mother,
totally rejected, finally committing suicide. This film, the
theme of which was the fall of the Japanese family-system
and its mutual-obligation structure, showed off Kinoshita's
experiments in dynamic technique. His style here somewhat
reminds one of Dos Passos' in *U.S.A.*, where newspaper
clippings of current events are used to highlight or counter-
point the events in the story. The opening shows newsreel
clips of postwar Japan—war trials, the Emperor, May Day
riots, disasters, crimes, etc.—then a title, "Life is not easy,"
succeeded by "All over Japan there is darkness," then a cut
to the main title, "A Japanese Tragedy."

Once the film starts, the crosscutting of newspaper headlines also takes the story from the specific to the general.
When the mother, out of desperation, takes a trip with her
fat businessman friend there is a cut to headlines about business scandals. In the middle of the film, Kinoshita uses titles,
just as in silent picture. There is also much crosscutting between stories and superb use of flashbacks. Scenes differing
in time are cut together so that a happening in the flashback
is followed by a contemporary shot, as if it were a direct
reaction-shot to the flashback.

While some directors were thus exposing postwar Japanese
life, others were examining, and in large part condemning,
the past. Shin Saburi's *Twenty Years in the Storm* was a
study of the changes, mostly for the worse, in prewar, wartime, and postwar Japanese society. *Reeds That Rustle in the
Wind* (Kaze ni Soyogu Ashi), filmed in 1951 by Masahisa

Sunohara, accurately showed an intellectual's stand against Japan's militaristic policies between the Manchurian Incident and World War II. In 1953, Kaneto Shindo remade a general favorite, *A Woman's Life*, based on a Maupassant novel, which showed the life of a Japanese woman from 1927 to 1953. There was strong evocation of the past, but again Shindo pushed his re-creation of the actual too far. The unpleasant aspects of the story were almost repulsive in their horror and ugliness—they turned audiences against the film, not against the conditions Shindo was trying to criticize.

Sometimes the directors, rather than concern themselves with analyzing the entire postwar scene, attacked specific injustices. Yoshimura's 1950 film, *Spring Snow* (Shunsetsu), was a character study of two young lovers—a railroad conductor and a girl office-worker—sharply outlined against their social environment. The highly realistic love story was projected against the background of society's injustice as the two experienced it: the small, petty difficulties which make their lives the more difficult.

In 1952, Yoshiji Imaizumi's *Eighty Percent of the Village* (Mura Hachi-bu) was based upon an actual incident. A rural-high-school girl discovers that in an election the ballot boxes were stuffed by supporters of the district's representative in the Diet. She writes a letter to a newspaper exposing the deed. The reaction of the people in the village where she lives is almost overwhelmingly against her. They say that she is young and "only a woman" and that "even if this is true, why bring shame to our village by exposing such things?" The girl is ostracized by the village and only a few rally around her. The film's trenchant criticism of feudal survivals was very strong, and when the unit went to the actual village for location shooting, it was violently attacked by hired thugs.

Kaneto Shindo's 1953 *Epitome* (Shukuzu) was about the daughter of a family whose poverty forces her to become a geisha. There was a general exposé of the world of the geisha, insisting upon the sordidness behind the glamorous façade. Again, it was so excessively explicit that there were parts where one could scarcely bear to look at the screen. As a whole the film attempted to move beyond realism to naturalism and was, in some parts, quite successful.

Another geisha story was Yoshimura's *Clothes of Deception* (Itsuwareru Seiso), made in 1951, about two sisters. The elder completely ignores her responsibilities in an effort to take advantage of as many men as possible. Finally she is

wounded by one of her lovers. The film was much like
Mizoguchi's *Sisters of the Gion* except that the two sisters' characters were reversed and life in Kyoto's Gion was brought up to date by showing its postwar deterioration.

The postwar Gion geisha was again seen in Mizoguchi's *Gion Music* (Gion Bayashi), a 1953 film about two geisha, one old and experienced, the other young. The latter rebels against her environment, encouraged by the elder, who thinks herself too far gone to change her way of life; yet she resists in her own way and refuses to become a common prostitute, the lot of many geisha after the war. The younger, soon lost in the upside-down world of the postwar geisha, is actually the daughter of a former patron of the elder's, and their mutual sacrifices constitute a very severe criticism of the geisha tradition.

Of course there were also those directors who were interested in special pleading and who, by pushing polemic, weakened the effectiveness of their pictures. In a number of these films there was only one answer, usually no more than implicit, to the genuine social problems they treated: revolution, a revolution which would end every injustice, or at least so the makers implied.

Satsuo Yamamoto's 1950 *Street of Violence* (Boryoku no Machi) was based upon an actual attempt to suppress a journalist's investigation of collusion between a rural police chief and the local gangster "boss." The theme was supposedly "the democratization of local government," but the methods proposed resembled those of the Communist union which produced the film.

Imai's *And Yet We Live* (Dokkoi Ikiteiru), made in 1951, was one of the first major examples of the postwar Italian influence, the direction being patterned after De Sica's in *Bicycle Thieves*. The story, about the struggle of day laborers to achieve dignity and a standard of living above the starvation level, was persuasively presented, though many felt that Imai's compromise with the star system inherent in his use of the Communist Party's Zenshinza theatrical troupe considerably invalidated his message, even though the ensemble gave the acting a rare unity in style.

The Sunless Street (Taiyo no Nai Machi), made in 1954 by Satsuo Yamamoto, was an adaptation of Sunao Tokunaga's 1929 proletarian novel about a prolonged strike at a printing plant. There was a conscious application of Soviet "socialist realism" to Japanese technique, with a very idealized portrayal of the working class spouting their all-knowing and inherent folk wisdom, as against the all-black capitalist adversaries and their bootlicking lackeys. It had a final scene where, as anti-union forces try to steal the red flag, it is passed from hand to hand with as much commotion as the jacket-snatching climax of René Clair's *Le Million*. The only difference was that the scene in the Yamamoto film was not supposed to be funny.

Along the same general line was Hideo Sekigawa's *My Crime While at the First Higher School* (Waga Ichiko Jidai no Hanzai), made in 1951, which showed the sufferings of a Communist-oriented student during his attendance at Japan's most famous college-preparatory school. The leftist sentimentality of this film was fully matched by Fumio Kamei's 1953 *A Woman Walks the Earth Alone* (Onna Hitori Daichi o Iku), whose exposure of horrifying working conditions in Japanese mines was moreover greatly weakened by the quite apparent calls for violent revolution.

The postwar spirit was, with reason, so gloomy, so critical of crumbling institutions, so pessimistic in outlook, that one of the few signs of health in the industry was this very awareness of the wretchedness of life. On one point, however, everyone was united. This was the idea that only in youth, in the coming generation, lay any hope at all. This idea was responsible for the enormous number of films about young people, from children to teen-agers, which filled the screens and continue to this day.

The cycle of films about children began in 1947, when Yasujiro Ozu made his first film in five years, *The Record of a Tenement Gentleman* (Nagaya Shinshi Roku), which was about one of many homeless boys who roamed the streets directly after the war. The boy meets his father, but eventually rejects him to go off on his own and make his own life.

Hiroshi Inagaki, the sword-drama specialist, turned to children in 1948, making *Children Hand in Hand* (Te o Tsunagu Kora), which was based on an earlier Mansaku Itami script about mentally-underdeveloped children and appealed to the charitable instincts of the audiences, something very difficult to do successfully in the early postwar years of economic and social upheaval in Japan. He followed it a year later with *Forgotten Children* (Wasurerareta Kora), about a school for the mentally retarded, with a plea for special attention lest these children be discarded by society when they grow up.

Another film which treated the rehabilitation of war orphans was Hiroshi Shimizu's 1948 *Children of the Beehive*

(Hachi no Su no Kodomotachi), made entirely on location and using not even one professional actor. Shimizu himself collected an actual gang of ten lost children and made them the leading actors. Although he had specialized in pictures about children before the war, never before had he come so close to reality. The picture created something of a revolution in Japanese technique, the use of non-professional actors being rare in Japan, and it also helped create public interest in the rehabilitation of war orphans.

In 1952, Shimizu made another film about wandering gangs of war orphans, *Children and the Statue of Buddha* (Daibutsu-sama to Kodomotachi). In it the homeless orphans acting as tourist guides around the historic city of Nara develop a feeling of affection and respect for the many art treasures of the city, particularly the great statue of the Buddha. Shimizu was so carried away by his subject in this film that he could not resist sentimentalizing, something he had so far avoided.

Abandoned children again came into their share of attention in Minoru Shibuya's 1953 *Topsy Turvy* (Yassa Mossa), based on a popular newspaper serial about an orphanage for the illegitimate children of American servicemen. Another school picture was Imai's *Echo School* (Yamabiko Gakko), made in 1952, about a junior-high-school teacher in the mountain area of northern Japan and how he devoted himself to the pursuit of knowledge amid poverty. Imai's *Blue Mountains* (Aoi Sammyaku), made five years earlier, was a jump from the children's-film genre to the youth-film genre and was the more successful. It too was about school, this time a provincial girls-high-school which goes coeducational after the war. It was a very joyful film and at times its excellent humor was slightly satirical as it focused on teachers, pupils, and the PTA. Youngsters in love opposed their feudalistic elders, but the tone was light and quite different from Imai's later, and heavier, polemic.

Another 1948 youth film was Kinoshita's *Apostasy* (Hakai), about a young schoolteacher, a member of Japan's pariah class, who tries to teach the meaning of freedom and equality among human beings and runs into opposition from the established heads of the community.

Minoru Shibuya's *Crazy Uproar* (Tenya Wanya) was a very clever 1950 film about what happens when an *après guerre* girl invades a small, backward mountain town in Shikoku. Another comedy of that year was Naruse's *Conduct Report on Professor Ishinaka* (Ishinaka Sensei Gyojoki),

about the humorous experiences of young intellectuals in
a provincial city. Gosho too turned to regionalism in his
Dispersing Clouds (Wakare Kumo) in 1951, which was about
a young girl student and a middle-aged woman, focusing on
the elder's dreams of youth and the younger's sentimentality.

Life Is Beautiful (Inochi Uruwashi), a 1951 film by Hideo
Oba, was less sanguine about the future since the story was
about a family who lives near a spot favored by young
suicides and must continually save people. It did show, however, that the postwar pessimism was just as strong in the
provinces as it was in the cities.

One of the very best films of the entire youth cycle was
Imai's *Until the Day We Meet Again* (Mata Au Hi made),
which won the *Kinema Jumpo* "Best One" Award for 1950.
Set in the spring of the final year of the war, it nevertheless
managed to reflect well the postwar atmosphere of hope in
the young, coupled with sorrow for the many young who
died in the war. According to some critics, Imai never again
equaled the quality of this tender story of a boy about to
leave for the army, and his girl, forced to remain behind.
The film followed them to the bitter end, the boy dead at
the front and the girl killed in an air raid, and was, in the
very best sense, a powerful anti-war picture.

Such worthwhile films as the above, however, were only
a part of the genre. By 1950 the youth cycle had brought
forth a bastard which was soon to usurp popular interest: the
teen-age sex film, which had a long if not particularly good
pedigree. In part it was a continuation of the prewar
"student" genre, in part a harking back to the adult sex
comedy, which, thanks to the intervention of the politically
minded censors, had risen from the tendency film.

After the war, amid all the confusion, it was not uncommon, particularly among the young, to confuse freedom with
license. The films were quick to realize this, exploiting it in
pictures which in turn created even more confusion. The
man who dubbed this era *Kasutori Bunka Jidai*, the Age of
Rotgut Culture, was no more than telling the truth. In the
movies, despite the continual rise in quality of Japanese
pictures, the biggest tendency of 1950, as noted by critics
and public alike was the boom in the teen-age sex picture.

One of the earliest was Yoshimura's *About Twenty Years
Old* (Niju-sai Zengo), which, supposedly a picture for high-
school students, actually stressed sex in a most adult way and
very effectively paved the way for what was to come. *Bad
Girl* (Furyo Shojo) and *Black Flower* (Kuroi Hana) were

both about sexy teen-age girls, and the fact that in both films the rôle of the sexiest was played by Yoshiko Kuga, a daughter of a former peer, only increased the titilation. Koji Shima's *Teen-Ager's Sex Manual* (Judai no Seiten) had Ayako Wakao, soon to become the top teen age star, carrying on in a girls' high school and went on for several sequels with similar titles. *Virgins' Clinic* (Otome no Shinsatsushitsu) and Hideo Oba's *A Virgin's Sex Manual* (Otome no Seiten) did justice to their titles, while, for many, the newcomer Machiko Kyo in her many and more adult-oriented sex pictures epitomized postwar sexual profligacy. In one of them, Keigo Kimura's *Bitch* (Mesu-inu), the character she portrayed had relations with great numbers of men.

The popularity of both teen-age and adult sex films was such that even some of the better directors were tempted. Naruse turned out one on young streetwalkers in *White Beast* (Shiroi Yaju), while Toyoda made one of his most unimpressive films in *Whisper of Spring* (Haru no Sasayaki). Even less noteworthy was Kinoshita's *Youth* (Shonen-ki), though both of the latter directors were to redeem themselves later in films about young people.

It goes without saying that kisses, novel though they had been in the immediate postwar era, no longer satisfied sophisticated audiences, and so the films went farther and farther toward a complete exploitation of sex. These products had titles like *Confessions of a Gynecologist* (Aru Fujinka no Kokuhaku), *Sex Manual for Married Women* (Hitozuma no Seiten), and the explicitly titled *Male Virgin* (Dotei). The indefatigable Koji Shima made something called *Night Widows* (Yoru no Mibojin), since in Japan widows, once having had it but later denied it, are thought the sexiest things around. Even the old Shimpa standby, *The Golden Demon* (Konjiki Yasha), was sexed up and dressed in modern clothes.

The film which went furthest was probably the best of its kind, though certainly not the best picture its director ever made. It was Mizoguchi's 1950 *Picture of Madame Yuki* (Yuki Fujin Ezu), the story of a woman who finds that spiritual love leaves her completely cold and more or less falls in love with the sexual act itself. It had more bed scenes than were ever shown before on the Japanese screen and contained a good performance by Michiyo Kogure, in the rôle of the middle-aged woman. Mizoguchi, through his feeling for the woman's touch and his creation of atmosphere did much to make it an accurate portrayal of one type of postwar emancipation.

While not unconscious of the changes in postwar Japan
and not at all hostile to the social-film genre, some directors sought to explore the more eternal aspects of Japanese society rather than its transient and superficial problems. The most eternal aspect of Japan is its traditional family life, and it was to this subject that the more thoughtful of directors turned again and again. Those most interested were the *shomin-geki* specialists, Ozu, Gosho, and Naruse, who after 1950 raised the genre to its highest form.

Naruse launched the *shomin-geki* revival with his 1951 *Repast* (Meshi), a film which also provided the director with his first escape from a fifteen-year period of relative mediocrity. The film was about a poor white-collar worker, the average Japanese "salary-man," and his wife who after a few years of married life decide to break up because they just cannot make a go of it. They finally understand, however, that at least they are not alone in their plight, that things are not so bad as all that, and that love and enjoyment can come from the simple things in life. This film proved one of the most perfect expressions of the perennial Japanese *shikata ga nai*, "it can't be helped," philosophy. It also differed somewhat in feeling from the typical *shomin-geki* of, say, Ozu's. In the Naruse films, although things appear quiet and commonplace, one false move (ever so dangerous because Naruse's characters are moved by instinct) would bring disaster. In an Ozu film, on the other hand, things appear and *are* basically quiet.

In 1952, Naruse made one of his best films, *Mother* (Okaasan), which was essentially an extension of the mood of *Repast* and, though a *haha-mono*, was one of the very best. A widow, Kinuyo Tanaka, faces life with her three children, the story being told through the eyes of eldest daughter, played by Kyoko Kagawa in one of the most sensitive teenage performances in the Japanese cinema.

Lightning (Inazuma), made in the same year, continued the trend of his earlier pictures, this time concentrating on everyday life among stepchildren. The mother has been married to various men, all of whom have left her with offspring. Most of her children are rather rough types, but the heroine, Hideko Takamine, is gentle. Here was an almost perfect realization of Fumiko Hayashi's novel, but at the same time nothing filmic was violated to make the picture more literary. It was a balanced union of literature and cinema, a very rare occurrence in any country.

Naruse's 1953 *Older Brother, Younger Sister* (Ani Imoto)

had a very strong story about the interrelationships between
a brother and his two sisters in a working-class family. The
older sister goes to work in a cheap restaurant so that the
younger sister can go to school, but since she gradually becomes a prostitute she consequently, if unintentionally, prevents her sister's marrying the boy she loves. Naruse tells his
story in the most economical of ways, putting his camera in
close and shooting the picture in the most intimate of close-
ups. Attempting to move from realism to naturalism, Naruse
is occasionally at fault in manipulating his characters a
bit too obviously. As a rule they lack the intelligence and the
capacity for self-examination that are found in Gosho's,
though the characters of both are from the same social level.
Naruse's people are caught by fate; they lack the inclination,
maybe even the intelligence, to search for escape. Gosho's
too are trapped, but they struggle, often in vain, for
release.

The difference is seen in one of Gosho's best films, and one
of the really important postwar Japanese films, *Where
Chimneys Are Seen* (Entotsu no Mieru Basho), which shows
shomin-geki at its purest and in the very best postwar form.
Shown abroad as *Three Chimneys* (despite the fact that there
are four chimneys in the film) and third-prize winner at the
Berlin Film Festival in 1954, it tells the story of people in
an industrial section of Tokyo and the factory chimneys
under which they live. The chimneys are more than merely
symbolic of industrial Japan: they are symbolic of an attitude
toward life, an attitude which has long been identified with
Gosho himself, the attitude shown when the husband looks
once more at the chimneys, so placed that they never appear
the same to people in different places, and says: "Life is
whatever you think it is. It can be sweet or it can be bitter
—whichever you are."

The story, taken from a novel by Rinzo Shiina, is about
a couple, long married but childless because they feel they
cannot afford a baby, whose lives are suddenly invaded by
an abandoned child. At first they attempt to get rid of it but
little by little become attached to it. Episodic in structure
but with each event relating directly to the central philosophy
of the film, it is one of those movies which one cannot
adequately summarize. Nothing is irrelevant, every detail
adding to the effect of the whole world which is created.

Ozu, who had made the *shomin-geki* his own, continued
in it after the war for a few years, until he moved the genre
up the social ladder, with a whole series of pictures about

the upper middle-class, beginning with *Late Spring* (Ban-shun), a film which was awarded *Kinema Jumpo's* "Best
One" Award for 1949. A college professor lives in Kamakura with his twenty-seven-year-old daughter. His wife having recently died, he now begins to think that it is time for his daughter to marry, before she is too old. At last she agrees and they find her a husband. Before her wedding they take a trip together to Kyoto, as if to sever old relationships be-fore her new life begins. Then, after she marries he returns to his now-empty house and his new life alone. This film marked the emergence of Ozu's new postwar style. There was a virtual elimination of plot in the interests of creating character and atmosphere. Yet, with almost no story in the usual sense of the word, the film's development was quite complex.

His 1951 *Early Summer* (Bakushu), again a *Kinema Jumpo* prize-winner, continued Ozu's experiments in the *shomin-geki* genre. This time it was a study of interrelationships among a middle-class family of six. Again the setting was Kamakura and again the subject was marriage and the result-ant breaking of the home. Unlike *Late Spring,* however, the emphasis shifts from a family to four ex-classmates from a girls' high school. The plot, seldom important to most Japanese directors, was in this film insignificant to Ozu, who emphasized character, mood, and observation.

The 1952 *The Flavor of Green Tea and Rice* (O-Chazuke no Aji) showed a middle-aged middle-class married couple in trouble as they seek to avoid the responsibilities of married life and yet remain faithful to each other. The couple, Shin Saburi and Michiyo Kogure, have lost their individual per-sonalities, and the film shows their attempt to find themselves again. Devoid of plot, more so than perhaps any other Ozu film, it was the unusually profound presentation of character that held its audience, the characters coming alive in a way seldom seen on the screen.

Ozu's 1953 film, *Tokyo Story* (Tokyo Monogatari), called *Their First Trip to Tokyo* abroad, was about an elderly couple who come to visit their children in Tokyo only to find them completely engrossed in their own lives, with no time to spare for their parents. The only one who pays any attention to them is the widow of a son killed in the war. Back home again, the mother falls ill, and the children come to the family home for an ironic contrast to the parents' trip to the city.

Not everything connected with the *shomin-geki,* however,

was of the calibre of the films by Naruse, Gosho, and Ozu.
From 1951 Toho was active in the production of salary-man
comedies, a continuation of the prewar genre with everything brought up to date. White-collar workers had always
been a part of the *shomin-geki*, but this salary-man development moved eventually in the direction of cheap comedy
and was hence a degeneration. Soon all of these films, having
failed to attract the better directorial talent, were dominated
by poorly executed slapstick, outdated comedy routines, and
a general lack of competence. Typical examples were Kozo
Saeki's *Tomorrow Is Sunday* (Asu wa Nichiyobi) and
Shunkai Mizubo's *Young Company Executive* (Botchan Juyaku). The better ones, like Masahisa Sonohara's *Third-Class
Executive* (San-to Juyaku), owed whatever appeal they had
to the rising comic talent of the actor Hisaya Morishige.

Fortunately the Japanese film did not have to depend on
the salary-man comedies for its laughter. Good comedies were
and are made in Japan, though they are few in number. The
best, indeed, have a national style which is at the same time
universal in its appeal.

One of the earliest of the postwar comedies was Torajiro
Saito's *The Emperor's Hat* (Tenno no Boshi), made in 1950
and incorporating a plot which before the war would have
constituted a severe political crime. A man working in a
museum steals the Emperor's hat from its display case and
with it gets a job as a hatter's sandwich man. The plot
revolves around the reactions of the public, police, and central
characters to this bit of lèse majesté.

In 1953, Kon Ichikawa directed a rather free remake of
Yutaka Abe's very successful silent comedy *The Woman
Who Touched the Legs*. In it he attempted to break away
from the stringing together of unrelated jokes found in the
usual Japanese comedy in favor of a more integrated, wittier
form. Another of the better comedies was Kinoshita's
Carmen Comes Home (Karumen Kokyo ni Kaeru), a 1951
film about a strip-tease artist, Carmen by name, who returns
to her rural home with a friend and fellow stripper. Their
gay postwar manners embarrass and even frighten the simple
country people in her home town. Although not a musical,
songs were used in the early René Clair style, as a kind of
inner monologue or to comment on the action, and the film
was particularly amusing in its attack on the notion that anything that comes from Tokyo is the best of Japanese culture.

Much more highly developed than the simple comedy is
the filmic satire, and here the Japanese can make a real con-

tribution to the world's cinema. Though the form rarely appears, when it occurs it is almost invariably of the very best. In the postwar era Kon Ichikawa, Minoru Shibuya, Kimisaburo Yoshimura, and especially Keisuke Kinoshita contributed greatly to the genre.

One of the earliest was Yoshimura's 1949 film, *Waltz at Noon* (Mahiru no Embukyoku), which was about relatives fighting over an old lady's fortune. The family were former peers, and prewar types were contrasted with postwar, all set in the ruins of the large burned-out foreign-style family mansion.

Ichikawa contributed *Mr. Pu* (Pu-san), a 1953 satire on contemporary life in Japan based on a famous cartoon character. In it the young director showed the gradual evolution of talent which had the critics calling him the "Japanese Frank Capra." Somewhat less satirical and closer to simple film comedy was Minoru Shibuya's 1952 *No Consultation Today* (Honjitsu Kyushin), about a doctor who tries to close his clinic for a day and is constantly interrupted by a variety of patients who just cannot wait. He becomes involved in all kinds of doings which constitute Shibuya's comment on postwar life.

It is in the work of Kinoshita, however, that film satire finds its finest form. His 1949 film, *Here's to the Girls* (O-josan Kampai), was a relatively minor effort but at least indicated the director's latent satiric power. The story of a low-class roughneck and his love for a girl from an impoverished aristocratic family, it was itself almost a burlesque on the old Shochiku "woman's film."

Much more successful was *Broken Drum* (Yabure Daiko), which starred Tsumasaburo Bando as a newly-rich construction-company owner who tries to run his modern family along feudal lines. He is forever proclaiming his own virtue and issuing commands to his patient and ultra-individualist family, which then does just what it intended to do all along. Hence the broken drum of the title, the father issuing commands to a perfectly unresponsive family. There was also rich satire on the airs put on by the new-rich snobs in Den-enchofu, Tokyo's most elegant residential district.

Kinoshita's best satire, and the greatest made in Japan, was the 1952 *Carmen's Pure Love*, a sequel to the earlier comedy *Carmen Comes Home*, created after the director had made a trip to Europe, where he had the opportunity of meeting his idol, René Clair. Again Hideko Takamine was Carmen the stripper, but this time she was also a satiric symbol of

Japan. The film was full of the old René Clair spirit including actors who sang as they went about their business, satirizing bohemian types, sporting ultra-Americanized types, and every other kind of postwar personality. The fluid plot parodies mother love, excessive patriotism, marriage, and the atom-bomb scare. Here Kinoshita rejects the past but also sees no road to the future; he only suggests that one must look at all the signboards before choosing a path.

There are numerous excellent satiric touches in this sharply edited film, among them being the widow of an army officer who tries to run her house like an army post; an avant-garde artist's studio so filled with mobiles that there is no room to walk; and one wonderful comic sequence in which a pro-militaristic election candidate's procession gets mixed up in a demonstration of "Mothers Against War."

Another genre which was rising fast in postwar Japan was the anti-war film, a genre which made its first appearance in 1950, partly as a consequence of the American war pictures shown for the first time in Japan, and partly because of the outbreak of the Korean War and the widespread Japanese desire to stay out of it at any cost. Another reason was the 1949 release of *Paisà* and *La Grande Illusion*, the latter having been banned in prewar days. These two films received, respectively, the first and second "Best One" *Kinema Jumpo* Awards in the foreign-film category for the year and had the effect of reinforcing Japan's official promise never again to interest herself in war.

The initial anti-war pictures were essentially non-political. There was no big message, only an exposure of the horrors of war. Hideo Sekigawa's *Listen to the Roar of the Ocean*, showing how a unit of drafted students was wiped out, was based on the diaries of dead soldiers. The first picture since the end of the war to feature battle scenes, its tremendous grosses helped save the young and feeble Toei Company. Similar in structure to such wartime pictures as *Five Scouts*, it no longer allowed the horrors of battle to obscure the horrors of the Imperial Army. Especially interesting was Sekigawa's vigorous use of contrapuntal montage. Scenes of the soldiers' privations were followed by flashbacks of peacetime Japan; a wounded soldier's sufferings were crosscut with his friend's attempt at a humorous song; shots of men dying evoked scenes of the Imperial Army marching in full-dress review.

Senkichi Taniguchi's *Escape at Dawn* (Akatsuki no Dasso), also made in 1950, was the story of a group of "consolation

49. *Our Neighbor Miss Yae*, 1934, Yasujiro Shimazu. One of the finest films about the middle-class. Yumeko Aizome, Den Ohinata, Akio Isono, Yoshiko Okada.

50. *Sisters of the Gion*, 1935. Kenji Mizoguchi. Perhaps the best of the prewar films. Yoko Umemura, Isuzu Yamada.

51. *Wife! Be Like a Rose!* 1935, Mikio Naruse. Husband, wife, and mistress: a problem film. Sachiko Chiba, Heihachiro Okawa.

52. *The Village Tattooed Man,* 1935, Sadao Yamanaka. The search for the truth of human existence. Fujiko Fukamizu, Chojuro Kawarazaki.

53. *The Great Bohdisattva Pass,* 1935, Hiroshi Inagaki. The superproduction. Naoe Fushimi, Denjiro Okochi.

54. *Osaka Elegy,* 1936, Kenji Mizoguchi. Reality on its own terms. Eitaro Shindo, Isuzu Yamada, Kensaku Hara.

55. *Theater of Life*, 1936, Tomu Uchida. A successful attack on the values of an overly-commercial society. Isamu Kosugi, Reizaburo Yamamoto.

56. *Humanity and Paper Balloons*, 1937, Sadao Yamanaka. The contemporary hero in a period setting Sukezo Kuketakaya, Chojuro Kawarazaki, Kanemon Nakamura.

57. *Many People*. 1937, Hisatora Kumagai. The social-problem film. Koji Shima, Sadako Sawamura (*c*).

58. *Children in the Wind*, 1937, Hiroshi Shimizu. One of the many fine films about children. Bakudan-kozo, Masao Hayama.

59. *Young People*, 1937, Shiro Toyo-da. The most successful of the liter-ary adaptations. Yuriko Hanabusa, Haruyo Ichikawa, Den Ohinata.

60. *The Summer Battle of Osaka*, 1937, Teinosuke Kinugasa. The last of the period epics.

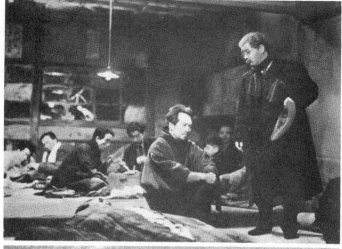

61. *The Naked Town*, 1937, Tomu Uchida. A film about the middle-class during the '30's. Koji Shima, Isamu Kosugi.

62. *The New Earth*, 1937, Mansaku Itami & Arnold Fanck, The first coproduction. Setsuko Hara.

63. *A Pebble by the Wayside*, 1938, Tomotaka Tasaka. A boy and his teacher. One of the more successful literary adaptations. Isamu Kosugi, Akihiko Katayama.

64. *Earth*, 1939,
Tomu Uchida.
The new realism.
Akiko Kazama,
Isamu Kosugi.

65. *Five Scouts*,
1939, Tomotaka
Tasaka. The most
important Japanese
war film. Isamu
Kosugi (*c*).

66. *Spring on
Lepers' Island*,
1940, Shiro
Toyoda. A cry
for humanism in
an age marching
toward war.
Shizue Natsu-
kawa (*r*).

67. *The Story of
Tank Commander
Nishizumi*, 1940,
Kimisaburo Yoshi-
mura. The human-
istic ideal at war.
Ken Uehara (*c*).

68. *Horse*, 1941,
Kajiro Yamamoto.
The documentary
approach. Hideko
Takamine.

69. *The War at
Sea from Hawaii
to Malaya*, 1942,
Kajiro Yamamoto.
A dramatization of
"the Navy Spirit as
culminated at Pearl
Harbor."

70. *There Was a Father*, 1942, Yasujiro Ozu. The obligations to family and society. Chishu Ryu (*l*).

71. *Musashi Miyamoto*, 1942, Hiroshi Inagaki. The period hero during wartime. Haruyo Ichikawa, Chiezo Kataoka.

72. *The Life of Matsu the Untamed*, 1943, Hiroshi Inagaki. The rickshaw man and his young friend. Tsumasaburo Bando, Hiroyuki Nagato.

73. *The Blossoming Port*, 1943, Keisuke Kinoshita. A social satire in wartime. Chieko Higashiyama, Mitsuko Mito.

74. *Sanshiro Sugata*, 1943, Akir Kurosawa. The emergence of a powerful new director. Ryuno suke Tsukigata. Susumu Fujita.

75. *Army*, 1944, Keisuke Kinoshita. Three generations in the Imperial Army. Kinuyo Tanaka (*c*).

76. *The Men Who Tread on the Tiger's Tail*, 1945, Akira Kurosawa. The Kabuki transformed. Enoken, Denjiro Okochi.

77. *A Ball at the Anjo House*, 1946, Kimisaburo Yoshimura. An evocation of the past and the postwar present. Masayuki Mori, Keiko Tsushima.

78. *Four Love Stories: 1. First Love*, 1947, Shiro Toyoda. Young love amid the ruins. Ryo Ikebe & Yoshiko Kuga (c).

79. *Drunken Angel*, 1948, Akira Kurosawa. An allegory of the postwar man, Michiyo Kogure, Toshiro Mifune.

80. *Late Spring*, 1949, Yasujiro Ozu. Father and unmarried daughter. Setsuko Hara, Jun Osami, Chishu Ryu.

81. *Stray Dog*, 1949, Akira Kurosawa. Cops, robbers, and postwar society. Toshiro Mifune, Takashi Shimura.

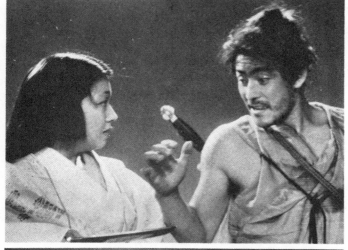

82. *Rashomon*,
1950, Akira Kuro-
sawa. The most
famous Japanese
film ever made.
Machiko Kyo,
Toshiro Mifune.

83. *Early Sum-
mer*, 1951, Yasu-
jiro Ozu. The
postwar film
about the middle-
class. Kuniko
Miyake, Chieko
Higashiyama,
Chishu Ryu.

84. *The Idiot*,
1951, Akira Kuro-
sawa. Dostoevsky
in Hokkaido.
Setsuko Hara,
Yoshiko Kuga.

85. *Clothes of Deception*, 1951, Kimisaburo Yoshimura. The geisha in the postwar world. Machiko Kyo, Ichiro Sugai.

86. *Mother*, 1952. Mikio Naruse. The daughter prepares for her wedding. Kyoko Kagawa, Kinuyo Tanaka.

87. *The Moderns*, 1952, Minoru Shibuya. The postwar generation. Isuzu Yamada (*u*), Ryo Ikebe (*l*).

88. *The Flavor of Green Tea and Rice*, 1952, Yasujiro Ozu. The Japanese family and its individual members. Koji Tsuruta, Shin Saburi.

89. *The Life of a Woman by Saikaku*, 1952, Kenji Mizoguchi. The classic novel on the screen. Shown abroad as *The Life of O-Haru*, Midori Komatsu, Kinuyo Tanaka.

90. *Carmen's Pure Love*, 1952. Keisuke Kinoshita. Japan's greatest film satire. Toshiko Kobayashi, Hideko Takamine.

91. *Living*, 1952, Akira Kurosawa. Perhaps the single finest postwar film. Takashi Shimura (*r*).

92. *Ugetsu Monogatari*, 1953, Kenji Mizoguchi. Cinema at its most evocative. Machiko Kyo, Masayuki Mori.

93. *Tokyo Story*, 1953, Yasujiro Ozu. The family system in flux. Haruko Sugimura, Chishu Ryu, So Yamamura, Shiro Osaka, Setsuko Hara, Kyoko Kagawa.

94. *Gion Music,* 1953, Kenji Mizoguchi. A severe criticism of the geisha tradition. Chieko Naniwa, Michiyo Kogure.

95. *Where Chimneys Are Seen,* 1953, Heinosuke Gosho. If at first you don't succeed, try, try again. Hiroshi Akutagawa, Hideko Takamine.

96. *Gate of Hell,* 1953, Teinosuke Kinugasa. Full color and the period-drama. Kazuo Hasegawa, Machiko Kyo.

girls" in China near the end of the war and of a Japanese soldier's desertion because of his love for one of them. There was an honest portrayal of army cruelty and a very impressive final scene where soldiers are ordered to shoot down their fleeing comrade. They refuse but do not have the further courage to turn on their commanding officer, who eventually shoots the soldier himself.

Before long, however, the anti-war genre, always so amenable to propagandistic manipulation, began to acquire political direction. In 1952, Satsuo Yamamoto made *Vacuum Zone* (Shinku Chitai), an exposé of the brutality and corruption of the Japanese army shown in its most revolting form. The strongest anti-military film ever made in Japan, it also contained definite indications of Yamamoto's political affiliations. Sekigawa's *Dawn, Fifteenth of August* (Reimei Hachigatsu Jugo-nichi), based on the actual event of a group of military fanatics' attempting to continue the war just prior to the surrender announcement by the Emperor, likewise used a condemnation of the military to expound political opinions.

From the immediate postwar position of complete distrust of the military, the Japanese treatment of soldiers and sailors in films split into two largely political directions. The first affirmed that the military, even some of the officers and the fanatic *kamikaze* volunteers, were really anti-war and peace lovers at heart. The second suggested that the military knew what it was doing, that the aim had been the greater glory of the nation, and that the tales of wartime horror had been greatly exaggerated.

Films like Kosho Nomura's *Military Police* (Kempei) and *Combat Nurse* (Yasen Kangofu), both made in 1953, while pretending to condemn war, actually glorified it. Others sympathetically re-examined the wartime leaders and found them guiltless. Kiyoshi Saeki's *Tomoyuki Yamashita* (Yamashita Tomoyuki) had Sessue Hayakawa in the title rôle and followed the hero's career from his capture of Singapore to his execution in the Philippines. The film particularly sought to excuse him from responsibility for atrocities committed under his command in the final days of the Philippine campaign. There seems to be good evidence of Yamashita's guilt, but the film sought to drum up as much sympathy as possible and consequently used one of the oddest trios of villains (all three actual personages) ever seen on the screen: the drunken, whoremongering Field Marshal Terauchi, who, says the film, got Yamashita into the mess; a vindictive and advancement-seeking American prosecutor who will stop at nothing in order to secure a conviction; and, by implication, a jealous and revengeful MacArthur.

Admiral Isoroku Yamamoto also came in for whitewashing in Inoshiro Honda's *Eagle of the Pacific* (Taiheiyo no Washi), which followed the admiral's career from Pearl Harbor to Midway Island and insisted that he was opposed to war all along and had proposed peace discussions any number of times. Yutaka Abe's *Battleship Yamato* (Senkan Yamato), also made in 1953, featured the final voyage of that ship before it was sunk by American planes, and was designed as a eulogy to the spirit of the old Imperial Navy. The special effects were unusually poor, but wartime nostalgia built the film into a big success.

From the treatment of war, either from the right or the left, it was but a step to expressing resentment against the United States. Moreover, a perfectly good reason for disliking Americans was on hand in the atom bomb and what was left of Hiroshima and Nagasaki. The authentic Japanese attitude toward not only the bomb but their surrender itself had been one which the Occupation never fully understood. Initially, the occupying Americans had expected resentment and were puzzled and a bit disquieted when they could discover none, not realizing that the Japanese thought of the surrender, once it was proclaimed, as inevitable. The often-noted passivity of the Asian was not so much the cause of this attitude as was the uniquely Japanese inability to cry over spilt milk, the widespread "it can't be helped" philosophy, and the knowledge that Japan would either cooperate with the Occupation or else.

After the Occupation had packed up and gone home, however, a resentment which would have seemed perfectly natural five years before did flare up. The spark was more or less artificially ignited and busy hands fanned the blaze which, to some disappointment, never did grow into the overwhelming conflagration so confidently expected.

In 1953 the Japan Teachers Union decided to go in with Kaneto Shindo and make a film version of the bestselling *Children of the Atom Bomb* (Genbaku no Ko) by Arata Osada. Shindo made a faithful film version, using the name of the book, and showed the aftermath of the bomb without any vicious polemic. The picture's weakness, as one would have expected from a Shindo film, was its coupling of the most lifelike naturalism with truly excessive sentimentality.

The Union was not at all satisfied, saying that he had "made [the story] into a tear-jerker and destroyed its political ori-

entation." They decided to back another version which
would this time "genuinely help to fight to preserve peace." They found their man in Hideo Sekigawa, who turned out *Hiroshima.*

The film, which used over twenty thousand extras, had scenes in which Americans (not shown) are reported to have said that the bomb was nothing more than a simple scientific experiment and the Japanese were nothing more than experimental animals; had dialogue suggesting that the bomb would not have been dropped if the people had been other than Japanese; and ended with scenes where American tourists are busy buying souvenir bones of persons killed in the explosion. As a whole, the picture was composed of two contrasting and interwoven sections: first, a well-made, dramatically moving, documentary-like reconstruction of the explosion; second, a tedious, statically filmed, polemic-filled tract which gave the film its message and its inherent anti-American meaning. The picture was financially successful, however, and opened the way for the spate of other films supposedly expressing the American terrorization of Japanese innocence.

Of all the so-called anti-U.S. films which blossomed in the wake of the Occupation, *Red-Light Bases* (Akasen Kichi) received the most public attention, although in retrospect it was more naive than "anti." It was in general a poorly constructed film, without much drive, which confined its political content almost entirely to scenes between U.S. soldiers and their "pom-pom" girl friends. Actually, the film exhibited little propaganda and much bad taste. It fit precisely into the current sex cycle and was like the many other films dealing with whores except that it replaced the customary Japanese patrons with American soldiers.

There was, to be sure, an amount of anti-Americanism implicit in merely showing these relatively common occurrences on the screen and thus calling attention to them, but this was merely incidental. The big point was the exploitation of sex. Toho, however, began to have its doubts about the foreign reception of the film even before it was released and with the most transparent guile decided to allay suspicions by calling it a "Japan-U.S. goodwill" film. As such it was shown to the foreign press, which, unusually sensitive at the time, made a tremendous fuss about it. The foreign colony in Tokyo at once took the matter up, animated in part by a feeling of personal resentment against one of its number, the featured actor, an American who often took the rôle of the

unsavory foreigner and who later, upon being indicted as
a professional confidence man, fled the country.

Taniguchi, the director, was most disturbed by all the uproar, and Toho was even more so when word came that the *Chicago Tribune* was allegedly going to disrupt Toho's export efforts. There were a few other more genuinely anti-U.S. pictures during this period, particularly *Hiroshima* (which in an edited version got itself shown all over America), but *Red-Light Bases* was chosen as the scapegoat while others went unnoticed.

Two of the worst were the work of Hideo Sekigawa. *Mixed-Blood Children* (Konketsuji) completely ignored the official and public indifference to Japanese social conditions, which was at least partially responsible for the fact that there were, it has been estimated, as many as twelve thousand orphans or abandoned children of mixed American-Japanese parentage in the country. Instead, America was blamed and blamed and blamed. *Orgy* (Kyoen) showed the Occupation's brutal "colonization" attempts at Nara, the cradle of Japanese culture. In this film Sekigawa would have had his audience believe that U.S. soldiers made it a rule not only to sleep with Japanese whores by night but to go about by day raping schoolgirls.

While these two films were ignored by the foreign press, the rumpus over *Red-Light Bases* went on and on. Shochiku, which had just climbed on this newest of bandwagons, hastily descended and issued orders that its just-completed *The Thick-Walled Room* (Kabe Atsuki Heya) should not be released. And it was not until three years later, in 1956, that it was seen. At the time, Shiro Kido, head of Shochiku, delivered himself of a number of "reasons" why the film was not being released, among them being the fact that "motion pictures are a vehicle for the expression of emotion and not theory" and that "no matter how agitated the world, film art must remain calm."

Actually *The Thick-Walled Room* was a lot calmer than the others. It was based on published abstracts from the diaries of war criminals and, though its theme that most of those imprisoned were innocent while the real criminals had escaped was debatable, it was still one of the few Japanese motion pictures to bring up the question of responsibility for the war. The main character in the film was a soldier who is ordered by his superior to kill an innocent Indonesian civilian who has done nothing in any way hostile to the Japanese troops quartered in his home. Is this man's deed then a personal crime? Is it his superior's? Or is it Japan's? While the film did not answer these questions, it at least asked them. Later, however, it somewhat seriously compromised its honesty by showing a regional war-crime trial being held with both judge and prosecutor the same person, and implied that this was widespread.

All the same, the film was definitely better than most others in its genre. It was a particular improvement on the many *haha-mono* of the period which showed how mother still loved and waited for her imprisoned boy, no matter how many people he had tortured, and which sought to prove that imprisoning mothers' sons was very immoral since their captivity caused mothers so much anguish. The result was such titles as *Mothers in a Storm* (Arashi no Naka no Haha), *A Mother Calls Tearfully* (Haha wa Sakebinaku), and *Sugamo-Prison Mother* (Sugamo no Haha).

Another casualty to the anti-American scare was Tadashi Imai's 1953 film, *The Tower of Lilies* (Himeyuri no To), which has received a reputation abroad, where it has never been seen, as being the most scurrilous of anti-American projects. If it is "anti" anything, the film is anti-war. It is the story of the girls of the Okinawa Prefectural First Girls High School, often called the Lily School, who just before the pending American invasion are mobilized as special combat nurses. Under the American attack they are all killed, and in memory of their heroism a monument is erected, called the Tower of Lilies. In the film Imai had almost nothing to say about the enemy, and the terrific pounding given the area by the American forces is not implied to have been one of terror against the civilian populace; rather, it is presented as a straight battle between opposing military forces. Still, given Imai's self-avowed political consciousness, one would have expected some suggestion that the terror was in some way the result of Japan's aggressions and that the enemy ships had ample motivation for the horror they caused.

The film was a spectacular success in Japan, particularly with women audiences, since Imai had not spared the sentiment. In addition there was tremendous public nostalgia at seeing the film's detailed treatment of civil-defense activities. Part of the success of the film too was due to its coming on the heels of the boom in U.S. war pictures showing how Japan was defeated. Particularly popular was *The Sands of Iwo Jima*, which on occasion was double billed with the Imai film. The question remains, however—as it does with all of Imai's postwar work—just how leftist-inspired the film

was. Taken by itself, its anti-war sentiments seem genuine;
and if it was created with ulterior political intentions, a number of opportunities for anti-American touches were strangely neglected.

Amid all of this leftist and near-leftist anti-American film-making during the period one might perhaps wonder if there were not at least a few anti-Soviet films. There were, but they were few indeed. Kunio Watanabe's *Repatriation* (Kikoku), released in 1949, was an omnibus of six stories about repatriates from Soviet-occupied territory. It showed how the repatriates were forced to join the Communist Party, showed people dying from previous Soviet mistreatment, and was, in part, a protest against the extremely slow repatriation of Japanese from Russia. In 1952, Yutaka Abe made *I Was a Siberian POW* (Watakushi wa Shiberiya no Horyo Datta), which was based on newspaper accounts of interviewed returnees. It was full of the horrors of Russian prison camps but was thoroughly naive in its whitewashing of the Japanese military.

While the war was being fought over again on the film front, the industry was also concerning itself with several other genres. The Occupation, in its avowed intention of stamping out the period-film, had acted as willing midwife to the gangster film. While this new genre never replaced the period-film, as the Occupation had hoped, it soon developed enough of a following to ensure its continuance, the fans coming from that vast audience which demands action and violence, period or not.

One of the reasons for the popularity of the gang films, which the Occupation all but openly sponsored, was that films with crime subjects had been severely censored before the war. Thus the first of the gang films were a definite novelty, and furthermore, the film companies were not slow to realize that these provided vehicles for those period stars now temporarily out of work. In addition, public interest was quickened by the crime waves which most large cities experienced after the war.

The gang film has grown so fast that today, with the exception of the period-film, it is the largest genre in the Japanese cinema. Toei has built its production foundation upon the pattern of period-film in the Kyoto studios and gang film in the Tokyo studios. Its popularity is such that it very conveniently allows the same actor to alternate between sword in the obi and pistol under the arm.

It should be noted, however, that among all Japanese film

genres the gangster movie has produced the smallest number of worthwhile pictures. Most of them are nothing but cheap imitations of French and American originals. Apart from its poor quality, what distinguishes the Japanese gangster film is its overemphasis on violence and sadism. Such scenes occur in similar films produced in other countries, but usually they are in some way required by the plot. In the Japanese gang films, violence is thrown in, quite irrelevantly and for its own sake, serving no other purpose than inflaming its thrill-seeking audience. Perhaps for this reason, the few fairly decent films which have emerged from this mass of meretricious hackwork are none too representative of the genre.

Senkichi Taniguchi, who had early proved himself a good hand at melodrama, made *Beyond Hate* (Nikushimi no Kanata e) in 1951, about an escaped prisoner who, thinking that his wife has been unfaithful, flees to a remote mountain locality where he is finally tracked down after defending himself with a hunting rifle. In the following year Kimisaburo Yoshimura made *Violence* (Boryoku), which documented Osaka low-life extremely well and showed what could be done with a fairly ordinary crime story. In all, however, this genre, ironically one of the few real influences fostered by the Occupation which still survives, is utterly worthless.

Not so the period-drama, though one should constantly remember that the average period-film is creatively just as moribund as the gangster film and that the sole exceptions fall entirely in the category of the completely off-beat period-drama; such exceptions belong only nominally in the genre. The obvious example is Kurosawa's 1950 film, the now world-famous *Rashomon*, which, though classified as a period-film since it is set in the early Heian period, is in actuality just about as far away from the standard Japanese period-film as one can get. It was a highly adventurous undertaking, extremely advanced for its audience, and quite experimental in its technique. Those in the West who instantly concluded that all Japanese films were "like *Rashomon*" were, as time richly proved, completely mistaken.

Based on elements taken from two stories by Ryunosuke Akutagawa, one of the greatest names in modern Japanese literature, this film marked the first attempt to adapt his works to the screen. A samurai, his bride, and a bandit meet in the thick wood. The girl is violated, the lord killed, and the act is witnessed by a woodcutter. The film's plot consists of separate versions of this story, each from the viewpoint of the person telling it. In one version the girl is raped

against her will; in another she lures the bandit and makes
him kill her husband; and in one memorable scene the ghost
of the husband is called forth to speak through the lips of a
seer. The audience is left with the feeling of the essential
relativity of truth.

Many Japanese who saw the film were intensely confused
by this relativism and insisted: "There must be a correct
solution; now, just who *was* telling the truth?" So, for those
who had missed the entire point of what Kurosawa was trying to show, a number of Japanese theaters provided *benshi*-
like explanations about the film. The critics, somewhat less
confused, noted its "silent-film style direction" and "its
wonderful balance of realism and impressionism," though
some, like Tadashi Iijima, thought the film failed because of
its "insufficient plan for visualizing the style of the [original]
stories. Although we are impressed by its artistic power, it
remains a most valuable failure." Tatsuhiko Shigeno, a critic
for *Kinema Jumpo*, objected to the over-noble sentiments
and the attempts at poetic speech and big words continually
used by lower-class people, who really would not have used
them. He also thought that the script was too complicated,
that the direction was monotonous, being on the same key
throughout, that there was too much cursing, and that there
was a tendency to overact.

Despite popular and critical misinterpretation in Japan,
and contrary to a curious myth which has apparently spon-
taneously sprung up in the West, *Rashomon* was from the
very first a financial success in Japan. It was given a Holly-
wood-style première at what was then the best theater in
Japan, the Imperial Theater in Tokyo and, despite its heavily
intellectual orientation, earned large box-office receipts all
over the country. Long before it won the 1951 Venice Festival prize it had won back its production costs; theater managers considered it the eighth ranking commercial hit of
1950 and Daiei's annual report showed that of the fifty-two
pictures distributed by the company that year it was the
fourth largest grosser. The other first three were all Kazuo
Hasegawa vehicles.

The story prevalent, particularly in America, that *Rashomon* was unappreciated in Japan is simply not true, though
its receiving the Venice top prize gave it an even higher
reputation, besides giving the entire period-drama genre a
terrific artistic boost. Kurosawa himself has said: "Receiving
the prize was entirely unexpected....Of course, there's nothing like happiness, so I'm happy, but if I'd made something

reflecting more of present-day Japan, such a film as *Bicycle Thieves*, and then received a prize, there would be more meaning to it and I'd probably be happier."

Before *Rashomon*, the postwar period had produced almost no other exceptional period-films. Somewhat interesting was Kinoshita's 1949 version of Japan's favorite summertime chiller, *The Yotsuya Ghost Story* (Yotsuya Kaidan), which, this time. did not include any ghost at all, being much more concerned with the human elements than with the mysterious or the horrifying. Perhaps the only other was Yoshimura's *Ishimatsu of the Forest* (Mori no Ishimatsu), another remake and the director's first period-film. He was mainly interested in presenting the traditional period-story as present-day commentary in disguise. This he brilliantly succeeded in doing. Moreover, the whole cult of the classic hero came in for attack when Yoshimura satirically showed that Ishimatsu owed his heroic reputation entirely to good public relations.

After *Rashomon*, the atypical period-film became more and more frequent. A few were failures, like Keigo Kimura's *Beauty and the Bandits* (Bijo to Tozoku), which took what inspiration it had directly from Kurosawa but was really just another sex vehicle for Machiko Kyo as the lady chieftain of a band of robbers. Yoshimura's *A Tale of Genji* (Genji Monogatari) was much more successful and was praised for its delineation of characters all well-known to the audience and for its careful re-creation of period. It became Japan's top-grossing picture up to that time thanks largely to Daiei's publicity (the film had been made to commemorate the company's tenth anniversary) and the fact that teachers took students by the busload to give their charges an educational, historical experience.

Daiei, emboldened by success, kept one eye on the money-making formula period-piece and the other on the new international market, and in 1952 let Teinosuke Kinugasa make *Dedication of the Great Buddha* (Daibutsu Kaigen), a film which did no credit to its director, "the prewar founder of the spectacular period-drama," who was to. have somewhat better luck in the following year's *Gate of Hell*.

In the same year Satsuo Yamamoto made *Storm Clouds over Hakone* (Hakone Fuun Roku), a period-film about a peasant revolt in the region near Mount Fuji, occasioned by high officials' depriving the farmers of their water rights. It was very much in the style of the tendency period-films of the late 1920's, though now the message could be driven home with much more force.

The year 1953 saw the release of Akira Kurosawa's period-film parody, *The Men Who Tread on the Tiger's Tail*, which had been completed just as the war was ending but not previously released. It showed that even during the war Kurosawa had affirmed his humanistic values, though the Occupation had prohibited release because the film apparently stressed the feudal code in the relationship between Yoshitsune and his retainer Benkei. Of course, on the suface it *was* feudalistic, because Kurosawa had borrowed his plot from the Kabuki drama *Kanjincho,* but his whole approach was to show the basic equality of all human emotions irrespective of social position. The comedian Enoken was particularly good as the embodiment of the spirit of the common man and of his right to human dignity.

Another atypical period-film was Kenji Mizoguchi's *The Life of a Woman by Saikaku* (Saikaku Ichidai Onna), released in 1952, known abroad as *The Life of O-Haru,* and winner of the Venice International Prize for that year. It told the story of the beautiful daughter of a wealthy merchant who becomes a palace wife, and then shows her fall to concubine, cook, bath-woman, and finally cheap harlot. There was a criticism of feudal society from the woman's viewpoint and an exceptionally good performance from Kinuyo Tanaka.

A year later Mizoguchi followed this with the deservedly much praised *Ugetsu Monogatari,* one of the director's best films and one of the most perfect movies in the history of Japanese cinema. Based on a story by Akinari Ueda, the picture tells a timeless legend about a potter, caught in the civil wars, who, having gone to the city to sell his wares, falls in love with a beautiful and mysterious girl only eventually to discover that she is the ghost of a princess who, chaste during her life, must now live on, seducing and destroying. Freed at last, the potter returns home and finds his wife awaiting him, but when he awakes in the morning he discovers that she has been dead for some time, that she too was a ghost.

Impossible though it is to give anything of the flavor of the film in a resumé, one may note that in it Mizoguchi also saw a parallel to postwar Japan and that in a way the film represents his commentary on postwar life. As a period-film it was most unusual, fitting into no category at all, self-sufficient, nearly allegorical, and a film experience both beautiful and disturbing.

While truly extraordinary films like *Ugetsu Monogatari*

back-
ground

were being made, the period-film genre as such was having the best time of its postwar life and, while creatively moribund, in box-office terms it was both alive and kicking. Talents such as those of Kurosawa, Mizoguchi, and Yoshimura, by breaking down the sharp division between the period-film and the film about contemporary life, could ignore the old formulas and escape from the clichés, but within the rigid limitations of the standard period-film there was no room for art at all; it could merely repeat endlessly what it had already shown, and after the Occupation, there was always a loud, enthusiastic, money-paying, and usually juvenile audience clamoring for more.

After 1951 the period-film turned spectacular, and pictures like Hiroshi Inagaki's *Kojiro Sasaki* (Sasaki Kojiro), devoted to the life of Musashi Miyamoto's chief rival, and Daisuke Ito's *Five Men from Edo* (O-Edo Go-nin Otoko) proved tremendous box-office successes, both pointing to the fact that ready cash was to be had in the traditional period-drama. Some maintain that the financial success of *Rashomon* was due almost entirely to people's thinking that it was a standard period-film.

With the audience willing to go to almost any period-film, the makers did not have to worry too much about whether the product was any good or not. There were, however, a few changes in the old patterns. Toei created a switch by orienting the period-film toward child audiences and making the heroes boys in such films as *Whistling Boy* (Fuefuki Doji). This was in part due to the extraordinary popularity of Kinnosuke Nakamura and Chiyonosuke Azuma, both very young and both appealing to the younger teenage audiences. One of the reasons for their popularity was that they were almost alone in the field; the other period-stars, Kazuo Hasegawa, Chiezo Kataoka, Utaemon Ichikawa, and the like, were all in their fifties or sixties and had become famous during the silent era.

One of the few other changes was the development of the "series picture," somewhat like the old-time serial except that each chapter was about an hour in length. Thus such a series usually had the same central characters in the manner of Andy Hardy or Tarzan or Ma and Pa Kettle.

The more forward-looking of the company heads saw that the industry was in something of a dilemma simply because it suffered from an embarrassment of riches. The home market was clamoring for more period-drama, and the international market was apparently willing to create an opening

for the exceptionally good films. The Japanese attitude toward this open-armed foreign market was not, however, to
be fortunately resolved.

After half a decade of near-disastrous exporting policies
which came perilously near ruining Japan's foreign market,
the various companies finally put their heads together and,
late in 1957, came up with UniJapan Film, an "Association
for the Diffusion of Japanese Films Abroad, Incorporated."
This government-supported organization hoped to be able to
contribute "to the expanding of international friendships and
the exchange of cultures with far-off countries by means of
the color and sound of motion pictures." This was later,
however. As of 1953, the industry was facing a double demand, that of the home audience and that of interested foreigners. There was much turmoil and not a little discussion.
One of the few involved who knew what was going on was
Nagata of Daiei, who, clearly seeing the possibilities of both
markets, set out to do something about them.

For some time Daiei had been experimenting with Japanese-made color film but found it severely lacking in quality.
Because of this, Nagata turned to Eastmancolor and, although
this film was still in a somewhat experimental stage, sent two
of his people to America to make tests. This move was
inspired both by his seeing that color was the coming thing
and by his announced desire to break even further into the
international market.

His investigations amply paid off. In 1953, *Gate of Hell*
was released and proved the answer to his every prayer. This
picture was ordinary enough for the home market and was
exotic enough for the foreign market. What made it important was its incorporation of the most beautiful color
photography ever to grace the screen. Based on a Kan Kikuchi story about palace intrigue and lost love, it was directed
by Kinugasa, starred Hasegawa, and was photographed by
Kohei Sugiyama, the triumvirate that had been together since
their early Shochiku days and had created some of Japan's
most spectacular period-films.

Daiei, now definitely on top, set what was shortly to become a pattern, representing as it did the perfect compromise
between the exoticism which it was believed the West hun-
gered after and the mediocrity which it was thought was all
that Japan would happily consume. The industry was elated.
The days of big business were finally here.

11 soft focus: 1954-59. THOUGH THE INTERnational reception of *Rashomon* was a surprise to the industry, it was a welcome one since, even before the war, the Japanese had been trying to send their pictures abroad. The films they had managed to send, *Crossroads* and *Wife! Be Like a Rose!* among them, had been few and far between. In 1937 they sent *Moon over the Ruined Castle* (Kojo no Tsuki) to Venice, but lost to Duvivier's *Carnet de Bal.* Undiscouraged, they sent *Five Scouts* the following year and had the pleasure of seeing it win the Popular Culture Award, making it the first Japanese film to win a foreign prize.

The end of the war soon brought a movement to establish Japan as a "leading cultural country," and during the Occupation the Japanese press was full of discussions as to how Japan could raise its prestige abroad. Those in the film industry naturally turned to motion pictures as one of Japan's major culture vehicles, and it was obvious that film festivals were the perfect medium. The only question was how. Japan had not been invited to participate, and even if it were, what would it send?

The constant refrain among Japanese producers, directors, and critics was that the main purpose of showing Japanese films abroad was to introduce Japanese customs and culture to the world. Seldom indeed did these discussions once suggest that a film should be shown abroad because it was a work of art or because it might entertain someone. Rather, the cinema was to be Japan's cultural emissary, and the industry stuck to this concept with the evangelistic zeal of a

true missionary. The new Japanese way of life was to be the
salvation of the world. This theme was inescapable; hence the suspicion of the period-film, within the industry, since it did not show modern Japan, and the near hysteria when it was discovered that the period-films were successful abroad.

On the other hand, there was the constant suggestion, put forward individually, in various places and at various times, that films about contemporary life would never succeed abroad "because foreigners will think it funny when Japanese in Western clothes sit on *tatami*. It won't look civilized to them." Nagamasa Kawakita, head of Towa, the largest film-import company of Japan, suggested early in 1950 that the first exported Japanese films should be travelogues and that subsequent non-travelogue features should insist upon an amount of scenery. Another suggestion, often heard, was that the best Japanese films to send abroad to a certain country would be those which most closely resembled the recent, successful films of that country.

In line with these suggestions, in 1950 the small Toyoko Company made Victor Hugo's *Les Misérables* (Re Mizeraburu) in two feature-length parts, the first directed by Daisuke Ito, the second by Masahiro Makino. The novel was moved to Meiji-period Japan with Sessue Hayakawa in the Jean Valjean rôle. It constituted Japan's first attempt to crash the postwar foreign market and was markedly unsuccessful. No foreign contracts were signed and no foreign festivals entered.

In the meantime Nagata of Daiei, the first member of the industry to leave Japan since the end of the war, had gone abroad to look things over in the United States. He returned with Japan-distribution contracts for Samuel Goldwyn and Walt Disney productions and, once home, decided that Japan must enter international festivals as soon as possible, one of his main incentives coming while in the United States, where someone asked him: "Are movies made in Japan too?"

When an invitation came from France for Japan to send one feature to the 1951 Cannes Festival, everyone was delighted. The Motion Picture Association of Japan met and decided to send Imai's *Until the Day We Meet Again*, which had won the *Kinema Jumpo* "Best One" Award of the previous year. Then, to everyone's consternation, it was discovered that Toho was in such financial difficulties that it could not raise the money to have a print prepared with French subtitles. Also, Yoshinobu Ikeda, head of the Motion Picture Association, had objections, saying that the story of the Imai film very much resembled that of a certain Romain Rolland novel. Others thought that this was fine, that it would make the film all the more likely to win a prize because the French would not be slow to praise such skilled imitation. Ikeda won, however, when he pointed out that the resemblance might cause copyright complications. So a short subject was sent to Cannes. Very shortly afterwards the once-long-hoped-for occurred again. Venice sent an invitation to Japan. Again consternation in the Japanese industry; again the Imai film; and again an embarrassing lack of funds in the Toho coffers. In the meantime, at the urging of the Venice sponsors, Giulliana Stramigioli, head of the Italifilm branch in Japan, had viewed a number of possible Japanese entries and taken a definite liking to one Daiei film, because of its "strangeness." The film was *Rashomon*.

Some time before, Nagata had more or less accidentally signed a one-year distribution and production contract with Kurosawa and his associates from Toho who had left their mother company to form the independent Motion Picture Art Association. A businessman's businessman, Nagata was nevertheless always overwhelmed by genuine artists, being fascinated by both them and their work. Despite his reputation as a maker of the most uninteresting and most financially successful of pot-boilers, Nagata had always liked to use his commercial talents to help men of genius—hence his long association with Mizoguchi and his continually going out of his way to give that director everything he needed to make good pictures.

Yet when Kurosawa had wanted to make *Rashomon*, Nagata had objected, holding that it was just too off-beat. The Toyoko Company had felt the same two years earlier, when it canceled a contract with Kurosawa to make the same film just as shooting was about to begin. Kurosawa campaigned heavily, and finally Nagata agreed to go along, but with many objections since it was his money that Kurosawa was using. When Miss Stramigioli said that she thought the finished film ought to go to Venice, however, Nagata thought he could not possibly agree. He was afraid of failure and the consequent humiliation, but worst of all was the fact that the film had not been made "especially for export." This was the era, however, when Westerners' opinions were listened to most carefully, and so Nagata reluctantly took the plunge, and was forced into his present greatness.

To everyone's intense surprise *Rashomon* won. It was a stroke of real luck—and luck was something which both Na-

gata and Daiei needed and could now take advantage of.
Not owning any of its own theaters, Daiei had concentrated
on getting contracts with independent exhibitors by offering
favorable rental rates and a steady supply of pictures under
the slogan "Quick but Skillful." Though it has lost the contracts of such big period-stars as Bando, Kataoka, and Ichikawa, it had managed to sign up Kazuo Hasegawa and, upon
his return from long exile abroad, Sessue Hayakawa. It was
also beginning to cash in on the immediate success of the
former dancer Machiko Kyo, whose career was launched
with a series of sex films. These pictures exploiting Kyo
were accompanied by an extensive advertising campaign,
which made her the first Japanese actress to have public attention drawn to her alleged sex appeal. Before Machiko
Kyo appeared, the more domestic aspects of female stars
had been stressed.

Now that Nagata saw foreign gates opening wide in invitation, he at once began making pictures for what he thought
was the international market. In 1952 he imported one Paul
Sloan, a one-time director of Hollywood Westerns, and put
him in charge of *Until Forever* (Itsu Itsu made mo), which
had the English title of *Forever My Love*. It starred two
relative unknowns, Chris Drake and Mitsuko Kimura, who
had been a *Life* cover-girl. The shooting schedule called for
two months, but because of the usual delays and disputes
which seem to plague production when Japanese film people
work with foreigners, half a year was required. The story
was about a GI who falls in love with a Japanese girl whose
family wants her to marry a rich Japanese boy. The soldier
is sent to Korea, gets wounded, and is returned to Japan just
in time for an earthquake to kill the girl. The climactic earthquake scenes were laughed off the screen in Japan, and the
picture never did get abroad, an RKO distribution contract
coming to nothing.

Undaunted, Daiei announced a new "coproduction,"
which was issued under the title *Two Persons' Eyes* (Futari
no Hitomi), starring Hibari Misora and Margaret O'Brien.
Little Margaret comes to Japan to visit her father and makes
friends with a Japanese girl who is the leader of an all-child
orchestra which plays to collect money for the building of
an orphanage. Equally a failure was Tomotaka Tasaka's *I'll
Not Forget the Song of Nagasaki* (Nagasaki no Uta wa
Wasureji), which was about an American buyer who visits
a Japanese family to return a music manuscript found on a
wartime battlefield and becomes interested in the sufferings

of atom-bombed Nagasaki. Director Tasaka was still too sick from his own atom-bomb wounds to make much of a film out of the story.

In the meantime Japan had gone on winning unexpected prizes at festivals. Kohei Sugiyama had won the photography prize at Cannes in 1952 for his work in Yoshimura's *A Tale of Genji,* and Mizoguchi's *Ugetsu Monogatari* had won Venice's Silver Lion a year later. Looking at his failures with one eye, his successes with the other, Nagata sent *Gate of Hell* to Cannes, where it won the 1954 Grand Prize and a year later received an American Academy Award.

The victory of *Rashomon* had been cause for truly national jubilation. Some critics even compared the film festivals to the Olympic Games and felt that Japan must enter with no other idea than to win for the glory of the motherland. Each failure to win a festival prize was regarded as a national disaster. Director and producing company issued public apologies, and when the Japanese delegates got back home, they filled the popular and trade press with articles on "What I Learned at Cannes [About How to Produce Prizewinners]." The Japanese critics were completely confounded by the foreign success of *Gate of Hell,* however, since it had made no one's "best ten" list in 1953, and their attitude was that of the insulted and injured, since these foreigners seemed to suggest that the Japanese critics did not know their business. Many were the articles suggesting this and claiming that Japan had suffered a national insult. One critic pointed out that "in the same way, foreigners—forever souvenir-hunting —always pick Japanese-style paintings on silk rather than our oils on canvas." Daiei, however, was not complaining—not in the slightest.

After this, Daiei launched a regular program of color-film productions and thus became the first Japanese company to go in for color on more than an experimental basis. Of course, the technically successful *Gate of Hell* had not been Japan's first color film. There had been various prewar experiments and directly after the war a few scenes of the 1946 film *Eleven Girl Students* (Juichi-nin no Jogakusei) were shot in the integral tripack dye coupler reversal Japanese process called Fujicolor In 1951, Shochiku, noting the box-office success of foreign color pictures in Japan, used Fujicolor for Kinoshita's *Carmen Comes Home* in celebration of its thirtieth anniversary as a corporation.

Since the Fujicolor process was by no means perfect, they took separate black-and-white footage. Actually, only

two color prints were turned out for initial release because
everything was hand processed and this took time, about one month per print as against the few hours required by foreign color processes. In addition, the cost was the equivalent of forty cents a foot against the then current cost of five cents a foot for black and white. Yet, despite all the technical defects—which extended to a poor reproduction of reds, an overall flatness of all colors, and an inability to shoot in artificial light—the process was regarded as a success, as indeed it had to be if Japan was to keep up with world film technology.

The second Fujicolor full-length feature, again produced by Shochiku, was Noboru Nakamura's *Natsuko's Adventures* (Natsuko no Boken), made in 1953. Though it revealed a much improved color process, the desire not to show Fuji-color in a bad light by straining its capabilities severely limited the movie. In the same year Sakuracolor, made by Fuji's only domestic competitor, revealed equally poor quality in Toei's *The Sun* (Nichirin). Noting his competitors' fail-ures, it was at this point that Nagata had decided that the Japanese color processes simply were not good enough and had dispatched his emissaries to America.

Despite its technical failures, *Carmen Comes Home* made money and helped Shochiku reassert itself as leader in the industry. The company had been in a bad way for some time, and the only thing which saved it was that Toho, its chief rival, was having even more trouble. One of the reasons for Shochiku's difficulties was that its staff was too long accus-tomed to making the old-style "Ofuna flavor" films (so called because of the distinctive quality of the women's films made in Shochiku's Ofuna studios) to satisfy modern film-audiences. Even during the war Shochiku had not been able to modernize itself to the extent of making good govern-ment-policy films, and after the war it found itself still out of step. The result was that the 1949–50 period was one of depression for Shochiku, with many severe financial losses. Had it not been for Toho's endless labor troubles during this period, Shochiku would have perhaps had even a worse time of it. It had its eyes partially opened in 1950 when Kimisabu-ro Yoshimura and Kaneto Shindo got mad and left to form their own independent company because Shochiku manage-ment so vehemently opposed the kind of social-criticism films they wanted to make. Things finally got so bad that even Ozu, the last of the great prewar Ofuna directors, decided to move elsewhere. Now thoroughly alarmed, Shochiku wooed him back, giving both him and Kinoshita—their only two remaining important talents—more freedom.

Financially, Shochiku's recovery came through its successful melodramas and gang movies. It also modernized its old Ofuna-flavored tear-jerkers, and by 1951 had developed its very profitable teen-age genre. Too, it was considerably helped by the return of Shiro Kido, Matsujiro Shirai, and others following their pardon after having been exiled from the film industry by the Occupation. Kido hit precisely the brave-new-world note Shochiku was striving for when he was able to say: "The greatest needs of the public were still laughter and tears, as we had always given them, but what was required was an updating of methods that cause the public to laugh and cry." This *a posteriori* wisdom was what the company had come to expect from Kido, and its stockholders, each clutching a fat dividend, the first in a long time, were completely appeased.

Toho, in the meantime, had been having worse difficulties. After four years of internal unrest it was almost bankrupt and in 1948 could make only four features. Then, in 1950, as a consequence of its failure to pay admission taxes, converting the money to meet its payrolls, the Tokyo Metropolitan Tax Office stepped in and issued an order putting up for sale Toho's four biggest and best Tokyo theaters. The once-proud Toho went around literally begging for money and was saved only by making a half-payment within the week and promising to pay the rest soon.

As if this were not enough, Toho's four biggest directors —Kurosawa, Kajiro Yamamoto, Naruse, and Taniguchi—had earlier decided to leave and form their own independent company. And then, only a month after its tax troubles, Toho had yet another strike. This time the call was "Down with the rationalization program! Eliminate amateur management!" The strike failed, but only because the union was now as weak as the management.

The day was saved by the reappearance of Iwao Mori, formerly exiled from the industry by scap, and he soon had the company back on its financial feet. In the meantime, Ichizo Kobayashi, the organizer of Toho, was still having grandiose dreams and in 1951 came up with the idea of a "Greater Toho Bloc," which, he thought, would certainly give him major control of the industry. He planned to line up with Shintoho and Toei to create the most powerful motion picture company in Japan's history, and if the two smaller companies had not had the foresight to see that they

would lose everything by placing themselves in the hands of
Toho, Kobayashi's plans might well have come to something.
As it was, he instead organized the Takarazuka Motion
Picture Company, which was designed to take advantage of
the many popular actresses then under contract to his Takarazuka girl-operetta troupes, the films being used to fill out
the cheaper parts of the overall Toho program. A bit later,
in 1952, he bought out the facilities of the independent company Tonichi and turned it into the Tokyo Motion Picture
Company.

Kobayashi was not about to give up his monopolistic hopes,
however, and began to talk about a Toho "five year plan,"
the main point of which was to raise the number of Toho-
owned theaters to an even hundred through a policy of
building first-class theaters in every possible major location,
which would then make the Toho chain the largest in the
country. The plan also included a blueprint budget of a half-
million dollars for a complete modernization of production
facilities. After all of this, Kobayashi said, they would turn
to the problem of increasing the quality of Toho's pictures.

Toho's bastard child, Shintoho, was none too healthy, and
as the parent prospered, the offspring sickened. Although
from the very beginning Shintoho lacked the good writers
and directors it needed, the popularity of the old and established stars who had come from Toho sustained it for a
time. By the beginning of 1951 the company was in such
financial difficulties that it had to close down its studios. A
month later the gates were open again but the old Shintoho
independent spirit and most of its stars were gone. The new
policy said to make them cheap and fast, and they did, turning out complete features in less than fourteen days each. In
addition, the management got its hands on a number of prewar Nikkatsu films, which it released to fill the holes in its
own schedule.

Even so, the company was continually running out of
money and having to halt production. Finally a management
committee from Shintoho asked the president of the Asahi
Breweries to help them out, and he, completely out of his
field, called in his good friend Kyusaku Hori, head of Nikkatsu, which was now only a chain of theaters. Toho instantly saw Shintoho slipping from its grip and brought court
action to have the contracts abolished under which Toho
rented studio facilities to Shintoho at a low cost. Next, the
latter company's stockholders revolted. They felt that Hori
might try to take over the company, and in their haste they

elected Munehide Tanabe chairman of the board. A few
months later Tanabe had total control of Shintoho, reaffirming the Toho ties. By an odd coincidence, Tanabe also turned out to be the younger brother of Ichizo Kobayashi, head of Toho.

Under Tanabe, Shintoho was able to continue on its somewhat feeble way into the postwar world. This would never have been possible, however, had it not been for an increased demand for domestic films, which even the three big wartime companies could not fill. Here too many smaller independent companies organized to cash in on the picture demand.

Between 1947 and 1949 about thirty-five companies had appeared—many never to make a picture. Kazuo Hasegawa, Hiroshi Shimizu, Kimisaburo Yoshimura, and Masahiro Makino all created their own, and any number of top Toho talents, fatigued and angered by the endless bickerings between labor and management, withdrew to form their own organizations. Among the more interesting of these was the Motion Picture Art Association, formed by the producer Sojiro Motoki and the directors Kurosawa, Taniguchi, and Kajiro Yamamoto, and later joined by Naruse. The company managed to stay alive only four years because the recovered Toho offered its old talent such tempting terms. Yet during its lifetime the company produced such excellent films as *The Silent Duel, Stray Dog,* and *Rashomon.* Another independent responsible for some exceptional films was Studio Eight Productions—they used the English name—formed by Heinosuke Gosho, Mitsuo Miura, Shiro Toyoda, and others. It lasted until 1954 and produced *Where Chimneys Are Seen.*

After 1950 there was another eruption of independent companies, but these were much more interested in politics than in ready cash. One of the reasons for the appearance of these small concerns was that the Toho union was no longer under left-wing domination and many leftist workers quit the company as the tide turned against them. Another was the 1950 SCAP purge of Communists from all of the mass-communication fields, with the result that thirteen persons from Toho, sixty-six from Shochiku, and thirty from Daei, plus many in the newsreel and short-subject fields, found themselves jobless. Not knowing what else to do, they formed independent companies. Critic and producer Akira Iwasaki long affiliated with leftist movements, wrote that, as a consequence of the Hollywood Red purge, the Truman government "began to try the same thing in its colonies....First it tried to conduct a Red purge of French studios, but because the French film people stood together, the Americans were unsuccessful. Next, they thought, let's try Japan, that should be good. And so two thousand Japanese police in steel helmets, American soldiers with automatic weapons, and the commander of the First Cavalry in an airplane [attacked]. It wasn't too skillful but it was a success....From this grew the need for an independent movement in Japanese films." Elsewhere Iwasaki goes on to claim that the use of troops in the big 1948 Toho strike was personally ordered by Truman to show his "tough policies" in an election year.

Iwasaki himself organized one of these leftist independents, Shinsei Motion Picture Productions, for the specific purpose, as stated in the prospectus, of producing "democratic pictures with a left-wing flavor." He was joined by directors Tadashi Imai, Teinosuke Kinugasa, Fumio Kamei, and Satsuo Yamamoto, as well as the actress Isuzu Yamada, but had trouble getting finances because of the company's political orientation. Eventually he managed to produce Yamamoto's *Street of Violence*, the commercial success of which was the main impetus for the subsequent creation of many other left-wing "independent" groups.

Soon the Hokusei Motion Picture Company, the importer of Soviet films in Japan, began to distribute the work of these small production units, its first such film being Shinsei's second feature, Imai's *And Yet We Live*. Production costs for this film were raised by selling stock for fifteen cents a share at left-wing meetings, and its publicity was full of widows and poor workers who had sunk their savings into this stock because of their faith in "democratic films." Though Hokusei began big and hoped to become one of the major film distributors of Japan, by 1953 their overemphasis on left-wing subjects had cost them their audience, and the popularity of double bills had forced them into becoming suppliers of the relatively unprofitable lower half. Later Hokusei reorganized on a smaller scale as the Dokuritsu—meaning Independent—Motion Picture Company, and still later, in the fall of 1957, again reorganized, this time as a "new film studio," backed by its former president and its former board chairman and calling itself the Daito Motion Picture Company.

One of the reasons why Hokusei had so much difficulty and eventually failed in its attempts at being a major distributor was that though there was now room for another major company, a rival of much greater strength for this position had now appeared. This was Toei, an abbreviation for Tokyo Motion Picture Distribution Company, which had been formed out of the small Toyoko and Oizumi production companies. Together they represented all that was left of the studio facilities of Shochiku's once powerful prewar satellite, Shinko. The new Toei at once took the place that would have been Shinko's had it still been around —manufacturer of the cheapest films in Japan.

At the head of Toei was Hiroshi Okawa, who had come into films through the Toyoko Railway Company, from where the company's money had originally come. He was a big-businessman with heavy stakes in railway and truck transportation, rubber companies, and baseball teams, in short, just the kind of man to make the new company a success. Gradually Toei collected many of the people who had been with the old Shinko period-film studios and added such costume stars as Chiezo Kataoka and Utaemon Ichikawa, giving them big places on the board of directors. One of old-timer Shozo Makino's sons was named head of production.

Toei had its difficulties, among them a throttling contract with Toho, which insisted upon Toei's films forming the lower half of a double bill, but after Okawa had gotten rid of that, the specter of bankruptcy disappeared and Toei's stock rose in one year from four to twenty-five cents the share. Completely oriented toward the conventional period-film, Toei soon began making money hand over fist by taking full advantage of the double bill. This institution had been well established before the war, and now that distribution companies and theaters, despite the internal difficulties within the various producing companies, had more to offer their customers, it was again being used to stimulate the market artificially.

The main impetus for double bills came from the theater owners themselves; fearing saturation in the number of theaters, they felt they had to give the audience more for its money. There were obviously four ways in which films for double-features could be obtained. One was revivals, but you can only revive a picture a certain number of times before people tire of it. Another was mixing domestic and foreign pictures, though this tended to run into audience opposition since each category has its own fans, those liking foreign films being much the smaller. Yet another way was to run programs with films from two or more distribution sources. This method also tended to break down the "exclusive contract" system which has been in force for many years in

Japan, whereby an exhibitor usually relies on one and only one distributor for his annual supply of films. Finally, one could perhaps find a company ready to step-up production so that it could turn out two features weekly instead of one.

By the middle of 1952 all five major companies were making one feature a week and were growing optimistic about the possibility of being able to make two. Shochiku hit upon the idea of turning out two films a week by making one of them much shorter than the usual feature and was soon monthly grinding out four- to six-reel "sister pictures," or SP as they are still called in Japan. These had the double advantage of providing a training ground for new actors and directors and at the same time giving Shochiku complete control of a large number of two-bill programs. Toho countered at once with BP, or "brother pictures," but the triumph, and the novelty, was momentarily Shochiku's and Toho soon had to drop out.

Seeing what was happening, Toei's Okawa did some fast figuring and then marched into the double-feature field with a plan for Toei to furnish both halves of the double bill to theaters throughout the entire year; thus theater owners could look to one source alone for all their pictures. This was block booking with a vengeance: 104 pictures in each block to be booked completely unseen by the theater manager. So that his company could handle the increased production, Okawa demanded an increase in action pictures, which are easy to photograph, and also pushed the production of "series" films in installments, each running four or five reels. This latter move allowed for every kind of economy since sets, costumes, and actors remained the same.

By 1953 hardly a theater in Japan was not running double-features, but while some producing companies were rubbing their hands with glee, others, like Daiei and Toho, were regarding the entire trend with suspicion and despair. The reason was that neither could adjust to double-feature demands. Daiei was in the midst of a "big picture" production campaign and had fixed its gaze steadily if unrealistically on the foreign market. It was most loath to lower its aim to the domestic field and the double bill. Toho simply was not yet in shape to compete, as it had discovered disastrously when it tried its "brother picture" production program. So the laurels went to the new Toei, which by 1954 was able to complete a production program allowing it to release one new double bill every week, a feat requiring 104 pictures a year.

The institution of the double-feature in Japan was actually
a sign of prosperity, unlike the scourge of double bills in America during the 1930's and the late 1940's when Hollywood was losing money by the fistful. Nor was this the only sign of prosperity. By the end of 1953 every studio had bought lots of new equipment of every kind and technical quality was up. Two dozen new Mitchell cameras had been bought and the companies were able to retire their oldest cameras: spring-wound newsreel Eyemos or even older adapted silent cameras, some made as early as 1918. Foreign exchange having become available for import purchases by "non-essential" industries, everyone could now more or less buy freely, if they had the money.

Most of the companies had money enough to invest in this much-needed new equipment. For one thing, taxes were lower. The Occupation-imposed admission tax of 150 percent had been reduced to a hundred percent in 1950. This saving should have gone to the public, but instead the industry for the most part kept its admission price at the same scale and merely pocketed the tax saving to meet increased costs. Later, when the tax was reduced to a fifty percent maximum and as low as ten percent for the cheapest admissions, the companies found themselves embarrassed with even further riches.

The economic recovery of Japan had been greatly accelerated by the Korean War. Coming in 1950, at a time when the country needed more money and needed it fast, it occasioned a financial boom which materially aided the Japanese in realizing the long-hoped-for, bright, new, postwar era. Among its results was a mushrooming of amusements and entertainments. The public took to pin-ball with an enthusiasm which still persists, the hot-spring resorts became crowded for the first time since the end of the Pacific War, coffee shops opened by the thousands, and the race tracks were filled daily with those who wanted to become richer even faster.

The films too profited. In October, 1945, there were only 845 theaters in operation in the entire country. By January 1957, there were over six thousand, and building continued at the rate of two new theaters opening somewhere in Japan every day. Likewise, box-office receipts were growing. In 1951, foreign pictures grossed $12,150,000; Japanese pictures, $19,620,000. By 1953 the figures were $24,210,000 and $39,020,000, respectively. With the doubling of the market in two years, and the ultra-rapid emergence of the fifth major power, Toei, it was obvious that there might be room for a sixth major producing company.

This was precisely what Nikkatsu thought. Having re-treated from the production scene a dozen years earlier, all but forced out of business by the wartime formation of Daiei, it continued as a theater-holding company after the war, mak-ing its money by showing American films. Kyusaku Hori, head of Nikkatsu, had noticed the sharp rise in business done by Japanese films after 1951 and decided that if Japanese pictures could provide greater profit to the exhibitors than foreign films, Nikkatsu could make still more money by resuming production itself.

The profits from exhibition allowed Hori to build the big Nikkatsu International Building not only to house Nikkatsu's home offices but also to provide "class" rental office space, luxury shops, and for the first time a modern hotel to rival the older and more famous Imperial. Hori was just as proud of his new building, located right in the center of downtown Tokyo, as he was of his subsequent production activities, saying: "I'm not a movie man. I'm a man of the world of high finance. Films are a minor business, something to be entrusted to a Nagata or a Kido."

Originally, Nikkatsu had wanted to tie up with Shintoho, but when this plan fell through due to the objections of the Shintoho stockholders, Nikkatsu decided to resume produc-tion by itself. It managed to snare a number of Shintoho technicians who, feeling that their former company was on the rocks, were quick to leave it, and erected brand-new studios along the Tamagawa River, very near their prewar studios, which were now occupied by Daiei. With eight stages, six new Mitchell cameras, and Western Electric re-cording equipment, Nikkatsu was at last back in the produc-tion business.

The other five production companies were most unhappy at this move. Accustomed to splitting the profitable film market five ways, they were all agreed that a six-way split would result in no one's having enough. By the early part of 1954 they had already decided what steps to take against the resuscitated Nikkatsu. They composed the "five-company agreement against Nikkatsu," which corresponded exactly with the prewar "six-company agreement against Toho" and to the silent era "four-company agreement against Makino." In each case, these ferociously unfair boycotts succeeded in holding off the new companies for a while, but in the end the newcomers triumphed, at which point they were directly welcomed into the fold, slapped on the back, and made one of the tribe.

In the case of Nikkatsu, the other five took more than usual care of their personnel, attempting to discourage desertion by explicitly forbidding people under contract to one company to hire themselves to another, a practice which had heretofore been not uncommon. Naturally, one of the first results was that Nikkatsu, forced into theft, began to steal stars left and right. Interestingly enough, when it came to plugging the loopholes in the action against Nikkatsu, it was Toho, the victim of the prewar boycott, which formulated most of the agreement, apparently relying on the rich experience it had formerly acquired in boycott-breaking. As an empty gesture of good will the five invited the new company to join the Motion Picture Association of Japan and subscribe to the contract upholding their agreement, but this Nikkatsu refused to do, one of the provisions being that new people developed by any one company were not allowed to move to another during their initial three years of work.

This was one of the provisions that eventually helped Nikkatsu break the agreement. These new people, poorly paid under the industry's common-contract provisions which called for a three-year incubation period, realized that they could do better elsewhere. The new stars, already popular, were not about to wait three years before they cashed in on their popularity; hence they listened all the more attentively to the beguiling voice of Nikkatsu. An added incentive was that Nikkatsu, beginning work in the summer of 1954, offered the only fully air-conditioned sound stages in Japan at a time of year when the temperature on most Japanese stages had been known to rise to 120 degrees Fahrenheit on hot days. In addition, the dining rooms and dressing rooms were much superior to those of other companies. Daiei, for example, had experienced an attack of severe food-poisoning among its studio employees because of unsanitary conditions in the studio commissary, and was finally forced to clean up its studios and modernize its buildings only because so many visiting foreigners were shocked at the appearance of the studios where so many prize-winners had been made.

Even with the young talent, however, Nikkatsu's success was not immediate. It suffered from lack of good directors, the eternal complaint of a new company. Though it had Tomotaka Tasaka, he was past his best days. It also had young Kon Ichikawa, but he too had seemingly lost some of his power. Consequently, the company got off to a rather slow start. Only eleven films were made in 1954 and only one of them, So Yamamura's *The Black Tide* (Kuroi Ushio), could be called a hit. In 1955, however, everything was changed. There were many box-office successes and a schedule of one film a week was maintained, all in all a rather amazing achievement for a production company which had started right from the bottom.

Despite box-office appeal, the early Nikkatsu product achieved little critical success, although some of their initial releases were quite good. One of the reasons was that the Nikkatsu product had, and still has, no especial flavor. Most Japanese film companies like to create and push their own particular kind of film, for example, Shochiku's woman-oriented "Ofuna flavor" movies and Toho's pictures appealing to the urbanites. Nikkatsu, however, in aiming its films to appeal to every taste, scattered its shots too wide. The critics particularly disliked being unable to pinpoint a "Nikkatsu flavor," since the supreme pleasure of the Japanese critic is to classify and correlate. But Nikkatsu had its reasons: it was looking for a place in the market and for that reason it shopped around and purposely avoided specializing.

While this youngest company was attempting to appeal to all elements in Japan's vast established film audience, the next youngest, Toei, was already looking beyond the average audience to appeal to groups who had the greatest unexploited ticket-buying power. Okawa of Toei, like Hori of Nikkatsu, prided himself upon being a businessman and not a movie man, and his business acumen was amply proved when he hit upon just those segments of film audiences not yet fully exploited: children, young teen-agers, the poorly educated, and the farmers.

He was vastly successful and today, among all six companies, Toei commands the most loyal audience. People who go to its films seldom go to those of any other company. Before the war, companies like Zensho and Daito appealed to this audience by producing largely silent period-films, but until Toei appeared, these people had been neglected. Having no idea whatever of the meaning of the words quality or intelligence, they were completely satisfied by Toei's innumerable standard period-dramas and responded by making Toei's biggest stars, Kinnosuke Nakamura and Chiyonosuke Azuma, phenomenally popular. By the end of 1956, six-year-old Toei emerged as leader of the Japanese industry in terms of box-office receipts. The company was quite accustomed to receive a box-office gross of 250 percent

on the original cost of any film. It also released the three
biggest money-makers of that year, all of them standard
period-dramas.

Toei was also successful in pushing "exclusive contracts"
with exhibitors, under which theater owners agreed to show
only Toei pictures, excluding all others. By the autumn of
1957, out of the 2,100 theaters with which it held various
kinds of exhibition contracts, there were 730 "Toei only"
motion-picture houses. In exclusive contracts Toho was
second with a mere 168.

The biggest reason for the spectacular financial growth of
Toei was its championship of that production and exhibition
policy that now threatens to destroy the artistic status of the
Japanese cinema. One of the most objectionable and important aspects of this ultra-commercialized policy was the
double-feature, which had never before been so ruthlessly
pushed. By the end of 1956, only three percent of Japanese
theaters had a single-feature policy; eighty-three percent
showed double-features; and fourteen percent had triple bills.

This led to a big production race, with all the major companies except Shintoho trying to release eight features a
month from the beginning of 1957 and all but Toei showing
the strain. Nikkatsu dropped out of the race first and was
soon followed by Shochiku and Daiei, leaving by June only
Toho and Toei in the race. Various reasons were given
to cloak the failure. Kido of Shochiku announced that his
company was moving "from quantity to quality" and in the
future would abandon double-features. He also said that he
had the cooperation of Nikkatsu and Daiei in making such
a move. Whatever Hori of Nikkatsu may have felt about the
worth of quality over quantity—since he himself had been
among the first to install a double-bill-production policy in
emulation of Toei—Nagata of Daiei was squarely behind
Kido since he had long stood out against double-features.

One of Nagata's main reasons was that directly after the
unexpected and more or less accidental success of *Rashomon*
he had announced a "big productions, few in number" policy,
seeing a chance to escape some of the competition at home
by doing battle in the international market and reasoning
that there was a chance to make bigger money on a film
successful abroad than on the biggest films at home.

As Nagata evaluated the international market, he decided
that the success of *Rashomon* lay entirely in its exoticism,
and he therefore decided on more large-scale period-films.
Little by little, however, it became abundantly clear that

Nagata had been wrong and that his policy of producing
special period-films "that appeal to foreigners" was rather
disastrous. Some years later, in 1958, things had come to such
a pass that, on the occasion of the Second Japan Film Week
in New York, Shiro Kido could come to the astonishing
conclusion that the industry should stay away from traditional "samurai-action pictures" and should produce more
"modern, exportable, films." The aim was the same, to make
something they thought foreigners would like; the product
was different, modern-day Japan was now on the block.

As of 1955, however, Nagata was just learning the extent
of his misery. He failed to win anything abroad and the films
in question, apart from not selling in foreign countries, had
only a moderate success in Japan—because the quality was
poor, not because they were made for export. At the same
time this concentration of resources on a few films for foreigners resulted in a neglect of Daiei's weekly bread-and-
butter product and a consequent fall in overall quality. Too,
despite its frequent announcements claiming sole concentration on "big, quality pictures," Daiei's actual output
showed an almost total concern with slickly-made but essentially trite adaptations of fiction appearing in second-rate
magazines. The company's more constructive efforts were in
introducing the color film and in helping turn the eyes of
other producers to markets abroad. Daiei also served as example of how not to make a coproduction. The other companies, profiting by its mistake, took a look at *Until Forever* and the Margaret O'Brien number, and then decided
to embark on a few collaborations themselves.

The first serious postwar attempt at coproduction came
from two men who, though not outside the film industry,
were not in active production either. They were Yoshio
Osawa, former head of Toho and currently the main supplier
of imported motion-picture equipment in Japan, and Nagamasa Kawakita, a Toho executive and now head of Towa,
Japan's most important distributor of European pictures.
Both had helped coproduce Japan's first such venture, *The
New Earth*, and, undismayed by its fiasco, continued to
believe that if the right foreign director were found, success
would be theirs. The man they finally selected for the job
had always been a favorite in Japan, Josef von Sternberg.
He was also an old acquaintance, having been in the country
when the two producers' *The New Earth* was being filmed.
Though both knew that he had been thoroughly rejected
by the American film industry, they could not bring them-

selves to believe that Hollywood's reasons for the rejection
had been quite sound, and consequently gave him a free
hand in production.

The Saga of Anatahan (Anatahan), released in 1953, was
based on a true story of a woman and ten men on a small
island during World War II and their resultant sex struggles.
Von Sternberg took a year to make the film, but, since he
had lost his touch decades before, the picture was a failure,
handicapped as he was by his inability to communicate with
his Japanese co-workers. Von Sternberg went home, the
film was shown in Japan, America, and elsewhere, failed to
make money or win critical acclaim, and quietly disappeared.

The next company to take up coproduction was Toho.
Earlier, President Kobayashi had promised that as soon as he
had all his theaters built he would start improving production, and toward the end of 1954, when his theater plan was
completed, that was just what he did. He allowed such films
as Akira Kurosawa's Seven Samurai and Mikio Naruse's
Late Chrysanthemums (Bangiku), and cemented American-
Japanese ties by selling an American film company Japan's
first science-fiction film, Godzilla (Gojira), as well as Toho's
first color period-film, Musashi Miyamoto. The former played
all over America after being remade in Hollywood as Godzilla, King of the Monsters; the latter made somewhat more
of a splash by winning an Academy Award as Samurai.

Then Kobayashi tried a coproduction, the 1955 Italian-
made Madame Butterfly (Chocho Fujin). It looked as though
Toho was making a good deal. All it put up was Iwao Mori
to help with the script, several carpenters and prop men,
Kaoru Yachigusa for the title rôle, a few other actors, a
Takarazuka chorus, and $550,000. In return it received ex-
hibition rights for Japan and East Asia. The picture, however, turned out to be an inept and garish pantomime accompaniment to a relatively inferior and much-cut performance
of the opera. No matter how appropriate the visuals may
have been to Puccini's score, the Japanese were confused by
Italian ideas on Japanese behavior, architecture, and landscape
gardening, being particularly mystified and somewhat upset
by Kaoru Yachigusa's apparently being able to speak Italian.
The picture had no great success, though originally there
was a curiosity value which drove people into the theaters
in Japan, if not in the rest of East Asia.

Shochiku too wanted to get into the act. Disregarding the
examples set by Daiei, Messrs. Osawa and Kawakita, and
Toho, it began negotiating with the French Pathé Overseas.

Again, as with *Madame Butterfly*, these coproductions were not so much strict business ventures as they were answers to Daiei's apparent international success. As Daiei's two closest rivals, both companies had to do something to maintain their domestic prestige after Daiei's winning streak at the foreign festivals. It seems strange that they should both pay vast sums which they knew there was little hope of recovering from the limited rights assigned. But as they did purposely take such losses, one can only somewhat weakly suggest that the saving of face was somewhere involved.

The Pathé-Shochiku film, *Unforgettable Love* (Wasure-enu Bojo), called *Printemps à Nagasaki* in France, was budgeted at one million dollars, or enough to make fifteen average Shochiku features. Director Yves Ciampi and stars Danielle Darrieux and Jean Marais appeared in Japan with much attendant publicity. Then the many difficulties which plagued the production of the film began. The Japanese claimed that they were being treated as inferiors by the French. They also objected to the payments made to the French stars and technicians, often five to ten times higher than their Japanese peers were getting. It is scarcely surprising that the resulting picture was as bad as it was: one might have expected it to be even worse. Again a synthetic story (French boy, Japanese girl); again fuss made over quaint Japan (Miss Darrieux in a geisha wig); again a full-color tour of Japan's scenic spots; and, yet again, the death of the heroine. This last was standard procedure for coproductions. Fanck's *The New Earth* had its climax on a smoking volcano; Sloan's *Until Forever* featured a final earthquake; and Ciampi's *Unforgettable Love* got rid of its triangle during a studio-made typhoon. The fate of Japanese girls who love foreigners was made obvious: they always die in natural disasters.

Despite its coproduction failures, Daiei was anxious to try again. This time it looked to Hongkong and interested the Shaw brothers, producers responsible for many Hongkong films, to the extent of their putting up thirty percent of the money, and made *The Princess Yang* (Yokihi), a rather dull if pictorially beautiful reworking of Chinese history. Toho too cooperated with the Shaw brothers a year later, in 1956, in *The Bewitching Love of Madame Pai* (Byaku-Fujin no Yoren), called *Madame White Snake* in America. In both films the directors—Mizoguchi in the former, Toyoda in the latter—were largely wasted, though each was given his first chance to work in color. The box-office returns were not

impressive, but at least Daiei and Toho each received the
dubious prestige of having made yet another foreign co-production.

The battered palm remained Shochiku's, however. It had had a part in making *Unforgettable Love*, which was the most expensive picture ever made by Japanese. Though its failure did little to help the ailing Shochiku, there was a general feeling that not all was lost. Shochiku had kept up with Toho and Daiei and, despite the millions gone forever, had kept its face as well. Whatever else it retained, however, Shochiku had lost its position of preeminence in the Japanese film world. In 1956, for the first time since the end of the war, Shochiku's total receipts failed to total the highest of any Japanese film company. Toei and the double-feature were just one of the reasons. After a brief revival in the early 1950's Shochiku had begun its decline in 1954 and now it was falling from the highest position any company had ever achieved in the Japanese film industry.

The beginning of the end happened to coincide with Shiro Kido's being moved up to the position of president of Shochiku, but this was simply circumstance, not cause and effect. Kido was the only head of a movie company who had ever had practical production experience. Others had been concerned only with the business angles of film production, Nagata for example, whose only real production ties were as a location manager. Kido was also the only Tokyoite among the six major-company heads and was certainly the only member of the intelligentsia among them. Upon assuming the presidency, Kido again sought to widen the appeal of the type of productions Shochiku made and at the same time attempted to "update" the very outmoded "Ofuna flavor"—he had tried the same thing with some success in 1950.

If Shochiku was further down than ever before, however, it at least had the consolation of being able to look below and see a company in even worse difficulties. This was Shintoho. Since declaring its independence from Toho, it had been in continual financial trouble. In 1952 Tomoyoshi Hattori was brought in as a new head, but he seemed rather ill-prepared for the job, his only previous experience in film production having been in the making of home movies. One of the few things he did before he was deposed was to make a valiant stand against the double-feature, maintaining that Shintoho "would never" lend itself to such a dubious enterprise. "Could never" would perhaps have been the more accurate, since under any circumstances Shintoho would have been unable to make the necessary number of features, even if it had had an adequate outlet. Some felt that if Shintoho wanted to make valiant stands, it should have started a bit nearer home. Due to an utter lack of money, its studio facilities were very poorly maintained. This extended as far as the studio toilets, which had an unsavory reputation, in part brought about by stories like that of Setsuko Hara, who, working on the Shintoho lot, one day decided to use the facilities during a brief break when the lights were being set. She found herself unable to enter because of the stench and general untidiness. Angry, she climbed into her car and was driven home, used her own personal facilities, which were naturally above reproach, and three hours later returned to the waiting crew and cast.

By the end of 1955, Shintoho was in serious trouble. Losses were mounting daily as every picture failed to earn a profit due to insufficient bookings. In desperation, the company called in Mitsugu Okura, who owned the small Fuji rental studios and thirty-six theaters, put him in charge of everything, and all but gave him the company. He seemed at first a rather unlikely choice, having a number of business failures to his credit. But he had once been a *benshi*, had had a lot of experience in exhibition, and it was thought that he, perhaps, could do something.

When he came in, Shintoho was losing $100,000 a month, and one of the first things Okura did was put a stop to this. He was able to do so by switching Shintoho's production policy from pictures which appealed to white-collar workers and the more sophisticated urbanites (a carry-over from Toho days) to pictures which would bring in children and the relatively uneducated laborers and farmers. These films were bloody *chambara* sword fights, sex exploitation, gang films full of literal violence, ghost stories, and military films verging on the ultra-rightist. Discovering that the pro-military films were successful, Shintoho decided to push further in this direction. At the same time, seeing that the widescreen era was about to break in Japan, Okura reasoned that few things fitted wide screens better than war.

Thus Shintoho signed up with the French Cinepanoramic system, a process somewhat equivalent to what was once Republic's Naturama, imported two sets of lenses, and decided to make *The Emperor Meiji and the Great Russo-Japanese War* (Meiji Tenno to Nichi-Ro Daisenso). Okura liked nationalistic subjects, for political and commercial reasons, but when the budget was figured out, his staff revolted. The sum of $560,000 was needed, and as that was all that Shintoho had left in the world, the risk was thought too great, even for the greater glory of the Emperor Meiji. Okura was reasonable and merely announced that if the picture lost any amount whatever, he would reimburse the company out of his own pocket. This mollified and inspired both stockholders and the company workers. They set to work at once, using every penny of Shintoho's capital. It was the equivalent of a suicide charge.

The production taxed Shintoho's facilities so much that while the film was being shot all other production had to come to a halt. There was neither enough electricity nor lights to go around. When it was completed, Shintoho made thirty widescreen prints and called its process *Daishinesuko*, which means "Bigger CinemaScope." Since hardly any of its contract houses had converted to widescreen, and Shintoho could offer them no future program guarantee in widescreen, the film was booked into foreign-picture theaters which already had widescreen facilities. The première came and everyone held his breath. Then they let out a long sigh of relief. The picture was an astonishing success. It took in over $1,300,000—the biggest gross of the year—and Shintoho was saved.

A static and almost excessively reverent film, *The Emperor Meiji* showed a very paternalistic emperor concerned over the welfare of country and soldiers. He refuses to eat anything but what the common soldier eats; he refuses to change into a summer uniform, saying that, after all, his men are uncomfortable too; he will not take a vacation because his men cannot take vacations from the war. The long, slow palace sequences were intercut with scenes of frantic action, Japanese soldiers dying like flies, Russian battleships firing and being fired upon, explosions, gunfire, and battle after battle. Almost everyone liked the film, even the critics, and many felt it would be almost unpatriotic to criticize it.

They still felt the same when Shintoho decided to press its advantage and in 1958 released a sequel, *The Emperor Meiji, the Empress, and the Sino-Japanese War* (Tenno Kogo to Nisshin Senso). Again, the same reverence; again, royal concern over the common people; and, again, an object lesson on how not to make a film. The cycle continued with the 1959 *Greater East Asian War and the Far East Military Tribunal* (Daitoa Senso to Kyokuto Saiban).

Those who failed to appreciate the finer points of these productions held that it was merely widescreen that had made them, particularly the first, so successful. Others, with some reason, felt that they would have packed the houses no matter how they had been shown.

There could be no doubt, however, but that widescreen was the thing. *The Robe* had opened in Japan at the end of 1953 and soon broke postwar box-office records wherever it was shown. Widescreen had been seen before when a Tokyo theater masked off the top and bottom of the 3-D *Man in the Dark* and projected it on a long screen to make not only Japan's first widescreen film but maybe the world's first widescreen 3-D process. (The 3-D films had no more success in Japan than elsewhere in the world, but even so, Toho went to the trouble of making several using what it called To-Vision.)

By the end of 1954, one hundred theaters had anamorphic lenses on their projectors and, by the end of 1955, five hundred. Shochiku, pioneering in widescreen as it did in sound and color, made the first Japanese picture in an anamorphic process, *Birth of a Revue* (Rebyu Tanjo), using Grandscope, a process that its own technicians had developed. An Eastmancolor short featuring an all-girl dancing team from Shochiku's International Theater, it was made in a ratio about equal to CinemaScope, but was shown only in the theaters specializing in foreign films. The reason was that though over a thousand theaters had widescreen equipment in 1956, these all showed nothing but foreign films. Japanese films were long in converting to widescreen because at a cost of about $1,500 per theater, small theaters simply did not have the money to convert.

Toei was the first company to solve the problem. With its ever-growing number of "exclusive contract" theaters, it could guarantee a steady flow of widescreen pictures. This is why Toei was the very first to launch a full-scale widescreen production program and the first to promise to make all pictures in widescreen. Toei helped its contract theaters by freely lending them the money to buy the necessary equipment. This naturally made the theaters even more in debt to Toei and ensured even greater "cooperation." The company's first widescreen offering was the 1957 *Bride of Otori Castle* (Otori-jo no Hanayome), a very ordinary period-film using the technically rather poor Toeiscope. Its slogan was "Picture Size Three Times as Large; Interest One Hundred Times as Great." One naturally doubts the veracity of the latter statement; even the former was not true, as the picture size was only twice as large.

Both Shintoho and Toei were making their initial wide-screen films at about the same time, and thus it was that the first battle of the big screen was fought by the poorest and the richest of Japan's film-producing companies. They were at least on a level so far as the value of their products went, both purposely appealing only to the lowest of intelligences. In the meantime, however the other four companies were not to be outdone in this matter of widescreen.

Shochiku, having invested in Grandscope, decided to improve it. The initial short subject had used lenses of poor quality and, unable to perfect them, they imported some made by Bausch and Lomb. The result was an Ofuna-flavor comedy about youth called *The Embraced Bride* (Dakareta Hanayome).

Toho was the only company successfully to use an exclusively Japanese developed anamorphic system and had been experimenting with it from 1953. The first feature made in this Tohoscope was *Three Types of Girls Make a Big Hit* (Oatari Sanshoku Musume), which itself made a big hit thanks to the popularity of its stars—Japan's most popular teen-age singers—and thanks to its being the third in series of "Three Girl" films. The system was patterned after Cinema-Scope, using identical lens and the same aspect ratio, the idea being a compatibility with what Toho thought was probably the safest of the widescreen systems.

Nikkatsu originally planned to use the Japanese-developed Koniscope, with a negative that had, instead of four perforation holes on each side, only one, located on the line between successive frames. The photographed image covered the entire film from edge to edge without the interference of sprocket holes. This larger image was then squeezed onto regular thirty-five millimeter stock in the manner of Super-scope. But for its first picture it imported foreign lenses for a regular anamorphic process called Nikkatsuscope and made a very run-of-the-mill period-film, *A Young Samurai in the Moonlight* (Gekko no Wakamusha).

Daiei decided to import VistaVision, making arrangements with Paramount to use the system. This of course required the purchase of special cameras and printers. The first picture using the system was Daisuke Ito's *Flowers of Hell* (Jigoku-bana), a Machiko Kyo period-film. All the other Japanese production companies experienced a budget rise of from ten to twenty percent thanks to widescreen. Daiei, however, found that its budgets went up fifty percent.

Widescreen, a problem and something of a challenge in all

film industries, was particularly troublesome to Japanese film-makers because the proportions did not lend themselves well to Japanese sets. The rooms of Japanese houses are small and hence difficult to photograph, the wide angle always wanting to take in more than is actually there. Also, since so many scenes occur with the actors sitting on the floor and the camera in a low position, there is considerable distortion in widescreen. With all the difficulty and expense created by widescreen, one might wonder just why the Japanese bothered to enter the field. Japanese films continued to make money whether in widescreen or not. Kinnosuke Nakamura's youthful fans, as well as the more serious film-goer, were alike unconcerned over widescreen. When the companies were asked why they were embarking on widescreen programs, the ready answer was: "To get the jump on television. We don't want to wait for it to catch up to us, as they did in America."

Though television in Japan had not yet represented the threat to the industry that it did in the United States, the film-production companies continued to regard it with marked distrust. When television began in Japan, in 1953, there were only 866 TV sets in the country. By 1959, however, there were close to two million, increasing at the rate of 150,000 every month.

From the very first, Japanese TV made a place for theatrical films, but, originally, the companies were very reluctant to release their pictures. Gradually, however, since there are no union problems on Japanese TV rights, and since such rights brought in extra revenue, all of the major companies began letting TV use their products. Most of the pictures originally shown on television were only about a year old. It was common for TV to use the films directly after theaters were finished with them. There is and was nothing like America's use of prewar pictures. For one thing, few prewar prints or negatives exist, having been destroyed in the war or by the Occupation; for another, films from the immediate postwar era are in such poor condition, if available at all, that the sound track becomes unintelligible when distorted by TV. Japanese film artists received no additional payments for TV-shown pictures, nor was there much prospect of establishing such a royalty system. But finally, noticing the world-wide tendency of film industries to regard television as a deadly enemy, after the summer of 1956 the companies refused to release their films to TV. This delayed opposition arose in part as result of a poll in which TV

viewers listed their program preferences. First was theatrical
motion pictures, followed by professional wrestling and *sumo;* in the thirty-fifth place was live television drama. Seeing this, the film producers thought, and rightly, that if the public liked films so much it could just as well come to the theaters to see them.

One of the results of this was that television turned to American-produced TV films. They could get a half-hour film for under $300, while the Japanese film companies originally demanded $1,500 for each showing of a feature film. A few of the American films were shown with specially enlarged subtitles, but most of them were dubbed, using a crude if inexpensive process in which synchronization was more of an accident than a requirement. The mistakes inherent in this system were many and frequent, but at least it was better than the *benshi,* revived on several occasions, who explained and interpolated, with the original English dialogue faintly heard in the background.

The Japanese film industry, following with the most rapt attention every horrible detail of what television was doing to Hollywood, was just on the point of observing that it could not happen here when TV struck. In 1957 the January movie-house receipts, usually two to three times higher than those of any other month, fell off from twenty to twenty-five percent. Hasty polls showed a considerable reduction in movie attendance by those who owned television. The film companies reacted at once. Rather than continue their stand-off fight, the first thought was to join the enemy, and by the middle of the year each of the six major film companies had organized a prospective television broadcasting company, Toei leading all the rest in applying for one of the two remaining commercial TV channels in Tokyo. The shortage of channels forced the companies to triple up, and this move secured a fraction of a channel for all six companies when two new Tokyo channels were awarded. Fuji Television, for example, was backed by Toei, Shintoho, and Nikkatsu.

While all six companies were in a dither about the new enemy outside the industry, they failed to see that inside the industry there were forces aimed at breaking up the lucrative six-company cartel. They found out only by accident when a newspaper got hold of the story. Actually this new dissension in the ranks was top secret since the maneuvers were so delicate that any direct countermove would ruin them. The dissension came from within Daiei. One of Nagata's most trusted employees, his managing director, Masashi Soga,

resigned just at the time when his boss was to be away on a
trip to America, to form a seventh major motion-picture company. The newcomer was called Nichiei, an abbreviation of Nippon Eiga.

The revolt was short lived. Just ten months later the new company was bankrupt. During the filming of its second and final production, entitled *Vice* (Akutoku), many of its office personnel had to appear as extras and members of the board had to help in the actual shooting. Even when the film was finally finished there was no way to distribute it. Shochiku had agreed to buy Nichiei's first picture but was not interested in the second. Eventually Daiei had its revenge. It offered to buy the film outright but offered only slightly more than what the film had cost to make, thus leaving the already poor company nearly broke.

If Nichiei had been successful with its original plans, it would have been the first time that a major company was launched with neither strong backing nor prestige and immediately assumed an important status. Other majors had been formed by the gradual amalgamation of smaller companies and had taken time to grow. They had in their background at least something of a tradition and a defined place in the hierarchy of the industry. Nichiei was too much of an upstart, and this simple fact was very much against it. Thus this would-have-been seventh major film company joined the ranks of the independents and then quietly folded. So many changes had already taken place in this minor sector of the industry, the independents, that one more or one less company would scarcely be noticed

By the end of 1955, independent production was no longer significant in the Japanese film world. Though earlier films like *Vacuum Zone* and *Children of the Atom Bomb* had made money, playing in as many as a thousand theaters when there were only four thousand in all Japan, later films, like Satsuo Yamamoto's 1954 *The Sunless Street,* were tremendous commercial failures. With the big companies deliberately pushing them out for commercial reasons, these left-wing independents could not even hold what market they had: the public was refusing to pay to see out-and-out propaganda pieces.

Too, the whole tone of the independent organization was changing. The initiative to produce independent films shifted from left-wing companies to Shingeki drama troupes and actors' group. Both were willing to cooperate with the big companies for distribution services. The actors' production groups were largely a financial proposition designed to get better deals for their members under the theory that "in union there is strength." This also allowed them financial savings in combining their personal management staffs and in creating advantageous tax situations. Some groups were composed only of stars, while others were made up only of by-players. Some were mixed in membership with members of varying experience and varying jobs in films.

The major film companies soon put a stop to this, and independent production in Japan all but ceased. Kido claimed that, thanks to the breakdown of the feudal family-system within film companies and the resultant lack of loyalty among the stars, not one "star who is really a star" had been developed in Japan in the past fifteen years. He said that they never stayed long enough with one company to become fully developed by that company's resources. Nagata for once agreed with his rival and delivered himself of a full pronouncement: "Although we read film advertisements in the newspapers, we can't tell what company made what picture if we don't look for the company's trademark. That's what the constant interchange of stars has done to destroy the particular 'color' of each company. To allow each company to develop its own 'personality' [in terms of the type and style of film it makes], talent can no longer be freely exchanged."

In the middle of 1957 all the major Japan film companies, including Nikkatsu, which, after the Nichiei scare, had been warmly welcomed into the fraternity of the Motion Picture Association of Japan on its own terms, decided on a policy of "no lending" of personnel. Nobody under contract to one company would be allowed to work for another. In addition to contract limitations, there was a handy clause which read that even if a person's contract expired, no other company would be allowed to grab him. This "exclusive-use system," which was really a revival of the industry's family system, applied even to bit players and general employees. The bargaining power of the actor was reduced to nothing, and Shochiku was even thinking of refusing employment to extras who worked in other companies' pictures.

The announcement of this new feudal policy was followed by each company's accelerating a new "new face" campaign, each planning to hoard new talent, safe in the knowledge that it could no longer be stolen. This mutual-exclusion policy soon became known as the "six-company agreement," and though talent and technicians unanimously objected, pointing

out that it would prevent any crossbreeding of ideas among
artists under contract to different companies and would most severely interfere with the activities and income of free-lance artists, the film companies paid no attention whatever. They had finally achieved just what they wanted: stability and the elimination of competition in as many areas as possible.

This was essentially a retreat to the feudal era and a dividing of the film world into separate and closed self-sufficient communities. Free-lance actors, who usually form a large part of any cast, would not be used; talent would be severely restricted in all its activities; and the film world of Japan would cease to be an entity—rather it would be six entities, each sealed off in an even greater seclusion than that of the "closed nation" policy of the Tokugawa era.

12 long-shot: 1954-59. (cont.). EIGHT YEARS after the war, the Japanese motion-picture industry had attained a kind of stability. The novelty of relative financial security was such that all of the major companies took further steps to rationalize the industry, resolving that at almost any cost they would never be poor again. The two main ways in which the industry sought to safeguard its financial position were, first, by introducing a production-line method of film-making and, second, by staking off sections of the market as a company's private territory and fitting production plans to that particular audience.

The production-line technique very much resembled that of other industries, automobile manufacturing, for example. If a film was successful, it was analyzed and broken down into its component parts; these were rearranged in a new script and a new film was constructed. In his *The Rise of the American Film*, Lewis Jacobs describes the process, though he was talking about the American industry in the early 1920's and not the Japanese industry in the late 1950's. "When a second-rate director was assigned to a film, the safest procedure was to instruct him to imitate the style of a more talented director as closely as possible. It was not uncommon for a director to be told outright to copy the effect or trick or mannerism of some more distinguished craftsman. Indeed, if a lesser director who was getting a relatively low salary could do this effectively, he was a great commercial asset to his employer. At the same time, of course, the more esteemed directors were continually asked to repeat their own successful efforts." This paragraph perfectly describes conditions in Japan during the present age of the omnipresent double-feature, except that in Japan it is carried even further. Often the publicity department thinks of a highly salable title, and then the head of production orders a film to fit the title.

The division of the market into six spheres assured each major company of its own private, and presumably loyal, audience, and had as one of its effects a partial removal of inter-company rivalry, hampering greatly the healthy principle of competition. Thus, Shochiku aimed for the woman audience, with "home drama" dominating its production schedule; Toho chose the city people, particularly the white-collar workers, with its "salary-man" films; and Daiei went after the teen-age audience with its youth films, sexy or otherwise, also making period-drama which would particularly appeal to the city storekeepers. Toei concentrated exclusively on juvenile-oriented period-drama and modern thrillers for children and rural audiences. Shintoho saw money in pictures that the ultra-conservative would favor, particularly military films and those which recalled the good old days; at the same time it found a ready market among the urban lower classes for its films accenting sex and violence. Nikkatsu's policy was a carefully planned lack of policy. A newcomer still trying to get established, it usually made pictures to cash in on a quick yen whenever it could.

All these policies were successful in that each company indeed did attract the type of audience it wanted. But of course things were never completely rigid. Each studio made many films which naturally included audiences not within its supposed sphere of influence. The better directors, too, were not going to let company policy determine the content of their films if they could help it. In most of these cases their films were successful despite their often going against the commercial market. In general, however, the result of this striving for security within the industry was a complete commercialization of the film product.

An example is the biggest commercial success in the post-war history of the Japanese cinema, the Shochiku film *What Is Your Name?* (Kimi no Na wa), in three feature-length installments. It may be regarded as the supreme triumph of the "Ofuna flavor" home drama, a eulogy to Japan's traditional family values, which put Shochiku way out in front as the leader in terms of box office until a year later when the old Ofuna tricks lost their magic. Like *A Japanese Tragedy*, it paid tribute to the traditional Japanese virtues

and cashed in on them, but unlike the Kinoshita film, it was
an uncritical affirmation of the semi-feudal.

The film was based on a popular radio serial which was a variation on the film version of *Waterloo Bridge,* and was complete with bridge. During an air raid on Tokyo, a young couple meet and fall instantly in love. They part, promising to meet again—on the bridge—but unfortunately neglect to tell each other their names. After the war, and after much waiting and dreaming, the young girl—Machiko by name— marries. The marriage does not work out, however, and she decides to get a divorce, only to discover that she is pregnant. In the meantime, the young man has been waiting too and finally, at the end of the third installment, he finds her again —on the bridge.

The original radio version was extremely popular. So much so that during its broadcast time the women's side of the public baths was always empty. The film version, its three parts released in late 1953 and early 1954, was also popular, grossing over four million dollars; this means that the total attendance at these three pictures ·was over thirty million, more than one-third of the population of Japan. The theme song of the film became a tremendous hit. The "Machiko-maki," a kind of kerchief the heroine wore over her head in the picture, was taken up by millions of Japanese girls and even extended to Korea, where the film was never shown. There were also "Machiko" kimono, bathing suits, bathrobes, harmonicas, pencils, dolls, handkerchiefs, perfume, neckties, tearooms, chinaware—all bearing her name and/or image. There were special sightseeing trains and buses which took thousands of sightseers to view the locations used in making the film. All in all, it was a tremendous success, so much so that Shochiku was able to use the profits in modernizing and reequipping its production facilities, as well as setting up the Shochiku Motion Picture Science Institute for the purpose of studying technical problems in film-making.

Needless to add, *What Is Your Name?* had a vast number of imitations, and the Japanese screen was filled with pairs of searching lovers missing each other by seconds, losing all chance of bliss on earth because he, or she, was held up by a traffic light. The commercialization of the love story, how-ever, is but one facet of greater commercialization which seized the Japanese film industry of the 1950's in its firm if financially remunerative grasp. Another facet was the rise of the ghost and science-fiction monster films.

Ghost stories have long been as popular in the Japanese

film as they have been on the Japanese stage. The origins of
the film ghost, despite the vast number of spirits in the Noh, lie in the Kabuki, in one play to be precise, *The Yotsuya Ghost Story*. It became the custom to perform this as well as other ghost plays during the summer heat of the O-Bon, a Buddhist observance held to honor the souls of the dead. The festival occurs in July and the ghost dramas created a psychological form of air-conditioning by thoroughly chilling the spectators. When the public discovered that the motion picture houses were just as sweltering as the drama theaters or the *yose* halls, there arose a demand for ghost films which continues even to this age of the artificially refrigerated movie house.

In the summer of 1957 one company alone—the sinking Shintoho, always looking for a fast profit—flooded theaters with ghost films, which included such typical titles as *The Bewitched Spirits of the Castle of White Wax* (Byakurojo no Yoki) and *The Seven Wonders of Honjo* (Honjo Nana Fushigi), all containing the traditional Japanese ghost, usually female, with a heavily scarred face, blood running from the mouth, no legs, and long disheveled hair These spirits usually return to haunt men who have done them wrong, or to redress old wrongs. They never return simply to haunt at large, and all have a single purpose—revenge. Thus the Japanese ghost film is simply one facet of the revenge theme, one of most important plot movers in all traditional Japanese drama and literature. The trouble with the ghost-film genre is that the stories are all alike. The audience knows precisely what to expect since it probably saw a different version of the same story the year before. The films are made cheaply and unimaginatively, yet the audience, responding to a well-known stimulus, is apparently thoroughly and delightfully chilled each summer.

The Japanese monster picture is a somewhat more recent development, having had its beginnings in the 1954 *Godzilla*, a film which the Japanese critics, though criticizing the picture's exploitation of the atom-bomb scare, praised for an "intellectual content usually lacking in foreign pictures of the same genre." America had a chance to sample this intellectual content when Columbia bought the film and revamped it, showing it under the title of *Godzilla, King of the Monsters*. A dinosaur-like creature, patterned after that in the American *The Beast from Twenty Thousand Fathoms*, ravages Tokyo after having been awakened from a long sleep by the Bikini bomb explosions. He is finally taken care

of by a self-sacrificing Japanese scientist, who dissolves the
monster and himself in Tokyo Bay. The Japanese success of the film was such that a year later Toho brought out *Godzilla's Counterattack* (Gojira no Gyakushu), a quickie which ignored the monster's official demise in the former picture, changed the locale to Osaka, and spent much less time and ingenuity in the destruction of miniature sets. In the same year the Abominable Snowman, again a man in a monster suit, made an appearance in *The Monster Snowman* (Kyojin Yukiotoko), and a year later another prehistoric monster, this time a pterodactyl, appeared in *Radon*.

Honshu and Hokkaido having been successfully ravaged by Godzilla, Radon was given the southern island of Kyushu, where she spread the greatest havoc in trying to find a place warm enough to lay her eggs. She chose a volcano, to her eventual regret because the Japanese Security Forces, complete with an "Honest John," were on hand to blow her up.

The monster genre had obviously also become the science-fiction genre, and soon the screen was littered with transparent men, invisible men (a slight difference, but telling), and, with a bow in the direction of Universal, shrinking men. Daiei made a science-fiction number for the foreign market called *Space Men Appear in Tokyo* (Uchujin Tokyo ni Arawaru), which, in full color, solemnly warned against any more atom-bomb tests. Foreigners never had a chance to enjoy the film, however, since Daiei was never able to sell it to anyone.

Foreigners had ample opportunity, however, to view the much more pretentious *Earth Defense Force* (Chikyu Boeigun), made in 1958 and released abroad as *The Mysterians*. With one eye firmly on the foreign market (some snippets of Japanese culture and lots of English spoken) and the other just as firmly on the yen-paying customers at home (plot complications, all leading nowhere, and a favorite Japanese science-fiction stance: Japan, saviour of the world), Toho achieved a kind of myopic intensity, but that was all. Again, foreign invaders from outer space; again, monsters ravaging; and, again, Japan leading the world in the pursuit of true peace, ending on a slightly naive note of optimism when the main characters, gazing aloft at the recently installed satellites, reassure each other that with these "guardians" overhead, there will never be another war.

Slightly more sophisticated, if equally commercial, entertainment was available in the series of the "Three Girl" musicals which soon proved among Toho's biggest grossers.

The three girls were the phenomenally popular Hibari Misora
and two other singers of only slightly less appeal, Chiemi Eri
and Izumi Yukimura. The latter was a real modern girl who
sighed over James Dean and sang in English; Chiemi Eri was
the comic lead, slightly muscular and straight from the
country. Hibari Misora was the true daughter of Japan, not
much given to popular American songs nor James Dean but,
on the other hand, not overtly scornful of either. The trio
made a number of films, all with such typical titles as *Toss-
up Girls* (Janken Musume), *Romance Girls* (Romansu Musume), and later two of the girls continued in such films as
Festival of Romance (Romansu Matsuri). The plots were
always similar if not identical. There was much business
backstage at one of the big revue halls; a mix-up over boys,
with the correct males allotted only at the end; and usually
a reel-long singing finale with the girls and their boys on
bicycles, motorboats, or water skis.

Perhaps even more typical of the commercialization of the
Japanese film was the fad of the *taiyozoku* films during the
summer of 1956. The concept of the *taiyozoku* (literally,
"sun tribe") is usually credited to Shintaro Ishihara, a young
man who received one of the more coveted literary prizes,
the Akutagawa Award, for his short novel *Season of the Sun*
(Taiyo no Kisetsu), which was a violent, adolescent outcry
against tradition and the older generation. At the end of the
novel there is a scene where the boy, at the funeral of the
girl whom he made pregnant, cries out: "You people don't
understand anything." And it was this theme which was soon
taken up by young people whose anarchistic ideas allowed
them to think themselves members of the *taiyozoku*. The
same attitude was noticeable all over the world, finding expression in James Dean, Marina Vladi, and films like *Avant
le Déluge*. In Japan alone, however, the attitude became a
fad of some proportions.

Nikkatsu was not slow in making the Ishihara novel into
a film, and its success was such that Daiei bought the rights
for Ishihara's next, *Punishment Room* (Shokei no Heya), and
gave it the benefit of full publicity. Again the story was
about sex and lawless youth. A student puts sleeping pills
into a coed's beer and then rapes her. She falls in love with
him (all raped heroines fall in love with their attackers in
Ishihara's novels), but he spurns her and eventually gets badly
beaten up in the torture room of the title.

Though the novels had not aroused much public resentment, the films did. The *Asahi* newspaper said that because

the crime (sleeping tablets in beer) was so easy to imitate by the boy on the street, the film should have been cut before release. Other critics pointed out, quite accurately, that while Nikkatsu's *Season of the Sun* had merely claimed to be representative of the rather small *taiyozoku* clique, Daiei's *Punishment Room* announced that it was representative of the life of all present-day students. Daiei, however, could not have cared less. Seeing the *taiyozoku* pictures as a logical extension of its teen-age sex films, it was delighted to note that the movie was playing to standing-room-only from morning to night because of its uncommon attractiveness to girl high-school students.

The critics reserved their really big artillery for Nikkatsu's *Crazed Fruit* (Kurutta Kajitsu), based on yet another Ishihara novel. Though this was the worst in terms of social irresponsibility, it was cinematically by far the best. About a girl summering by the seaside with a foreigner, it showed the havoc she introduced into the Japanese family system by having sex with two brothers perhaps simultaneously and certainly repeatedly. It created an aura of sexuality quite rare in films and was so unambiguous in its presentation that Eirin, the film industry's self-censorship board, stepped in and ordered two scenes cut. So they were, but the result was that the film became even more salacious. One of the cut scenes showed one of the brothers taking off the girl's bathing suit. The substituted scene was merely a shot of the sun and the sea over the gunwale of the boat they were in. The sound track was left intact, however, and so the girl's petulancies followed by her softer sounds of acquiescence, unaccompanied by any meaningful image, gave lively imaginations the freest play.

This time there was violent public protest. Housewives picketed theaters, and local governing bodies instituted special bans to keep anyone under eighteen from seeing these films. This was the height of the *taiyozoku* craze, and despite all the publicity efforts of the film companies, the excitement subsided rather suddenly. Nikkatsu's *Backlight* (Gyakkosen) was based on a novel by "the female Shintaro Ishihara," a girl college student named Kunie Iwahashi, and Toho's *Summer in Eclipse* (Nisshoku no Natsu) was not only written by but also starred author Ishihara himself. After that the companies who had more *taiyozoku* films to make quietly shelved them and the fad was over.

One of the few results of these pictures was that they succeeded in placing Nikkatsu firmly in the public eye, something company president Hori had long desired. Many people wanted to know why Eirin had not more severely cut these films, and it soon became known that Nikkatsu was not even a member. This fact showed the Japanese government that the industry could not, after all, adequately police itself (which was the sole purpose of Eirin) and gave rise to Cabinet demands for the restoration of government censorship, which of course brought panic to the industry. One of the results of this was that for the first time Nikkatsu was accepted as a fully equal sixth company, and that the administration of the Eirin code was taken out of the hands of motion picture company employees and given to representatives of the general public. Though Hori had answered critics with "Among the hundreds of thousands who have seen these pictures, it seems strange that there should be such a fuss if it influences five or six people in the wrong way," he now saw the light and agreed to shelve the *taiyozoku* concept, though this was over the protests of such new directors as Hiromichi Horikawa, Yoshio Kawazu, and Yasushi Nakahira (the latter had made *Crazed Fruit*), since they all believed that *taiyozoku* represented an important and necessary genre and thought its banishment a severe loss.

Shochiku, caught without a *taiyozoku* picture on its production schedule and unable to cash in on the sudden boom, announced in weighty moral tones that it would never lend itself to the production of such dirt, but later made a half-hearted attempt in *Sun and Rose* (Taiyo to Bara), a very inferior Kinoshita film which dressed itself up in the borrowed sex and violence of the *taiyozoku,* meanwhile satisfying public opinion by wagging a heavy moral finger at its young culprits.

It was the violence and implicit lack of social responsibility in the *taiyozoku* films that had angered so many Japanese. The sex they were able to take quite in their stride so long as it was not violent and ill-mannered, like rape. Thus the industry, which had by now come a very long way from the time when it was nervous about showing a kiss on screen, was safely able to substitute nudity for picturizations of a socially irresponsible younger generation.

One of the first actresses to appear nude was Yukiko Shimazaki, in Satsuo Yamamoto's *To the End of the Sun* (Hi no Hate), a left-wing independent film, Yamamoto's apparent theory being that if polemic would no longer draw an audience, a nude would.

The company that really cashed in on nudes was Shintoho,

which, in the person, or rather the body, of Michiko Maeda,
had a star who consisted almost entirely of mammary
glands. *The Revenge of the Pearl Queen* (Onna Shinjuo no
Fukushu), made in 1956, was the first of the cycle. It proved
so successful that other companies started making similar
films and rumor had it that talent scouts were going about
Japan looking for bigger bosoms to bare, a search quite
necessary since in Japan large breasts are the exception rather
than the rule.

Not to be outdone by any newcomers, Maeda got the jump
on her rivals in *Woman Diver Trembles with Fear* (Ama no
Senritsu) by going whole hog and showing practically everything. Eventually, however, after even staid Shochiku had
made a nude film starring its very own *nikutai joyu* ("flesh
actress"), Nikkatsu braved opposition with Hisako Tsukuba
and in the 1957 *Resistance through the Flesh* (Nikutai no
Hanko), showed the heroine absolutely naked, watched her
climb into bed, and then closed in for a long and loving close-
up of a hairy underarm.

Not all the exploitation lines, however, were new. Shintoho
was continuing its financially successful preoccupation with
the war. Its 1956 *God of War Admiral Yamamoto and the
Combined Fleet* (Gunshin Yamamoto Gensui to Rengo Kan-
tai) was particularly successful despite the fact that the use
of the word *gunshin* offended many people who believed,
and hoped, that this word, coined by the militarists as the
supreme title of respect for a military man, had been dropped
from the language at the end of the war. The picture showed
that Yamamoto was hostile to the idea of war with the
United States, but that, if come it must, he was going all out
for the motherland. All the characters behaved in this way,
and the film was full of bit actors possessed by an overwill-
ingness to die. The critics' attitude was the same as the
audience's, one of the better-known critics writing: "Maybe
some of the aims of militarist Japan were wrong, but it is
certainly a beautiful thing to see the resolve with which
these young men [suicide troops] carry out their task with
devotion, removing all obstacles that stand in the way of
their objectives. Futile though their deaths proved, their
deeds were glorious." Another Shintoho glorification of Japan at war was the moneymaking *The Emperor Meiji and
the Great Russo-Japanese War*, the advertisements for which
had testimonials of old generals and admirals seeing the film
and bursting into uncontrollable tears. A somewhat lighter
view was that of a Tokyo critic who described the film as

"a rather advanced form of *kami-shibai*," the humor of the
observation lying in his comparison of the tableau-like scenes
of the Shintoho films with the so-called "paper theater" of
Japanese children, a diversion consisting of placards accompanied by a storyteller.

At the same time that Shintoho was turning out one war
picture after another, a number of military documentaries,
quickly pieced together from Japanese wartime footage and
materials borrowed from the United States, were shown. The
films all capitalized on growing wartime nostalgia, particularly
among ex-servicemen, but one of them accomplished what no
feature film had ever fully achieved. *Blitzkrieg Operation
Number Eleven* (Dengeki Sakusen Juichi-go), made in 1957,
was actually billed as "Not a record of Japan's defeat in the
Pacific War, but a record of the glorious victories of the
army, navy and air force. See the brave deeds of your fathers
and sons. Free stills of any scene in which your relatives and
friends appear. War wounded admitted free." The picture
was precisely what it said it was. It followed each Japanese
campaign up to the point where the tide turned and then
jumped over to a new battle. There was a careful avoidance
of shots of Japanese casualties, though the wounded in hos-
pitals were shown, as well as services for the dead. *Kamikaze*
operations too were shown in detail, but there was no mention of the desperation that had made the *Kamikaze* possible.

Shintoho and the documentaries were by no means alone
in cashing in on nostalgia for the war. In 1954, Nikkatsu
reedited the 1942 propaganda film *Generals, Staff, and
Soldiers* of Tetsu Taguchi and released it under the title *War
and Generals* (Senso to Shogun). Later it made *Human
Torpedoes Attack* (Ningen Gyorai Shitsugekisu), which
showed how suicide torpedo pilots willingly sacrificed their
lives to sink an American cruiser transporting a load of atom-
bomb parts. Thus their sacrifice saved thousands of lives—
for the time being. Yutaka Abe in 1956 made *The Last
Charge* (Saigo no Totsugeki), about Japanese troops who,
with no chance of escape, are ordered to fight until the end.
Though theoretically critical of the military system, Abe
could not hide his respect for it. Hiroshi Noguchi's *Weep!
People of Japan; the Last Pursuit Plane* (Nake, Nihon Kokumin, Saigo no Sentoki) said that it was a shame that these
nice young people must be sacrificed but never once questioned the system which called for suicide squadrons.

Not all military pictures, naturally, were quite so jingoistic.
Kiyoshi Kusada's *The Last Women* (Saigo no Onnatachi)

gave a most unpleasant picture of the Japanese national character, showing both civilians and the military becoming like beasts as their island is bombarded prior to the American invasion. It also contained a reconstruction of the famous incident in which groups of women living on Saipan were herded together and, under the grip of propaganda which declared that they would be raped to death by the invading Americans, committed suicide by the hundreds.

From 1955 there was also military comedy, one of the first being Shochiku's *The Privates' Story* (Nitohei Monogatari), a farce inspired by American films of the Willy and Joe variety. Poorly made, these films were a strange mixture of barracks humor, military nostalgia of the American Legion type, and a laughing exposure of the injustice and cruelty of the army, scenes of the most barbarous torture being hoked up with slapstick. These films were all enormously successful at the box office, pointing again to the fact that as military nostalgia becomes stronger and stronger, pleasant memories of military service gradually exclude the attendant horror.

At the same time, however, none of the films exploiting wartime themes show a friendly attitude toward Japan's present security forces. The older Imperial Army virtues were truly Japanese, this attitude says, while the present-day army is much too tainted with foreign influence to be accepted on the same terms. The temper of the Japanese populace in the mid-1950's was such that no film which in any way favored the Self Defense Forces and rearmament could have been successful at the box office; hence none were made. The few pictures which used Self Defense Forces for other than minor characters have shown the new military in an unfavorable manner. Minoru Shibuya's *Medals* (Kunsho) was about an ex-general whose whole life is bound up in rearmament, who sinks his funds in staging a comeback through the Self Defense Forces, and who fails. Though the film was actually about the Self Defense Forces, it was also passionately against rearmament and was timed to coincide with a public debate on an increase of the Self Defense Forces. Concerning this new military and the entire question of rearmament there is a conspiracy of silence in the films as elsewhere. If for this reason alone, it is difficult to see the nostalgia of wartime Japan, as pictured in the movies, as anything like a reawakening of old warlike instincts or anything of the sort.

Most of the many war films of the 1950's were frank audience exploitation, but there were exceptions, among them

Kon Ichikawa's *Harp of Burma* (Biruma no Tategoto) and *A History of the Pacific War* (Taiheiyo Senki). The latter was a documentary compiled from wartime newsreels, extremely well edited by Hiroshi Okada. The former was based on a novel originally written to introduce children to certain Buddhist tenets, which was about a Japanese soldier's decision to remain in Burma after the war and not return home with his unit so that he can become a mendicant priest, traveling about the country and tending the unburied war dead.

Originally the film was to have been directed by Tomotaka Tasaka, who had made Japan's best war pictures, but because of his continuing illness the picture was given to Kon Ichikawa. In spite of the many and various vicissitudes which the film underwent, including a hack editing job by Nikkatsu, the picture was thought good enough to win the 1956 San Giorgio Prize in Venice, an award given the film which best shows "men's capacity to live one with another."

Besides sex and war, another favored exploitation theme in the commercial Japanese film was the use of exotic and foreign locales. By 1955, dollars were available and a number of the companies set about spending them. Mizoguchi's *The Princess Yang* and Toyoda's *The Bewitching Love of Madame Pai* were both set in ancient China and both failed to come up with anything more than the kind of gaudy family scenes one finds hanging in Chinese restaurants—as tasteless as Chinese pastry. Daiei went further afield and shot *Buruba* in Hollywood, in an "African jungle" set since the story was about a Japanese Tarzan. For Shintoho's *Passion in Rio* (Rio no Jonetsu), the unit went as far as Brazil. But neither of these latter films was successful, since both failed to make enough to cover the additional expenses required for their foreign locations.

Tokyo-Hongkong Honeymoon (Tokyo Honkon Mitsu-zuki Ryoko), a Shochiku film, costarred Japanese and Chinese actors in parallel stories of a Japanese couple honeymooning in Hongkong and a Chinese couple in Tokyo—a sort of small-screen *Cinerama Holiday* with slightly more plot. In 1958, Toho went all the way to Cambodia to make *Beautiful Sorrow* (Utsukushiki Aishu), which had the English title of *The Princess of Angkor Wat*. In it, the "beautiful sorrow" belongs to a princess who longs for Japan. The reason is that when she was little a handsome Japanese soldier saved her from the perils of war and escorted her back to the palace. Now, fifteen years later, he returns. They

meet. She remembers him but he has no idea she is a princess.
Finally she divulges and offers her arms, her lips, and her
throne. In Japan, Cinderella is usually male.

As the rationalization of the market continued there was
many an attempt to discover more "proven properties," and
this led to frequent remakes of past hits. The process, sometimes difficult in the West, is never a problem in Japan because, for one thing, revivals of older Japanese pictures are
very infrequent and, for another, no additional payment or
clearance is needed; in Japan things are bought outright.
Among the films remade in the middle 1950's were Kajiro
Yamamoto's early and successful *Botchan*, from the Soseki
Natsume novel of the same name; Kinugasa's *The Sun* (Nichirin), which twenty-five years before had run into censor-
ship trouble since it dramatized events happening during the
"Age of the Gods"; Gosho's 1945 *The Girls of Izu*. Daisuke
Ito remade Tomotaka Tasaka's prewar *The Life of a Woman
in the Meiji Era*, and in 1955 Ito did his own 1927 silent *Serv-
ant* over again as *The Servant's Neck* (Gero no Kubi).
Later, Inagaki made a second, and much inferior, version of
The Life of Matsu the Untamed (sent abroad as *Rickshaw
Man*), and Tomu Uchida remade Inagaki's 1935 *The Great
Bodhisattva Pass*. In the same year there was a new version
of *The Naked Town*, and a year later, in 1959, Uchida's 1936
Theater of Life was redone. Not one of the remakes was
better than or even equal to the original.

Period-drama meanwhile—in the manner of Hollywood's
Westerns—proved the most stable and sure product of all.
Yet, it too was undergoing a kind of change now that Toei,
with its series of short feature-length period-films, was setting the pattern for profit making. One of its biggest money-
makers was *The Red Peacock* (Beni-kujaku), in five parts,
which began showing during the New Year holidays of 1955.
Starring Kinnosuke Nakamura and Chiyonosuke Azuma, its
spectacular box-office record showed that Toei was on the
right track so far as making money went, though film critics
were of the opinion that Daiei was making the more competent period-pictures. One of the reasons was that Daiei had
both Kinugasa and Daisuke Ito, who, even though no longer
great nor even very good, could still turn out commercial
products better than others in the field. In addition, Mizoguchi's highly creative experiments in the field of the period-
film helped considerably to raise Daiei's reputation. Among
its standard period-films were *Princess Sen* (Sen-hime), a
thoroughly uninteresting story dressed up in garish colors,

and three long feature-length films constituting the *New*
Tales of the Taira Clan (Shin Heike Monogatari), based on
Eiji Yoshikawa's historical novel, published in English trans-
lation as *The Heiké Story*.

As always during the postwar era, the best period-dramas
were the off-beat experiments by men who specialized in
films about contemporary life, in particular the period-films
of Kurosawa and Mizoguchi. The year 1954 saw the completion of *Seven Samurai,* the biggest—and, some think, the
best—film Kurosawa has ever made. Lasting three hours and
twenty minutes, it took over a year to photograph and cost
about $500,000, making it the largest-scale picture and biggest
spectacular ever made by the Japanese industry up to that
time. It was so big that Toho thought of abandoning the
production entirely. At one point the front office actually
became so nervous that Kurosawa sent them an ultimatum:
abandon the production or get another director who would
finish it quickly. This quelled the front office for a time, long
enough for Kurosawa to finish the film.

In it, the director made many technical experiments, one
of the most original being his use of super-powered telephoto
lenses to get a feeling of intimacy. These lenses cause things
on a line to and from the camera to "pile up," and this effect
causes them to seem much closer than they really are. The
intimacy was heightened by a frequent dependence on close-
ups, often recalling their use in Carl Dreyer's *Jeanne d'Arc.*
Kurosawa also used deep focus, low-key photography and
slow motion to accent the death and killing scenes. Throughout, editing was used with a vigor that one thought had died
out with the silent Soviet films.

In addition, Kurosawa's re-creation of the historical period
made everything look as if it really belonged to the Sengoku
era. The clean, pretty, romanticism of the average period-
film was completely missing. What one saw on the screen
was so compelling, so real, so very believable that it had an
immediacy one does not at all expect from costume-films.
Though the story—leaderless samurai band protecting a
village from marauding robbers—was somewhat suggestive of
a tendency picture, the emphasis had moved from vague
feelings about revolution to a solid, humanistic call for cooperation among men. Though the film has been criticized
for repetition in the endless attacks upon the village and
interminable counterattacks by the villagers and samurai,
Kurosawa knew precisely what he was doing. The West,
having seen only a much-cut print under the title *The*

Magnificent Seven, has not yet seen what Kurosawa intended to show. The complete three and one-half hour film has
an epic-like quality, due in part to skillful repetition of events,
which in the opinion of many puts it among the best films
ever made not only in Japan but anywhere in the world.

Even more visually brilliant, though perhaps not so emotionally satisfying, was Kurosawa's 1957 *Castle of the Spider's
Web* (Kumonosu-jo), which, like all this director's period-
films, was another successful attempt to leap beyond the
narrow restrictions of the average period-picture. In this case,
he fully adapted *Macbeth* to a Japanese setting, betraying
neither Shakespeare nor the Japanese milieu in which the
play is set. Using only a handful of components—drifting fog
and smoke, rainy forests, the shining surface of armor, the
sheen of natural wood, the dead white of human skin—Kurosawa created a film with a definite texture. Great imagination
was used in creating a real world governed by laws which,
though quite different from ours, were quite believable
through their consistency. The film constituted a real triumph
of style.

Kurosawa's other 1957 film was *The Lower Depths* (Don-
zoko), another of the director's successful experimental
period-films adapting foreign concepts to Japanese settings,
in this case a removal of Gorky's play to Edo during the
final days of the Tokugawa period. In this film Kurosawa
tried a new production method. The cast and crew, with
lights, full costume, make-up, and camera positions, rehearsed
for forty days before starting the actual shooting. Another
innovation was that there were no leading characters, the
film being entirely a series of vignettes. One of the most important results was an ensemble effect rare on the screen, an
acting unit, one part very carefully balanced against the
other. Another result was that the film had a real style, a
consistent set of rules governing characters, camera movement, formal composition, and editing. These rules all unified
the film, making it a bit more consistent than life itself, and
gave that higher realism which we usually call art.

In spirit, the film was very close to Yamanaka's *Humanity
and Paper Balloons.* Again, the lower depths of Tokugawa
Japan were examined with candor and realism. Death is never
horrible when life is barely worth living and the serenity
brought by the itinerant Buddhist priest is but transitory. In
the final sequence, a drinking party, with songs and dances,
has just begun when news of yet another death, this one a
suicide, is brought. Kurosawa cuts to a close-up of one of his

actors looking straight into the camera and saying: "What a
shame. Just as the party was getting started." Then with one
stroke of the Kabuki clapper, the *hyoshigi*, the end title appears. Kurosawa, by refusing to pontificate, by refusing to
sentimentalize, by eschewing even irony, has shown us that,
indeed, ours is a floating world, illusionary at best and always
transitory.

Kurosawa was not alone in period-drama experiments. In
1954, Kenji Mizoguchi directed *Sansho the Bailiff* (Sansho
Dayu), a Heian-era story about two children who set off
with their mother to a remote region to find their father, a
noble who has been banished for protecting farmers. The
person they trust to guide them separates them from their
mother and sells them as slaves to Sansho, a tyrant in control
of a distant region. When, after many years, they finally
escape, the sister feels that she is a burden to her brother and
commits suicide. Later he becomes a great lord in Kyoto and
uses his power to displace Sansho; then he sets out for a final
reunion with his mother, now old and blind.

As in *Seven Samurai*, the period is presented with a genuine
feeling for realism. The false romanticism of the standard
period-drama is missing and there is not one sword fight. The
hero wins by having righteousness on his side. Again, Mizoguchi insisted upon the "humanistic tradition," and no matter
how dark the future of the children, there is always reason
to hope. The photography in this film, the work of Kazuo
Miyagawa, who had filmed *Rashomon*, was particularly fine,
providing a beauty which contrasted greatly with the
ugliness of the subject matter. It was full of rich blacks and
whites and had a "liveness" to it, a living quality which was
entirely missing from the color of *The Princess Yang* and the
New Tales of the Taira Clan.

Mizoguchi's other 1954 film, *A Story from Chikamatsu*
(Chikamatsu Monogatari), found the director's realistic
period-style at its highest. Both the script and the direction
pointed up the contemporary meaning in the old and traditional Kabuki story of the flight of the oppressed lovers, the
chase, their final capture and crucifixion. The film represented
Mizoguchi's style at its most painterly. The influence of the
graphic arts, always strong in Mizoguchi's work, was readily
apparent but was quite different from that seen in, say, *Gate
of Hell*. In the Kinugasa film, the influence consists of literal
copying of the attitudes and tableaux seen in Japanese paintings; in the Mizoguchi film, the graphic arts have been fully
"cinematized." The result was a film of great subtlety, with

any number of sensuous love scenes which never so much as show the lovers kissing. Instead, we see the movements they make in relation to each other, the slight glance which tells so much more than the actual embrace.

Just as subtle, and even more explicit in its condemnation of feudal society, was Tadashi Imai's *Night Drum* (Yoru no Tsuzumi), a 1958 film called *The Adulteress* in foreign showings. The story was a familiar one: a wife is unfaithful and, under the social code of Tokugawa society, she must commit suicide. Imai's interpretation, however, was radically different from that of the usual period-film. The husband forgives her completely, only to find himself in the position of having to exact a penalty that he does not believe in. Her death will supposedly clear his name, but he does not feel the need of having his name cleared. He loves her.

Told in a series of very ingeniously constructed flashbacks which purposely fragmentize the story, the past and present are freely cut together and one of the results is an immediacy of experience and a feeling of the inexorable which at times lifts the film to nearly tragic heights. The last reel is entirely epilogue. Society insists that the other man be punished as well. Having been forced to murder his wife when she is unable to commit suicide, the husband dutifully goes in search of his rival, finds him, and kills him. It is then and only then that the husband realizes what has happened. Acting according to a social rather than a moral code, he has done everything which society says he ought. Then, in a shattering final close-up, he suddenly realizes that in doing so he has ruined his own life.

Along with Kurosawa, Mizoguchi, and Imai, both Kimisaburo Yoshimura and Keisuke Kinoshita also contributed greatly in creating period-drama meaningful to contemporary audiences. One such film was the 1957 *An Osaka Story* (Osaka Monogatari), the film on which Mizoguchi was working when he died and which Yoshimura completed. The story was about the rise of the merchant class in Osaka during the Genroku period. Being unable to pay his land rent, an impoverished farmer flees to Osaka, where he and his family starve until, through bribery, he gets the concession of sweeping up waste rice from a loading pier. After ten years, through unbelievably miserly ways, the farmer becomes a very rich man, but gradually this very penuriousness destroys both him and his family.

The film was filled with excellent satire on the inception of capitalism. The farmer enshrines the brooms first used to

sweep up the rice; he refuses to let his wife and daughter call
in a hairdresser although they are one of Osaka's richest
families; finally he refuses his wife medicine and she dies.
The film, however, was no melodrama on the evils of money;
it was rather an essay poking fun at Osaka's famed concern
for cash.

Equally successful was Yoshimura's 1955 *The Beauty and
the Dragon* (Bijo to Kairyu), a period-film in which the
famous Kabuki play *Narukami* was brought thoroughly up
to date. Somewhat in the manner of *Henry V*, the film opens
with a reconstruction of a classical performance of the play,
accurately recreating a historical presentation in the proper
style; it then moves, as a film, into a more cinematic interpretation. As in the Olivier movie, the acting style shifts from
stage technique to cinema technique, and Yoshimura's aim,
like Olivier's, was not a total reconstruction of the past but
the use of a historically literal presentation as means toward
something more modern in conception.

The film was highly praised by the Kabuki authorities, not
because it was a literal reproduction, but because it was a
freely-interpreted performance which was completely in the
spirit of the original. Nobuko Otowa's interpretation of the
princess who sets out to tempt the self-righteous priest was,
on the outside, perfectly correct as to period, but, under-
neath, the princess has the mind of a postwar woman. Some
film critics, however, did not prove so understanding and
completely misunderstood the director's use of satire, through
which he commented on present-day events. So they accused
Yoshimura of "disrespect for the classics." Still, if we are to
have Kabuki in the films, Yoshimura showed how to make it
a thoroughly cinematic experience.

Keisuke Kinoshita went even further in the excellent *The
Song of Narayama* (Narayamabushi-ko), a 1958 film based
on Shichiro Fukazawa's prize-winning short story about the
people in a remote section of the Japan Alps who traditionally abandoned their aged on the top of a high mountain.
The heroine, near seventy and ready for death, finally forces
her reluctant and loving son to carry her to the top of the
mountain, there to die of starvation and exposure. A near
folk-myth, the story was a very sobering legend, almost allegorical and always explicitly symbolic of the common lot.
This being so, Kinoshita chose to tell the story with
deliberate theatricality.

It opened like a Kabuki—the curtain drawn to disclose the
first scene—and throughout used *nagauta,* the voice and sam-

ısen accompaniment that describes and comments on the action. The visuals in the film were handled with an effortless virtuosity. Division between scenes often consisted of sudden light changes at which whole sections of the scenery slid away; intimate conversations were accented by careful spotlighting; the entire background would drop to reveal the next scene.

Yet Kinoshita did not forget that he was making a film and there was nothing stagey about his style. The moving camera was used to superlative effect; both color and wide-screen were employed in the most imaginative fashion, and the pacing and general tempo of the film was cinema at its most creative. Perhaps the greatest strength of this film, however, was that the highly artificial form which Kinoshita chose to use was completely right for the content of his story. Since he was filming a myth, he was able to move beyond reality, and create a style which was precisely adapted to the sober truth of what he was saying.

Not all off-beat period-films were successful. Minoru Shibuya's *Christ in Bronze* (Seido no Kirisuto) was a study of the Tokugawa suppression of Christianity, showing the sufferings of the faithful and the treachery of an insane Portuguese missionary. Not the least of its absurdities was the proposition that Japanese believers invariably make better Christians than foreigners. Somewhat more successful was Tomu Uchida's *Bloody Spear at Mount Fuji* (Chiyari Fuji), the first picture made by the director after having been detained for ten years in Red China. The story, about how a spear carrier fumbles his way toward revenging the death of his lord, was rather dull, and the film's strength came from the fact that it was an odd combination of genres: it was a *shomin-geki chambara*. A year later, in 1956, Uchida made *Disorder by the Kuroda Clan* (Kuroda Sodo), which was centered on a historical incident of rebellion against the dictatorial powers of the Tokugawa Shogunate. Again, Uchida's interest was in reality and character rather than in mere swordfighting, but even so the end product was so much like the standard period-film that most viewers did not appreciate the difference.

There were in addition some experiments in new directions. In 1954, Eisuke Takizawa, long one of the better directors of the ordinary period-films, made *Six Assassins* (Roku-nin no Ansatsusha), a reinterpretation of the events during the change-over from Tokugawa rule to modern Japan. Usually, films concerned with this subject show merely the total virtue of the Imperial faction. This film suggested a more disinterested and consequently truer approach. A scholarly samurai is assassinated because of his advocating the introduction of Western learning in Japan. His young friend feels obligated to revenge his death but, in so doing, becomes mixed up in the liberalization movement and eventually realizes that the old ways of revenge no longer have a place in new Japan. Another off-beat period-film was Kiyoshi Saeki's 1956 *Samurai of the Earth* (Daichi no Samurai), which was the story of the opening of the northern island of Hokkaido. Somewhat like those American Westerns that focus on pioneers rather than gun-slingers, it showed battle-loving samurai forced to become hardworking farmers and finding in this new struggle something that they like. It was full of what could be termed "the Japanese pioneer spirit," a very rare thing in the Japanese film.

One of the reasons for the revival of the period-film, both good and bad, in the early 1950's was perhaps in part due to an inclination to escape into the past, an inclination which was evidenced in the fields of literature and art as well as the film. Just as the public was anxious to relive the more pleasant aspects of the past war, they were equally ready to dream of the even earlier times when Japan and the rest of the world were much more calm. The good old days were symbolized for many Japanese by the Meiji period and perhaps for this reason *Meiji-mono* became very popular after 1953. One of the leaders in the movement back to Meiji was Shiro Toyoda, who now carried his interest in literary adaptations from the contemporary to the Meiji-set story. His 1954 effort, *A Certain Woman* (Aru Onna), was a failure due mainly to the fact that the film was turned into a vehicle for Machiko Kyo. His 1953 *Wild Geese* (Gan), however—shown in America as *The Mistress*—was an unqualified success.

Based on an Ogai Mori story, *Wild Geese* contained such excellent period-atmosphere that some critics believe it the best *Meiji-mono* of the postwar era. A young girl, Hideko Takamine, has been badly treated several times by men. The mistress of a man older than herself, who already has a first and legal wife, she lives alone in the house he has given her and dreams of a life with a student who passes the house frequently. Her love is never consummated; just as she finally gets to know him, he is called abroad to study.

Almost as powerful was Tadashi Imai's *Muddy Waters* (Nigorie), which won a *Kinema Jumpo* "Best One" Award in 1953. Based on three short stories by the woman writer

Ichiyo Higuchi, it was a study of three different women and
their place in Meiji society. There was an unloved wife, forced into marriage; an oppressed maid in a rich merchant's house; and a cheap prostitute who searches for a better life. There was also an excellent capturing of the Meiji flavor, and this film more than any other showed that Imai's talent was not confined to the loud "protest" pictures which his comrades were always encouraging him to make. Particularly fine was the camera work, the soft and romantic texture of the image, the beautiful dolly shots, and the excellent deep-focus work.

Another Ichiyo Higuchi story was used by Gosho for his 1955 *Growing Up* (Take-kurabe), the story of a young girl doomed from birth to a life of prostitution, and her gradually growing awareness of her fate. Though the critics objected to the "overliterary approach," something very rare in Gosho, it was, as a *Meiji-mono*, one of the finest due to its excellent sets, its superb photography, and the nearly perfect performances of everyone from Isuzu Yamada as the aged prostitute to Hibari Misora, the teen-age idol in her only serious rôle, as the young girl.

Somewhat less satisfying, though well received, was Kinoshita's *She Was Like a Wild Chrysanthemum* (Nogiku no gotoku Kimi Nariki), based on a Sachio Ito novel about an old man's returning to his hometown after having been away for sixty years. As he revisits the places he knew as a boy he recalls his youth, and most of the picture is from there on a series of flashbacks, principally dedicated to the story of how he loved his cousin when they were both very young though she was to have an arranged marriage and he was to go away to school.

Though in 1955 widescreen was beginning to influence the Japanese film, Kinoshita deliberately restricted the standard dimensions by enclosing all of the flashbacks in an oval-shaped vignette, much like the typical photographs of the time. In fact, the photography with its rich blacks, surrounded by the white oval frame, well suggested the quality of the photographs made at the time. An added strength in the film, besides marking one of Kinoshita's rare excursions into *junbungaku*, was that its evocation of area was excellent. Kinoshita is perhaps the most sensitive of Japanese directors in his use of regional characteristics, both geographical and temperamental.

Among the less successful *Meiji-mono* were Yoshimura's *Before Dawn* (Yoake mae), a story of intellectuals during the Meiji Restoration and their casting off feudalism in search

of a new life, and Taniguchi's *Fog Horn* (Muteki), a remake of an early Minoru Murata film based on a Jiro Osaragi novel about a rather singular love triangle between a
foreign trader, his mistress, and their footman.

From the Meiji period, those directors interested in the
junbungaku literary movement made the natural move up to
the Taisho period, and one of the finest results of this change
of period was Toyoda's 1955 film, *Grass Whistle* (Mugi-
bue), based on a Saisei Muro novel. A sentimental, talented
son of a Buddhist abbot has only one real confidant, a rakish
fellow-student who is also interested in writing. The two
quarrel over their rival affection for a restaurant-keeper's
daughter. Later the friend dies and when at the end of the
film, both the girl and abbot's son go to the grave, the boy's
mixed emotions prevent him from coming to an understanding with her. The film was an excellent example of what the
Japanese call "remembrance of youth pictures," and the
period-atmosphere was perfect.

In 1957, Naruse, who had been specializing almost entirely
in contemporary-life stories, made the Taisho-period *Untamed*
(Arakure), shown in America as *Untamed Woman*. Based
on a Shusei Tokuda novel, the story was about a strong-
willed and independent girl who refuses to believe that it is
a man's world—an almost heretical opinion in prewar Japan.
She runs away from an arranged marriage and becomes the
second wife of a petty merchant. When he proves too over-
bearing she leaves him to work in a small resort-hotel, eventually leaving—after more self-centered men—to open up a
tailor shop with a man with whom she has fallen in love. At
the end of the film he too has proved a disappointment and
she is planning to run off with one of his apprentices. The
girl was one of the strongest characters Naruse ever created.
She had more plain will power than all the people of his
other films put together. That she was not even stronger was
perhaps due to Hideko Takamine's introducing a definitely
postwar strain of neuroticism into her performance, a quality
which gave such pictures as *Floating Clouds* (Ukigumo)
added strength, but which seemed out of place in this film.

This *Floating Clouds*, based on a Fumiko Hayashi novel,
was one of the strongest of the *junbungaku* series with
modern settings and won the *Kinema Jumpo* "Best One"
Award for 1955. It was the story of a man and a girl who
first met during the Indonesian campaign. After the war they
continue to meet until she discovers that he has long been
married. Not knowing where to turn, she becomes the mis-

tress of an American soldier and finally becomes a prostitute, all the time cherishing the great love she feels for the married man. At last, after she has stolen some money for him from a rich uncle who has turned his military commander's talents into cash as the leader of a "new" religion, they run away together to a small island, where she dies. He approaches her bier and very slowly paints her face to make her look young, as when they first met. Then he collapses in sorrow over her dead body—the first time he has shown sincere affection. The film was outstanding for a number of reasons, one of them being the accurate portrayal of postwar life, another being the performances of Hideko Takamine and Masayuki Mori in the leading rôles. It was also filled with an eroticism not often seen in Naruse's films though its thesis, that love is an illusion, is common to most of the director's other pictures.

Another of Fumiko Hayashi's works was the basis of Yasuki Chiba's *Downtown* (Shitamachi), an excellent adaptation about a poor working woman who finds love only to lose it when the man is accidentally killed. Again the feeling of the period just after the war was beautifully captured and, again, the impermanence of love and the tragedy of being a woman were emphasized.

Shiro Toyoda brought this theme up to date in his 1957 *Snow Country* (Yukiguni), based on the Yasunari Kawabata novel. In the rather literal film adaptation, an artist staying at a hot-spring resort has relations with one of the local geisha. He keeps returning from time to time, but since he is married and since he is by nature laconic, there is little chance of their making their attachment legal or even permanent. Toyoda had wanted to make the novel into a film for twenty years, and when Toho finally gave him the chance he himself worked for four years on the preparation. Despite the strength of the film this elaborate preparation seems to have been insufficient. If anything the picture was less successful as a novelistic adaptation than many of Toyoda's others. Talky, discursive, with an ending different from the novel, it yet contained a number of scenes of psychological revelation, feelings shown rather than talked about, which are Toyoda's speciality.

Much more successful was his 1955 *Marital Relations* (Meoto Zenzai), to which Toho gave the English title *Love Is Shared Like Sweets;* a tender love story based on a Sakunosuke Oda novel. The wayward son of a well-to-do Osaka family is keeping company with a lower-class geisha. Thanks to his attentions, she loses her position in the geisha house, and, about the same time, his outraged family finally kicks him out. They have nothing but each other and at the end of the film go off together in the snow, trying to find their future. Light in spirit, it was in a very Japanese tradition and its humor was never exaggerated. Of the film Toyoda has said: "My interests are in strong, living personalities among the common people—those who after being kicked and kicked, never fall or sink. I mix this with their brightness and humor, and compound it with the speedy tempo of modern life."

Equally fine was Toyoda's next film, the 1956 *A Cat, Shozo, and Two Women* (Neko to Shozo to Futari no Onna), which was based on the Junichiro Tanizaki novel about a man who is much more fond of his cat than either of his wives. As in *Marital Relations* the emphasis was upon the young man—again perfectly played by Hisaya Morishige—and his dilemma. Dominated by his mother, terrorized by his first wife, a traditional Japanese type, and horrified by his second, a mambo-crazed modern girl who wears a bathing suit under her dress and eats butter for breakfast, he turns to the cat, Lily, for true affection and understanding. It is to Toyoda's credit as a director that the film was never once grotesque. It was instead warm, moving, and awfully funny, a winning combination of comedy and impeccable taste.

Another exceptionally tasteful film was Senkichi Taniguchi's *The Sound of Waves* (Shiosai), given the English title *The Surf* by Toho, based on the Yukio Mishima novel. The story was about the love affair between a young fishing-boy and a diving-girl on a small island in the Ise region. There were occasional lapses—as when Taniguchi went back forty years to borrow the old trick of superimposing the heroine's face on the scene to show that the hero is thinking of her—but most of the time the picture was distinguished by its tasteful restraint. This was particularly true of the nude love scenes between the two youngers, which were a far cry from the obviousness of the usual teen-age sex picture. In this film Taniguchi showed a delicacy of touch which had never been suggested in his previous pictures, and this was instrumental in making *The Sound of Waves* Taniguchi's best film since *Escape at Dawn*.

Another Mishima novel, *Kinkaku-ji*, was brought to the screen in 1958 by Kon Ichikawa in the uneven but extremely powerful *Conflagration* (Enjo). Based on the true story of the young student-priest who purposely burned Kyoto's

famed Golden Pavilion, the film, like the novel, was cold,
dispassionate, clinical, but the story was told with such visual invention, and such pictorial beauty, that one was moved by the telling if not by the story itself. Moving through expertly controlled flashbacks, the film showed the events leading to the burning, achieving a kind of formal perfection rare in any film. Cameraman Kazuo Miyagawa, who filmed *Rasho-mon*, here used widescreen as it has seldom been used before or after, capturing, in black and white, textures and surfaces so perfectly that the screen at times almost resembled a bas-relief. Though the film repelled some, not only for its cold-ness, but also because of its insistence upon pathological details, its astonishingly outspoken symbolism, its single-minded pursuit of disease, it was so beautifully conceived that it afforded a fascinating experience if not a profoundly moving one.

Excellent portrayals of the problems of adolescence were not, however, entirely confined to adaptations from literature. One of the best original scripts on the subject was *The Story of Fast-Growing Weeds* (Asunaro Monogatari), a 1955 film directed by Hiromichi Horikawa about the first three women in the life of an adolescent and how the varying relationships helped him to mature. The script was by Akira Kurosawa and was very near perfect; Horikawa, however, was guilty of not fully developing what Kurosawa had given him. Another young-love story was Imai's 1957 *A Story of Pure Love* (Junai Monogatari), about two young lovers both sick because of the evils of present-day society. The girl is a victim of atomic-radiation disease; the boy is a social rebel who makes a living by picking pockets. Imai contrasts their relative purity with the corruption of society and approves their revolt. But, as always, when the director chooses a social theme, he is more interested in propaganda than people. Imai, though all tied up with political considerations, also obviously and personally believes in revolt as an ethical neces-sity; he himself, as a person rather than a Party affiliate, feels compassion for those suffering.

Much more socially conscious and much more of a protest film was Imai's *Darkness at Noon* (Mahiru no Ankoku)—no relation to the Koestler novel—which won the 1956 *Kinema Jumpo* "Best One" Award. Based on a case pending before the Japanese courts, it took a stand and even suggested a verdict while the case was still being heard. Five youths are accused of a brutal murder and the police "force" confessions from them. While the film did treat real problems—since the

Japanese police apparently continue to be overzealous in obtaining confessions—it also unfortunately presented everything in terms of black and white. Like most Japanese films of protest, from the tendency movement to the present, it refused to look beyond the immediate evils of a social condition and took a vehement stand without once asking why this condition was possible or how it could be corrected. Akira Iwasaki, the film critic, called the film "the Japanese Sacco-Vanzetti, Tom Mooney, and Rosenberg cases all rolled into one," and while this is an overstatement, the theme was explosive enough for Toei to refuse to book the film, having allegedly received threats from high government sources. Eventually however, Imai and Toei got together and the director abandoned independent production for the security of a Toei contract. For all of his faults, Imai in the past had frequently showed a well-rounded approach. In this film, however, he sacrificed technique in the heat of argument and was not above using tear-jerking of the most unabashed *haha-mono* variety to win sympathy for his characters.

Another film suffering from the same faults was Imai's 1955 *Here Is a Spring* (Koko ni Izumi Ari), based on a supposedly true story of how an amateur orchestra brought good music to the masses. Especially interesting was the film's suggestion that only in the Japanese peasant and laboring class is there any real appreciation for the inner substance of music. It preached not enjoyment but unquestioning respect for the masterworks and showed one peasant face after the other lighting up to the strains of the *Turkish March*. When the orchestra played selections not identified in the preceding dialogue, subtitles showing the name of the composer and the work were superimposed for the benefit of the audience. In all, the movie was a perfect example of Imai's "people's film."

If Western classical music was necessary for the people, so was Shingeki. This was the point that Satsuo Yamamoto set out to prove in his *Duckweed Story* (Ukigusa Monogatari), of 1955. A provincial touring Kabuki company escapes from the rigid conventions of feudal drama into the socially oriented realism of left-wing Shingeki when they are forced to share their theater with the headquarters of a striking miners' union. The workers end up getting Art; the players get the working Gospel. The film was filled with the most arrant propaganda for the left-wing theater. The enlightened workers have to show the Kabuki actors how to act and must then provide them, for apparently the first time in their lives, with an acting philosophy. The Kabuki people in the

film were properly grateful, but the Kabuki fans of Japan
severely attacked the film for its anti-Kabuki stand.

Social criticism need not be so vehement, however, as So Yamamura discovered with his second film, *The Black Tide*, which was a fictionalization of the mysterious death of a president of the Japanese National Railways. A reporter searches for the truth rather than use any of the various versions which have been created to support existing editorial policies. The pictorial creation of the newspaper world was very effective, though Yamamura continually weakened the film by narrating parts which could have been dramatically presented. Then, having failed to dramatize his points about the freedom of the press, he has his characters talk about them.

Somewhat more effective was Yasuzo Masumura's 1958 *Giants and Toys* (Kyojin to Gangu), shown abroad as *The Build-Up*, a very fast moving and at times trenchant attack on the advertising racket in Japan. A very slick advertising director takes an unknown girl from the slums and turns her into a national celebrity, only to have her walk out on him at the end. Until the plot turned melodramatic, this unusually fast-paced film bravely attacked a prevailing materialistic social philosophy and, with an honesty rare on film, showed the cynicism and corruption of the world of mass communication.

Another critical film was Masaki Kobayashi's *I'll Buy You* (Anata Kaimasu), a 1956 movie about the overcommercialization of Japan's professional baseball world as rival teams outbid each other for the services of a high-school star. The corruption of the baseball world is such that an exposé had been long overdue, though Kobayashi lacked the power to present a really smashing indictment. Still, the picture opened up new directions for the sports-*mono* by suggesting that sport is not always the purification ritual that many Japanese apparently believe.

Much more powerful was the same director's 1957 *Black River* (Kuroi Kawa), which had as its object the corruption centering around American bases in Japan, the whores, petty gamblers, and gangsters who preyed on the American soldier stationed in Japan. Though weakened by some melodramatic touches, the picture was notable for its extremely cinematic exposition of what so easily could have become merely a static and preachy indictment. It was moral without being moralistic, and Kobayashi was obviously concerned with pictorial as well as ethical values. Further, the picture was studiously just. The villain was not America for having camps in Japan but the Japanese social system, which permitted such lawless behaviour to go unpunished. Equally just was Kobayashi's 1959 *The Human Condition* (Ningen no Joken), about the treatment of Chinese in a Japanese wartime prison camp. As social criticism its weakness was perhaps that it forgot its "message" and turned into melodrama. Yet even this fault—if fault it is—occurs so rarely in Japanese social-criticism films, most of which push "message" to the exclusion of everything else, that it at least had the charm of novelty.

Social criticism, again somewhat muted, was also seen in Kurosawa's 1955 *Record of a Living Being* (Ikimono no Kiroku), called both *I Live in Fear* and *What the Birds Knew* abroad. A seventy-year-old ironworks owner becomes obsessed with the idea that the atom bomb will destroy Japan and attempts to trade his property for a farm in Brazil, where he can retire with his family, including both wife and mistress. The family objects and in a rage he burns down his factory. Sent to a mental hospital, he is confined to a small cell and as the picture ends he looks out of the hospital window at the sun and screams: "Look! The earth is burning! It's burning!" Supposedly a protest against atom warfare, the picture wastes all of its efforts in a wandering story that lacks direction. Kurosawa fails to make the fear of the atom bomb a universal phenomenon by showing it only through the distorted imagination of his crazy old man. Actually, as shown in the film, none of the people involved were particularly worth saving from atomic extinction. The entire family was motivated entirely by greed for money, and the old man was plainly insane from the first sequence on. The argument against the atom bomb was never fully thought out, with the result that nothing really comes off and there is a failure—a truly Japanese failure—to bring things to a full and satisfying conclusion.

Another film which suffered in the same way was Kaneto Shindo's *Gutter* (Dobu), a 1954 picture about a mentally retarded girl and her oppression by society. Though one of the best of the *lumpen-mono*, its conclusion was sticky with sentiment and its criticism of society got lost in the invariable flood of tears. The picture did show, however, that Shindo can hold his own as one of Japan's best pictorialists. His images had a strength that made one remember them: the girl in front of the railway station, all dressed up, trying to attract men so she can make money; her two friends sound asleep, so poor that they must cover themselves with a boys' festival cloth-kite for a blanket; the scene, rich in burlesque over-tones, when the rich brothel-owner comes to look over the land where the lumpen have built their shacks. The film was also interesting as a combination of realism and stylization, the latter coming from films like De Sica's *Miracle in Milan* and rather akin in style to the Berthold Brecht "Epic Theater" approach.

Jukichi Uno—who played one of the young men in *Gutter*—later turned director and in his first picture, *How Sorrowful* (Aya ni Kanashiki), experimented in a kind of higher realism, a realism of character rather than of place and event, an attempt to describe one person completely, giving everything it was possible to know about him. Based on the "first-person novel" (*shishosetsu*) of Akira Kambayashi, it was the story of a novelist whose wife is confined in a mental hospital. His love for her drives him to write about her, though he runs into trouble when her parents accuse him of cashing in on her misfortune.

While the young Uno was creating a new realism, one of the oldest talents in the Japanese industry, Yasujiro Ozu, was busy testing the limits of naturalism. In his 1957 *Tokyo Twilight* (Tokyo Boshoku) he did not attempt to create character; he merely observed it, and the acting was kept on the same key throughout the film in the belief that this was the way the characters would have behaved in real life. The dialogue seemed hardly written; it seemed collected—snatches of words from real life. The camera too was more intimate than ever, with full-screen images of the actors' faces, play-ing almost directly into the lens, a technique which all the movie textbooks say to avoid.

The plot had something of a Shimpa flavor. A young girl, unadjusted to society, lacks the power to rebel; instead, she exists from day to day, carrying on a tentative affair with a student younger than she. Living with her father, she gradual-ly becomes aware that her mother is not dead, as had been supposed, and begins to search for her, her life thus achieving some direction. Actually finding her mother only leads to more disappointments, however, and this fact, coupled with complications arising from an abortion, conspire to make her kill herself. And—as in all Ozu films—life goes on.

Ozu designed both this film and the 1958 *Equinox Flower* (Higanbana) as answers to the increasing criticism of "O-funa flavor" pictures and attempted to bring the quality up to date. The question of just how successful he was became one of the biggest cinematic battles of 1957-58, the main

point being, did these films represent reality or merely a
fabricated world, a genuine slice of life or the latest twist of
the family-film?

Though one often hears Ozu criticized for being always
the same, *Tokyo Twilight* was quite different from any other
of his films. Much more Ozu-like was the 1956 *Early Spring*
(Soshun), one of his best *shomin-geki* pieces. The theme—
like that in *Tokyo Twilight*—was that Tokyo corrupts people
and yet they are held to the big city by ties which are none
the less strong for being invisible. At the end, the young
couple does escape, when the man accepts a company transfer, and they go to the country to find a happiness they did
not know in Tokyo. Yet in the final scene, as they look out
of the window of their new house at a passing train, the
husband says: "If we got on that, tomorrow morning we'd
be in Tokyo." She replies: "Yes. But three years aren't long.
They'll pass quickly." The camera lingers on her face looking longingly after the passing train.

In this two-and-a-half-hour-long picture, Ozu prolonged
the film beyond its customary length because he wanted to
give all his actors a chance to develop their parts fully. The
result is a multitude of well-played, fascinating characters
who have reality and are played with a unity that one would
hardly expect possible in a star-oriented film industry. Ozu's
"world" was never more alive than in this picture.

Reflections of this world were also seen in Kinuyo Tanaka's
second film, *The Moon Doesn't Rise*, made in 1955, which
contained the careful delineation of character usually associated with Tanaka's work and incorporated much of the
Ozu flavor—Ozu himself having helped with the script. Kinoshita's 1957 *Times of Joy and Sorrow* (Yorokobi mo Kanashimi mo Ikutoshitsuki), called *The Lighthouse* in foreign
showings, contained something of the same flavor with its
story of a family who moved from one remote lighthouse to
another. The director took nearly three hours to encompass
twenty years in their lives, yet the film did not drag, mainly
because Kinoshita exercised such fine discrimination in showing only those scenes which carried the lives of his characters
onward.

Other films too were giving the *shomin-geki* a new direction. Yuzo Kawashima's *Our Town* (Waga Machi) followed
the lives in a single neighborhood from the Meiji era to the
present day. Tomu Uchida's 1955 *Twilight Beer Hall* (Taso-
gare Sakaba) showed one day in a cheap beer-hall from opening to closing. The film was episodic in character with

various little stories about the employees and the patrons, representing a cross section of postwar life as viewed by Uchida after ten year's absence from Japan. *Will-o'-the-Wisp* (Onibi), a 1956 film by Yasuki Chiba and the first in Toho's short "Diamond Series" films, was an excellent forty-six-minute movie which showed that the short feature need not be the worst. A bachelor who collects bills for a gas company tries to seduce a poor married woman as payment for an outstanding bill and in so doing gets mixed up in her and her husband's double suicide.

Another direction for the *shomin-geki* was shown in Tomotaka Tasaka's 1955 film, *The Maid's Kid* (Jochukko), the story of a young girl fresh off the farm who comes to the city of her dreams, Tokyo, only eventually to learn that the superiority of urban life is a relative matter. Her employer's young son, after making friends with the lonely maid in Tokyo, runs off to the farm to see all the wonderful things she has told him about, and she, formerly so awkward and embarrassed by Tokyo, now sees that her employers when they come for their son are equally ignorant of farm customs. Here, as in his prewar work, Tasaka was concerned with details and thus created the definitive portrait of the thousands of young girls who come from the depressed farming areas of the north every year to become Tokyo's new supply of maids. In showing this he was considerably aided by a perfect performance from Sachiko Hidari as the girl.

Kinoshita's *Clouds at Twilight* (Yuyake Kumo), made in 1956, was also about awakening to reality and leaving illusions behind. The eldest son is full of romantic dreams and ambitions. He looks at far-off people through his telescope and constructs stories about them; he and his friend imagine all kinds of fantasies; he longs more than anything else to be a seaman and go away to distant and exotic places. Gradually, however, the responsibilities of the small family business become his, and when his father dies he must prematurely enter the adult world. In a wonderful final scene, what it means to be an adult suddenly comes upon him as he looks over his small childish world and says: "Goodbye—to everything I loved; to the girl I saw in my telescope; to my sister; to my friends; to my hopes of becoming a seaman." There has seldom been a better pictorialization of the tremendous change required of the Japanese when he leaves a very free childhood for the narrow restrictions of adult society.

In 1957, Kinoshita took great delight in showing just what those restrictions were, in the *shomin-geki* comedy *Candle in*

the Wind (Fuzen no Tomoshibi), which was about a thoroughly revolting middle-class suburban family and what
happened when they won a lot of money. Some young thugs,
bedraggled remnants of the *taiyozoku,* set out to burgle the
happy prize-winners but, though they hang around all day
long, never get the chance. Friends and relatives have gotten
there first and already begun the work of depredation.
Toward the end of the film, the family is so upset that there
is nothing to do but weep, and this they do in a delicious
parody of the endless crying scenes in the usual Shochiku
family-film.

Gosho's 1957 film, *The Yellow Crow* (Kiiroi Karasu),
called *Behold Thy Son* in America, was also about maturity
attained, though this film was not nearly so persuasive as the
Kinoshita one. A young boy has formed an idealized image
of his father, who has yet to be repatriated from Russia.
When they finally meet they fail to get along together.
The boy withdraws more and more into himself, and the
picture is concerned with how the two gradually develop a
love for each other. Children's problems had been much
better handled by Gosho in *Growing Up,* and due to a
weak script the eventual reconciliation in *The Yellow Crow*
was too fast to be convincing. There was, however, at least
an attempt to introduce psychological elements into the
usually tear-laden home-drama genre.

Much more successful was Gosho's 1954 film, *An Inn at
Osaka* (Osaka no Yado), which was a real slice-of-life presentation of existence in Japan's commercial center. As one
Japanese review said: "The emphasis here is on money in
the money capital—Osaka. Although the major figures are not
materialistic, they find they cannot live without money." This
gradual discovery undermines both the morals and the ideals
of everyone in the film. The man transferred from Tokyo,
the maids at the inn, the geisha who entertains—all are completely controlled by the need for money and all are controlled at the expense of both their instincts and their better
natures. An extremely powerful and a very sad film, it is—in
its very understatement—one of the very best of the indict-
ments of postwar Japan.

In the same year Gosho also made *The Valley between
Life and Death* (Ai to Shi no Tanima), in which the mutual
suspicions of a man and wife force the former to hire a
detective to follow the wife wherever she goes. She, made
miserable by this constant attendance, makes friends with the
detective, and eventually the husband's suspicions are ironical-

ly confirmed by her first infidelity—with the detective. A somewhat more typical film was *The Cock Crows Again* (Niwatori wa Futatabi Naku), a satirical revival of the *lumpen-mono*, about three girls, one illegitimate, one a cripple, one an abandoned child, who start off to examine life. They become involved with a gang of lumpen and eventually discover hitherto untapped hot springs—one of the few ways of making a fortune in Japan since resort towns always flourish wherever there are hot springs.

Altogether, however, there was much less comedy—and considerably less satire—in this period than in the preceding, one of the reasons being that the "straight" dramatic film was including more comedy and humor, examples being *Early Spring, Marital Relations, An Inn at Osaka,* and *A Cat, Shozo, and Two Women.* One of the finest Japanese comedies ever made, however, was the 1955 *Police Diary* (Keisatsu Nikki), a 1955 film of Seiji Hisamatsu's. It was a collection of short sketches based around a rural police station in northern Japan: the thief who steals only from temples because religious articles have a certain scholarly fascination for him; the labor-union official from the city who tries to get credit for rescuing a girl from being sold into prostitution; the poor drayman who gets the job of carrying his girl friend's large dowry to the home of her husband when her parents force her to marry against her wishes. We laugh with these people because their entanglement with the law seems so petty. Even then, however, the police are most reluctant to "do their duty." The community is in reality too well organized to need a police force. Actually the police's only real duty is the maintenance of the town's fire engine, but this too is superfluous since the truck is so old that it breaks down as soon as it gets out of the fire station.

Another outstanding comedy was Yasuki Chiba's *Large Size* (Oban), a 1957 film in several feature-length parts. Set in the 1920's, it was about a rather heavy (large size) man whose ambitions are equally big. He is a go-getter of the mythological American type whose constant energy in life and business is completely foreign to the traditional social ideals of the Japanese. Even in love he considers no woman beyond his ability, and here too he is generally successful for, as the picture delicately hints, he is large size all over. He is constantly losing everything—women and money both—only to gain back even more through sheer energy and determination.

Other comedies included *Bundle of Love* (Ai no Nimotsu),

a 1956 Yuzo Kawashima film which is a satirical treatment of
the *haha-mono:* a family begins to feel the pressure of over-
population due to its large number of children. Satsuo Yamamoto also dropped polemic long enough to make *Uproar
Over a Typhoon* (Taifu Sodoki), about a small town hit by
a typhoon which realizes that it could have had its disaster
recompensation greatly increased had its school been
destroyed. This oversight on the part of the typhoon the
town officials remedy themselves by tearing down the school.
Certain teachers, however, mobilize to put a stop to the graft.
Yoshitaro Nomura's *A Tale of Dung and Urine* (Funnyo-
dan), a 1957 film, was based on an Ashihei Hino novel about
a simple but honest collector of night-soil who runs into
trouble with gangsters. The film was distinguished by a
climactic sequence in which the aroused and united night-
soil collectors run through the city dousing their opposition
with the day's collection.

Social problems were not all treated humorously, however.
Among the more serious was Kimisaburo Yoshimura's 1954
Cape Ashizuri (Ashizuri Misaki), a study of left-wing
students in the 1933–34 period and the violent police suppression of their activities. Based on autobiographical stories by
Torahiko Tamiya, the film kept close to the original and,
instead of making violent propaganda, presented a gentle but
forceful protest against excessive injustice. But the most
moving of all the pictures dealing with the problems of the
1930's subordinated the political and social questions to those
concerned with character. This was Kinoshita's extremely
fine *Twenty-four Eyes*, which won the *Kinema Jumpo*
"Best One" Award for 1954. It then went on to win the
Hollywood Henrietta Award, and the French critic Georges
Sadoul said, upon viewing it out of festival competition in
1955, that it would certainly have won the highest award
had it only been entered.

Beginning in 1927, the film shows the life of a woman
teacher and her pupils through the following two decades of
Japanese life, showing how the big events of history made
themselves felt in a small island community. There was a
deliberate dropping of experiments in form and technique to
meet realism head-on in one of Japan's greatest lyrical
pictures. The film was also a triumph of casting, using
amateur children picked up on the spot with an excellent
matching of the child actors who played the various children
at different age levels, and incorporating a truly beautiful
performance by Hideko Takamine as the teacher. Though

the film was sentimental, it was a sentimentalism dictated by the situation and not forced on the plot in an effort to milk tears; for once in the Japanese film, the sentiment was called for by the emotional situation.

Another 1954 Kinoshita film was *The Garden of Women* (Onna no Sono), which was an exposé of conditions in an upper-class, feudalistic girls' boarding school in Kyoto, with an interesting treatment of the girls' emotional problems somewhat suggestive of the German *Mädchen in Uniform*. Here Kinoshita's realism underwent a change of pace, and in contrast to the lyricism of the earlier film, there was a stronger, rougher approach. Again, the film was a study of the teaching profession, but this time it took the form of a protest against feudal survivals. The characters were very sharply, almost coldly, drawn: the spinster teacher who once had a baby; the girl forced to go to school by her father so she would be kept away from her boy friend; the rich girl with extremely left-wing ideas. When one of the girls commits suicide because she is thought to be one of the teachers' spies, the girls break out into open rebellion.

Milder in its social protest was Imai's *Rice* (Kome), a film which showed the life of farmers from rice planting to rice harvesting, and which took over half a year to film. The impetus behind the film was Toei, which desperately needed a prestige film to raise its status in the industry. So Imai was called in to make another *Earth*, the prewar Tomu Uchida film, and though he did not succeed, his results were praised in Japan—for intentions rather than for achievement. This 1957 film was designed to examine the social problems of rural life, particularly the tensions between the farmers and the fishermen in the nearby coastal villages, and the surplus of sons. Though Imai tried for a lyrical realism completely opposed to the polemic of *Darkness at Noon*, his success was but partial. This, however, did not discourage the critics, especially those of the *Kinema Jumpo* school, who have long shown a tendency to confuse slow pace and loose direction with lyricism.

One of the perennial problems of Japan is the family system and what it does to the individual. In this film Imai showed social pressures within the family gradually killing his heroine, and in Naruse's 1954 film, *Sounds from the Mountains* (Yama no Oto), the director questioned the boundaries of the family system. A woman is married to a man who no longer loves her and who in fact has a mistress. The wife wants an abortion because she refuses to bear a child by her

unloving husband, while the mistress is determined to have
a child by him. The wife stays on in the house because she and her husband's father have developed a platonic friendship of considerable depth. The parents, too, feel closer to her than they do toward their own daughter. What makes the picture outstanding is the subtlety with which Naruse makes his characters reveal emotions they are trying to hide. The emotions are examined on several levels, beginning with the obvious, the surface emotion, and working inwards. One of the ways in which Naruse does this is through repeated use of close-ups so that the camera has almost microscopic properties, catching the hidden reactions that would have been unnoticed in a medium- or long-shot.

The family system even lost Shochiku's long-standing support in Noboru Nakamura's *White Devil-Fish* (Shiroi Magyo), a 1956 film which was one of the first heartily to approve of a "good girl's" refusal to follow her mother's advice. Many previous films had showed daughters refusing to follow parental desires, but in these pictures the girls were either all bad or else, if good, had to pay for their misdoings. Nakamura's film, however, took a direct stand for modern youth. In the same year, however, Shochiku reversed its position with *Tears* (Namida), called *Bliss on Earth* in the United States. Here feudalism won out and the film pushed the message that arranged marriages are really the best. In Kimisaburo Yoshimura's *Night River* (Yoru no Kawa), shown under the title of *Undercurrent* at the 1957 New York Japanese Film Festival, the heroine longs for freedom in very traditional Kyoto and wants to become a "new woman." Though she succeeds to the extent of identifying herself with the parading workers on May Day, she finds the conflict between modern social ideas and the facts of her own feudal background too much for her. Somewhat the same problem arose in Heinosuke Gosho's 1957 *Dirge* (Banka), about a lonely young girl in a small Hokkaido port city who discovers a kind of escape in adultery, only to find herself responsible for the wife's suicide.

Toyoda's 1957 *Evening Calm* (Yunagi) has its heroine rebelling against the fatalism and traditions of Japanese society. Her mother runs a whorehouse in Yokohama, and though she has a number of brothers and sisters, she does not really know who they are since her mother had children by a number of men. She rebels and tries to find personal happiness outside the milieu of her own family, and in part succeeds. The final scene shows her clerking in a bookstore, independ-

ent and relatively happy, refusing to help a foreigner who
is attempting to find some material on the Yoshiwara, once Japan's largest licensed quarter.

This heroine's problem was shared by the girl in Naruse's *Flowing* (Nagareru), a 1956 film based on an original by Fumi Kota. The film was praised by Japanese critics for its wonderful creation of the geisha world, but Naruse was also criticized for failing to develop the characterizations in a deeper manner and for his inability or reluctance to show social conditions as the base of the problem which faces everyone in the film: the end of a way of life, the disintegration of the world of the geisha.

In 1954's *Late Chrysanthemums*, Naruse had already looked at this world of the geisha in an adaptation of some of the stories of the director's favorite writer, Fumiko Hayashi. A retired geisha, now middle-aged, has gone into business and become a success. With her money she tries to recapture her youth and young loves. Another geisha owns and operates a small restaurant along with her husband; yet another loses her only son when he leaves her to become an older woman's paid lover. Though all of the ex-geisha are searching for love, none of them find it. They are shown as having worn out the tricks of their trade; everything is fake as they try to live a life that is false and to assume personalities which are not their own.

Kimisaburo Yoshimura examined the same problem from a lighter viewpoint in his 1955 *Women of the Ginza* (Ginza no Onna), which was about life in a high-class Tokyo geishahouse just off the Ginza, Tokyo's fashionable shopping center and main street. The film's tone was good-humored, but rather than rely on funny incidents, Yoshimura treated rather serious events in a humorous style and intended to offer a combination of satiric comment and reality. His 1957 *Night Butterflies* (Yoru no Cho) dropped several rungs in the social ladder and took up the lives of the women who run Ginza bars, the so-called "madames" ubiquitous to Japanese nightlife. In the 1958 *Naked Face of Night* (Yoru no Sugao), he turned his attention to the world of the classical dance and so candidly showed its bloodthirsty rivalries and tooth-and-claw machinations that several leading dancers complained.

Probably the best of all these films examining the problems of women in postwar Japan was Kenji Mizoguchi's last film before his death, the 1956 *Red-Light District* (Akasen Chitai). Originally, Mizoguchi planned to make the film in a semi-documentary fashion, filming extensively on actual locations. But at the time legalized prostitution was encountering so much public opposition that the brothel owners, fearful of attracting further attention to their operations, refused to cooperate, and Mizoguchi had to retreat to the studio to make his picture. The finished film appeared during the heated and widely publicized Diet debates which were shortly to result in Japan's anti-prostitution law, and was a box-office smash. It was also a success in the United States, where, playing under the title *Street of Shame*, it was the very first outstanding film on Japanese contemporary life to command a large American audience.

In it Mizoguchi continued and concluded his presentation of the Japanese woman and her problems. At the time of his death the most experienced director in Japanese films, having been active for thirty-five years in the industry, Mizoguchi in both period and contemporary pictures was also one of the finest directors, having done much to shape the past and indicate the future of the Japanese film.

The future is probably less problematical than it is in other countries. At present the Japanese industry creates not only more films than any other in the world, but it also—despite ups and downs—manages to maintain an extraordinarily high level in the pictures made by its score of top directors. From its rich and varied heritage—with its many mistakes, its many triumphs—the Japanese industry is at present in a unique if anomalous position. It has managed to retain a nation-wide audience and to let its products be occasionally seen overseas. The various misfortunes suffered by the industries of other countries have left the Japanese relatively unscathed. One of the last of the film industries to attain an individual flavor, it may well be one of the last to survive in this modern age.

97. *Wild Geese*, 1953, Shiro Toyoda. The past recaptured. Shown abroad as *The Mistress*. Hiroshi Akutagawa, Hideko Takamine.

98. *The Tower of Lilies*, 1953, Tadashi Imai. The tragedies of war.

99. *A Japanese Tragedy*, 1953, Keisuke Kinoshita. A highly successful experimental approach to the postwar scene. Keiko Awaji, Yuko Mochizuki.

100. *Muddy Waters*, 1953, Tadashi Imai. The exploitation of women. Chikage Awashima (*r*).

101. *The Sound of Waves*, 1954, Senkichi Taniguchi. A film version of Yukio Mishima's novel. Akira Kubo, Kyoko Aoyama.

102. *Seven Samurai*, 1954, Akira Kurosawa. The period-film as it should be done. Shown abroad as *The Magnificent Seven*. Toshiro Mifune, Minoru Chiaki, Takashi Shimura.

103. *Gutter*, 1954. Kaneto Shindo. The idiot prostitute and her boy friends. Nobuko Otowa, Jukichi Uno, Taiji Tono-yama.

104. *Sansho the Bailiff*, 1954, Kenji Mizoguchi. The past viewed with the realism of the present. Kinuyo Tanaka (*c*).

105. *An Inn at Osaka*, 1954, Hei-nosuke Gosho. An authentic slice of life. Nobuko Otowa, Shuji Sano.

106. *A Story
from Chikamatsu*,
1954, Kenji Mizo-
guchi. The wife
and her lover: a
realistic period-
film. Kyoko
Kagawa, Kazuo
Hasegawa.

107. *The Valley
between Love and
Death*, 1954, Hei-
nosuke Gosho.
Tribulations and
the silver lining.
Kyoko Anzai,
Hiroshi Akuta-
gawa.

108. *Musashi
Miyamoto*, 1954,
Hiroshi Inagaki.
The standard
period-drama.
Shown abroad as
Samurai. Rentaro
Mikuni, Toshiro
Mifune.

109. *Sounds from the Mountains,* 1954, Mikio Naruse. The married couple breaking up. Setsuko Hara. Teruko Nagaoka. So Yamamura.

110. *Twenty-four Eyes,* 1954, Keisuke Kinoshita. The life of a schoolteacher and her pupils. Hideko Takamine (*c*).

111. *The Beauty and the Dragon,* 1955, Kimisaburo Yoshimura. New directions for the period-film.

112. *Grass Whistle*, 1955, Shiro Toyoda. Young lovers separated by their dead friend. Kyoko Aoyama, Akira Kubo.

113. *Record of a Living Being*, 1955, Akira Kurosawa. The H-bomb and human dignity. Toshiro Mifune (*c*), Bokuzen Hidari (*r*).

114. *The Maid's Kid*, 1955, Tomotaka Tasaka. The country girl in Tokyo. Sachiko Hidari.

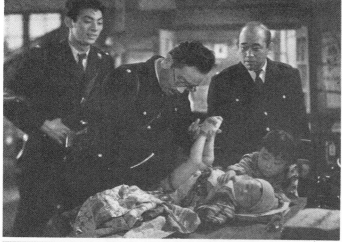

115. *Police Diary*, 1955, Seiji Hisamatsu. A wry look at the officers of law and order. Hisaya Morishige (*m*) Taiji Tonoyama (*r*).

116. *Marital Relations*, 1955, Shiro Toyoda. The ruined geisha and her no-good boy friend. Chikage Awashima. (*u*), Hisaya Morishige (*l*).

117. *Growing Up*, 1955, Heinosuke Gosho. Two prostitutes: old and young. Isuzu Yamada, Hibari Misora.

118. *Floating Clouds*, 1955, Mikio Naruse. A backward look at the immediate postwar world. Hideko Takamine, Masayuki Mori.

119. *She Was Like a Wild Chrysanthemum*, 1955, Keisuke Kinoshita. A boy's first love affairs. Shinji Tanaka, Noriko Arita.

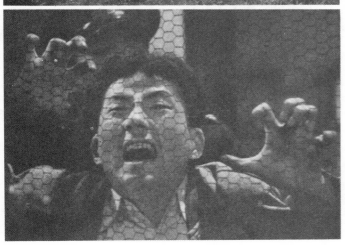

120. *Darkness at Noon*, 1956, Tadashi Imai. Police pressure and the far left. Kojiro Kusanagi.

121. *Early Spring*, 1956, Yasujiro Ozu. The dilemma of the white-collar worker. Ryo Ikebe, Chikage Awashima, Chishu Ryu.

122. *Sudden Rain*, 1956, Mikio Naruse. The married couple agrees to get along Setsuko Hara, Shuji Sano.

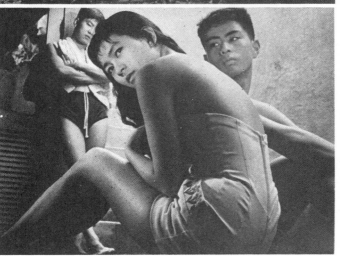

123. *Crazed Fruit*, 1956, Yasushi Nakahira. Sun, sea, and juvenile delinquency. Shown abroad as *Juvenile Passion*. Yujiro Ishihara, Mie Kitahara, Masahiko Tsugawa.

124. *Harp of Burma*, 1956, Kon Ichikawa. The soldier who became a priest. Shoji Yasui.

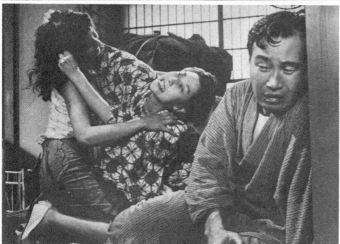

125. *A Cat, Shozo, and Two Women*, 1956, Shiro Toyoda. About a man who loves his cat more than either of his wives. Kyoko Kagawa, Isuzu Yamada, Hisaya Morishige.

126. *Red-Light District*, 1956, Kenji Mizoguchi. The last of the prostitutes. Machiko Kyo, Aiko Mimasu, Ayako Wakao, Kumeko Urabe, Sadako Sawamura, Eitaro Shindo.

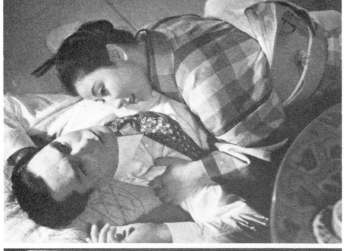

127. *Night River.*
1956, Kimisaburo
Yoshimura. A
modern girl in old
Kyoto. Ken Ue-
hara (*l*), Fujiko
Yamamoto (*u*).

128. *Flowing,*
1956, Mikio Naru-
se. The geisha in
a society of
changing values.
Hideko Takamine,
Isuzu Yamada,
Kinuyo Tanaka.

129. *The Castle
of the Spider's
Web,* 1957, Akira
Kurosawa. Mac-
beth in medieval
Japan. Shown
abroad as *The
Throne of Blood.*
Toshiro Mifune.

130. *Tokyo Twilight*, 1957, Yasujiro Ozu. Daughter, mother, and the break-up of the family. Setsuko Hara, Isuzu Yamada.

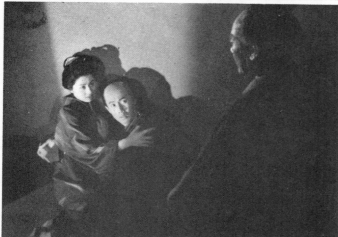

131. *An Osaka Story*, 1957, Kimisaburo Yoshimura. The rise of a middle-class family. Kyoko Kagawa, Raizo Ichikawa, Ganjiro Nakamura.

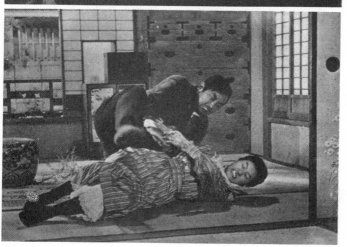

132. *Untamed*, 1957, Mikio Naruse. The Japanese woman fights back. Daisuke Kato (*u*), Hideko Takamine (*l*).

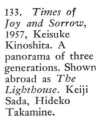

133. *Times of Joy and Sorrow*, 1957, Keisuke Kinoshita. A panorama of three generations. Shown abroad as *The Lighthouse*. Keiji Sada, Hideko Takamine.

134. *Rice*, 1957, Tadashi Imai. Peasants, crops, and taxes. Masako Nakamura, Yuko Mochizuki.

135. *Black River*, 1957, Masaki Kobayashi. Gangsters and soldiers. Tatsuya Nakadai, Ineko Arima.

136. *Snow Country*, 1957, Shiro Toyoda. The patron and the geisha: an adaptation of the Yasunari Kawabata novel. Ryo Ikebe, Keiko Kishi.

137. *Downtown*, 1957, Yasuki Chiba. Lives of the poor but rich in heart. Toshiro Mifune, Isuzu Yamada.

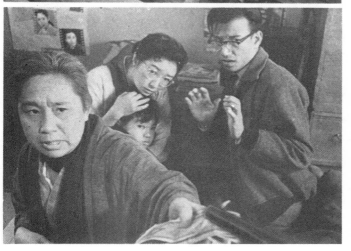

138. *Candle in the Wind*, 1957, Keisuke Kinoshita. The Japanese family at bay: grandmother and the married couple. Akiko Tamura, Hideko Takamine, Keiji Sada.

139. *The Lower Depths*, 1957, Akira Kurosawa. Gorky in the Tokugawa period. Toshiro Mifune, Isuzu Yamada.

140. *Night Drum*, 1958, Tadashi Imai. The adulterous wife and her forgiving husband. Shown abroad as *The Adulteress*. Ineko Arima, Rentaro Mikuni.

141. *The Life of Matsu the Untamed*, 1958, Hiroshi Inagaki. The director's remake of his 1943 film. Shown abroad as *Rickshaw Man*. Toshiro Mifune.

142. *The Song of Narayama*, 1958, Keisuke Kinoshita. A legend about old age and death. Kinuyo Tanaka, Teiji Takahashi.

143. *Conflagration*, 1958, Kon Ichikawa. The story of the boy who burned the Golden Pavilion. Raizo Ichikawa.

144. *Three Bad Men in a Hidden Fortress*, 1959, Akira Kurosawa. The period adventure-film. Toshiro Mifune, **Minoru Chiaki, Kamatari Fujiwara.**

part two

foreground

13 content. THE content of the Japanese film is not radically different from that of films in other countries. The average period-film finds a ready equivalent in the American Western; the home drama is much at home in France; *Stella Dallas* and René Clément's *Gervaise* alike are *haha-mono*. The main difference, perhaps, is in the attitude of the Japanese film-maker and his audience, the singular way in which both tend to think of the film product.

The non-Japanese film-maker thinks of his film as an entity, standing by itself. To be sure, if he is making a Western he realizes that he is working in a genre, but otherwise he does not usually tend to see his film as belonging to a given category. The Japanese film-maker, on the other hand, is conscious not only that he is working in a given genre but also that within this genre he is specializing in a rigidly defined type, or *mono*, which, in turn, is often even further subdivided.

The Japanese tend to classify to such an extent that they have a category for everything, Japanese or not. Any film with a self-sacrificing heroine is a *kachusha-mono*, named after the heroine of Tolstoy's *Resurrection;* the type of film in which Marilyn Monroe appears is a *monro-mono;* Harold Lloyd has given his name to both a comedy genre and also to rimmed spectacles which are still called *roido*.

The largest genre division, as has earlier been indicated, is that between the *jidai-geki*, or period-film, and the *gendai-geki*, or film about contemporary life. The period-film is distinguished by both period and content. The former is usually the Tokugawa era; the latter is always feudalistic and

was developed from the popular arts of the period, the *kodan*,
the *naniwa-bushi*, and—to a much lesser extent—the Kabuki.

Both the *kodan* and the *naniwa-bushi* are recited stories, complicated in plot and endless in number, most of which Japanese know from earliest childhood. When the *kodan* tales appear on film, the audience comes to the theater already knowing the basic story. A certain prior knowledge is assumed by the film-maker and there is no attempt made to provide full exposition since it is familiarity more than novelty which entrances the Japanese audience. Still, the *kodan* stories on film often concern themselves with underdeveloped phases of a well-known character's life, the movie often becoming a series of such tidbits, the better-known connecting sections left out, to the complete bafflement of anyone not familiar with the character.

The favorite stories are, naturally, those most often filmed. These usually center around a beloved feudal hero: Musashi Miyamoto, Mataemon Araki, Chuji Kunisada, Jirocho of Shimizu, the Soga brothers, or Komon Mito. Year in and year out these characters appear on the Japanese screen. Though there may be new interpretations and new minor characters, the story is basically always the same because the audience will have it no other way. The hardiest of the perennials is the Kabuki play, *The Loyal Forty-seven Ronin*, of which one or even two film versions are made every year.

All of these period-stories share a majority of elements, one such being a respect for the *giri-ninjo* conflict: the battle between obligation and human feelings, the contention between duty and inclination. There are various ways of treating this conflict. Sometimes duty means doing bad, personal belief and emotion symbolizing the course of action which would benefit society. Sometimes duty means doing good; human feelings and inclination would demand a bad action. At other times the "social" evil of refusing to do one's duty is outweighed by the humanity and the righteousness of the opposing course of action. Sometimes the audience does not know whether an action has been performed for the sake of duty or for the sake of human feelings; or it knows which action is for duty but does not know which action has been performed. In any event, the action in either direction is usually compelled by forces outside the characters involved, because the governing philosophy is that an individual's ability to influence his future is almost non-existent. Hence, the course of action is usually compelled by fate.

A variant of the *giri-ninjo* conflict is seen in the common

and popular *isshoku ippan,* "a meal and a night's lodging,"
dilemma. A man accepts this minor form of hospitality and
thus becomes terribly involved, because he is inescapably
obligated to pay back the favor. The wandering samurai who
receives a meal and a bed finds that in the morning he is expected to participate in an attack on the host's enemy, who
usually turns out to be the samurai's friend.

Another variant is the *oyabun-kobun,* "gang boss and
underling," relationship, which is always of the greatest use
in moving the period-film along. Here, unswerving loyalty is
owed, the samurai to his lord, the gang member to his boss.
Something gets in the way and *kobun* finds that he must
oppose his lord, or—as in *The Loyal Forty-seven Ronin,* the
lord is killed and his samurai must avenge him. This compulsion for revenge animates all period-films. Often it takes
the form of direct retaliatory murder. Sometimes it is a bit
more subtle. The loyal forty-seven *ronin* all commit suicide
before the grave of their maligned leader.

Another favorite device is the *migawari,* when one person
substitutes for another. Persons openly or covertly offer
themselves for sacrifice in place of a friend or relative to
whom obligation is owed. This nicely thickens any revenge
plot and, despite the fact that the gesture is usually an empty
one, brings on massive complications. In the same way, minor
infractions of the social code—the love of the villain for the
wife of the dead lord of the *ronin* in *The Loyal Forty-seven
Ronin*—bring on major catastrophes. The answer and solution
to such problems is usually suicide since it alone will "clear
the name" of the person and because suicide—by period-film
standards—is so ennobling an act.

Many period-film stories are set in the later Tokugawa era,
that period just before the nineteenth-century restoration of
the throne and the "opening" of the country. These usually
hinge on the rivalry between the Imperial forces and those of
the Shogunate. Although history favors neither, tradition in
the film says that the emperor's side was the right one. To
suggest otherwise before the war would have been dangerous,
but even in the postwar world, the imperial side is constantly
favored. If one is not certain, one can always tell which side
is favored by the number of fighters left alive on each side
after a sword fight. It is nothing for one of these *chambara*
heroes to kill from twenty-five to fifty people in every film,
and all by himself. The enemy gang attacks the single hero
who—if it is a musical period-film—will sing while he slashes,
missing neither note nor man.

Pointless killing is one of the main features of the Japanese film, whether *chambara* or modern gangster movie. Innumerable people are killed to no apparent point. In fact, looking at the general run of Japanese pictures, the feeling of the cheapness of human life is unescapable. Apart from excessive killing, Japanese films also tend to accentuate the attendant gore. Gushing blood, open wounds, and the like abound in the average Japanese adventure film, period or modern. There are also all kinds of torture and various varieties of suicide. Often the violence goes beyond the bounds of plot necessity. For example, a man falls dead toward the camera. He has been fatally shot or stabbed. This, however, is not enough. Right in the foreground, next to the camera, is a fire into which his head drops. As we watch the fire burn away his face, horses trample upon his body—all in full detail. In Nikkatsu's 1955 *Beyond the Green* (Midori Haruka ni), made especially for primary school children, there was a scene in which a gang of children, having finally captured the villain, pin him to the ground while the heaviest of their number climbs onto a seven-foot ledge and jumps off onto the man's chest, to the accompaniment of the sound of crunching bones.

Before the war, the period-film—not always completely gruesome but almost always filled with aimless slaughter—comprised half of the total film production of Japan. After the war, however, thanks to the Occupation's stand on the period-picture, there was very little activity in this genre. In the past five years, however, period-films have come to represent about one-third of the total production.

The other two-thirds are films about contemporary life, and these *gendai-geki* are subdivided into many different categories. The prevalence of the *haha-mono*, or mother films, has already been indicated. With their constant theme of the sufferings of mother for husband and/or children, they have a great appeal for women in general and before the war were among the most common of the *gendai-geki* genres.

In the usual *haha-mono* there is no escape for mother. She must sacrifice and suffer. It is all part of her life. If she has any happiness, it is only in the hope that her husband may reform. There is very slight chance of this. It is not even socially desirable in a totally male-oriented society. Another possible reward for her sufferings is that they may bring success and/or happiness to her children. But seldom do the children understand what mother has had to go through for their sakes. And even if they do, they often despise her for it. In many films the suffering mother is a widow who is forced to become a prostitute to support her child. When the script-writer wants to make things really difficult for mother he calls in the dead husband's senile parents. They move in, disrupting her business ventures and vastly increasing the obligations she is obliged to meet.

But there are also problems with the children. In a foreign film when a child "betrays his parents" and runs away, the mother feels that she has some connection with her child's departure and that perhaps he will be happier away from home. She gradually comes to see things from her child's viewpoint. Not so the Japanese mother in the *haha-mono*. It seldom occurs to her that the child's happiness may be at stake. She feels totally betrayed and the only remedy is a complete reconciliation in which all the old relationships are restored. The mother in foreign films finds happiness through adjustment; the Japanese film mother almost never realizes that any adjustment, other than her child's, is called for. Mother's attitude may be unreasonable but, as the critic Tatsuhiko Shigeo has pointed out, in Japanese films the highest attainment a woman can reach is not in becoming a wife, as in American films, but in becoming a mother.

In postwar Japanese films, mother still reigns but her position is no longer supreme. In fact, mother rôles are now only about four percent of the total female rôles in Japanese movies. Even princesses and geishas are higher, at about seven percent each. Most frequent of all is the wife; eleven percent of all female rôles in the Japanese films belong to her.

The *tsuma-mono* or wife picture is, generally speaking, a postwar development. Of course wives were featured in pre-war pictures, but seldom did the film focus on them as individuals unless they also happened to be mothers. In such cases the fact that a mother is also a wife was irrelevant. To speak of a mother in a *haha-mono* is to speak of a person who occupies a definite place in the family; she is a unit in the Japanese family system and, as such, though thoroughly representative of all mothers everywhere, is scarcely treated as an individual. In the *tsuma-mono*, on the other hand, it is a concern for the wife as an individual which animates the film. Her problems are personally hers and though she may represent young or old wives everywhere the emphasis is upon her as an individual and not as a unit in the family system.

The wife's problems are not too varied as seen in the Japanese film. Usually the *tsuma-mono* wife is concerned with her attempt to defend or find her individuality. Very often her problems arise from an empty married life. She thus seeks

other ways in which to expand her personality. Sometimes
the plot hinges on the wife's or the husband's inconsequential
affair with another person and comes to a climax when both
discover their old love for each other.

The clichés of the *haha-* and *tsuma-mono* are many, though
just how well the genres may be handled is seen in films like
Kinoshita's *A Japanese Tragedy* or Ozu's *The Flavor of
Green Tea and Rice.* More often than not, however, both of
the *mono* degenerate into the most unabashed of tear-jerkers,
the kind of films the Japanese call *o-namida chodai eiga* or
"tears-please films," the kind that the critics sometimes
measure as one-, two-, or three-handkerchief pictures.

Chikamatsu, the most important of Kabuki playwrights,
and the one whom the Japanese delight in calling "the
Shakespeare of Japan" had a few words to say on tear-jerking, a practice which he himself scrupulously avoided: "I take
pathos to be entirely a matter of restraint... It is essential
that one not say of a thing that it is sad but that it be sad of
itself." The very sage advice is usually disregarded in films
and one of the results is the deluge of tears which all too
frequently accomplishes the end of a Japanese film.

Japanese pictures as a whole are much more concerned
with trivial emotionalism than with any higher tragic feeling.
The usual word for tragedy in Japanese is *higeki,* and the
literal meaning of this word, "sad play," comes much closer
to what it really is. The truth is that not only in the movies
but also in every form of Japanese drama there is really no
need for a word fully to describe a play that deals with, say,
the subject matter of *Phèdre* or *King Lear* because such
emotional heights are completely missing. To the Japanese,
Hamlet is little more than a faithful son avenging his father's
death; one who loves his mother not in Olivier's Oedipus-like
fashion but merely as every good boy should. One of the
many reasons for this lack of what the Occident considers
the higher emotions is that the individual and his problems
are—in art if not in life—continually sacrificed to the well-
being of society, and in Japan society means the family
system. The penetration of this system into Japanese film
stories is complete, not only in such obvious forms as home
drama, but also in every other genre as well.

In gang pictures, for example, the members are always in
a family relationship to each other, the *oyabun-kobun* relationship. In period-films the unattached swordsman (*kobun*)
under obligation assumes a "son-like" attitude toward his
"father-like" benefactor (*oyabun*). Again, in geisha stories,

the owner is always called mother, and the girls refer to each
other as sisters—as they do in real life. In the white-collar-
worker films, the company manager plays father while his
wife is a mother to the company employees. This relationship
is insisted upon not only during the working hours: marriage
to the president's daughter is frequent in this kind of film.

Although the continual triumph of tradition in Japanese
pictures seems unusually reactionary to Americans, who make
a virtue of rebelling against certain types of tradition, it is
dictated by forces similar to those in America which demand
that in all films righteousness and happiness triumph. In Japan the established view is that justice and the well-being of
society depend on the maintenance of established ways and
that to break them is to threaten society. In America there is
the fear that showing evil in any way triumphant would
threaten the basis of society; to suggest that the happiness of
the individual is not identical with the highest aims of society
is to threaten society itself. Naturally, such are the views of
the moral and ethical purists in their respective countries.
Reality is far different, and this fact every film-maker of
integrity knows and shows in his pictures.

Yet, in Japan, devotion to the myth is extreme. Shiro Kido,
the Louis B. Mayer of Shochiku, believes so strongly in the
traditional family system, what he considers the "healthy
family life," that he advocates it in all Shochiku productions
with an almost religious fervor. The difficulty is that such
an attitude no longer reflects the reality of Japanese life and
that it appeals to an ever decreasing audience. Kido knows
this very well and yet he is apparently willing to sacrifice
commercial considerations to further propagandize the system.

In addition to those mentioned above there are many, many
other film categories. *Meiji-* and *Taisho-mono* have been
touched upon earlier, as also have the nonsense-*mono* and the
salaryman-*mono*. The sports-*mono* has long been popular in
Japan though it is seldom concerned with the quieter athletic
activities, nor indeed, with any which cannot be used in action
dramas. Thus, the greater number of these films is entirely
concerned with judo, American-style professional wrestling,
and *karate*. Despite Japan's universal passion for baseball,
films about this sport are rare.

One of the more interesting genres is the *shakai-mono*, or
social genre, of which Kurosawa's drama of insanity in the
hydrogen-bomb era, *Record of a Living Being*, is an example.
Interesting though it is, this genre has in the last ten years
gone into almost total eclipse. In 1946 it composed twenty-

one percent of all Japanese pictures. A decade later it was
only two percent. In the same period, action-dramas rose from four to thirty-four percent. The action-drama as a category includes a number of genres, among them the form of melodrama. The Japanese, using the English word "melo-drama," mean something different from what might be expected. The Japanese melodrama is usually a love story with little adventure thrown in. A long-suffering heroine under-goes various harrowing vicissitudes and comes out happy.

In all of the various genres, however—and in all of Japanese drama—the themes are dissimilar to those of the West in that a film's initial assumption is not based upon a relative and philosophical good and evil but upon an absolute and social good and evil. Thus *Rashomon* with its multiple worlds of reality presented a line of thought completely foreign to the Japanese. In the Japanese world of drama there is only one reality, and for this reason Japanese drama but rarely pene-trates beneath the surface of existence. The status quo must be unquestioningly accepted and the characters, particularly in the period-film, the Kabuki, and the Bunraku doll-drama, must be meaninglessly sacrificed. Thus, Chikamatsu's lovers always face a problem surmountable only by death. They are always tormented by the inescapable pressures of society, which drive them to destruction. Many of these pressures in Chikamatsu revolve around money, the recognition of the development of a capitalist society from a feudal society. By merely showing the death of hero and heroine, there is protest in his work though it never comes near the surface.

This conflict between resignation and social protest has long been inherent in Japanese drama. The Noh, for example, represents resignation, while its sister, the Kyogen or comic interlude, is a form of social protest and is often full of scenes ridiculing Buddhism. This conflict continues into the Japa-nese film.

One of the ways in which the Japanese escape the pressures of their own society is by a retreat into nature. No other people on earth make more of nature: their literature is full of appreciation of it; going out into the country is a national passion; nature is even brought into the house in the form of miniature trees, flower arrangements, and gardens which seem an extension of the dwelling itself. Though this extreme admiration for the more aesthetic aspects of nature (typhoons and earthquakes, equally natural, are not admired) definitely represents a retreat from the rigors of Japanese society, it is equally true that the feeling for nature also represents much more than this. It is a complex of emotions and the fact that one can get away from the world of man by turning to nature is but one of its attributes.

This attitude toward nature permeates Japanese art, the earliest poems as well as the latest films. It has developed the poetic form known as the *haiku*, a poem in which the essence of a natural situation is fully suggested with an absolute minimum of words. These poems are necessarily static. They describe an occurrence or, more often, the conjunction of two occurrences, and from this conjunction a third image arises in the mind of the reader. In the famous Basho *haiku* the pond is still; then in the midst of this stillness there is suddenly heard the splash of a jumping frog. This tiny splash is all that signifies movement and life. It is heard but for an instant and then all is still again. Even before one has heard it, it is gone. It is like life, fleet and evanescent; it is followed by the silence of eternity.

Taihei Imamura, the motion-picture critic, has pointed out that the Japanese film is full of *haiku*-like images. He says that the Japanese film, particularly at its most documentary-like, is an avoidance of dramatic construction and "an escape to nature," an escape from descriptions of events and people into descriptions of natural scenes. "Japanese films in general portray scenes merely as a part of nature and not as a part of society. A situation which elucidates a man's behaviour and its necessity is never shown in Japanese movies." While this generalization is a bit sweeping, the observation remains valid. Japanese films are filled with little vignettes of nature and these small scenes often have no direct relation to the story as such. Foreigners who were puzzled at Hiroshi Inagaki's intercutting his love scenes with shots of running water in *Musashi Miyamoto* (better known abroad as *Samurai*) failed to make the connection which Inagaki expected of his audience: earthly passion was being contrasted with the standard poetic image for the impermanence of life on this earth.

Almost any Japanese film includes visual metaphors of this sort. Gosho's *Where Chimneys Are Seen* uses the varying aspects of chimneys viewed from different angles to suggest that people see the same things very differently. Kurosawa in *Drunken Angel* has his tubercular hero gaze at a broken doll floating on an oil-covered pond, and thus suggests the corruption of innocence, which is one of the picture's main themes. In *The Lower Depths* he uses the caw of distant crows (a traditional poetic image) to emphasize a character's suddenly feeling the fragility of life.

Critic Imamura gives a particularly beautiful *haiku*-like image which occurred in the opening scene of Sadao Yamanaka's prewar *The Village Tattooed Man*. A rough outlaw is walking through the precincts of a temple when he meets another outlaw. They pass each other, their sleeves brushing. "Just at this instant, the grand temple bell strikes the hour, breaking the stillness of the surroundings. Stabbed mortally with a dagger, one of the men falls; the other hastily disappears through the gate. As the camera is turned upon the prostrate figure of the man, the resonant reverberation of the bell slowly dies out, tranquility returning to the temple precincts." The Japanese, says Imamura, associate the long reverberation of the temple bell with death. The dagger flashed just as the bell was struck; the man died just as the last reverberation ceased. The transience of life has been symbolized.

This kind of montage is, to be sure, not unknown in the West, but it is very common in Japan and so uncommon elsewhere that almost every book in English on film aesthetics can find no better example than the scene in Basil Wright's *The Song of Ceylon* where the sound of a bell startles a bird and the camera follows its flight as the sound of the bell dies away. Alistair Cooke has called this "one of the loveliest visual metaphors I have ever seen on any screen," and so it may be. The point, however, is that this kind of thing is very rare in the West and yet so common in Japan that even the dullest of the period thrillers make constant use of it.

Often nature—the physical environment—literally dominates Japanese films. It sets the atmosphere, and, to the Japanese director, atmosphere is often more important than plot. Kinoshita in his pictures constantly uses nationally known scenery as locations, making the scenery itself comment, often ironically, upon the action. *A Japanese Tragedy* is set in Atami, the Miami Beach of Japan, and the tragedy is played against scenery representing the most obvious kind of pleasure that money can buy. In *Carmen's Pure Love*, the heroine's penniless friend wants to abandon her baby in front of the Diet Building, for after all, does it not represent the welfare state? In the 1955 *Distant Clouds* (Toi Kumo), a widow meets the man she once loved. They meet in a place they both knew but now the trees are dead and the grass is dry. Since the audience too knew the location when it was in full flower, the utter bleakness and sterility of the lovers' fate is emphasized in a truly moving sequence.

Ozu treats environment in yet another way. Very often he

cuts back to the setting where important action has previously occurred. This time the setting is absolutely empty.
In the few seconds it appears on the screen, it serves as an
abstraction to recall the scene that was played there. There
is no need to make any reference to the dialogue of the
previous scene, no need to flashback to a recapitulation. Just
a simple short shot of the "dead" set recalls everything.

The effect of the elements and the seasons upon human
behavior is something else no good Japanese director misses.
Ozu's *Late Spring* is set in that season which occurs just before the violence of the monsoon, a season of quiet and content and stillness. The season is an obvious parallel to the
story, in which a daughter passes from the quiet content of
unmarried life with her father into the stormier existence of
a late marriage.

The dramatic value of rain every film-maker knows.
Perhaps they know it too well in Japan. It rains frequently
in Japan and even more frequently in Japanese pictures. In
fact, a scene in the rain is almost obligatory. It is a sure sign
that a film is Japanese, just as you would expect a portrait
of Stalin in every early postwar Soviet film, and Vera Hubra
Ralston in most pictures made by Republic.

The seasons affect the Japanese film in another way. Films
with winter settings are apt to run as much as ten minutes
longer than those with summer settings, even though the
films are of the same basic script. One of the main reasons
for this is that the Japanese house during summer is completely open, both to the outside and from room to room.
In the winter, however, there are so many doors to open that
much additional footage is required. In the films of other
countries doors are no problem since entrances and exits
rarely interrupt the scene. In Japan, however, both are fully
shown and in Japan no one just opens a door and comes in.
The door is opened formally and then closed formally behind
one. This takes time enough in Japanese life but in the Japanese film the time devoured is incalculable.

For reasons like this, foreigners are often heard to com-
plain about the slow tempo of Japanese films. One should
point out that this tempo is the tempo of Japanese domestic
life (as opposed, to be sure, to the helter-skelter rush of
public life in big modern cities) and that slowness in films is
usually dictated by the tempo of national life or by ineptness
on the part of the director. Junichiro Tanaka, long a leading
editor of critical film magazines, in writing on the wartime
releases in Japan of Manchurian and Chinese films, says that

these pictures met with little success because they "lacked a **326** truly cinematic speed," and both bored and irritated the **fore-** Japanese audiences with their apparent slowness. Tempo, like **ground** so many other things, is relative it seems.

What is generally inferior in Japanese films is not tempo, nor style, nor attitude, nor artistry, but—in a special sense— the content itself: that is, the story, the plot, what the film is about. Japanese films say things well but what they have to say is often not worth hearing. In other words, the Japanese film suffers from local complications of precisely the same malaise that affects other films of other nations: a lack of good scripts.

Given the conditions under which Japanese script writers work, their very low level of performance is not surprising. Payment conditions are such that if a writer wants to make a living entirely through writing for the films he must average at least six full scripts a year since he receives as low as five hundred dollars—or as high as fifteen hundred dollars—per script. There are only about one hundred and thirty full-time script writers in the industry and the demand is so great that many do not even have time to correct their work. Many a picture has been turned out on an incomplete first draft. Sometimes the unfortunate scenarist will be handed a title, thought up by the head office and regarded as "catchy," and will be required to write a script that fits it. All in all, the script writer's life, never too easy in any film industry, is a particular burden in Japan.

Though many script writers feel that originals are easier to write, more fun to conceive, and ultimately make better films, less than a third of all Japanese scripts are originals. The remainder are adaptations of one kind or another. One of the main reasons for this is that when polls are taken, about half of the audience usually replies that they go to see a film because they read and liked the original. Only about twenty percent say they go because they like the stars appearing. Naturally, film companies then insist upon adaptations because such materials have already been "proved" and have aroused an amount of public interest. So important are successful literary works as sources for films that a number of studios have placed sure-fire popular writers on their boards of directors and given them well-paying administrative jobs in order to get complete monopoly of their output. Thus a top commercial writer like Matsutaro Kawaguchi works as a Daiei executive; Kazuo Kikuda is with Toho.

Commercial literature continues to appear in Japan in serial form in both magazines and newspapers. Though now almost completely vanished from Western journalism, serials have remained the rage in Japan for over half a century, and film versions of popular serialized novels have been a part of the industry since its infancy. When Eiji Yoshikawa's prewar best-seller *Musashi Miyamoto* first appeared, the Nikkatsu, J.O., and Daito companies all rushed to film it. Sometimes film versions are made even before the serial is finished. Yoshikawa's *The Heiké Story* was still running in newspaper form after three full-length films had been devoted to it.

Apart from the adaptation of popular novels, there is the movement, previously discussed, called *junbungaku* (or "pure literature"), which uses first-rate Japanese contemporary or near-contemporary literature as a basis for films. Though these films, at first almost entirely the work of directors Shiro Toyoda and Heinosuke Gosho, initially did badly at the box office, after the war some of the biggest film hits have been a part of the movement. Toyoda thinks the reason for this is that the sufferings of war brought the Japanese audience closer to an examination of those deeper emotions which typify most *junbungaku* films. The directors, too, have become more sure of their talents and hence are no longer afraid of really adapting instead of merely photographing a well-known novel.

The majority of Japanese film adaptations are those of novels, commercial or not, and there are almost no adaptations of stage plays. One would perhaps think that in a country with some of the most developed theatrical techniques in the world, adaptations of the traditional theater would be a natural and common occurrence. Such, however, is not the case. There have been, for example, extremely few film adaptations of Noh plays, and the Noh has had almost no influence on the film art of Japan. One of the reasons is that the form of the drama could not be further removed from the requirements of films and that, consequently, a total adaptation would be necessary. Another is that only a relatively few Japanese ever see, or care much about seeing, Noh. They know that it exists and they know it to be a part of their culture, but at least some people believe, as was once told the authors, that "Noh is something that foreigners see when they come to Japan."

Despite all the nonsense written about the influence of the Noh on the Japanese film, the leading Noh critic, Michizo Toita, has rightly said: "One must look hard, almost invent, influences if writing on this subject....Movies in their early

stages were often cheap imitations of Kabuki but although
Noh is greater in its stage art, I know of no instance of its theories and techniques having been really utilized by film-makers." If there is any Noh influence it tends to be very oblique. In *The Castle of the Spider's Web*, Kurosawa consciously used some elements of the Noh. Scenes with the witch (the film used one instead of Shakespeare's three) were reconstructed from the director's recollection of a Noh play he had once seen. The make-up of Isuzu Yamada, who played the rôle equivalent to Lady Macbeth, the background music, and the general timing of the intimate scenes were all caught by the Noh fans who saw the picture but by no one else. The elements were all consciously and experimentally included. Their appearance was most unusual and not a common thing at all.

The Kabuki influence is more pronounced but not nearly so much so as foreign critics like to proclaim. For one thing, the content of the Kabuki drama is very slight. Everything depends on the actor's performance, and the Kabuki style of acting is simply too big for films. For another, Kabuki incorporates and relies greatly upon dancing and singing, neither of which are appropriate to the realism of Japanese films. The use of Kabuki elements in such films as *The Beauty and the Dragon* and *The Song of Narayama* is a very rare occurrence indeed. That acting in ordinary period-films seems so expansive to foreign audiences is due more to the blustering way of the samurai and to the native Japanese inability to hold back emotion than it is to the influence of the traditional stage.

Still, if Kabuki plays themselves have little to offer the films —and Kabuki staging and acting even less—themes and stories borrowed from the Kabuki have found an occasional place in the period-film. Even here, however, the connection with Kabuki is slight. If the period-film has a historical precedent in the classical theater it is in the Kabuki *aragoto*, rough-house plays generally about famous swordsmen. This Kabuki genre is full of action, expansive posturing, and stylized swordplay—the kind of Kabuki that Japanese like to show foreigners. Some, however, think that even this link between Kabuki and the period-film is suspect. Tsuneo Hazumi, the film critic, has said: "Unfortunately, there has never been any real connection between Kabuki and films.... The Kyu-geki [the earliest word for period-films], a poor substitute for genuine Kabuki, was acted by rural troupes which had no connection with the great Kabuki traditions and none of its art. The film star Matsunosuke was essentially an imitator of Kabuki rather than a performer of it." And even Matsunosuke, though his pictures were little more than photographed theatrical tableaux, considered himself in revolt against the traditional theater.

Shimpa and Shingeki have given something to the film but not so much as might be expected, perhaps because, as translator and literary critic Donald Keene has pointed out, "on the whole, modern Japanese drama and poetry have not been the equal of the novels...." Most early Shimpa plays dealt with Meiji problems in Meiji settings and, with no vital creative impulse of their own, had to look elsewhere for inspiration. Consequently, after 1890, Shimpa playwrights relied more and more on "proven" popular novels or sensational news items from the daily press. Though the Shimpa attitude of sentimentality for its own sake found a secure place for itself in the Japanese film, relatively few films nowadays use Shimpa stories. On the contrary, a majority of Shimpa plays today are based on successful films.

Shingeki, though it furnishes some plays to the films, is much more concerned with static discourse than with action and characterization. It too, like the Shimpa, is fond of adapting novels to the stage and continues to exist completely separate from the films, rather like the "little theaters" in various European countries.

Even television has proved a poor source for scripts, in contradistinction to America. The economics of Japanese TV have prevented the creation of many high-quality original plays. Instead, television has relied most often on relaying theater performances, though there is also a quantity of low-grade serial-drama. However, there is also a tendency to adapt radio dramas to the screen. In fact, about thirty to forty radio serials are turned into films every year since in Japan radio serials do not run indefinitely as they do in the United States. These films often turn into multi-part features such as the previously mentioned *What Is Your Name?* Shochiku's *The Flower of This Generation* (Kono Yo no Hana), made in 1955–56, appeared in ten parts, each feature-length.

One of the few remaining sources for film scripts is foreign literature, and here Japan has not been backward in taking what it wanted. The early Shimpa, like some of the early literature reformers, tried to turn foreign works into something Japanese by changing the locale, the characters' names, and other surface details. Even now, the inability of the Japanese to handle anything without sooner or later nationalizing it—or, perhaps better put, the peculiarly Japanese genius for assimilating and incorporating—remains much in evidence in these adaptations of foreign models. The incorporation is usually complete. Most Japanese, for example, are convinced that *Auld Lang Syne* is a traditional Japanese melody recently picked up and appropriated by the Scots. In precisely the same way a character by the name of Shirano Benjiro once became so popular that most of those in audience would have expressed disbelief upon learning that he was really the creation of a Frenchman named Rostand and that the French insisted upon pronouncing his name Cyrano de Bergerac.

Besides the foreign adaptations already mentioned in this book, one might add that in the early days a majority were Russian—no Dostoevsky but lots of Turgenev, Gorky, and Tolstoy. *Resurrection* was a great favorite and was done yet again as recently as 1950, this time as a vehicle for Machiko Kyo in Hokkaido. Hauptmann and Schiller also proved popular. *The Robbers* was made into a 1955 period-film by Tatsuyasu Osone, and a year later Tomu Uchida took *William Tell* as the basis for a tendency-film-like period-drama: peasants rise against the cruel lord, etc.

Sometimes, rather than go to all the trouble of adapting foreign literature, someone will simply remake a foreign film. In the silent era, Hotei Nomura's *The Cry of the Nation* was *The Covered Wagon* in Manchuria. When Sumiko Kurihara became Japan's first vamp—a bit late, in 1924—she did so in a remake of Gloria Swanson's *Hummingbird*. After Douglas Fairbanks had made a big hit in Japan, Makino Productions turned out *Robin Hood's Dream* (Robin Fuddo no Yume), copying even the sets and costumes. A bit later *The Hunchback of Enmei-in* (Enmei-in no Semushi) appeared, lacking nothing except the original's Lon Chaney. Griffith's *Broken Blossoms* was remade twice, both films being set in Yokohama's Chinatown, and even Chaplin's films were closely duplicated in Japanese settings. The tendency is still lively. As late as 1955, Hiroshi Noguchi made *Duel in the Setting Sun* (Rakujitsu no Ketto) which was *High Noon* all over again, this time in a period setting.

If one is inclined to wonder at the worth of these adaptations and to question their too-ready acceptance by the Japanese, one can do no better than to quote the words of Shiji Inoue, a noted Japanese geographer who, though not speaking of the films, might well have been in his elucidation of an attitude rampant in the Japanese academic world: "The Japanese universities introduce foreign ideas through translations of the transactions of learned societies, the papers of foreign professors. What happens then, in many instances, is that a Japanese study of the subject in question, in much greater detail than the original but in fact departing little or nothing from the conclusions thereof, is thereupon presented to an admiring Japanese world as a thoroughly Japanese example of superior Japanese scholarship. This kind of comparison between Japanese and foreign cultures shows, to Japanese eyes, the superior quality of Japanese scholarship. It is not a genuine comparison but of this fact there is blissful ignorance. As a result, the extension of foreign culture in Japan progresses at snail's pace."

Since the Japanese industry refuses to allow too many original scripts and demands mostly "proven" material, it is forced into adapting novels, foreign or Japanese, and since there are just so many novels, the industry time and again has found itself faced with an acute shortage of material. In the early 1920's, the critic Yoshio Ishimaki was writing: "In the contemporary motion picture world, the greatest trouble faced by not only Japanese but producers all over the world is the problem of scenarios. In Japan recently this difficulty has become too obvious and may plague us forever." He then points to the sameness of the scripts, the poverty of the scenarios written by actors for themselves, the extreme tendency to adapt inappropriate foreign literature and films, and the constant remakes of the same picture.

To his list one might add two items of particular relevance to the 1950's. One is that nowadays the script writer is often given only two weeks in which to do a complete script; consequently, he presents very inferior work, usually falling directly into a *mono* of some kind, and the script becomes at once rigidly defined. Another is the "rationalization of product" tendency which attempts assembly-line methods in film-making, beginning with the script.

Still, the problem of content is one which Japan shares with all the other motion-picture industries of the world. It is by no means a new problem and has existed concurrently with the art of cinema ever since pictures first moved. At least a part of the art of the cinema consists of seeing the world from an angle which removes this problem and which gives back to overused content its original power, and beauty. This the exceptional Japanese film has done and continues to do.

14 technique.

IF the content of the Japanese film is conditioned by the peculiarly Japanese outlook on life, the shape which the finished film finally takes is even more influenced by the exigencies of the Japanese production system and its various techniques.

The production schedule of the average Japanese film, for example, is by Western standards extremely short. While months of careful planning are required abroad, the preparatory period for the production of a Japanese film (the time from the selection of the cast, director, and crew, to the beginning of shooting) is customarily ten days, though a "super-production" may take twenty days or more. The shooting schedule itself varies with the director and the kind of picture. Toho allows fifty days for its average film; Shintoho insists that the picture be shot in thirty. The time spent shooting is, of course, directly related to the length of the final film. Fully half of Japan's features are from eighty to a hundred minutes long and only five percent run over 110 minutes. These latter are usually pictures by name directors who are often given as much time and footage as they need.

After the cameraman is finished, the editor of the average picture seldom has more than four or five days to get it into final shape, and many films are released after the editor has worked on them only two days after the end of shooting. Because of the pressure of time, the editor must begin to work on a final cut as soon as he gets his hands on the first day's rushes. Things at the Toei Company are so thoroughly organized that the precise lengths of films are often decided in advance and the editor, instead of cutting as continuity, style, and tempo demand, very often prolongs or shortens shots without regard for their optimum effectiveness so that the film comes to just the right total length.

With everyone falling over each other to save time, one of the strangest contradictions is the amount of time it takes to have film processed. For all of the industry's concern for quick production, Japanese laboratories are extremely slow in delivering rushes. Three days are usually required for what in other countries is only a matter of hours. This lengthens schedules inordinately, which means that corners must be cut in other departments. An enormous amount of time is also lost while shooting because of the *kakemochi* problem. This word describes the actor who is appearing in two or more productions at the same time and shuttles back and forth between them. The entire unit may be kept waiting for an actor to return from another studio; or it may fill in by jumping about and shooting around the missing actor.

Seldom is a film made in Japan that keeps to its shooting schedule. Most end up in a frantic race against time, working day and night, sleeping in the studio and eating meals on the stage. During these rush periods no one can go home. They are locked in, as it were, until the job is done. The studios very often favor this because in many cases overtime payments are not made and the harassed studio head always knows that even if the day's shooting does not get done, he can still keep them on the set all night and it probably will not cost him a penny.

One might perhaps think that the technicians, or at least the actors, would put down their feet and demand some kind of compensation, since all of this labor would be completely unnecessary were the studios to make some kind of realistic scheduling procedure. They do not, however. Under standard Japanese contract conditions, whether by picture or by a fixed period of time, no provisions are made for overtime payments. If people under contract work a full day and are then called out for work at night, they receive no extra compensation. Permanent studio personnel who are paid on a time basis, however, receive some overtime pay. But there are ways to get around this. Nikkatsu hires even such regular personnel as grips and art-department men on a short-term contract basis, thus doing away with the necessity of paying them overtime.

This contract basis makes things easy for the personnel department. It is much more difficult in Japan to fire a regular employee than to break a contract with him. Even in other studios, however, the amount that non-contract people receive for overtime is really only a token amount.

Working conditions in Japanese studios would further horrify the foreign professional film-worker. Not only is everyone supposed to work three or four days and nights in a row, taking cat naps when not on call, but everyone also regularly works a seven-day week, and only a few of the national holidays are observed. Yet, the seven-day week is not quite so bad as it sounds. About one-third of an average Japanese film is shot on location, often far away from the studio. This means that when the weather turns bad on a day scheduled for location work there is seldom an alternate schedule for shooting indoors and so everyone gets the day off—with pay. On other occasions the script may not be ready by starting day and so both cast and crew are packed off to a hot-springs hotel where they wait and enjoy themselves on a kind of paid vacation until the script arrives for location shooting.

The number of people involved in a production, whether in the studio or on location, is not so many as one might expect, given the Japanese penchant for overstaffing. A breakdown of the staff (applicable to most productions except for the very cheap and the very expensive) would include: one director and three or four assistants; one producer and his assistant; three or four from the business office; one cameraman and his four assistants; one lighting supervisor and from six to ten electricians; three or four sound-department people; two from the art department and one or two carpenters; two propertymen; one greenman; one continuity man or script girl; one man to take stills; two automobile and truck drivers; a publicity man; two dolly pushers; and for costume pictures, one to three costume fitters, one make-up man, and from one to four hairdressers. In addition, of course, there is the cast and the entourage that always follows the Japanese actor around wherever he goes.

One of the things that most impresses the foreign observer on the Japanese film set is the general youth of the crew. Though one can easily find, usually among the prop-men and hairdressers, people who have been working in the industry since the 1900's, most of the people are very young. The grips are usually in their twenties, as are many of the art-department people. The assistant directors and camera assistants are equally young. Most studio personnel are retired at the standard age of fifty-five though often older people are given other than crew posts. When Daiei sent a unit to

Hollywood to film *Buruba* in a rented jungle setting, one of
the things most impressing them was the extreme age of people involved in making American films. Michio Takahashi, the cameraman, complained that the abundance of men in their fifties doing even the lowest-ranking jobs kept deserving young people out of the industry and added that Hollywood studios reminded him of an old people's home where easy work is provided for the senile.

Given the often near-primitive conditions of filming in Japan, however, youthfulness is a great asset. The grips, for example, are given no mechanical apparatus for carrying equipment; they must depend upon pure muscle. The lighting grids above the sets have no hand rails and seldom even a floor. The electricians must crawl about, up and down, over and across, on all fours. With such a lack of fundamental safety devices one might be led to think that the job of a grip is not a thoroughly safe one. One would be right: it is not. The ease with which one can fall from a grid is a danger not only to the men above but also to the actors below. The accident rate in studios is not inconsequential.

In the happy family which is the Japanese film studio all the help is organized into unions on an industrial basis, so that producers are never plagued with the jurisdictional disputes that often hold up or limit production in Europe and America. Each person, to be sure, has his own job, but no one hesitates or is angry when for some reason a person is called upon to do a job outside his department. Often, each director's crew is fixed; even the electricians, grips, and assistant prop-men are the same for each picture. Shochiku—stronghold of feudalism—will not even use script girls; all the continuity is handled by male assistant directors. (At the other end of the scale, however, Toho has female grips.) Furthermore, Japanese film companies are often family affairs in a further sense. Nagata's son, for instance, is in charge of Daiei's Tokyo studios.

In a paternalistic society almost no one is ever fired from a job and advancement is slow but sure. If a person proves too incompetent, he is merely kicked upstairs. The assistant director eventually becomes director, the lowest prop-man finally gets to be head prop-man, and the film loader after some years ends up a full-fledged cameraman.

This last is not the precise equivalent of the American director of photography or the British lighting cameraman. The man in charge of photography in a Japanese unit is called simply "the photographer," or perhaps "the cinématographer"

would be a better term. He has no operator to run his camera
for him. Instead, he must do all the framing himself and during a take—no matter what kind: stationary, pan, dolly, or crane—he mans the camera. His arms do the panning; his eyes do the following. He usually has four assistants to help him. The chief assistant pulls focus, another changes magazines, another takes light readings, and the fourth—and lowest —runs errands. The photographer himself does the actual photographing. Japanese camera crews are always shocked to learn that an American director of photography is not often permitted to touch the camera, all physical manipulations being in the hands of the camera operator and other assistants. Yet even if the Japanese cinématographer had an operator, he probably would not use him. If he himself had three arms, he would prefer to follow his own focus on those shots requiring focal adjustment. The reason for this extreme possessiveness was explained by one of the best Japanese cameramen, the late Mitsuo Miura, when he said that he always did everything himself because there was no one he could trust to the job; that only he, himself, possessed the technique necessary to get what he wanted.

Before the war most technicians, especially cameramen, closely guarded their "secrets" and there was very little interchange of information. Apprentices were told the master's findings with all the ceremony surrounding an initiation rite. Now, however, there is a much wider dissemination of technical knowledge, though the apprentice still learns most from his master.

The Japanese cinématographer, however, does not reign completely supreme. For one thing, he has much less responsibility for lighting than does the foreign director of photography. Lighting is largely in the hands of a lighting supervisor, whose nearest Hollywood equivalent would be the "gaffer," a simple technician. He often designs the lighting plot and oversees its execution. The cinématographer will make the few adjustments he considers necessary, but the basic responsibility for illumination belongs to the supervisor. Top cameramen, of course, tend to treat the lighting supervisor as they would an assistant and demand this effect or that. Less established talents, however, merely handle the camera and accept what the supervisor offers them.

In practice, the lighting supervisor often has little to do. Production is so formalized that lighting set-ups, particularly for the program pictures, are never designed, they just happen. Everyone in the crew knows where each light should

go and since the Japanese use less lighting equipment and
make set-ups quicker than elsewhere, an electrician often
holds the light in his hands instead of placing it on a floor
stand. If the cameraman, the director, or the lighting supervisor wants a change, he turns to the electricians, tells one
to stand here and the others to stand there, and the new
lighting set-up is completed. Even the microphone is seldom
placed on a boom. It is usually taped to the end of a bamboo
pole and held by hand, even for static shots on the sound
stage. Sometimes, rather than use a boom, a grip holding the
microphone in his hands is suspended over the set from the
grid.

It is not surprising that visitors to the studio come out
believing that most of the technical equipment of the Japanese studios is both poor and out-of-date. This is not so,
though it would have been a decade ago. In the past seven
years there has been a tremendous improvement in equipment. Literally dozens of new Mitchell cameras have been
imported, and today almost every Japanese film is shot using
that American camera. A Japanese manufacturer, sensing
profit, has been turning out an almost exact copy of the
Mitchell (without permission), but though it looks the same,
its technical inferiority has resulted in its failure to find a
market.

Given decent equipment, the Japanese technicians can
usually turn out a technically superior film. During the war
a Hollywood committee, including Frank Capra and Alex-
ander Korda, viewing twenty of the top Japanese films made
just before the war and sent abroad for propaganda and
commercial reasons, were unanimous in praising the high level
of technical quality. And, as thousands of postwar film-goers
know, the technical level of the Japanese product can be
extraordinarily high. Still, one must also note the fact that
such films represent less than five percent of the entire film
output. These pictures are technically on a par with foreign
pictures today—but there is still the other ninety-five percent
to think about. Technically as well as artistically, the gap
between the "good" Japanese films and the daily product
off the assembly line is unbelievably wide. Just as Japan
makes some of the world's best pictures, as a candidate for
turning out some of the world's worst it is also almost without a peer.

As one might imagine, the reason for the usual low technical level is that everything is rushed so. Equipment is used
to the limit, and it is not unusual for a different unit to be

working concurrently on every stage in the studio. Often
carpenters are at work on another set on the same stage where a crew is shooting. The hammering stops only for sound takes. Time is so short that very often the studio carpenters work directly from a rough sketch that lists no specifications or measurements. They build by instinct. The set designer himself is often little more than a quick-sketch artist who supervises the carrying of props from the warehouse. One thing that helps avert chaos is the module construction of Japanese houses. All the component parts have fixed measurements, that is, doors are always the same height; room dimensions are always figured in units of *tatami,* two-inch thick straw mats which measure approximately three by six feet.

Too, one must take into consideration the actual appearance of modern Japan. As one walks the streets of any Japanese city, one is immediately struck by the insubstantial appearance of many Japanese modern foreign-style buildings: teahouses, coffee-shops, small stores, and the like. They are made of painted wood or stucco or plaster, or strips of plastic and metal covered with neon. The genuine Japanese urban street tends to look just like a movie set—ready to be struck at a moment's notice. Naturally, when the studio carpenters rebuild modern Japan for the screen (the flats which form walls are made by pasting old newspapers together until a fairly rigid sheet is obtained) the end result looks precisely the way modern Japan tends to look: jerry-built, utterly insubstantial, and ready to collapse on the slightest provocation.

The continual rush which allows the carpenters to hammer away just out of camera range also accounts for the "bad" films' badness in other ways. Very often only one take is made of each camera set-up. This tendency is largely dictated by the heavy shooting schedules which the units must meet, but it is also caused by the Japanese obsession to conserve negative. Though raw stock is now relatively inexpensive in Japan, this miserly attitude toward its use dates back to pre-war days when the film-stock costs were often forty percent of a cheap production's budget. The lengths to which this obsession goes can be seen in the special training given to all the clapper boys in pulling their slates quickly out of the frame after the sticks have been banged together. The tendency reaches the lunatic fringe when, to save those few frames each take, contests are held among the clapper boys to see who is quickest on the draw.

One should also observe that very often only one take is

actually needed because the Japanese director more often than not tends to visualize and even edit his film in advance. Visualizing in his head and editing in his camera, the Japanese director sees his films already cut in terms of a close-up here, a two-shot there, a cut-away there, and back to an establishing shot here. Most directors consequently shoot as they visualize, seldom employing alternate angles for the same scene and with very little overlap from one shot to the next. On the surface this simplifies the editor's job because there is only one way to edit a shot and variations are seldom possible. If two shots do not fit together well, however, he must simply move on to the next. There is no time to experiment with variant arrangements and little additional footage to do so if the opportunity appears. This accounts for the roughness of most Japanese film editing.

The cheaper Japanese pictures are shot with a ratio often lower than three to one, that is, one foot of usable footage out of every three exposed. Of course, the better directors, as a matter of assuring quality, insist on shooting more. Still, Kinugasa in making *Gate of Hell* which in release had a length of about eight thousand feet, exposed less than thirty thousand. A number of directors, however, have developed their own techniques for getting away from the limits of the "final editing in advance" technique. Kurosawa, for example, favors the multi-camera set-up in which he stages a scene and then films it with from two to four cameras in varying set-ups, all turning at once, very much like the usual live television method. This, of course, eats up film but it does prevent lapses in continuity. It also saves time by eliminating the need to run through the scene again each time a change of angle is needed. Kurosawa is well aware of the limitations of this method and uses it only where it is an asset. One obvious limitation is that it prevents the lighting and action from being adjusted to the needs of each set-up. Another is that it throws great responsibility on the actor who, first time through, must be perfect.

Shiro Toyoda gets around the problem by adopting the process used by most European and American directors. He shoots an entire scene in a master take and then closes in for shorter takes from different angles. Heinosuke Gosho shoots from less of a detailed plan. He breaks up his scenes into innumerable separate shots and angles, eventually discarding what he does not need. He gets variety by breaking everything into very small bits and using only what best fits together.

The better directors also manage to escape from the rigidity of common studio methods to the extent of an experimental approach, when an experimental technique has a place in the film they are making. Thus Kinoshita borrowed the dynamic montage of Eisenstein to give a broader meaning to *A Japanese Tragedy*. A simple synopsis of the story makes it sound like a standard *haha-mono* and the use of "tragedy" in the title would seem almost too grand for the apparent small scope of the story. But Kinoshita makes it a genuine Japanese tragedy in the widest sense by editing. He cross-cuts his simple story with newsreel and other footage showing that the actions of the mother and her children reflect the political and social events of the day.

Yasujiro Ozu eliminates fades, dissolves, and even a moving camera, telling everything through straight pictorial content and simple editing, feeling that this austere film vocabulary better suits what he is saying.

In *Stray Dog*, Kurosawa completely eliminated dialogue for a whole reel simply because it was not needed. It was not a detailed study of a mechanical process as in, say, the opening safe-cracking sequence of Jules Dassin's *Rififi Chez les Hommes;* it was merely an absence of talk, Kurosawa having reasoned that dialogue added nothing here.

Directors even make use of the obviously eccentric and get away with it through an entire picture. The whole crazy world in Kinoshita's *Carmen's Pure Love* was filmed without once leveling the camera off on the horizontal. Each shot appeared on the screen slanted off the perpendicular, as if one were looking at the picture with one's head tilted. The amount of slant took on meaning in indicating the director's comment on just how crazy he considered each action.

In *Mother,* Naruse had great fun with the mechanical nature of the motion picture. The film proceeds normally until, all of a sudden, scenes start appearing on the screen upside down. The audience is confused but just before it has begun to think that the projectionist has made a mistake, Naruse cuts back to a normal view, a little boy looking at the world as he stands on his head. Later, when things are coming to a climax, just as we hope that all of the difficulties of the characters will be solved, the title "The End" flashes prematurely on the screen. We think the film has ended too soon; then Naruse cuts to his central characters leaving a theater. The title we saw belonged to a movie that they were seeing, and we feel all the closer to his wonderful people be-

cause we thought when we first saw "The End" that we
would have to leave them too soon.

If the better directors have found ways of beating the Japanese system and turning out good films in spite of shooting schedules and the extreme rigidity of film-construction methods, they are presented an even further challenge in the matter of sound and sound recording. Of all of Japan's film arts and techniques sound is the most neglected. An imaginative use of the sound track is all but unknown in Japan and technically it comes off the worst of all the film crafts. Things change slowly in Japan and it would appear that the film technicians are still not at all sure that sound is here to stay. Hence dialogue recording and all the other sound elements, including music, receive the most secondary consideration. To be sure, actors, directors, and script writers know that the movies can talk; it is the technical elements that are ignored. Portions of many Japanese films are so poorly recorded even today that the audience cannot understand what is being said. *Rashomon* had a particularly bad sound track and a number of Japanese found that the only way they could understand it was to go to a foreign subtitled version.

Though all studios now use only the latest and most expensive recording equipment, and the mechanical reasons for poor technical quality are now absent, they are more than compensated by the uncraftsman-like and often frankly sloppy attitude of those in charge of sound. Nearly all scenes shot out of doors are post-recorded and in Japan where so much work is done on location these scenes make a sizable amount. Still, when the dubbing is made there is very little attempt made to match lip movement to dialogue and whole scenes are frequently out of synchronization. Sometimes, due to the speed with which Japanese films are edited, even dialogue shot simultaneously is out of synchronization because of the carelessness of the editor.

This attitude, alas, is also shared by the musicians who write Japan's film scores, though here there is at least some reason for their unoriginality, the lack of taste, and the often glaring inappropriateness of their finished product. For one thing, the film-makers in any industry tend to think of the music last and the composers are consequently given less time than anyone in which to finish their job.

The composer Ichiro Saito says, rather plaintively, that if a composer were given two weeks after seeing the completed work print he could do a much better job. "As it is now,

about the second week of a film's shooting, we are assigned
to a picture and must start writing. Not knowing precisely
how the film is going to turn out we have to proceed on a
sixth sense. Sometimes they call on the telephone and say that
it won't be necessary for us to see the daily takes, they'll
describe everything to us over the phone and we can take it
from there. So we write; and naturally the timing and
structure is changed in editing." Thus, with only three days
to complete the music and record it after the final work print
is approved, the main guide composers have is only the
scenario, and it is not at all infrequent for the music of a
film to be completed, orchestrated, and recorded without the
composer's having once seen the picture.

Another reason for the general worthlessness of most Japanese film scores is that, according to the film composers, a
number of directors order music directly and they usually
want something in imitation of famous existing works—something they can whistle. What they really want are "arrangements"—all the old chestnuts in a row much like the pianist
at the old Bijou playing "gems" as accompaniment to the
silents.

In a 1934 version of *The Loyal Forty-seven Ronin*, the man
who did the music used Schubert's "Unfinished" symphony
to back the climactic scene where the *ronin* attack their lord's
enemy. This continues to be highly praised by certain critics
for its "perfect union" of a Japanese dramatic classic with a
Western musical classic. A more famous and almost equally
imbecile example was the music for *Rashomon* during which
surprised foreigners found themselves listening to something
very much like Ravel's *Boléro*. The composer, the late Fumio
Hayasaka, was one of Japan's most respected and most
original composers, and moreover one of great personal integrity, but he was ordered by Kurosawa to write something
like the *Boléro* because the director felt that it would be
closer to the style of the picture. The critics agreed, finding
Rashomon to be "Kurosawa at his most Occidental."

Thus, one of the reasons that Japanese film scores tend to
strongly echo Brahms, Wagner, Strauss, Debussy, Ravel, and
early Stravinsky (or Shostakovitch, Khachaturian, Kabalev-
sky, and late Prokofieff if the production is "independent")
is that the composers are literally ordered to turn out music
like this. At the same time Japanese film companies are
notoriously adamant against the use of traditional Japanese
music.

Yasushi Akutagawa, one of Japan's better-known composers, claims that he finds a positive reluctance on the part of many directors to accept film music which is in any way related to the Japanese classical forms. One of the reasons is that, in Japan, Japanese music is taken completely for granted. There are at least a dozen nationally known magazines devoted to Western-style music but not one country-wide publication of any reputation devoted to Japanese traditional music. Another is that, no matter how exotic the style and action of period-films appear to Western audiences, to the Japanese this film style is a part of the realist tradition that was adapted from the West and therefore has only the slightest of connections with the classic Japanese drama. Because so much Japanese classical music exists only in relation to the classic drama, the use of this music in films would present a severe stylistic clash. The music is identified with classical acting but the acting on the screen is not.

One would think that perhaps an adaptation of Japanese classical music would then best suit the needs of the Japanese period-films, and so it would. Many composers are already agreed on this point, though the majority of directors are apparently not. Still, excellent period-film scores do get written. Two of the best are Fumio Hayasaka's music for *Seven Samurai*, with its strong folk flavor, and Masaru Sato's brilliant score for *The Castle of Spider's Web*, with its creative combining of classical Noh music and Western musical forms.

One might also mention that contemporary-life films are equally aided by scores using Japanese materials. One of the most exciting was Toshio Maiyuzumi's score for *Conflagration*, the credit music for which was a fascinating combination of Buddhist chants and *musique concrète*, prepared piano being used Noh-like as percussion *recitativo secco*. Likewise, Toru Takemitsu's excellent music for *Crazed Fruit*, with its electric guitars and ukeleles, perfectly captured the pathetic gaiety, the profound melancholy of a Japanese summer resort.

Most of the time, however, the Japanese film is accompanied by meaningless if musical sounds which add nothing to the effectiveness of the film. Since the composer has no control over how his score is cut, it is not uncommon for musical climaxes to occur when there is no need for them, and for cinematic climaxes to come when the composer is padding away at his most shameless. Since a composer can never be too certain of how his music will be used, most must plod along writing orchestrated piano music, risking a canon

now and then, and doubling celli with clarinets to give that
muddy sound so dear to the ears of film directors, and so
typical of Japanese film scoring. In Japan, where all the
leading composers write for the films, they have excellent
reason to refer to their products as "bread-and-butter music."

The composers, like everyone else, are in movies for the
money and yet, by Western standards, everyone is grossly
underpaid. For *Seven Samurai*, a very long film, Hayasaka
received approximately the equivalent of only one thousand
dollars, and was considered handsomely compensated indeed.
Most other composers get far less.

The budget for the average Japanese film is about eighty
thousand dollars and about thirteen percent of this, or a bit
over ten thousand dollars, is for the production staff. The
director is paid from this fund and usually gets from one to
five thousand dollars. Cameramen get approximately half of
what the director makes. Though this is no fortune by
Western standards, it is at least an improvement over the
early 1930's, when most top directors received a flat monthly
salary of $150.

The biggest single item in the budget is money given the
cast, which represents about twenty-eight percent of the
entire amount. Yet here too, a top star only receives about
eight thousand dollars per picture, while his equivalent
abroad often receives $100,000—twice what the Japanese film
star makes in a year. Obviously one must not conclude that
Japanese film people are penniless. Though Japan has the
highest standard of living in Asia and is not an inexpensive
country to live in, three hundred and sixty yen continues to
buy considerably more than its exchange rate equivalent—a
dollar—buys in America.

Unlike in many other countries, the films in Japan are
financed directly by the producing company out of its own
operating capital and usually without loans from outside
sources. This is partly possible due to the relatively inexpensive production costs of Japanese films, but another reason
is that the steady flow of films from Japanese studios is so
rapid that individual financing would be impossible. This, of
course, means that all the financial considerations involved
are entirely those of the producing company. In certain instances bank loans are secured, but these funds are part of
the company's operating capital and are not allocated to individual productions. Even in the more gigantic American
film companies, film financing is often on a picture-to-picture
basis, but in Japan no one ever has time to stop to think where

the money for just one film is coming from. From the wide-screen super productions of 1957–58—costing up to $300,000 each and the most expensive undertakings of the industry—to the average Toei short second-feature which is turned out for under $20,000, the view is always that of the total production schedule.

With all of this money going out, the main concern of the studio head is that it just as promptly comes back in again. This is yet another reason for all the hurry and carelessness in Japanese film-making. In today's inflated film market, the more you turn out, the more comes in.

Shochiku's super-spectacle 1956 version of *The Loyal Forty-seven Ronin*, an all-star affair lasting over four hours, made over $1,200,000, which is considerable in Japan where a picture has been outstanding if it does over $400,000. Shintoho's *The Emperor Meiji and the Great Russo-Japanese War* took in $1,400,000 and cost only a fraction of that. One does not need a smash hit to break even, however. If the average production cost of a Daiei or Toho feature is about $70,000, the average income from such a film will be about $190,000—which is not a bad return in a country where film rentals are at fifty percent of the gross.

Yet, in order to make this kind of money, each company must produce at least fifty-two films a year, and most companies attempt to make many more. A new product must be constantly before the audience. As we have seen, one of the results is a production schedule that makes it almost impossible to release a consistently high level product. Another is the use of careless, slapdash, and generally inferior studio techniques.

That excellent films continue to be made is not to the credit of the industry but to the credit of those few men, directors and producers usually, who have the integrity and sheer brute strength to fight against what is surely one of the most conservative, artistically reactionary, inefficient, and unprofessional film industries in the world.

15 **directors.** IN
Japan the director was very slow
to emerge as the controlling force
in production. In the early films
he did little more than read the
dialogue aloud while the actors emoted and created their own
business. He did not even get to select the camera position;
this was the responsibility of the cameraman, who chose the
spot and then indicated what was in frame and what was not.
Until the cinematic reforms of 1917, there was no director of
importance aside from Shozo Makino, and even he is remembered, not so much for his work as a director, but because, as
a producer, he so efficiently organized the various elements
that go into making a film. Thus, at a time when the director
already had an important and established position in the
West, the Japanese film director had little authority. A 1914
publication describes an early studio as "an old shanty
purchased for mere nothing, a kind of photograph gallery
combined with a stage ... Like a theatre it has its scenery, its
carpenters ... here human spectres move in front of the
camera, with faces whitened so as not to come out black in
the negative ... the raucous stage director piloting them
through rehearsal."

But once the director succeeded in gaining control of
production, he was much slower to relinquish his power to
the producer than was the foreign director. One of the consequences is that today the Japanese film director, as far as
having the final say goes, is among the strongest in the world.
The Japanese industry operates under what it calls the
"director system" rather than under the "producer system,"
which is so common in the West. What the Japanese mean

by "producer system" is that the responsibility for both the type and conception of a film is delegated by the company to an individual who selects the story, director, and cast, and who is in general responsible for the final shape of a given film. This system has been tried in Japan several times, notably by Toho, but never with success. The "director system" was found much more congenial to Japan.

Under this system, the head of the studio, or very often the head of the company as is the case with Shochiku's Kido and Daiei's Nagata, is the active director of policy as to precisely what kind of pictures will be made. The responsibility for delegating details to a producer is not exercised. The director is responsible for everything in a film and reports directly to the head of production. Hence it is called the "director system." A producer under this system is little more than an errand boy, since the two powers—director and studio chief—hold all the responsibility. To a Japanese director this means that his duties and responsibilities are greater than those of his foreign counterpart for he must assume some of the duties which elsewhere would be handled by a producer. In this connection it might be noted that in Japan film directors are not called *enshutsusha*, the Japanese word which would most closely correspond to the English meaning, but *kantokusha*, which has the wider meaning of superintendent, overseer, or person-in-charge.

Though the director is nominally responsible to the head of production, he is sometimes given a great deal of freedom. The top-line directors—certainly including those discussed later in this chapter and a few others—are generally given a free hand in producing what they want. Though the company retains some power to veto their ideas, it does not force them to do anything they do not want to—such is the respect with which top directors are held by everyone in the industry. On the other hand, directors of lesser rank must unquestioningly do what they are told. Sometimes they are handed a script and ordered to start production from scratch within a week. They have no right to object, and they do not. Hiromichi Horikawa, a former assistant to Kurosawa and one of the most brilliant new directors of the past five years, was actually suspended from Toho for a year because he was "too experimental." One cannot very well imagine this happening to a Kurosawa.

Directors in Japan often have a box-office appeal which in the West is usually exercised only by the stars. Despite the tremendous popularity of star Toshiro Mifune, who usually

appears in Kurosawa's films, the director's name is regarded
as a bigger draw and it is always given top billing, sometimes in type larger than the title. Even lesser director's names are included, no matter how small the advertisement or how inconsequential the picture.

There are not many top-rank directors, however, and new talent appears slowly and gradually. In Japan, feudal relationships are still strong and the apprentice system reigns supreme. Ninety-five percent of all the men who are directing features today worked first as assistant directors and were gradually promoted. Of the remaining five percent, none came directly to films from other fields; all came from the industry itself, from another job such as actor, script writer, or cameraman. The American practice of bringing in stage directors such as Joshua Logan, Elia Kazan, or Daniel Mann, simply does not exist in Japan.

Most Japanese directors started out as fourth assistants and gradually worked their way up to chief assistant. In the early days, promotion was rapid. Mizoguchi worked two years as an assistant before he was promoted to director; Gosho, two years; Ozu, four; Naruse, six; and Toyoda, less than a year. As the industry grew, more time was required. Kinoshita spent three years as an assistant cameraman and then worked seven more as an assistant director. Kurosawa worked seven years as an assistant. Today the average period of assistant directorship is fifteen years.

In the early days, too, one could be very young and become a director. Masahiro Makino was eighteen years old when he started to direct features in 1927. Of course the fact that he was working for his father's company helped. Directors without relatives had to wait a little longer. Toyoda and Gosho were twenty-three; Mizoguchi and Ozu, twenty-four; Naruse, twenty-five; Imai, twenty-seven; Kurosawa, thirty-three; and Kinoshita, thirty-four. Today most new directors are around forty.

Many directors are by no means satisfied with the present-day method of training through assistantships. Some think that the best way is to first become an established script writer, since most top directors today are able to write their own scenarios. Others think that only through formal academic training in film production can the young director be properly taught. Many criticize the apprentice system by saying that it actually constitutes inbreeding among directors (see Chart 1, page 430), that it keeps out new talent, and that it prevents new ideas from reaching the screen.

At first glance it would seem that these detractors are right.
Every year the same directors keep reappearing in the best-ten lists. In fact, those directors whom the authors personally consider the most excellent are coincidentally the same ones who dominate the "best film" lists. Ozu has won the *Kinema Jumpo* "Best One" Award six times. This is the equivalent of an American director's making six Academy Award pictures. Imai has won four times; Kinoshita, Kurosawa, and Naruse, twice each; Mizoguchi, Toyoda, Gosho, and Yoshimura, one time each. Despite the fact that there are almost two hundred active directors in the Japanese industry, there has been only one year since the end of the war when the above nine directors did not occupy at least half of the space on the ten-best-films-of-the-year lists. Their frequent appearance is described by the critical and the envious as being like a *noren-gai*, a place where all the old stores of established reputation are lined up in a row and where new businesses cannot hope to survive even though they may happen to sell goods of better quality.

And yet it is not just a set reputation that makes the critics choose pictures by the same directors year after year. The truth is—as the authors can verify after having seen hundreds of Japanese films—that the worthwhile films are turned out by a very small group of directors. This makes it very easy to predict who will take the yearly honors, and takes much of the surprise out of film-going in Japan. The industry has succeeded not only in stabilizing the commercial elements of film-making, it has even rationalized the quality.

The Japanese cinema is organized in such rigid forms that almost everything is predictable. Unlike in many other countries, there is never a sudden appearance of new talent or the excitement of an unknown creating something important. Everything develops slowly as the directors work their way up the ranks. There is literally no place for untried talent in the Japanese movie industry. Everything depends upon past reputation. The only time in the entire history of the Japanese cinema that there was anything like the excitement caused by the sudden appearance of a Welles or a Clouzot was the initial excellence of the first films made by Kinoshita and Kurosawa during the early 1940's. And this was due in part to the fact that the war caused the older, established directors either to retire or to go stale.

Yet, though the Japanese directors have more control of their product than most directors of other countries, the recent "rationalization" of the industry has weakened their

position. They are more and more tending to lose their power
both to individual producers and to the over-all production head of each company. According to Heinosuke Gosho, changing production methods are also weakening the influence of the director. One of the reasons that the Japanese director enjoyed much more control over everything that goes into making a film than his foreign counterpart was that due to his training as an assistant he had experience with all of the little things that make up a film as well as unusually close contact with technicians and their work. With color and widescreen, however, the camera positions, even the time of day for shooting, are taken out of his hands and made a technical rather than an artistic responsibility.

Many feel that the "director system" is directly connected with whatever is best in the Japanese film and that under a producer or any other kind of system the Japanese industry could never have produced its more excellent works. The "producer system" in essence means that rather than having a few geniuses making a few outstanding films, there will be a large number of merely competent directors turning out a predictable number of competent films. Obviously, as in any film industry, the really outstanding movie is the exception rather than the rule, and—just as obviously—it is usually the responsibility, if not the entire conception of a single man. It is these single men, all over the world, who have created the art of the film.

The nine directors to be treated in this chapter obviously did not singlehandedly create the art of the Japanese film, but they have certainly contributed more to it than anyone else. Viewing their work as a whole, one is continually impressed by its originality, its freshness, and its excellence. Each of these men has created a world of his own, one governed by the laws of his own personality. Each is, in his own way, the best that Japan has produced.

One might question the choosing of only nine directors for detailed treatment. One might think that there were others who could just as easily have been chosen. Such is not the case. A few of the most brilliant, like Sadao Yamanaka, have been dead so long that their achievements are visible only in archives, if there. Others have fallen off so sadly that their inclusion would not be warranted. Yet others are so erratic that their occasional excellence is seriously vitiated by their usual mediocrity. And of the vast majority there is simply nothing to say. Thus we have but nine men to represent

what is best in a country's films. If this seems an unduly small
number, however, try to think of nine directors from any other country whom one could put together on such a single plane of excellence.

KENJI MIZOGUCHI (1898–1956). It is commonly supposed that it was only with the exportation of *The Life of O-Haru* and *Ugetsu* that the West discovered the late Kenji Mizoguchi. Actually, he had been "discovered" once before, in 1928, when his *Passion of a Woman Teacher* (Kyoren no Onna Shisho), made two years earlier, was shown in Europe. Though the considerable impact made by this film on the few who saw it has been long since forgotten, it is not likely that anyone in the West will be able to think of the Japanese film and, for years to come, not also think of Mizoguchi.

Like many of the men who early contributed to the art of the film, Mizoguchi approached cinema through the two related arts of painting and literature. When still quite young he showed a decided interest in things pictorial, liked to draw and was early turning out cats and cherry trees. After graduating from a painting institute, one of the modern kind that specializes in Western-style art, he left crowded, modern Tokyo and traveled down to the graciously old-fashioned heart of Japan, the Kansai. He did not, however, live in austere Nara, nor in the culturally prodigious Kyoto, nor even in bustling Osaka. Instead, he lived in Kobe. Here, in this second-rate imitation of a Western port city, he got a job on a newspaper, where he largely wasted his talents designing advertisements. Returning at twenty-one to an even more crowded, even more modern Tokyo, he discovered that he could not find a job. After several months of looking, he finally gave up and began to spend most of his time with a friend who lived very near the Tokyo studios of the Nikkatsu Motion Picture Company. This friend, a samisen teacher, often used to go to the studios to give lessons, and Mizoguchi, having nothing better to do, would go along. In this way he eventually met Haru Wakayama, known as one of the new "progressive" directors, and became an actor.

When the *oyama* left Nikkatsu in a huff, they left some of their number behind, and the studio, very short of talent, rushed Mizoguchi into the breach as full director. And so, ironically, Mizoguchi, who became famous as a director of women and whose better films are concerned entirely with their problems, began his career as the rear-guard apologist for the use of female impersonators.

From his earliest films, his approach to cinema was definite-
ly literary. As early as 1923 he was translating Arsene Lupin
and American dime-novels into film. The 1924 *Turkeys in a
Row* (Shichimencho no Yukue)—starring Master Hiroshi
Inagaki, later to become a director himself—was based on a
children's comedy, and *Song of the Mountain Pass* was taken
from a Lady Gregory play, which was in turn influenced by
Yeats, who was in turn influenced by the Japanese Noh.
Mizoguchi's literary taste was eclectic, including Bernard
Shaw, Balzac, Sinclair Lewis, Kafu Nagai, and the "Boston
Blackie" stories, but he always knew precisely what he wanted
to film and how he wanted to film it. That the inspiration
was purely literary did not keep the final product from being sometimes close to pure cinema.

Here his inclination for painting was seen, his eye for
pictorial values, his insistence upon significant detail. This
painterly approach was what constituted the Mizoguchi atmosphere, and atmosphere was what Mizoguchi was famous
for, both in Japan and abroad. In this, of course, he resembled
European directors of two or three decades back and it is
perhaps this insistence upon atmosphere, plus the fact that
his later work was in the period-film, that make his pictures
seem anachronistic to the contemporary Japanese film scene.
As a director he was twenty years behind the cinematic times.
In a way, he was a man from the golden age of cinema.

One Japanese critic seems to have said precisely the right
thing when he observed that the locale is the real hero of a
Mizoguchi film, that the setting very often determines the
final picture, and that the director insists upon the supreme
importance of environment. This Mizoguchi did in a variety
of ways. One of the most important was the long-lasting
camera set-up. He said that he believed single set-ups held for
an unusually long time were extremely helpful in creating
atmosphere; almost any of his films contain a number of
them, particularly memorable being those in the lovers' flight
sequence of *A Story from Chikamatsu*.

Mizoguchi also said that he thought the long-shot—that is,
the camera far away from the objects photographed—was
very effective in obtaining what he wanted. In *Ugetsu* the
scenes in the enchanted mansion are often shot from across
a courtyard, and the charming scene on the lawn is prefaced
by an extraordinarily beautiful long-shot; the peach-blossom
garden scene in *The Princess Yang* is shot from very far away
indeed.

Camera movement was another way through which Mizo-

guchi suggested atmosphere. The final scene of *Ugetsu* is a
very fine example. The child places the food on his mother's grave and then, with the gentlest of movements, the camera begins to climb until finally the entire little settlement on the shores of the lake is seen in a shot which matches the opening of the film with its slow pan from lake to houses. In fact, almost any Mizoguchi film can be reduced to a catalogue of beautifully calculated effects which create the atmosphere of his film world.

This film world, despite its apparent diversity, is actually unified not only in form but also in content. Like any truly strong creator, Mizoguchi was continually saying the same thing over and over again. Whether this was apparent to him or not, a definite pattern of content began to be visible in his work. It took the form of what one might call a favorite myth.

Every director, really any creator of any kind, has a favorite myth. Von Stroheim's was that money corrupts; Marcel Carné is always concerned with love betrayed; John Ford's myth is that the quest is everything, that actually found, nothing. Actually, any statement of these governing myths or themes constitutes a damaging generalization but, in Mizoguchi's case, the elaboration may prove helpful. The favorite myth, the one seen at the core of most of his films, is that man's soul is saved by a woman's love. This is the myth of *Ugetsu* and *The Princess Yang*, where it appears in explicit form. *A Tale of Chikamatsu* seems concerned with the opposite until it is understood that neither man nor woman had any purpose in life before their illicit affair. With her love, and the resultant adversity, came fulfillment. Mizoguchi's last completed film, *Red-Light District*, is an ironic variation on the theme since all of the women are prostitutes. Love is an extravagance which they cannot allow themselves. They are continually thinking of and talking about love, ruining men left and right simply because they cannot afford this luxury. The corollary of the myth that woman's love saves man is that without a woman's love man is damned.

This was, however, by no means the only theme in Mizoguchi's work. One of the "founding fathers" of the tendency film, he had long been interested in social problems because they concerned human beings. It was during this period that he made his first two really famous films, *Tokyo March* and *Metropolitan Symphony*. The emphasis in both of these pictures was not upon the good proletariat and the bad bourgeois, but upon the good and bad in both. Mizoguchi's tendency pictures only said "this is the way things are," never "this is the way things ought not be." Both films ran into severe censorship difficulties and, like many other directors, he found that in order to be allowed to direct, he had to satisfy the army, the navy, and the government. He made a few of these "government policy" films before he discovered that, if he interested himself in periods other than his own, the government would let him do what he wanted.

In this way, by moving back to the Meiji period, Mizoguchi was able to express another of his main interests: the conflict between the ways of life in the Kansai and in the Tokyo-Yokohama area. Even now the difference is considerable. Tokyo is all modern and dirty and commercial and fashionable. It looks like Chicago or Liverpool. Kyoto, on the other hand, is still old Japan. Only in the Kansai, and in a few more isolated regions, are the graces of traditional Japanese living still observed. Many of Mizoguchi's finest films have dramatized this conflict. One of the best, *Sisters of the Gion*, was the story of the loving rivalry between two sisters, one "old-fashioned" and the other "modern." Earlier in the same year he had approached the theme from a slightly different point of view in his *Osaka Elegy*, showing the story of a modern girl struggling against the commercialization of Osaka life. When Mizoguchi died he was working on *An Osaka Story*, which took a similar theme and set it back in the immediate pre-Meiji period. Of the Meiji era the director once said: "It is my favorite period of all."

The Meiji era was, of course, that period during which Western influence, so destructive to the way of life which Mizoguchi's films celebrate, was first felt. Mizoguchi's reconstructions, however, were completely different from those of prior films set in this era. While others saw the period through the dim eyes of extreme nostalgia, Mizoguchi's was a sharp, clear, and realistic view. His realism was beautiful but it was also vital. Of it Akira Kurosawa has said: "Now that Mizoguchi is gone, there are very few directors left who can see the past clearly and realistically."

That Kurosawa and Mizoguchi, so different as creators, should have reached the same destination, the former through a very socially aware realism, the latter through books, painting, and an almost mystical love of the romantic, is perhaps indicative of the Japanese historical sense at its best. It is also indicative, however, of the universality of this world which Mizoguchi created in his films—a world two decades behind the cinematic times and yet timeless.

HEINOSUKE GOSHO (born 1902). Gosho, like Mizoguchi,
insists upon atmosphere, but his results are quite different.
Mizoguchi had the eye of a painter and was almost entirely
concerned with the pictorial. His atmosphere was one created
by craft, by the graphic elements of photography, by camera
viewpoint, camera movement, the use of color. Gosho, however, has the eye of a dramatist. The locale is important only
because it is a part of the characters who live and move within it. The raw material of his pictures, people, what they
are and what they do, creates the atmosphere of a Gosho
film. Consequently, while Mizoguchi interested himself in the
pictorial elements of each photographed scene, Gosho, using
editing as a base, is much more interested in the photographed
material itself and is especially careful with his scenario.

Always interested in literature, Gosho was one of the first
to bring to the screen what the Japanese call "pure literature"
—as opposed to commercial fiction. This has since created a
movement with which Gosho is always associated. His very
best films, *Everything That Lives, An Inn at Osaka, Where
Chimneys Are Seen,* and *Growing Up,* are all examples of the
interest which enabled him, along with Shiro Toyoda and
Mikio Naruse, to turn "pure literature" into film.

Gosho always tries to get the best possible script, sometimes writing it himself. In the same way, he likes to work
closely with his art director, showing an almost fanatical
concern over details. Even when forced to shoot in the
studio, he prepares the set with immense care. In the pre-
production stage of *Growing Up,* he managed to visit fifty
temples as research for the one finally designed for the film.
During one of the scenes, it is said that he himself polished
the wooden floor until it had acquired precisely the sheen
that he felt was needed. The result of all this care is the
typical Gosho production.

He has said that his philosophy of art is simple: "Only
if we love our fellow human beings can we create. From
this love of humanity streams all creativity." His, however,
is not the facile and optimistic humanism of a William Saro-
yan—though the two men have points in common. Gosho's
more closely resembles that of De Sica in his compassionate
portrayal of the common life, or Chaplin in his broad humanity. In fact, "Gosho-ism," now an accepted critical term
often used by Japanese writers on the film, has been defined
as a style incorporating "something that makes you laugh and
cry at the same time." Gosho further resembles Chaplin in
that his "love of humanity" contains not pity—he has already

gone through that—but compassion. Like other creators in this century, he finds human individuality the most precious thing in the world. When it is threatened the result is tragedy.

Believing in individuality, Gosho often draws from his own life and his own observations. He has said that "a director must live in modern society, and must be an active participant in all levels of that society's activities; the personality which he develops as an integrated person in society must be reflected in his work." Thus, Gosho's own life gives some clue to his work.

He was born to one of his father's mistresses, a geisha of famed and "ukiyoe-esque" beauty, but was made his father's heir after the death of the single legitimate son. At the same time, he was seeing something of the life of art and pleasure, since his grandfather, who had interests in the artistic world, often took the boy with him when he made calls. His father too, frequently took him along when he went to the geisha-houses and, in addition, often gave him passes to those theaters in which he owned stock.

Though the young Gosho had been initially interested in drama, his interest soon turned to the films and he used to make frequent contributions to the letters-to-the-editor columns of film magazines. Upon graduating from Tokyo's Keio University he made up his mind, braved considerable family opposition, and entered the Shochiku Tokyo studios, where he was assigned as assistant director to Yasujiro Shimazu. Shimazu provided the first and some say the only cinematic influence on Gosho's style. A leader in forming the modern drama and weaning away the Japanese cinema from the period-film, Shimazu made a place for simple stories of everyday life among the white-collar workers and the lower middle-classes, the kind of film which *Marty* perhaps best typifies and which thirty-five years later started winning prizes at festivals.

In 1925, Gosho received his director's certificate and began making his own films. His first big success was in *The Lonely Roughneck,* but in the same year a beloved younger brother was stricken by polio and this illness affected Gosho considerably. He himself says: "I lost my way for several years, and my personal life began to fall apart." Despondent, he even tried suicide, but in this, "as in all my efforts during the period, I failed." All this time, even at his lowest, he was "desperately searching for something different to get me out of my rut."

It was the coming of sound which, in part, gave Gosho the

impetus and the success he so badly needed. In *The Neighbor's Wife and Mine* he began the experiments in sound which he continues to this day. Though his idea of a talkie is still one containing a large amount of silence, it was to remain for him a problem in construction which thereafter kept him from the extreme introspection which had caused his earlier depression. Gosho continues to regard the integration of sound and silent-film techniques as the most important experiment that can be made in film production. In his pictures he continually uses various methods for retaining a silent-film technique, two of which are quite important to his style.

The first is his employment of pictorial symbols. A simple example of this occurs in *Growing Up* when the young heroine, designed from birth for a life of prostitution but never fully aware of it, innocently enters into a conversation with the adults who are deciding her precise fate. The camera, as the scene closes, turns and gazes at a bird in a cage. We have often noticed this cage throughout the film; there was even a small bit of business built around it. Now, however, at the psychologically proper point, Gosho makes his comment with a kind of cinematic metaphor, its brevity and lack of emphasis restoring to this notoriously trite symbol all of its original freshness and power.

The second of these methods is his use of both numerous close-ups and the number and rapidity of his separate shots. As early as 1925 he began using a great number of shots, saying that he was impressed with their importance in Lubitsch's *The Marriage Circle*, a film he saw twenty times and which, along with Chaplin's *A Woman of Paris*, he regards as the greatest foreign influence on his work. *An Inn at Osaka* is composed of over a thousand separate shots and *Growing Up* has even more. Gosho, in contradistinction to directors like Mizoguchi, is known as "the director who uses three shots where others use one."

Gosho's essential concern, in both his life and his films, has been the understanding of human life, the purpose of "the film director's life [being] to describe the real life around him and create works which express the true feelings of human beings.... All films, as all works of art, must touch the emotions of the audience and touch them deeply...." Thus Gosho, in perfecting the form of the *shomin-geki*, the drama of common people, raised it to the level of personal tragedy. His feelings made it impossible for him to create any war films acceptable to the government. He would turn any sub-

ject, no matter how military, into a simple love story or a
shomin-geki. The poor health from which he has suffered all of his life was all that saved him from official wrath.

Again, his extreme empathy with the common people led him to take an active part in the Toho strikes. Though politically uninvolved he felt that he too had to fight. "Of course I had to join, because I couldn't stand seeing people who had faithfully helped me make films get fired. I was no Communist, but I couldn't reject my friends' plight."

Gosho's belief in humanity is a very genuine thing. He seems to set the cameras rolling on life itself and then gently whispers to you that these people are really worth saving. And they all are, for even his villains, on those rare occasions when he has any, are both comprehensible and sympathetic. No one in Gosho's type of film is ever really to blame for what happens.

In *An Inn at Osaka*, though everyone accuses everyone else, no one is guilty. Money is the particular problem in this picture, and in it Gosho has used, as he occasionally does, fragments from his own life. When he was a boy in Osaka his grandfather once told him: "To have money doesn't mean that you can afford to be cruel to others. To make money is an important thing but one must stop short of becoming unbalanced about it." This bit of homely and prosaic philosophy became the theme of the very unprosaic *An Inn at Osaka*.

But beyond money and beyond Osaka is the austere law that slaughters the innocents and that orders Gosho's universe. And yet, in the end, there is always the faint light of hope. When the hero is finally transferred to Tokyo at the end of *An Inn at Osaka*, he says: "None of us can say he is happy or fortunate, yet things still seem promising ... we are able to laugh at our own misfortunes, and as long as we can laugh we still have the strength and courage to build a new future." And so it always is in Gosho's films. Something has happened, there is a sense of release. The circumstances remain the same but the outlook has changed and there is room for optimism.

Always busy with new films, new ideas, Gosho was the first important film director to become associated with television, writing story outlines for a weekly drama series. Still as busy in the films as ever, he continues to work, saying: "I thought I could not continue making pictures after I was thirty ... but somehow I continued. After I was thirty ... I knew I could make pictures until I was at least fifty years old. I was certain artistic senility would then grip me. Well, I am now past fifty and I still feel my work isn't done. I now plan to work in films until I am eighty. Or maybe I'll go right on working until I drop dead."

YASUJIRO OZU (born 1903). Considered by the Japanese as "the most Japanese of all directors," Yasujiro Ozu in his thirty-six years in the cinema has been more loaded with honors than any other director, having alone won six *Kinema Jumpo* "Best One" prizes. While entirely deserved, these various honors and his extremely high critical reputation have had the added effect of keeping his films off the international market: the Japanese themselves are very afraid that his excellence will not be recognized abroad and, in true Japanese fashion, prefer not to try rather than fail. Yet, when his *Tokyo Story* was shown at the 1956 University of California film festival, it was highly successful, and his films are eagerly awaited on the Hawaiian and West Coast theater circuits which Shochiku services. This success abroad is something which the producers prefer to ignore since they cannot comprehend it, one of the canons of the Japanese business world being that the West cannot hope to appreciate anything "truly Japanese."

His films, to be sure, are utterly Japanese. So much so that the man on the street will say of a new Ozu film: "That picture really has the Japanese flavor." This very quality is responsible for the fact that the younger generation thinks it fashionable to find his films old-fashioned and to pretend not to understand them. Actually, however, his films so faithfully reflect Japanese life that—more than any other director —Ozu is the spokesman for both the older and the younger generations.

One of these Japanese qualities is, outstandingly, his concern with home life. His later and best films are about nothing else—even their titles are similar. In every Ozu film the whole world exists in one family. The ends of the earth are no more distant than outside of the house. The people are members of a family rather than members of society, though the family may be in disruption, as in *Tokyo Story*, may be nearly extinct as in *Late Spring* or *Tokyo Twilight*, or may be a kind of family substitute, the small group in a large company, as in *Early Spring*. In any event, the treatment of the characters as basically members of a family rather than of a larger society, remains today one of the outstanding features of Ozu's work.

It is for this reason that Ozu but rarely treats romantic love—the staple of all motion-picture industries. He himself says, "I have no interest in romantic love," and proves this statement in his films. When he does occasionally treat romantic love he falters. His only interest in the various forms of love is in those which exist between members of a family, and he is successful with romantic love only when it finds an outlet in the form of family love, as between man and wife.

As a creator of the Japanese home drama at its best, he is much more interested in character and incidental incident than in action or plot, and has said: "Pictures with obvious plots bore me now. Naturally, a film must have some kind of structure or else it is not a film, but I feel that a picture isn't good if it has too much drama or too much action." With little or no interest in plot movement, Ozu concerns himself with character development, and all of his better films represent a leisurely disclosure of character, the like of which is rare in the films of any director.

In *Late Spring* the interest is in the relations between a father and daughter, and in their varying reactions to her coming marriage. In *The Flavor of Green Tea and Rice* we are shown a married couple who have no children to hold them together; we see how they lose their separate personalities and how in attempting to find a stronger basis for their marriage they find themselves, and each other, again. In *Tokyo Story*, Ozu examines the relations between three generations. The result is the creation of fully developed screen characters. One cannot say who is good or who is bad. One can only identify completely since one sees the entire character.

Naturally, character observed is built from one detail after another and all presented over a period of time. Just as naturally, since Ozu's films are essentially plotless, the director presents his characters in the most leisurely fashion. Hence, Japanese critics are forever pointing out that this slow pace would prevent a foreign audience's ever really appreciating these films. They are right in that Ozu's films have no violent action and therefore none of the breakneck pace so common in motion pictures. Yet, they are not slow. They create their own time and the audience is drawn into Ozu's own world, with its own way of reckoning the passage of time.

Actually, Ozu's characters and his tempo are in perfect synchronization with this time system that he has created. His is time as it actually is. It is psychological time, and so

clock time has no meaning. Critic Tsuneo Hazumi's remark
that "Ozu's world is one of stillness" is accurate only if one realizes that this stillness, this repose, is the surface which it presents and that, beneath this world, lies the thwarted yet potential violence found in the Japanese family system; beneath it lies also the quiet heroism of the Japanese faced with his own family.

Ozu illustrates his theme with a sobriety and cinematic economy that makes him, like Mizoguchi, something of an anomaly in the film world. He almost habitually shoots all his scenes from the same viewpoint, the eye level of a person sitting on *tatami*. The camera angle is correspondingly low, and for this reason Ozu was one of the first to construct sets with ceilings, since the ceilings show in low-angle shots. As early as 1930 he had begun to give up optical devices which other directors rely on. He says that his silent *Life of an Office Worker* "was a rare film for me—I used several dissolves. But this was the only time I ever did. I wanted to get the feeling of a morning beginning. The dissolve is a handy thing, but it's uninteresting. Of course, it all depends on how you use it. Most of the time it's a form of cheating." By 1932 he had decided not to use several more elements of the common cinematic technique. In *I Was Born But*, "for the first time, I consciously gave up the use of the fade-in and fade-out. Generally, dissolves and fades are not a part of cinematic grammar. They are only attributes of the camera."

Ozu was also one of the last important directors to convert to talkies, and he did so most reluctantly at that. Even after the conversion, however, his scripts continued to be written as silent, and silent techniques were used throughout. As of 1959, Ozu continues to pay more attention to the visuals of his work. Though no believer in either dynamic composition or montage, the composition of each of his shots has both beauty and effectiveness in its own quiet way. He uses no tricks in editing yet evidences a superlative ability for timing and arranging a rhythmic flow of images.

At the same time, he pays particular attention to the properties and other small details of the sets. These he selects and photographs so that they comment on character, selecting these details not because of what they add to reality but according to what they reveal about the personality of his people. Unlike Gosho's, Ozu's details emphasize character rather than environment.

Yet, despite the almost totally visual nature of Ozu's style, the dialogue in his films is the most interesting in Japanese

cinea, and many critics judge it with the standards usually
reserved for the most serious literature. Its strength is the
complete naturalness which it achieves without attempting
naturalism. Ozu's characters always say what is appropriate
to the situation, as if their conversation were stolen directly
from life. It could not have been better phrased by anyone
and yet the art with which it is said has no suggestion of the
"poetic" or the "artistic." In everything that Ozu does in
films, the parts fit so perfectly that one is never conscious of
the virtuosity with which it is done. His pictures are so
subtle—the precise opposite of Kurosawa's—that one never
thinks to praise the skill with which his effects are achieved.

Ozu, not unnaturally, considers the script the most important element in making a film and refuses to start shooting
until he has what he considers a perfect script. "For me
there's only one way—write and correct, write and correct,
day and night. In this way only can you make progress." In
practice this means that Ozu and Kogo Noda, who has done
many of the director's scripts, sit up over saké until the script
is done. "When a writer and a director work together, if
their physical constitutions are not similar, things won't come
out very well. With Noda and me, we see alike on drinking
and staying up late and I think this is the most important
matter. ... Although we don't write down the details of the
sets or costumes, they are in our two minds as one common
image—to the extent that we agree on whether to put *wa* or
yo at the end of a sentence. We think alike—it is an amazing
thing."

Ozu's attitude toward the films has always been that of a
perfectionist. After he became established at Shochiku, he
turned down six or seven pictures simply because he did not
feel he was ready to become a director. This easy-going attitude, a refusal to be pushed, reflects his whole approach
to film-making. It is also reflected in his refusal to be rushed
into talkie production, his extreme unwillingness to hurry
through a picture, his postwar decision to make only one film
a year and to take almost a year making it.

Having served a period as assistant to Tadamoto Okubo,
one of the first directors to make nonsense-*mono*, Ozu took
his time finding precisely where his talent lay. He made a
number of nonsense-comedy films but soon moved into the
social comedy. Then his interest turned to children and, at
the same time, to the lives of *shomin*, the lower middle-class.
This latter has remained his special province and his attitude
toward his characters has remained unchanged, despite the

advent of the leftist tendency film and the reactions that came with the war.

From the first he was above politics and completely avoided the false polemic inherent in the tendency picture. In this he contrasted strongly with Gosho, the other Shochiku *shomin-geki* specialist. He was perfectly aware of what he calls "the coldness of society," but his reaction took the form of satire. During the war he did not try to avoid government-sponsored "national-policy" subjects, as did a number of other directors, but took them on and still refused to compromise with reality. In films like *The Toda Brother and His Sisters* and *There Was a Father*, he took official subjects and bent them to his own way of thinking. The subjects therefore, while official, were treated in such a way that the official line was not pushed and was, in fact, inherently criticized.

It is Ozu's integrity and his refusal to compromise which make him one of the most respected of Japanese directors, and it is this, as reflected in the excellence of his films, that makes him the director most representative of the Japanese people. Yet, if recognition has come to him in Japan, it has yet to come from the outside world, kept in studied ignorance of his worth. He is one of the few remaining senior directors of Japan to remain unknown, while others of his generation —Gosho and Mizoguchi—have achieved foreign acclaim.

MIKIO NARUSE (born 1905). The film director, like any other artist, sees the world from an angle which becomes personally his own. This partial view creates a perspective which we thereafter associate with the director. Thus, we know what kind of film Marcel Carné or Luis Buñuel is likely to make next; we can usually recognize an Autant-Lara or a John Ford film after seeing only a few sequences; and we instantly notice the stylistic differences among the films of Mizoguchi, Gosho, Ozu, and Naruse. Each director has a strong personal profile, each illuminates a part of the world for us, and each insists upon an interpretation of this world which is so consistent that we speak of it as the director's style.

Naruse's view of the world, if one of the most consistent, is also one of the least comforting. Mizoguchi may show us that in beauty lies salvation; Gosho may permit his characters to hope; Ozu may take away everything, but he at least leaves his people the solace of each other's company. Naruse, however, believes that there is no escape. We are in a floating world which has no meaning for us. If we are fortunate we die. If not, we must go on and on. Happiness is impossible,

yet we find a kind of contentment if we are wise enough
never to hope.

This theme of expectations invariably ending in disappointment has run throughout all of Naruse's films, even from the early nonsense-comedy days. He himself speaks of his characters as being caught, saying: "If they move even a little, they quickly hit the wall. From the youngest age, I have thought that the world we live in betrays us; this thought still remains with me."

Naruse's personal life has been singularly unhappy, and this partially accounts for the extreme pessimism of his films. Both parents died when he was quite young and he was brought up by a not overly affectionate elder sister and brother. They did not have enough money to send him to school, so he took to reading in the library. He read extensively all during his childhood, mostly fiction, and conceived the great love of literature which remains with him still. He says that during this time "I had to immediately become an adult; it was the darkest period of my life."

When he was twenty-one, a friend of the family helped him get a job at the Shochiku Tokyo studios. There he was soon assigned to Yoshinobu Ikeda, one of the company's first directors and a specialist in nonsense-comedies. He remembers that at first he was such a low-ranking assistant that he was assigned to the light crew to help carry equipment.

In 1929, Kido of Shochiku told him to make a two-reel slapstick comedy. This film, thought of as a "test" of directorial ability, was edited by a Shochiku acquaintance, Heinosuke Gosho, who was anxious to give the young man a helping hand. *Mr. and Mrs. Swordplay* (Chambara Fufu) was considered successful and Naruse was allowed to continue with *Pure Love* (Junjo), only five reels long yet constituting a very successful lyric love story. It greatly impressed Yasujiro Ozu, also at Shochiku, who, like Naruse, was tied to slapstick and trying to get out.

Ozu escaped in the following year but Naruse had no such luck. Until 1934 he was stuck with nonsense pictures, melodramas, and tear-jerkers, the Shochiku staple products. Even later, when he was beginning to make a reputation for himself in the *shomin-geki* field, he remembers that "I was still considered only an assistant director." His work was, in general, thought inferior to that of Ozu, Gosho, Shimazu, and Hiroshi Shimizu, all of whom were working with the *shomin-geki,* and he had the further humiliation of seeing others promoted before him. "People who entered the studio after me began

to make pictures within two years; it took six years for me."
At the same time, his private life was far from happy. Extremely lonely, he made the studio his entire existence. Once a year his elder brother came to call. After a simple exchange of greetings, he was gone again. There was nothing to talk about and the two had never gotten on particularly well. Usually, after work at the studio, Naruse would go home to his tiny room, second-floor rear, and start on a bottle of saké. Always a heavy drinker, about half of his salary, the equivalent of fifty dollars a month, went to the corner liquor store.

By 1934, though his best pictures had made a great deal of money for Shochiku, Naruse was still working under a monthly-salary system and was earning only little more than one of the salary-men he was making films about. Eventually, relations with Shochiku became impossible. The company refused to let him make the kind of pictures he knew he made best and, at the same time, refused to pay him a living wage for making the kind of film that they themselves wanted. In the middle of 1934 Naruse left Shochiku and went to P.C.L., later to become Toho. At this time P.C.L. was a young, forward-looking company which was definitely interested in literary adaptations, and Naruse, having long had an interest in literature, was most enthusiastic about putting his favorite authors on film. Thus, initially at any rate, working at P.C.L. was quite different from working at Shochiku, which avoided like the plague anything it considered over the heads of its female audience.

At P.C.L., Naruse first made *Three Sisters with Maiden Hearts* (Otome Gokoro San-nin Shimai), a poetic treatment of *shomin* family life based on a Yasunari Kawabata story; the director still considers this one of his best films. A year later he made *Wife! Be Like a Rose*, a picture which won the 1935 *Kinema Jumpo* "Best One" Award and which was considered successful enough to be sent abroad. It was even shown in New York, where, according to a *Reader's Digest* article, it seemed more influenced by French than American techniques.

Emboldened by the first smile fate had deigned to give, Naruse married an actress and moved into that Japanese symbol of success, a Western-style house complete with bed and sofa. Fate, however, did not smile for long. From 1936, Naruse went into a slump which lasted fifteen years and was the most serious any major director has ever experienced. During this period he was simply incapable of turning out a really good film, though some, like the 1938 *Tsuruhachi and* *Tsurujiro* (Tsuruhachi Tsurujiro), were considered financially successful. A number of critics have laid the blame on the gradual breakup of his marriage. Whatever the reasons, once he and his wife had decided to part, Naruse went back to his saké and his cheap upstairs room.

He himself explains the fifteen-year period by saying that "there are times when a director must make a picture even if he doesn't want to....If you look at it from the outside, I fell into a slump at such a time. It's only recently that I've had the courage to refuse to make pictures....Not long ago, I was afraid. I used to vent my dissatisfaction with the content by concentrating on the technique. But this didn't work out. In the end, the film was just as bad as if I hadn't labored on it so."

In 1951, Naruse was finally given a vehicle which suited him. It was based on a novel by Fumiko Hayashi and was called *Repast*. The story of a married couple drifting apart, it contained elements that Naruse personally knew. Putting everything he had into the film he came up with his first postwar success. Later he was to use the same situation in two other films, *Husband and Wife* (Fufu) and *Wife* (Tsuma), the latter again based on a Hayashi story about the selfishness of a married couple. Of these three Naruse has said: "These pictures have little that happens in them and end without a conclusion—just like life." And indeed the films are "just like life," at least, just like the life that Naruse had experienced. His characters are so tied to their motionless environment and are so completely at the mercy of circumstance that they seem to negate the very concept of free will.

Looking at the later, and best films, one is struck again and again by the dark negation of Naruse's world. *Older Brother, Younger Sister* presents a family trapped by its own construction, each member unable to move because of the others. *Sounds from the Mountains, Late Chrysanthemums,* and *Floating Clouds,* all present characters so completely tied to their environments that they are motionless. *Sudden Rain* (Shuu) shows the boredom of a salary-man's marriage as it reaches its fifth year: again there are no children, and sterility, actual and metaphorical, becomes the theme of the film. *A Wife's Heart* (Tsuma no Kokoro) shows the family system to be so rigid that there can be no variation. In the 1958 *Anzukko* (the title refers to an alternate reading of the heroine's name) a girl, very unhappily married, finds some solace in visiting her father but must always return to her worthless husband. In the final scene—walking away, dejected and depressed, one of Naruse's favorite final shots—she is shown again returning to married life. In *Herringbone Clouds* (Iwashi Gumo), made in the same year, Naruse's farming family, try as it may, comes nowhere near achieving even contentment.

In Naruse's films, the family is usually held together by bonds so strong that no single member can break them. Life is a daily round of fixed customs and even the ways of expressing emotion are completely formalized. With all the dramatic elements eliminated from the endless round of days and years, even the slightest personal emotional reaction has a major and usually unfortunate effect. Tragedy is constantly hanging over Naruse's characters and they are never more vulnerable than when they for once decide upon a personal, an individual, course of action.

The girl in *Untamed* (shown as *Untamed Woman* in America) thinks of herself as completely free. She moves from job to job, from man to man, just as though she were not at the complete mercy of circumstance. Yet, at the end, in one of those long, quiet, resigned, final shots of which Naruse is so fond, we know that for her there is no hope. Those in his atypical *Mother* escape the tragedy which hangs over Naruse's people, but the lovers in *Floating Clouds* taste bitterness to the full when death intervenes. Yet even they attain a kind of serenity, a sort of resignation which, in the end, constitutes the greatest happiness they will ever know.

In the extremely fine conclusion to *Flowing*, only the elderly maid knows what will happen in the geisha house where she works. The others continue as they always have. The daughter, who will never again try to escape, happily works her sewing machine. The mother, filled with hopes for the future, practices her samisen. And in a long, unfolding final sequence, a kind of coda completely without dialogue, Naruse shows that their ignorance of approaching doom, their fortunate innocence, constitute a kind of beauty, a kind of strength. Happiness is impossible but contentment may yet be achieved.

It is the honesty with which Naruse treats his theme that commands our respect; it is his faithfulness to this theme which creates his style; and it is our suspicion that, painful though it be, he is telling the truth, that creates his greatness.

SHIRO TOYODA (born 1906). While still a boy, Shiro Toyoda decided to become a playwright. Fascinated by the theater,

he read drama, studied theatrical history, and went to plays
whenever he could. Wanting to become a part of the theatrical world, he asked a friend to introduce him to someone
in the profession. The best the friend could do was Eizo
Tanaka, a film director whose connection with the stage was
then tenuous. Still, this was better than nothing, and so the
young Toyoda called on the great man. He was told to start
writing film scripts: they were easier than plays and, besides,
said Tanaka, he could learn all he needed to know about
films in half a year. When the half year was over, Toyoda
had begun to find the films so interesting that he forgot all
about playwriting. Entering the Shochiku Tokyo studios in
1925, he became an assistant to Yasujiro Shimazu when his
chief assistant, Heinosuke Gosho, was promoted to director.
As a result, Toyoda's original infatuation with the theater
vanished and in its place grew his love for the motion
pictures.

Today, even after having become fully established as one
of Japan's leading directors, Toyoda still retains something
of this earlier infatuation. It was, in particular, the actors who
attracted him to the stage; as a film director, it is his concern
for the actor and the art of acting that has created his style
and accounts for much of the strength of a Toyoda film.
He personally believes that casting is the most important
element in a film, that in it lies the key to success. He has
consequently long insisted upon the right to cast his own
pictures and to reject stars when he feels they do not fit a
part. Because of his believing that the actor is the most important element of the film he has become known as an
actor's director and, certainly, he can obtain performances
which other directors cannot.

"What is important," says Toyoda, "is the unity of the
actors' playing—everything must be in the same style. Casting
is not just the director's concern. His selection must also
please the scenarist and the cameraman. In fact, a director
cannot cast a picture alone. He must take the advice of
everyone and must listen to their suggestions." Naturally, it
is Toyoda himself who in the end decides, but this kind of
diplomacy enables him to get the kind of performances he
wants, and this kind of tact has long made him the Japanese
actor's favorite director.

Once he has cast the person best for the rôle, Toyoda
achieves what he wants by merely guiding and suggesting.
"It is often better for an actor to draw on his imagination in
creating a rôle than to rely on actual experiences. In addition

to the danger of being too literal, if you know too much about the reality of a character, you will lose the courage necessary to create that character." For this reason, Toyoda is rather suspicious of pre-production rehearsals. Sometimes he uses them, sometimes he does not. Usually there is only a brief reading of the parts. The real work begins on the shooting stage. In this way be creates the feeling of spontaneity which he requires and which is so admirably presented in such films as *Wild Geese* and *Marital Relations*.

Another aspect of his interest in character is his reluctance to use more than a few characters in a film—two, three, or four at the most. Whereas many directors tend to use so many characters that they can only present their surface aspects, Toyoda, by insisting on only two or three, can probe deeply into each. *Snow Country* is a character analysis of two people; *Grass Whistle* is a searching essay on the meaning of three lives.

He reveals character by making his actors show what they feel. Though unusually dependent upon literary adaptations for his vehicles—he had a definite part in creating the *junbungaku* movement—he is by no means dependent upon the spoken word. His main concern is not with what his characters say but with that they show; his constant goal is rendering visible the psychology of his characters. Thus his films are filled with purely visual revelations of character.

There is a sequence in *Grass Whistle*, and a very talky one at that, in which the dialogue has nothing to do with what is really happening. Yoichi Tachikawa is dying and talking with Akira Kubo. Their conversation is of the most prosaic. Yet their faces are tortured, they are almost suffocating with what they want to say to each other and cannot because, both young boys, they do not yet know how to express these feelings.

In one scene of *A Cat, Shozo, and Two Women*, Isuzu Yamada comes back home in order to kidnap the cat. There is a short shot where she reflectively runs her hand along the staircase balustrade. This tiny strip of film tells us precisely what she is feeling: this is the house where she used to live; this is the bannister she used to touch every day when it was her house; now everything is different.

One could go on and on. *Marital Relations* is particularly rich in such scenes of psychological revelation. Further, Toyoda's films are so constructed that each of these scenes serves a double purpose. The attitude of a person is shown and, at the same time, the point of the scene is often that the

changing attitude of one person is being shown as contrast to
the changing attitude of another. Thus each of these scenes of psychological revelation also moves the story forward.

One such scene occurs in *Snow Country* (unfortunately cut from some prints shown abroad) where Ryo Ikebe asks Keiko Kishi to find him a geisha. Since she herself is a geisha, what he means (and his manner of asking makes it obvious) is that he wants someone to sleep with. Heretofore their relationship has been that of geisha and casual customer, a relationship devoid of meaning, devoid of sexuality. He has, however, let her know that he is more than interested in her. Her reaction has been that of the proper geisha: artificial laughter, simulated disbelief, childish petulance. Now, however, the relationship suddenly changes. Again, what they say has little to do with what they feel. He, certain of his advantage, cuts his toenails throughout the entire scene, punctuating his sentences with scissor snips. She, taken completely off guard, tries to retreat into the traditional geisha pose, fails, and must lose her temper to retain her self-respect. Their language is completely conventional and the meaning of the scene is entirely visual: two people are showing character, and at the same time, are showing attitudes in the process of changing. By the end of the sequence we are prepared to take the next step. She comes dead drunk into his room that night and flings herself on top of him.

This interest in showing human character has been Toyoda's from the very first. In his debut film, the 1929 *Painted Lips* (Irodorareru Kuchibiru), he opened every sequence not with the then-mandatory long-shot but, instead, with a close-up, since he wanted to show what was happening on the face. Later, he refused to film star vehicles, though he would use stars if he could do with them as he wanted. In both *Young People* and *Crybaby Apprentice* he used Sumiko Kurishima, still at the height of her fame, and made her into a real human being, quite separate from the "star personality" she usually assumed. Later, always looking for the right people for the right rôles, he used a number of Shingeki actors in *Nightingale, Spring on Lepers' Island,* and *Ohinata Village.*

Toyoda realizes, however, that even with perfect casting the director's responsibilities are far from over. The best performance in the world will count as nothing unless the director gives it its proper form, creating from it the single shots and sequences which make up the grammar of the film. Hence, Toyoda's concern with continuity. He now feels very strongly on the subject and believes that the

scenario offers nothing more than a hint of what is required.
When studying a script he therefore breaks down all of the
scenes into shots and then decides upon the value of each
one. He works out his continuity in advance and lets the
actors know what it will be. To this end he often constructs
charts, drawings, graphs, anything to get his ideas across. He
believes that "every motion, every emotion, must be planned
so that the total film has a place for it."

Unlike many Japanese directors who break down everything into close-up, medium-shot, and long-shot set-ups, and
then shoot only these parts, Toyoda first shoots the entire
scene in one master-shot. Thus the actor plays the scene in its
entirety and can build up emotion in a natural manner. Then,
when the necessary short shots, repeating the master-shot
actions, are inserted, there is a much stronger continuity of
mood and expression.

In creating what he thinks a film should be, Toyoda works
as closely with his cameramen and scenarists as he does with
his actors. During his early days at Shochiku, Toyoda wanted
to use Kinya Kokura, one of the company's top cameramen.
When he was refused and when the company kept insisting
that he direct only the cheapest of silents, Toyoda decided
to leave Shochiku and enter Tokyo Hassei. Shiro Kido, who
was perfectly aware of Toyoda's talent, at once panicked
and asked if there was anything he could give his discontent-
ed director. Toyoda said that if Kido thought a present was in
order he would rather like to have Kokura. Kido agreed,
only to discover that they were both going to Tokyo Hassei
anyway. They never returned to Shochiku and, instead,
enjoyed a long and fruitful collaboration elsewhere. Later
Toyoda worked just as closely with the late Mitsuo Miura,
one of Japan's best cameramen, and to this day continues
with Toshio Yasumi, one of Japan's leading script-writers.

In fact, Toyoda's entire career has been one of close and
thoughtful collaboration. From his scenarist, his cameraman,
and his actors, he is determined to draw the very best and in
this he is a "director" in the very best sense of the word: he
regulates, he guides, he trains, he gives directions. This attitude is entirely responsible for the excellence of the Toyoda
film, its fine polish, its expert craftsmanship, and its depth.
He leaves his imprint on everything he touches and precisely
what this imprint consists of was perhaps best expressed by
Akira Kurosawa, upon seeing Toyoda's section of the omnibus *Four Love Stories* (Yotsu Koi no Monogatari), for
which Kurosawa had written the script. Kurosawa did not be-

lieve his script had been used. He almost did not recognize
it. Then he went back to Toyoda, still in the screening-
room, and said: "Now I see what you've done. I understand
now. I described the love of these young people merely
psychologically; but you've described it physiologically."

Keisuke Kinoshita (born 1912). It has often been observed,
and with some justice, that the Japanese have little sense of
humor. They may have a lively sense of ridicule, but they
have little feeling for the ridiculous. They may throw themselves into the most purposeful sort of frenetic gaiety, but
there is little spontaneous wit. Humor often depends upon
an ability to see oneself as foolish and wit depends upon a
swift perception of the incongruous. Both qualities are somewhat conspicuously missing from the Japanese personality.
The spectacle of modern Japan, for example, strikes very few
Japanese as being incongruous, and almost no one as being
funny. One of the effects of this lack of humor is the almost
complete absence of real film comedy. Slapstick, comedy of
situation, comedy of manners are all present, but comedy of
character is rare and satire is almost unheard of. And both
would be even more rare were it not for the work of Keisuke
Kinoshita, one of Japan's most beloved directors and yet one
of the very few to see his country and his people as the
occasionally ridiculous and more than occasionally ludicrous
objects that any people are bound to be.

Kinoshita's best films often reflect his sense of the ridiculous; the essential incongruity of a situation rarely escapes
him. The pompous would-be-gentleman of a father in
Broken Drum, the strip-teaser living for her "art" in both
Carmen Comes Home and *Carmen's Pure Love,* the horrible,
domineering grandmother in *Candle in the Wind* are all comic
figures. And the situations in which these characters find
themselves are all truly comic.

The broken-drum of a father, a "level-headed businessman
type," confronts "art" in the form of his children with all
the terrified intensity of a man barehanded in a lions' cage.
The militaristic harridan of a mother in *Carmen's Pure Love*
makes the daughter and her fiancé endure a daily rendering
of the national anthem; Carmen and her fellow stripper, both
modern girls at their most dreadful, strike terror into the
hearts of the simple country people when they go home to
visit the folks. The typical suburbanites, including the horrible grandmother, are deluged with greedy relatives and im-
portunate gangsters once they win a very small sum of

money. In his films Kinoshita has created a comic rogues'
gallery, the personages of which live in the mind long after the films themselves have disappeared.

One might wonder, however, why the Japanese themselves so love Kinoshita if they are so deficient in just the sort of humor at which he excels. One reason is that the Japanese are always perfectly ready to laugh once the essential humor of a situation has been pointed out to them. Another, and more important reason is that, though the satire is often barbed, and the ridicule is both deep and painful, Kinoshita himself is no misanthropist. He is quite in love with his characters and he admires their faults no less than their virtues. Carmen may be ridiculous, but she is also intensely appealing; the martinet father finally comes to realize, not that he has been wrong, but that his family has been at least partially right; the horrible grandmother by attaining a measure of final serenity also achieves some dignity. For these reasons Kinoshita is beloved and for this reason Japanese critics may almost entirely ignore his comic and satiric achievements and label him as a "lyrical and social director." Thus he is universally respected (often for the wrong reasons) and continues to make films for Shochiku, a company which is in itself certainly no enemy to the feudally-based family system at which Kinoshita occasionally takes such telling shots.

The Japanese think of Kinoshita in the same way that the French tend to think of René Clair. The latter is a director who can turn out magnificent satire, as in *Un Chapeau de Paille d'Italie*, and—practically at the same time—create such haunting evocations of pure sentimentality as *Sous les Toits de Paris*. Though the French may praise the former, they give their hearts only to the latter. Fortunately for Clair, he can do two things equally well, and it is these two qualities which one also sees in the work of Kinoshita.

Like René Clair, Kinoshita is a stylist, one of the few in Japanese cinema. He always tells his assistant directors: "After you've read the script, the biggest problem is not how you are going to direct individual scenes, but in what style are you doing to make the entire film? It is always bad to consider a scene by itself. The worst directors are those who mix their styles." Kinoshita's style is always very strong. It may depend upon externals, a fondness for well-known locations, an addiction for railway trains, framing devices as in *She Was Like a Wild Chrysanthemum*, technical stylizations as in *Carmen's Pure Love* and *Sun and Rose*, or upon

the paraphernalia of the Kabuki perfectly tailored to the
exigencies of the screen, as in *The Song of Narayama*. More often, however, it is integral: an attitude, a way of looking at the world. If one were to personalize it, it would become a rather wry smile but a smile of sympathy, and above it the eyes would beam with the purest love.

Yet, despite Kinoshita's vast respect for René Clair, a director he admires to emulation, it would be a mistake to think of his work as anything but purely Japanese. Though he actually went to France in 1951 to meet Clair, his purpose in going included more than a pilgrimage to the idol's feet. "I wanted to live for a while in a nice democratic country, a country where no matter how poor the people are they at least have heat in the winter; a country where no matter what kind of work a person does he at least gets a day off.... I really went to France so that I could see Japan better."

This concern with and for Japan is seen at its best in films like *A Japanese Tragedy* and *Twenty-four Eyes*, intensely serious films which escape sentimentality only in that, unlike most other Japanese directors, Kinoshita insists upon a theme large enough to contain a tragic view of life. Japan's tragedy is not merely the tragedy of the mother. It is her story which reflects the larger tragedy of Japan. The young teacher in *Twenty-four Eyes* is more than merely pathetic since what she stands for—essentially, for everything that is fine and noble in the Japanese character—is so large that it is much more than mere sentimentality. Even when Kinoshita pulls out all the stops, as in *Times of Joy and Sorrow*, and the 1959 *Snow Flurry* (Kazahana), he is not sentimental. Sentimentality would not be enough: Kinoshita feels much more strongly.

In this he is rather like his teacher, Yasujiro Shimazu, a man who would tolerate no sentimental fuzziness and who used to make his assistants work until they knew films backwards and forwards. He was much more than a mere boss; he was a firm believer in the apprentice system and believed that he had a responsibility to teach his assistants more than they could pick up on the job. When work was over for the day, he would hand an assistant a newspaper clipping and tell him to make a script out of it, and to have it ready by the following morning. At other times he would pass on the responsibility for directing some scenes to his assistants. Thus it was no accident that Gosho, Toyoda, Kimisaburo Yoshimura, Noboru Nakamura, Hideo Sekigawa, Senkichi Taniguchi, and Kinoshita himself, all became better than ordinary directors.

As a director, Kinoshita himself is now rather like Shimazu.

He is a staunch defender of the present teacher-pupil method
of staffing and, like Shimazu, becomes angry when he cannot have exclusive use of his assistants. He also always refuses
to lend anyone to another director. At the same time he
takes extremely good care of those who belong to him. In
fact, his unit is often called "Kinoshita's classroom." Everyone from the lowest assistant to the highest star sits in front
of teacher and is called on from time to time. Though no
martinet, he is a careful teacher. "I think the most important
job of an assistant is to handle the slate. When I see how
he bangs the clappers, I can always tell whether he'll become
a director or not."

During Kinoshita's apprenticeship "the Kinoshita-held
slates were always perfectly centered and the sticks were
perfectly sounded." Having early conceived a passion for the
films and actually run away from home when parental con-
sent was refused, he worked himself up and out of an early
job in the processing laboratory of Shochiku, and was eventually in a position to combat the great Kido himself. "We
were at war. As soon as one of my scripts was returned
without comment I'd submit my next. I'd submit a tragedy,
then a comedy, then a melodrama. It was to make the head of
the studio remember the various talents that I possessed." His
various talents might well have gone unrecognized in a large
and complicated film industry had his devotion and energy
not proved equal to all the many obstacles put in his way.
Yet, from the first, he had very strong ideas on how films
should be made and what films should be.

It was for this reason that he first tended to collect people
around him and use the same people over and over again in
his films. Though not married—"I'm married to the films—
they are my entire life"—he believes in the family system.
His younger brother does his music for him; his sister has
written scripts for him; and her husband is none other than
his cameraman and best friend, Hiroshi Kusuda. He is also
very close to his actors. He even "arranged" the marriage
of one of his assistants, Zenzo Matsuyama, now a scenarist,
with one of his favorite actresses, Hideko Takamine.

One of the results of the "Kinoshita classroom" is the
stylistic superiority of the director's films. Another reason
for their superiority, however, is his shooting methods. "In
my direction I'm always changing my ideas and set-ups at
the last moment. I'm always getting sudden ideas on how to
experiment with actors and action. I never rehearse in advance. Shimazu used to say that so long as you've got some

kind of close-ups and long-shots in a scene, it'll come out all
right so long as the actors are properly directed. I think
exactly the same." This accounts for much of the spontaneity
of a Kinoshita film. He is constantly experimenting. In fact,
it might be said that he, Kurosawa, and Yoshimura are the
only conscious experimentalists in the Japanese film today.
"In every picture I try to do something that hasn't been done
before. I'm not like some directors who say: 'William Wyler
tried it this way, so I'll have a go in the same manner.' Just
because something has been done successfully by another
doesn't interest me."

One of the results is that each Kinoshita film is different
from every other. Yet all are characterized by the man himself, by a dedicated craftsmanship which is hard to find in
any country and exceedingly rare in Japan. Whether satiric
comedy or lyrical tragedy, the Kinoshita film is a unique
experience, perhaps because it is so very personal, because
it is so deeply felt.

AKIRA KUROSAWA (born 1910). The work of Akira Kurosawa—and, to a lesser extent, that of Kinoshita, Yoshimura,
and Imai—represents a break in the tradition of the Japanese
film. Perhaps, break *from* tradition would be the more descriptive term since Kurosawa has always deliberately refused
to make the expected kind of picture. He has consistently
confused critics and, sometimes, audiences by his continual
refusal to accept the prevailing philosophy of the Japanese
film. Rather, he has sought and found originality, and taken
together his films constitute an imposing experimental a-
chievement.

For this reason, the Japanese often call him their "least
Japanese" director and the description is apt. He is "Western" in that he is perhaps the only Japanese director who can
be called a creator in the pioneer sense of the word. Completely uninterested in the standard program film, he has
gone beyond the accepted confines of cinematic language as
the Japanese understand it, and in so doing has considerably
widened them.

Perhaps this was the reason that Kurosawa was the first
director to be "discovered" abroad and perhaps this was why,
once found, he was so quickly accepted in foreign countries.
On the other hand, Kurosawa himself—heartily sick of being
called "Western" by critics both at home and abroad—has
said: "I haven't read one review from abroad that hasn't read
false meanings into my pictures." He goes on to explain that

"I would never make a picture especially for foreign audiences. If a work can't have meaning to Japanese audiences, I —as a Japanese artist—am simply not interested."

Though Kurosawa may work entirely for the Japanese audience he completely disapproves of what they are usually given to see. In particular he dislikes the continual emphasis upon the fact that Japanese society is a sick society, though he himself does not deny the fact. He much admires the "healthy life" of those citizens shown in American films, and feels that one of the results of the pessimistic outlook of Japanese films is an invalidating weakness in the films' moral statement. "It is always said that artless simplicity is the truest Japanese way, but I am in strong opposition to such an atmosphere."

He himself has never made a weak film, and certainly artless simplicity is something of which no one could ever accuse him. Even when his films have been somewhat confused, like *Record of a Living Being*, they have also been so strong that at least while the film is unreeling one believes them. Even such hack work as *Those Who Make Tomorrow*, union propaganda made by three directors in less than a week, contains something of his style.

In contrast to the artless simplicity of the average Japanese picture, Kurosawa's films are heavily calculated and enormously artful. His interest in technique may call occasional attention to itself, as in the huge close-ups of *Seven Samurai* or the perfectly balanced composition of set-ups in *The Lower Depths*, but more often than not the mechanics and techniques of cinema are used entirely for psychological effect.

This has been true from the very first. It was in fact one of the points that Kurosawa made in the first film work he ever did, an essay on the "basic defects" of Japanese films which he wrote as part of his job application for P.C.L. He was hired, assigned as an assistant to Kajiro Yamamoto, and in 1943 was given a chance to direct *Sanshiro Sugata*. When the picture came out it was apparent that here was a talent who knew how to use the techniques of the film in a unique and personal way, who could use the vocabulary of the cinema to create a compelling psychological experience.

With each succeeding film he continued to experiment, changing his style with each new picture and in so doing upsetting the critics who, by the time of *No Regrets for My Youth* three years later, were saying that Kurosawa ought to return to the style of *Sanshiro Sugata*. The director, however, believed that in this former picture "for the first time, it could be said that I had something to say beyond the script's content," adding, "from this picture on, people began to be repelled by me."

By the time he had made *Drunken Angel*, only a very few critics were astute enough to know what he was doing. One of these few, Tsuneo Hazumi, said: "Out of an atmosphere of self-destruction and deterioration, a most important new Japanese film style is created." Most, however, were content to repeat what they had already said, that he was "Western," that he was "psychologically crude," and that he and his works were not "cosmopolitan"—whatever that meant.

If Kurosawa's results baffle his critics, his methods infuriate his employers. He is a perfectionist and will spare none of the company's money to get the results he wants. Nor is he one to take suggestions; he always knows precisely what he wants to do, which is something of a rarity among Japanese directors who more often than not hold meetings and make solemn note of any or all ideas.

He does, however, work extremely close with both crew and cast. When working on a scenario, Kurosawa likes to work directly with his script writers. They all sit around a big table, writing, talking, and exchanging ideas. Like Kajiro Yamamoto, his teacher, Kurosawa believes in the importance of the script and often quotes the former's words: "To understand motion pictures fully, one must be able to write a script." Having written some of Japan's finest, Kurosawa always knows what he is about and is usually able to help his scenarists out of whatever holes they get into. When *Rashomon* was first considered it was found to be much too short. Kurosawa sat down and introduced two new characters and also the opening and closing sections, including the baby part, which was his own idea.

While shooting, Kurosawa *Tenno*—or "Emperor Kurosawa," as he is often called—likes to spend all of his time with his cast and crew. "It is important, when you are directing a picture, to be close to [them]. When I'm directing I eat supper with them every night and until we go to bed we discuss various matters. That's the best time to give direction to your people."

While shooting, Kurosawa—in contrast to a director like Toyoda—thinks relatively little about continuity. He relies much more on editing to give continuity to his films. Also, rather like Kinoshita, he is sometimes apt to change his ideas on a film just before shooting it. One evening, just before

Rashomon was to go before the cameras, Kurosawa happened to see an early Martin Johnson picture and was particularly impressed with a sequence devoted to a lion on the prowl. He remembers: "I said: 'Well, Mifune, that's Tojomaru. Make the human like that animal.' " Later, he made everyone go see a film in which a black panther appeared and it became the model for Machiko Kyo's character in the film. Since this is the way that Kurosawa usually makes his films he is understandably amused when foreigners rave about the wrong things in his films. In this case he was particularly struck by the fact that so many found such ample evidence of Kabuki influence in the creation of the *Rashomon* characters.

While the film is being shot, Kurosawa is everywhere, supervising everything, and if he does not like the way a thing is done, then it is done over and over again until he is pleased. At the climax of *The Castle of the Spider's Web* he particularly disliked the faking of the arrows which fall around Mifune and finally transfix him. After shooting the scene in various ways, he finally decided to have real arrows shot at the actor. His interest was not in using the real thing simply because it was real but that the effect on film was greatest when real arrows were really aimed at Mifune. The actor and the bowmen went through with it—though the final transfixing scene remains a trick, realistic though it is—and Kurosawa again had his own way.

Once the film is in the can—and there is usually ten times more film than is needed since Kurosawa consistently shoots at a ratio of ten to one—the "Kurosawa family" breaks up and no one sees anything more of the director until he emerges with the finished print. Since *Living*, Kurosawa has undertaken his own editing and now does more of his own than any other director, feeling that only in editing can true continuity be achieved.

Ever since *Seven Samurai*, he has favored the multi-camera technique, using it for even the most intimate scenes, which considerably decreases some editing problems, though creating others. The director believes that using several cameras is useful in creating atmosphere and tone, "the catching of the actors when they are at their peak [which] usually only occurs once. If you have to do the same scene for different set-ups you lose naturalness and the basic tone changes from shot to shot due to the difference of time and circumstance." One of the disadvantages of the multi-camera technique is the fact that the composition cannot be designed for each

set-up, but this may be compensated for in the cutting. Anyone who has seen the brilliant editing of the 1959 *Three Bad
Men in a Hidden Fortress* (Kakushi Toride no San Akunin),
the pictorial magnificence of *The Castle of the Spider's Web*,
or the arresting stylistic unity of *The Lower Depths* is well
aware of the technical brilliance which Kurosawa's methods
can create.

Yet, in the best of Kurosawa's films, this mastery of film
style has but one purpose: it is meant to tell a story, and to
tell it in the most striking manner possible. The director is
frankly interested only in the psychological power carried by
his images. Precisely, he is interested in their carrying the
theme or "message" of his films. He is aware of the major
theme of his works and says that "every film-maker only says
one thing," adding that he usually says it over and over
again. "If I look objectively at the pictures I have made, I
think I say: 'Why can't human beings try to be happier?'
Living and *Record of a Living Being* are such pictures. *The
Castle of the Spider's Web*, on the other hand, states why
human beings must be unhappy."

This then is the famed "humanism" of Kurosawa. He is
concerned with the human lot above all else and he particularly insists upon the equality of all human emotion. All of his
films share this basic assumption. *Seven Samurai* shows what
can be accomplished when men forget their differences, and
it is honest enough to show that their sacrifice is usually for
nothing. *Stray Dog* shows the equality between opposites, in
this case between cop and robber, in a final scene where both,
covered with mud and undistinguishable from each other, lie
panting in a field of summer flowers too tired to move. *Rashomon* is, of course, the classic statement on the complete
equality of all things.

This theme is essentially un-Japanese and it certainly runs
completely contrary to the prevailing philosophy of the
Japanese film. Perhaps it is for this reason that the films of
Akira Kurosawa have taken so experimental and so original
a form: the thought behind them, and the personality of the
director, are so completely original that a new form had to
be created to hold them.

KIMISABURO YOSHIMURA (born 1911). One can usually recognize a Kinoshita film or a Kurosawa film after seeing only
a few shots. Their style, though often varying from picture
to picture, is distinctly theirs. One can, on the other hand,
seldom recognize a Yoshimura film; there seems an almost

studied absence of style. The reason, however, lies more in the director's material than in the director himself. Kurosawa usually chooses material which affirms his "humanism"; Kinoshita is interested only in that which lends itself to his very special view of the world. Yoshimura's material covers the widest range of any director in Japan. Remaining purposely unselective, he must adopt a style to fit the peculiar needs of each film.

One of Japan's most versatile directors—some say Japan's only really versatile director—Yoshimura can create almost any kind of film. He can make such period-spectaculars as *A Tale of Genji* and equally well can make such off-beat *jidai-geki* as *Ishimatsu of the Forest*, which used the genre to satirize contemporary society. He can make such socially-conscious protests as *Cape Ashizuri*, the 1954 film about left-wing students facing oppression in the mid-1930's; yet he can also make a film like *Night Butterflies*, which with utter seriousness (not entirely devoid of satiric touches) presents the sad lives of fashionable Ginza bar "madames." He can view the tragedy of postwar Japan with complete detachment and create the satiric comedy, *The Fellows Who Ate the Elephant*. At the same time he can involve himself to the point of earnestness and make films like *The Day Our Lives Shine*, a ruthless but also deeply felt exposé of postwar corruption.

Yoshimura has always refused to identify himself with any single kind of film and for this reason particularly resents those Japanese critics who are never content until they have classified the unclassifiable. He is constantly aware that he is being misunderstood and misrepresented and his battles with the press are consequently long and bloody. In speaking of *The Fellows Who Ate the Elephant*, he complains: "[They] called me a petit bourgeois for making a picture like this in times of national unrest. Now these same people look at my pictures and call me a red."

From the very first, Yoshimura proved quite unclassifiable. Though always fond of literature, he was never good at school and failed every placing examination in Kyoto University. Later, though he loved the films dearly, he failed all examinations given for assistant directors. Entering the Shochiku Tokyo studios, thanks to the influence of a relative, he was assigned as assistant director to Yasujiro Shimazu and later managed to get himself into the bad graces of Shiro Kido by doing everything wrong. Given a slapstick programmer, Yoshimura would turn it into a light comedy.

Given a melodrama, he would insert what he had understood
of Pudovkin's montage ideas, which he was then studying with the greatest attention. Shochiku's Kido became more and more angry, calling him "the strongest-willed director of them all," and sent him back to the ranks of assistant directors. Yoshimura could not fully understand why he was not promoted again. "It was said that I was talkative, insincere, and conceited. Even today Kido thinks these things about me. I wondered if I didn't have talent like the others. By 1936, I was the oldest assistant on the lot."

When he was again promoted to director, in 1939, his troubles only got worse. He was so interested in experiments that the picture itself often suffered. *Tomorrow's Dancers* (Ashita no Odoriko), a film supposed to glorify the Shochiku Dancing Team, made such extensive use of the moving camera that the audience all but became seasick. Later, in *Five Brothers and Sisters* (Go-nin no Kyodai), he ruined Keisuke Kinoshita's first produced script by unnecessary experimentation. Just one of the things he did was to shoot everything in long-shot; there was hardly a scene which did not contain full-length shots of the actors.

Even though his early films were not memorable, his refusal to conform to the cinematic style of the day was indicative of his entire approach to the film. Though he made more mistakes than most other directors, he also learned more than they did. His errors were always caused by his being carried away with enthusiasm for his subject. His 1942 *South Wind* went over twelve thousand feet and eventually had to be released in two parts. "I can't trim my own films. . . . The content was relatively simple but I got excited as I shot and it just got too long."

In 1944 he was drafted and sent to Southeast Asia, where, for him as for so many young men all over the world, the war proved a maturing experience. He distinguished himself by neglecting to relay news of the Soviet entry into the war, thinking it was merely more Allied propaganda; but, on the other hand, he learned a lot about films. In Bangkok he had ample opportunity to study captured enemy pictures, among them William Wyler's *Wuthering Heights*. Heretofore, Yoshimura's favorite director had been the eclectic F.W. Murnau, but now he carefully studied the Wyler film, making an elaborate shot composition and editing breakdown. Even now, like Mizoguchi and Ozu, Yoshimura likes William Wyler best among foreign directors.

Back in Japan after the war, he almost at once showed

proof of his new maturity by making *A Ball at the Anjo House*, a film which was a study in the decline of the older Japanese aristocracy. The original idea was conceived when Yoshimura was invited to a dance party held at a peer's mansion the night before it was sold, and many of the occurrences shown in the film actually happened that night. Yoshimura was so taken with what was happening that he stayed up until morning writing down ideas.

Once they were written, however, he could find no one to help him with the script until someone suggested Kaneto Shindo. This began one of the most successful film partnerships in the postwar industry, Shindo playing Dudley Nichols to Yoshimura's John Ford. From that time on, almost all (certainly all the better) Yoshimura films have been scripted by Shindo. The director explains the relationship when he says: "Because I work so fervently, I must know my limitations and my weaknesses. Because I understand these limitations, it is necessary for me to rely on outside help. Before I even entered the film world, I thought I could hang onto another fellow's shirt tails in order to do what I wanted, and even now I do this." Shindo's shirt tail has proved of the most durable quality and Yoshimura has returned the favor by acting as producer for most of the films that Shindo has directed.

It was also due to Shindo that Yoshimura finally left Shochiku, where he was just as unhappy as he had been before the war. The Shochiku board of directors, always clamoring for surefire box-office entertainment, had particularly attacked the two for their "dark outlook" on life. Yoshimura took these attacks in the most personal way but says that even so "without Shindo I would never have left." Both finally withdrew and formed their own Kindai Motion Picture Association, an organization which still functions, turning out the polemic-filled and occasionally near-propaganda efforts with which Shindo has associated not only himself but also Yoshimura.

In the meantime Shindo and Yoshimura had completed a scenario called *Clothes of Deception*, with which Shochiku refused to have anything to do, though both had put in over half a year of their own time on it. They shopped around the various companies and finally approached Daiei. Nagata, the head of the company, was at this time much troubled that *Rashomon* was taking so long to film, and was interested in making several cheap quickies to fill up the schedule. Yoshimura remembers that "because of his worry-

ing over *Rashomon*, Nagata came to like me and at Daiei if
Nagata likes you everything is all right." *Clothes of Decep-*
tion, a geisha film, was, however, no quickie. It took longer
to make than *Rashomon* and marked new directions for its
director. Praised for its exact and realistic creation of the
very special Gion atmosphere, it made Yoshimura something of a rival to Mizoguchi, and established his position as
a specialist in films about women.

Thereafter, working at Daiei, he came to make an unusual
number of films about women (as distinguished from
women's films) and upon Mizoguchi's death it was but natural that he should take over the directorship of *An Osaka
Story*. Some maintain that the Mizoguchi tradition is now
upheld only by Yoshimura and that this can be seen in such
films as *Night River* and the biting 1958 film about the
world of the Japanese classical dance, *The Naked Face of
Night*.

Yoshimura, however, does not consider himself a specialist
in anything and, as usual, resents any attempt to classify his
work. He feels that not only is any categorization a waste
of time, given the Japanese film, but also that the Japanese
film as a whole is scarcely worth taking that much time and
trouble over.

"We've got a poor tradition for making films. Japanese
fiction after a thousand years still lacks dramatic construction.
It's all just superficial prettiness. And this reflects over into
the films. . . . The Japanese novel has simply not developed
and the dramatic structure of film scenarios has no tradition
in Japan. . . . Foreign pictures are powerful in structure because they arise from a strong tradition in fiction. If you
make a Japanese picture with strong dramatic elements, it is
very dangerous, even revolutionary. The reason is that Japanese intellectuals don't like such things. Our whole trouble
in Japan is that, despite a surface affection, Japanese just don't
like new things. . . . Another problem is the Japanese respect
for authority resulting in blind mother-love, blind respect for
the male. Such things are thoroughly Japanese. In films such
themes are always sure to win the picture the special endorse-
ment of the Education Ministry."

Yoshimura's attitude in his films—as constructive as it is
revolutionary in the Japanese film world—is in essence completely opposed to that of, say, Ozu, whose virtue as a
creator rests precisely on what he does with the materials at
hand. Yoshimura, proven foe to the status quo, moves restless-
ly from theme to theme, from subject to subject. Yet, if his

fore-
ground

films as a whole lack the cohesion of Ozu's, they also offer something of a way out for Japanese cinema. In films like *Ishimatsu of the Forest*, Yoshimura has indicated one of the possible directions which the period-film might take; in *The Beauty and the Dragon*, he has created the only successful film version of the Kabuki ever completed. In *An Osaka Story*, he has recombined the forms of the *shomin-geki* and the period-film to create what seems a new genre.

In addition, through his experiments with editing, he has brought a new speed and lightness to the Japanese film. Back when he was an assistant director he used to handle most of the editing on Yasujiro Shimazu's films. During this apprenticeship he learned the art of cutting and Yoshimura's later films have become noted for their editing innovations. There is, for example, an extreme tendency in Japanese films to play every scene out even after it has made its necessary point. This fault arises from a false evaluation of naturalism, most directors firmly believing that everything they do should be "just like life." Yoshimura, on the other hand, very frequently makes a direct cut right at the high point of one scene, into another scene which is building up. This telescoping of effect, piling one dramatic point quickly on top of another, is a shorthand method of construction which gives his films their unusual pace.

Yoshimura has, all in all, opened more doors for the future than perhaps any other Japanese director. Ozu and Kurosawa open doors too; these they go through themselves and then slam behind them. Yoshimura, with his studied versatility, has managed, almost alone, to create new fields for the Japanese film to conquer.

TADASHI IMAI (born 1912). Like Yoshimura—and unlike Mizoguchi, Gosho, Ozu, Naruse, Toyoda, Kinoshita, and Kurosawa—Tadashi Imai is no stylist. Though Yoshimura, somewhat like Kurosawa, changes his style from film to film, Imai has never particularly cared to cultivate a strong, personal profile. He is much more interested in what he says than in how he says it. If he experiments at all, it is only to put over the full meaning of what he is talking about. The reason for this is that Imai has a "message." It is however, far removed from the simple faith of Kurosawa's humanism; it is resolutely political and continues to indicate the limitations of the director.

Imai's political direction was decided early in life. While still in middle school, he read stories about the poor and the

oppressed and, in the abstract, sympathized with them. These
generous emotions led him to join a left-wing study group while he was still in high school and this led to his arrest, though he was released because of his youth. While at Tokyo University he moved from a personal and deeply felt sympathy for the oppressed into something much more organized, and consequently much less personal: he joined the local Young Communist League and became very active in the bill-posting and pamphlet-distributing section. In the meantime he had been arrested once again.

His family, completely traditional (his father was a head priest of a large temple), was much worried about their wayward son. So they married him off, a common Japanese method for cooling hot blood. Consequently, Imai soon found himself a father. He also found that, though he had attended the most famous university in Japan, he had few job prospects of any kind: he had been twice arrested and, further, was well-known as a "red."

Though he originally had little interest in films ("...at college I studied history and was interested in politics ... but of course I liked the movies") about the only job he could find was with the J.O. Studios. His only connection with films had been when he had volunteered as projectionist for secret showings of Communist films at his university. But out of the five hundred who took the J.O. test, Imai was one of the five who were hired.

"At that time it was the belief of Osawa [then head of J.O.] that if the continuity were detailed enough anyone could direct a film. So I was immediately assigned to the productions office to write continuity." When it came time to direct his first film, however, Imai soon proved that the months spent writing continuity had taught him little. The film was *The Numazu Military Academy* (Numazu Heigakko). There were severe lapses in continuity, the fairly interesting subject—the clash between Shogunate and Imperial forces—was hardly developed at all, and the over-all direction was poor. Imai now says that it was an easy picture to make because he was not fully aware of a director's responsibilities. "I quickly read the script and at once decided that here should be a long-shot, there a close-up. Then I began to photograph the picture and soon discovered that things were not that easy."

Even now, though much, much better at it, Imai still makes pictures in more or less the same off-hand manner. "In my work, I never decide in advance on elaborate continuity. As

we come to each scene while we are shooting, I decide how
I'll do it. When the day's shooting is over and the next day's schedule is decided upon, without thinking any more about it, I go to bed. The next day, on the shooting site, before work begins, I talk things over in general with the actors. By the time everything is ready to go, I know how I'm going to do it." This method of directing obviously accounts for much of the roughness and lack of continuity in Imai's work. It also explains the pleasant spontaneity of such studio efforts as *Muddy Waters*, where everything is readily controllable and things can be easily adjusted to sudden inspiration on the part of the director.

One of the most arresting things about Imai's early films, however, was not that they were poorly made but that a man of Imai's convictions, and reputation, should have made them at all. From *The Numazu Military Academy* right through the war, Imai made films which were straight government propaganda, containing material which, one would think, any right-thinking young leftist would have avoided like the plague. The majority of Imai's wartime films were purposely made to glorify those very ultra-rightist tendencies within the nation which, both before and after the war, Imai so often fought against.

It is always difficult—and usually foolish—to attempt to reconcile inconsistencies in character, even—or particularly— when they are so glaring as in the character of Tadashi Imai. One can, at any rate, be fairly safe in saying that there was no Machiavellism involved: Imai is idealistic to the point of embarrassment. Nor was there any simple opportunism: Imai's integrity, no matter what the cause, is quite above re- proach. Yet, having said this, one must then accept the fact that Imai was just as dedicated to the Imperial cause during the war as he was to the Communist cause both before and after it. In way of explanation one can only again call atten- tion to the Japanese genius for the *volte-face*, and for the completely apolitical quality of the Japanese character. That this often approaches intellectual dishonesty no foreign ob- server of the Japanese can fail to appreciate. At the same time, however, it is equally apparent that the Japanese them- selves do not appreciate the illogic of their position and, far from believing in their own dishonesty, are acting in the best faith of which they are capable.

After the war Imai did another about-face, a real ideolo- gical somersault, and landed on his feet with *An Enemy of the People*, a vicious and almost personal attack on the Em-

peror-system, which also contained many indications of hav- **388**
ing been made as a call for pro-Communist political activity.
One might also add that it was made on direct order from
SCAP's CI&E as a part of its original program to have the
Japanese film industry turn out pictures criticizing various
aspects of old Japan and praising various aspects of the new.

Back among his leftist friends, Imai finally went all the
way and, at the urging of Communist director Fumio Kamei,
formally joined the Party. Since that time there is no doubt
and can be none of Imai's complete ties with the Communist
Party. Yet, even after having himself taken such an un-
equivocal position, his pictures continue to suggest the con-
tradictory character of the director.

The equivocal quality shown in these films puts any critic
in a difficult position. Take, for example, the 1957 *A Story
of Pure Love*. Imai contrasts the relative purity of his young
couple with the corruption of society and approves of their
eventual revolt. He shows his heroine suffering from a radiation disease, shows it to be as shocking and painful as it is, and
treats it as a tragedy. He does all this with a concern for
human beings as they are and with a very real compassion.
At the same time, the film is intended as Communist propaganda. If Imai were interested only in moral propaganda, if
he were interested, let us say, in revolt for its own sweet sake,
then what he says would be worth listening to. But the
propaganda is never that personal and therefore never that
valid. Imai is grinding an ax, grinding quite skillfully, but
grinding nonetheless. Thus, in this film, he approves of
rebellion not because it is an essentially noble human attribute,
but because it is politically convenient. The atom bomb is
brought in (in the novel from which the film was taken the
girl's disease is tuberculosis) not because its use at Hiroshima
was a moral crime but because the bomb has long been the
favorite weapon of Communist propagandists in Japan.

Yet, neither is it this simple. Imai, though all tied up with
political considerations, also obviously and personally believes
in revolt as an ethical necessity. He himself, as a person rather
than a Party member, feels compassion for those suffering
from radiation disease. Thus the difficulty in evaluating any
of Imai's postwar work comes when one tries to separate this
valid and personal opinion from the official Party opinion
when, for entirely different reasons, they happen to coincide.
It is a true moral dilemma and one which Imai has yet to
reconcile.

Imai's ambivalent attitude toward this dilemma is reflected

in the man himself. Though as Communist as it is possible to
be in Japan, his personal tastes are thoroughly bourgeois. He loves American film musicals, for example, and once called *Annie Get Your Gun* "unbearably enjoyable." His family and business life are utterly middle-class and he now turns out films, all of them leftist-oriented, for Toei, a company which within itself manages to contain almost every one of the vices of old-time capitalism at its very worst. Yet it is, perhaps, this ambivalent attitude which makes his good films so fine and which, incidentally, makes it impossible for him to turn out acceptable Party propaganda. Despite his full identification with the Party and its aims, he has yet to make a film which, on the Communists' own terms, might be considered effective propaganda. *And Yet We Live,* despite a total condemnation of capitalism, failed to spur audiences on to action; *Here Is a Spring* won more converts to the cause of serious music than to the cause of Communism; *Darkness at Noon* failed to influence any audiences and instead won all sorts of critical awards.

The reason why Imai's films even at their most polemical fail to win audience support for the "big cause" is that they are consistently over the head of the audience he is trying to reach. Though guilty of falsely glorifying the working class on occasion, he is honest enough never to fall into the worst faults of other directors of similar political ideas and lesser talent. Yet, for this very reason, he always fails to put the message over.

One can always recognize something of the truth in his work. He tries to avoid black-and-white characterizations and never once believes that workers are the fountainhead of all wisdom. What is particularly remarkable about such pictures as *Darkness at Noon* and *Here Is a Spring* is that, despite the workers in both, they require intellectuals to show them the right way. They cannot find it themselves because, although alert and responsive, their view is not broad enough; it requires the intellectual to give them the proper perspective. This, perhaps, is the reason that Imai's films fail as propaganda. In a way, they are too honest. The kind of people that Imai is ostensibly trying to reach remain completely impervious to this kind of appeal. It is even doubtful that they know they are being addressed. Therefore the really responsive audience for an Imai film is the intellectual —and he remains the darling of the intellectual bobby-soxers in Japan—but they are all in agreement with him from the beginning and so his films influence no one.

It is very doubtful that Imai, himself, guesses any of this. He says: "I want to make films not for cliques but for the entire film audience; I want everyone to find something they can like in my pictures." Yet, even so, his power as a director does not often lie where he apparently thinks it does.

Despite his pronounced desire to treat social problems in an all-encompassing manner, he is seldom successful. Perhaps it is because he is too tied to the Party, or perhaps it is because he himself cannot properly comprehend the big problem, or perhaps it is because his informal method of direction prevents his total control of a large production.

For whatever reason, Imai's best—and this best is of the highest quality—comes when the story is intimate and the concentration is on character. This accounts for the failure of certain efforts but also accounts for the extreme beauty of *Muddy Waters*, for the strength of *Until the Day We Meet Again*, for the power of *Night Drum*, and for the pathos of the 1959 *Kiku and Isamu* (Kiku to Isamu). In these films he is really concerned for the poor serving-girl, for the lovers soon to part, for the husband forced to exact a social penalty in which he does not believe, for the two mixed-blood children who belong nowhere. Their problems are human problems and Imai presents them as such, presents them for their own sake and not because they illustrate a political theory. If contemporary society is responsible for the serving-girl, and the unhappiness of the lovers, if feudal society is responsible for the husband's tragedy, then Japanese society past and present is unsparingly castigated. And one does not feel in these films, as one does in *Darkness at Noon* and *A Story of Pure Love*, that Imai has a universal panacea up his sleeve, ready to exhibit it and begin the soft sell at any moment. Rather, he seems to return to those generous emotions which originally interested him in the plight of the unfortunate; he seems to return to that state of innocence where his compassion was completely gratuitous, with no ulterior aim whatever.

No Japanese critic, incidentally, thinks of Imai in this manner. He is probably their favorite director, but never for the reasons given above. Perhaps they like him because he is Communist and all Japanese film critics (one might say almost any Japanese of any intellectual pretentions) still find it very chic to affect a leftist orientation. The critics call his style *nakanai* realism, which means realism without tears. In applying the term to such tear-jerkers as *Rice* and *Darkness at Noon*, they are even wider of the mark than usual.

Imai's extreme popularity with Japanese film critics (the *Kinema Jumpo* 1957 awards for first and second places went to *Rice* and *A Story of Pure Love* respectively) tells something about, and against, him. All the other directors included in this section have strong personal profiles, and they have equally strong moral convictions—whether they be as unified as those of Ozu, or as varied as those of Yoshimura. They are individuals. They are separate and distinct. It is perhaps for this very reason that the critics sneer at Ozu, laugh at Naruse, and ignore Kurosawa. Imai, who has deliberately abdicated his position as a free individual, and who has with full knowledge attempted to submerge himself into a social and political cause, is something that Japanese critics can understand. He is one of the boys, and in Japan if you are sufficiently gregarious you are automatically ensured of a relatively peaceful and popular existence.

Thus one might think of Imai as much more representative of the average film director in Japan than are any of the other eight treated in this section. He is typical in that at his best he is brilliant and at his worst he is incoherent. Like most Japanese directors, he is mercurial. He will turn out a scene which is magnificent and directly follow it with something which is acutely embarrassing. In other words, he lacks precisely what the other eight in this section have. He lacks a personal purpose, he lacks a personal view of the world, and his films consequently lack that personal angle of perspective which make them the director's own and which also sometimes makes them great.

Mizoguchi, Gosho, Ozu, Naruse, Toyoda, Kinoshita, Kurosawa, and Yoshimura, all represent what is best in the Japanese film today. In Tadashi Imai at his best we have something which is capable of comparison with the work of any of the above. At his worst we have what is wrong with the Japanese film.

16 actors.

FILM acting the world over is not so much a special acting technique as a compound of various acting styles. This is as true in Japan as it is anywhere else, with the difference that in Japan the choice of acting styles is considerably larger: Japanese film acting may reflect the highly formalized Kabuki, the conventionalized Shimpa, the naturalistic Shingeki, or various foreign acting styles, all the way from the Actors Studio "method" to the display of personal eccentricities exhibited by some foreign film stars and scarcely deserving the name of acting at all. A single actor will not, however, attempt to encompass all of these styles within himself. Rather, he will tend to specialize in but one. But, though he may specialize, he may also lend himself to one of the other styles. Koshiro Matsumoto, a leading Kabuki actor, has appeared in Shingeki; Yaeko Mizutani, a Shimpa actress, has played in Kabuki. Both appear frequently in the films.

Thus, today there is much more interchange among the various schools than ever before. Yet, this exchange does not too much affect the art of film acting in Japan because it is a one-way change. Koshiro may go from the Kabuki stage to the movie studio but the movie star may not make a like move to the Kabuki stage. The methods of both Noh and Kabuki artists require years of training, which the actors in most other fields do not have, particularly motion-picture actors.

The best film actors, in Japan as elsewhere, have come from the stage and Japan's finest film actors have, almost without exception, had Shingeki training. Some actors, like Hiroshi

Akutagawa, Masayuki Mori, and Hisaya Morishige, who
have had great success in the films, continue to return to the stage because they feel that constant film work, though much more lucrative than stage work, tends to limit their talent. The reason for this is the small number of film stars, their enormous popularity, and the consequent and constant call on their services.

Japan, which does so much to stretch one job into two, to hire three people where only one is needed, does precisely opposite with its actors. Stars who are established are so busy that they appear in two or three times as many films as their foreign counterparts. The actors have little chance to study on their own; hence they have no time for private improvement of technique. If they want to improve they must do so in public, while they are on the job, and the result is often a mediocre performance, confused and stylistically absurd, which practice off the screen could have corrected. Hence an occasional film star's return to the stage. A play, besides providing a sense of audience reaction, offers an opportunity for study and improvement which the film cannot.

Relatively few stars, however, are willing to take the time and trouble, their overwhelming fear being that if their face does not appear in a new film every few weeks they will be forgotten. Although there seems little to support such an attitude, it explains the reluctance of Japanese stars to appear at film festivals abroad. It explains why Jun Negami was in mortal fear when told that he would have to go to America for his bit as the boy in love with Machiko Kyo in *The Teahouse of the August Moon*. In the same time he could have starred in two Japanese feature films.

The average top star appears in from seven to ten films a year. Although these actors usually work on only one picture at a time, featured players often shuttle back and forth between rôles and studios. This practice has become so common recently that the airlines from Tokyo to Kyoto are loaded with actors hurrying back and forth during the production of pictures in which they concurrently appear. Thus it is not at all unusual for a supporting player to appear in twenty or thirty films a year. Though his fees may be only one-third those of the stars, he sometimes ends up with more money at the end of the year.

Before the war, all stars were paid a monthly salary by the studio to which they belonged. This was a fixed sum, unchanged by the amount of work they were called upon to perform. They received, for example, no extra compensation

for working eighteen hours a day—a not infrequent occurrence. Now, however, the stars often, though not always,
receive a lump sum for each film. Machiko Kyo, for example,
gets around $8,000 per film, which is more than any other
Japanese actress gets. That this amount is not equal to, say,
payments made in Hollywood, is shown in the fact that she
received from MGM $50,000 for her work in *The Teahouse
of the August Moon.*

The highest income among film stars is that of Hibari
Misora—$60,000 a year. With profit-participation deals some
U.S. stars get $1,000,000. The Japanese figures, however, are
those reported to the government for taxation purposes and
observers have estimated that in many cases the sum may
represent as little as sixty percent of the person's actual income. Still, it will be apparent that Japanese film actors do
not receive too much for their services, at least not by Western standards. And this is another reason that the stars are
so busy. They simply want to make money.

Out of their incomes the Japanese stars and bit players
must provide a number of things that the foreign film actor
takes quite for granted that he will receive from the studio.
In contemporary life films, the actor must supply his own
costumes; if he does not own the required clothes, he must
buy them. If the costume is unusual, however, the company
will sometimes "help out" and it will also often give a token
amount to cover "laundry expenses."

Among other expenses, the Japanese actor pays for the
services of a *tsukibito,* literally "attached person," a kind of
special servant who is also a general confidant. No matter
where the star goes, the *tsukibito* is sure to follow. On the
set his job is to help the actor with his make-up or costume,
run over his lines with him, fan him when he is hot, and have
a coat ready when he is cold. Most of the actresses tend to
choose decidedly plain young ladies given to tweeds and
sensible shoes for their *tsukibito,* though Hibari Misora owns
a man in his forties who follows after, handing things needed
and picking up things forgotten.

In addition, the Japanese star must be skilled in various
ways since he is often called upon to do things that would
fill his foreign counterpart with horror. Actors in period-
films must know a great deal about sword fighting, and it is
taken quite for granted that actresses in costume pictures
know how to ride a horse. Actors must also occasionally
perform mildly dangerous acts since Japanese stuntmen are
few in number and their bag of tricks small. Further, there

are seldom any stand-ins and the actors themselves must remain on the set while lights are adjusted.

Only very occasionally are doubles used. In *The Princess
Yang* there was a scene (cut from prints sent abroad) where
Machiko Kyo enters the bath nude. The scene was shot from
the rear and rather than show her in the flesh or in a skin-
colored suit, the company hired a strip teaser whose specialized job was showing off her body. Her hair was arranged in
the manner of the star's and the scene was made in long-
shot. Then Machiko Kyo took her place, now safely up to
the shoulders in the bath, and the sequence was continued.

Another burden of the Japanese film star is that he feels
his popularity to be most insecure. Both the press and general
circulation magazines give much more space to films and
film stars than do their foreign counterparts, and fan activities
in Japan are so extravagant as to make their American
counterparts look quite staid by comparison. Yet, despite his
very glamorous position, the star worries constantly. One of
the reasons is that he knows popularity is a short-lived affair.
The female star has an average professional life of only six
years, after which she must either change her type or else
face extinction. The male star specializing in contemporary-
life films has an effective life of about twelve years because
he does not age so quickly. The male period-film star can
continue for over thirty years and during this time he need
not once alter the type of rôle he plays.

With such insecurity in the top bracket, it is not too surprising that the stars themselves tend to hog the field and,
through constant activity in the films, restrict their own
number. Director Shiro Toyoda claims that the major fault
of the Japanese industry as a whole is its severe shortage of
stars. One gets tired of using the same people over and over
again, and audiences, he believes, get equally tired of the
continual parade of the same faces. More stars, he maintains,
would also allow for greater variety in casting. As it is, most
stars are hopelessly type-cast.

Hideko Takamine, one of the few actresses who can really
act, has said: "There are very few genuine actors and
actresses in Japan today. Most are lazy—they play for a
juvenile audience and therefore need not play well. Many of
them could do much better but they don't have to, so they
take the easy way out. Besides, very seldom does one get a
challenging rôle." Yasunari Kawabata, probably Japan's
greatest living writer, whose works have been used throughout the film *junbungaku* movement, says: "Japanese actresses

are always expert at playing *mizu-shobai* rôles [geisha, prostitutes, professional entertainers, etc.] but their playing of wives and young women is usually bad. It is because in real life, wives and young women hold back something in their emotions while *mizu-shobai* women show all."

Another reason that there are not more stars is that getting to be a star is quite difficult. One may work one's way up in the industry, as did Ryo Ikebe, from apprentice script-writer to actor. Or one may rely on personal introduction through friends, as Keiji Sada did. Or one may be related to someone in the films: Hiroshi Kawaguchi's father works for Daiei; Yujiro Ishihara is brother to Shintaro Ishihara, the novelist turned actor and director. Or one may be related to a star, one may be Isuzu Yamada's daughter, or Yuko Mochizuki's sister. To start from scratch, however, is extremely difficult though not impossible. Still, one must add, it is seldom necessary for actors or actresses to sleep their way to stardom as in—let us say—France.

Each studio maintains its own school for training likely star personnel. Students are kept busy all day long with various kinds of studies, confined to military-like barracks at night, and are paid eight dollars a month. "New face" contests too are frequently held. Here the competition is rough, the tests are academic and quite formal, full of questions which demand specific knowledge of obscure but general information.

Still, Toshiro Mifune got into the films as the indirect result of a "new face" contest, and Ayako Wakao came from the Daiei acting school. It is quite unheard of, however, for an actor to rise to stardom from nothing at all. No one in Japan was ever "discovered" diving into one of the better pools or sipping sodas in the corner coffee-shop. Likewise, those who leap to stardom from bit-playing or extra work are few indeed.

Here the Japanese production system keeps everyone in his place. Each studio has from 150 to 200 bit players on the payroll which form a kind of stock company from which bits are cast. Old studios like Shochiku have many bit-actors who have worked only there for twenty-five or thirty years. Extras are usually furnished by "extra brokers" who take as commission up to twenty percent of the extra's daily wage, which ranges from a usual ninety cents to a top of two dollars.

Under the star system genuine acting talent is usually more discouraged than otherwise and this is true in Japan as elsewhere. At the same time, the standard of film acting is

certainly no lower in the Japanese film industry than it is in
that of any other country. Still, one of the results of the star system is that Japanese screen acting has a heterogeneous quality to it which is essentially unstylistic. Though one may see strong performances, these tend to stand out and consequently call attention to themselves. Stylistic unity in the acting of a Japanese film is rather uncommon, if not rare. Only the best of directors can impose a style on their actors and, consequently, one of the ways of assessing greatness in a Japanese director is simply by observing what he has done with his actors.

Perhaps one of the main problems of the Japanese director is not how to bring out strong emotional reactions but how to suppress them since Japanese actors, as a rule, tend to overact. One might even venture that, as a people, the Japanese are more histrionically inclined than most: the playing of rôles in family life is common; hiding feelings is usually considered a virtue; and it is often thought equally necessary to counterfeit emotions. This has given the Japanese people a certain facility in the art of acting, that ability to step outside oneself and create the semblance of an emotion not actually felt. At any rate, overacting is much more common than "underacting" in the Japanese films and professional movie actors in Japan cultivate a personal quality or profile which is considerably stronger than those of actors elsewhere.

Most of the actors discussed in the following pages have molded rather strong personal styles for themselves. This style may be personal and creative, as with a Rentaro Mikuni or a Mori, or it may be essentially contrived and traditional, as with Kinnosuke Nakamura. Thus these actors discussed contain among their number some of the very best and some whose only reason for inclusion is their extreme popularity. In all, they may be considered representative of the Japanese film industry.

HIROSHI AKUTAGAWA (see Plates 95, 97, 107). One of Japan's leading stage actors (and son of the world-famous Ryunosuke Akutagawa, known abroad mainly as the author of stories from which *Rashomon* was made) is thirty-eight-year-old Hiroshi Akutagawa. He has made only a relatively few films but these have firmly established him with the movie-going public.

Beginning film work in 1950, he was soon featured in both *Where Chimneys Are Seen* and *Muddy Waters*. It was this latter Tadashi Imai film which made his screen reputation and, some say, has accounted for the popular reception given his frequent stage appearances with the Bungaku-za Shingeki troupe.

His acting style, seen abroad in such films as *Wild Geese* and Inagaki's 1958 *Rickshaw Man*, based upon acute understatement, finds its nearest foreign equivalent in the work of Montgomery Clift or, perhaps, Gérard Philipe. Proud, sincere, aloof, gentle, and ringing with integrity, Akutagawa's screen characterizations, with their emphasis upon intelligence accompanied by the shy awkwardness which in films always accompanies incorruptibility, have made him something of a screen anomaly: an extremely popular movie actor who rarely makes movies.

CHIKAGE AWASHIMA (see Plates 100, 116, 121). Entering Shochiku in 1950, Chikage Awashima made her debut in Minoru Shibuya's light-hearted comedy *Crazy Uproar*, and promptly received the Critics' Prize as best actress of the year. Since that time the almost invariable excellence of her performances has given her the reputation of being the best of the postwar actresses—a counterpart in excellence to Masayuki Mori.

Born in 1924, she studied at the Takarazuka Girls Opera School, where she became one of the leading Takarazuka stars along with Nobuko Otowa. Her greatest critical recognition came in 1955 when she played the geisha in Toyoda's *Marital Relations*, the film which also made Hisaya Morishige's reputation as a serious actor. Before that time, however, in addition to unchallenging rôles in costume drama, she had appeared in Kinoshita's *Carmen's Pure Love* and Imai's *Muddy Waters*, both of which greatly contributed to her critical reputation.

Though she has a decided feeling for comedy, her usual rôle is one in which her love is unrequited, yet where she is obviously a much better person than her husband or lover. Rather like Jane Wyman, she specializes in parts where the male lead misunderstands, though the audience understands and sympathizes completely. Unlike any Western counterpart, however, she brings to her rôles a depth of understanding and at times a wry kind of humor which makes all of her characterizations, even the most superficially written, both believable and moving.

SETSUKO HARA (see Plates 62, 80, 84, 93, 109, 122, 130). If the Japanese film had anything at all approaching a "woman's

woman," it would probably be Setsuko Hara. Like Joan
Crawford, her approach is almost consistently feminist and her presumably best-loved rôles tend to illustrate the idea that mother or, more often, wife knows best.

Born in Yokohama in 1920, she was introduced into Nikkatsu in 1935 by her brother-in-law Hisatora Kumagai, the director. Her youth and charm were such that Arnold Fanck soon chose her for the German-Japanese coproduction *The New Earth*. Now, though playing various kinds of rôles, her most common is that of a career woman in a man's world, or else the strong wife who brings her husband around to her way of thinking.

In Ozu's *Tokyo Story*, although the widow of a son of the family and thus related only by law, she is the only one of the children to observe the respect traditionally paid to elderly parents. In Naruse's *Sounds from the Mountains* she devotes all her energy to being a good wife, only to leave her husband when she realizes how hopeless it all is.

But, unlike Joan Crawford or Greer Garson, she is almost excessively subtle in her attacks on men, her main complaint being that they fail to understand, one, her business talent and, two, her true feminine delicacy. This type of rôle, very close to that of Maria Schell, has not unnaturally made her enormously popular with middle-aged women, whose spokeswoman she has become.

KAZUO HASEGAWA (see Plates 30, 96, 106). Though many actors have been in the films longer than Kazuo Hasegawa, he now has something of the reputation of the "grand old man" of the Japanese cinema—perhaps "grand old boy" would be better since he looks so eternally young. Appearing mainly in period-drama, he tends to be associated with the good old days; having appeared in many of Kinugasa's early and well-remembered silent pictures, he is often thought of as belonging to the golden age of the Japanese period-film.

This, however, does not prevent his remaining something of a matinee idol in Japan, where he is still a great favorite with the older women. Born in 1908 and entering the Shochiku Kyoto studios in 1926 while still a Kabuki apprentice, he has consistently played leads in costume dramas. The rôles in which the West has seen him, those in *Gate of Hell* and *A Story from Chikamatsu*, are rather typical of his work.

His charm lies not so much in the heroics of the typical period-drama star as in a quiet kind of *savoir-faire* which has long ravished his predominantly female audience. He has

therefore been compared to Charles Boyer and, though Hase- **400**
gawa continues to hold his age somewhat better, there are **fore-**
points of similarity. Both appear on the stage, Hasegawa **ground**
having organized the Shin Engi-za dramatic troupe with
Isuzu Yamada before entering Daiei, where he still remains;
both exude old-world gallantry and an aura of sexual prow-
ess; and both continue to be remembered and beloved by
audiences while others of less personal charm and, perhaps,
less talent, fall by the wayside.

SACHIKO HIDARI (see Plate 114). Despite the excellence of her
work in Tasaka's 1955 film, *The Maid's Kid*, Sachiko Hidari
had to wait until she received Ireland's Cork Festival acting
prize in 1957 for her rôle in *The Crime of Shiro Kamisaka*
(Kamisaka Shiro no Hanzai) before Japan took her talents at
all seriously.

Born in Toyama in 1930, she worked as a music and gym-
nastics teacher before entering films. In 1952 she joined the
independent Sogo Geijutsu Company as a "new face" and
was used mainly for decoration until Heinosuke Gosho gave
her small parts in *An Inn at Osaka* and *The Cock Crows
Again*.

Her career has been something like that of Jennifer Jones
in America. Cast mainly as merely a pretty young girl, she
has had to prove her ability by appearing in a large number
of films, mostly worthless except insofar as they were distinguished by her performances.

Most Japanese actresses' performances are mutually identical, but Hidari's are always distinct and individual. With
her appearance in Imai's *Darkness at Noon* both critics and
public finally agreed that she had emerged as a real dramatic
actress.

RYO IKEBE (see Plates 78, 87, 121, 136). Entering Toho
studios as an apprentice script-writer, Ryo Ikebe was discovered by director Yasujiro Shimazu and given his first
screen part at the age of twenty-three. From the first he was
taken up by the younger audience and made something of
a popular idol. Though he was used by such directors as
Gosho, Imai, and Kinoshita, it was not until he appeared in
Ozu's 1956 *Early Spring* that the critics finally decided that
he was something more than a teen-age favorite.

The first indication of his potential talent was in *The
Moderns*, a 1952 Minoru Shibuya film, where his boyish
charm and maturing technique created a very convincing

portrayal. One of Shiro Toyoda's favorite actors—he has
appeared in half a dozen recent Toyoda films—he is seen at his best when carefully directed, as in *Snow Country*, and at his worst in *The Bewitching Love of Madame Pai*, where both star and director floundered.

Now forty years old, he specializes in contemporary rôles, and is notoriously uneasy in period parts. One of the most sought after of leading actors, he remains something of a Toho creation and, as such, is the ideal contemporary urban hero, his qualities being almost perfect for the young white-collar worker rôle in which he specializes.

KYOKO KAGAWA (see Plates 86, 93, 106, 125, 131). Born in Tokyo in 1931, Kyoko Kagawa entered Shintoho in 1950 after graduating from high school, and in 1952 made her first important appearance in Naruse's *Mother,* following it with a leading rôle in Imai's controversial *The Tower of Lilies.*

Specializing in the rôle of the traditional Japanese girl, she was used by Mizoguchi in *Sansho the Bailiff* and *A Story from Chikamatsu* as well as by Yoshimura in *An Osaka Story.* Her usual rôle, even in modern settings, is that of the traditional daughter of Japan bound by all the usual conventions, but she also exhibits a genuine cheerfulness which is opposed to the false sweetness of so many Japanese ingénues.

Her talent is versatile enough, however, that she can handle equally well the completely opposite kind of rôle, for example her part in Shiro Toyoda's *A Cat, Shozo, and Two Women,* where she appears as the thoroughly modern second wife, given to mambo, eating butter for breakfast, and spending hours in the beauty shop.

CHIEZO KATAOKA (see Plate 71). A hardy perennial like Kazuo Hasegawa, Chiezo Kataoka, born in 1903, entered Makino Productions in 1927 after working in a third-class provincial drama troupe, and one year later organized his own independent Chie Productions with Mansaku Itami as the leading director. Together they made a number of films, and it is now commonly believed that the actor's best work was done during this period. Further, it has been said that without Itami's guidance Kataoka would have been nothing as an actor.

This impression has been further strengthened by his post-war work. Given a director like Tomu Uchida and a film like *Bloody Spear at Mount Fuji,* he almost invariably gives a memorable performance. Usually, however, he appears only in the wildest *chambara* or the most harrowing of detective dramas, where he is the most intrepid of samurai, the most indefatigable of sleuths.

His position in Japan is something like that of an older Errol Flynn. People often laugh at both, yet neither is insensitive as an actor. Flynn at his most swashbuckling shows strong evidence of talent, largely wasted though it be, and Kataoka at his most impossible is never completely bad.

MICHIYO KOGURE (see Plates 79, 94). One of Japan's most versatile actresses, and perhaps the most intellectual of all in her approach to acting, Michiyo Kogure invariably turns in an exceptional performance, whether in a modern rôle as that of the married whore in *Red-Light District* or in such typical period fare as *New Tales of the Taira Clan*.

Born in 1918, she graduated from Nippon University, where she majored in theater arts, and entered Shochiku, making her film debut in 1937. Marrying, she left films and went to Manchuria during the war but later returned to Japan to continue her career.

A favorite with directors because of her ability to create almost any kind of rôle, many feel that her really brilliant period was just after the war when she appeared in Kurosawa's *Drunken Angel* and Imai's *Blue Mountains*, for both of which she won a number of prizes.

MACHIKO KYO (see Plates 82, 85, 92, 96, 126). Along with Toshiro Mifune and Shirley Yamaguchi, Machiko Kyo is one of the few postwar Japanese stars well-known in the West. Her rôles in *Rashomon*, *Ugetsu*, and *Gate of Hell*, have built for her a Western reputation which later appearances in *The Princess Sen*, *The Princess Yang*, and *The Teahouse of the August Moon* have not been able to undermine.

Born in Osaka in 1924, she entered the Osaka Shochiku Girls' Opera as a dancer in 1936 and in 1949 signed a contract with Daiei. There she was at once "made over." Most Japanese female stars, since the introduction of film actresses in 1920, have been typed as typical, gentle, sweet home-bodies. Kyo, under Masaichi Nagata's direction, was the first star to be built on a glamour and sex-appeal campaign, her body being more often featured than her face.

Despite such good performances as those in Naruse's *Older Brother, Younger Sister* and Mizoguchi's *Red-Light District*, however, her Japanese critical reputation suffered greatly after her initial *Rashomon* dramatic success. Yet, such is the enormous prestige among Japanese of things foreign, particularly indications of foreign acceptance of things Japanese, that after her 1956 appearance in *The Teahouse of the August Moon,* her waning popularity rose to a phenomenal degree, assuring her of a long and active career in the films.

Toshiro Mifune (see Plates 79, 81, 82, 102, 108, 113, 129, 137, 139, 141, 144). The first Japanese actor since Sessue Hayakawa to achieve international fame, Toshiro Mifune was born in China in 1920 and, after graduating from the Port Arthur (China) High School, came to Japan, took the Toho "new face" tests in 1947, and failed.

He had been noticed by Kajiro Yamamoto, however, who decided that he was perfectly well qualified as an actor and turned him over to his ex-pupil Senkichi Taniguchi. This gave him his first big chance in the 1947 film *The New Age of Fools* (Shin Baka Jidai).

It was at this time that Mifune made the acquaintance of another of Yamamoto's former assistants, Akira Kurosawa, and the two began a series of films which, from *Drunken Angel* to *Three Bad Men in a Hidden Fortress,* have greatly contributed to the art of the Japanese film.

Mifune first received acclaim in the West for his uninhibited portrayal of the bandit in *Rashomon* and, since that time, has divided his work almost equally between period and contemporary dramas. Definitely a postwar type, Mifune's period-film character usually radiates raw masculinity. The typical period-hero loves his sword more than the old-fashioned Hollywood cowboy ever loved his horse and part of Mifune's popularity in period-films is his constant suggestion that he would like to go to bed with something more than a piece of cold steel. This quality, plus a genuine acting talent, has made him the perfect period-hero: the man of today reinterpreting the facts of yesterday.

Rentaro Mikuni (see Plates 108, 140). Born Masao Sato in the mountains of Gumma Prefecture in 1923, Rentaro Mikuni took his screen name from the hero he played in his 1951 debut, Kinoshita's *Good Fairy* (Zemma). An extremely versatile actor, he has appeared in a number of Naruse's films, including *Wife* and *Husband and Wife.* He tends to specialize in modern rôles, often comic, in which he plays the young man trying to get ahead in the world and usually failing. Occasionally he also appears in historical films, his excellent

portrayal of the husband in *Night Drum* being an example.
The West has seen him briefly in the opening reels of *Musashi Miyamoto* and as an army officer in *Harp of Burma*.

Notoriously indifferent to both publicity and public opinion, he emphasizes a kind of sloppiness in appearance both on screen and off which has endeared him to the young Japanese in the same way that Marlon Brando won the hearts of young America.

Very much attracted to those actors who practice "the Method," he also resembles Brando in his intensity, his concern for the art of acting, and his utter disregard for the proprieties of Japanese social life.

HIBARI MISORA (see Plate 117). One of Japan's most popular singers, Hibari Misora, born in 1938, is the idol of Japanese teen-agers, particularly the girls. Making at least fifteen films a year since her debut in 1949, she also appears frequently on radio and television, and makes Japan's best-selling phonograph records.

It was she the girls were waiting to see in Osaka when the ticket line panicked and crushed one of its number to death; it was she who had acid thrown in her face by a despondent admirer; and it was she who has had the dubious distinction of leading all of Japan's entertainment talent when it comes time to pay income tax.

Except for her one good performance in Gosho's *Growing Up*, most of her appearances have been in the most ephemeral of light romances, always with singing and dancing. No matter the film, her rôle is the same. She is the conventional, the traditional daughter of old Japan brought up-to-date. Though she likes to dance and sing and play with boys, she is never really frivolous: she really stands for reason, duty, obligation, and the most complete respectability.

YAEKO MIZUTANI (see Plates 10, 19). If Japan has a "first lady of the theater," it is probably Yaeko Mizutani, who has been acting since early childhood. After becoming one of the Japanese theater's first actresses, she made her film debut in 1921 in *Winter Camellia* at the age of sixteen. She was thus one of the first screen actresses as well.

Born in Tokyo in 1906 and appearing on the stage almost as soon as she could walk, she has become one of the world's most versatile actresses. Her more recent appearances in films however have been almost entirely confined to period-drama, where she has been seen in a number of costume program-

mers, as well as such box-office hits as the lavish 1956 *The*
Loyal Forty-seven Ronin. Like great actresses everywhere, actors
her difficulty on both stage and screen is finding parts worthy
of her great talent. Alternating in live drama with the Tokyo
Shimpa troupe and screen appearances, she is now all too
often confined to mother rôles.

YUKO MOCHIZUKI (see Plates 99, 134). Born in Tokyo in
1918, Yuko Mochizuki had a long stage career before making her film debut in 1949. After working with the Asakusa
Casino Follies, and the Shinjuku Moulin Rouge, both troupes
specializing in light comedy and adored by the prewar intellectuals, she joined various dramatic groups before her debut
in films, where she distinguished herself in bit parts before
receiving larger rôles.

An extremely versatile actress, she can handle almost any
kind of part, though recently her film appearances have been
limited mostly to mother rôles, such as those in Kinoshita's
A Japanese Tragedy and Imai's *Rice*. She brings to these
parts a talent not usually associated with the *haha-mono* and
further proves her versatility by, at the same time, appearing
in more romantic rôles on both stage and television.

MASAYUKI MORI (see Plates 77, 92, 118). One of Japan's most
intelligent actors, Masayuki Mori, son of the novelist Takeo
Arishima, was born in Tokyo in 1911. Quitting Kyoto University, he first made a considerable reputation for himself
as a stage actor, specializing in Shingeki, then made his screen
debut with Toho in 1942.

He even now occasionally returns to the stage and tends
to think of the films as a vehicle for what he has learned on
the stage. At the same time, however, he prefers films, largely
because they allow one to correct oneself instantly a mistake
has been made. Since one more take is always feasible, perfection is possible and Mori is a perfectionist.

Though extremely good at comedy, as in Kinoshita's
Broken Drum, he tends to specialize in the more somber films
about contemporary life. As the ex-army officer unable to
adjust to postwar Japan in *Floating Clouds*, or the dissatisfied
brother in *Older Brother, Young Sister*, he brings to these
rôles an acting intelligence which makes something of a part
in which a lesser talent would have failed.

An example of this is his playing of the emperor in *The
Princess Yang* and, to an extent, his rôle of the injured husband in *Rashomon*. Again, when the rôle itself has rich

possibilities, like that of the enchanted potter in *Ugetsu*, his expert reading of the part accounts for much of the beauty and power of the film.

HISAYA MORISHIGE (see Plates 115, 116, 125). Though Hisaya Morishige was widely known as an actor, a disc jockey, a vaudeville artist, and a stage and radio comedian, he did not achieve true film popularity until his appearance in 1955 in Toyoda's *Marital Relations*, a film which overnight established him as a tremendously versatile talent and made him one of the most sought after of Japanese film actors.

His appeal is very Japanese, one of the reasons being that he associates himself with the traditional popular arts of Japan, particularly the art of storytelling known as *naniwabushi*, having himself achieved a style which is known all over Japan as Morishige-*bushi*.

At the same time, on both stage and screen, he has brought to perfection his rôle of the *shomin*, the man of the lower middle-classes, the poor of pocket but rich of heart. Yet in all of his better films, such as *A Cat, Shozo, and Two Women* and *The Hotel in Front of the Station* (Ekimai Ryokan), this forty-five-year-old actor is also in habitual revolt against both class and tradition: he leaves his wife, refuses to support his child, and betrays a touching inability to take life seriously. There is something of Chaplin in him. He consequently appeals to all classes: both the critic and the man on the street praise and love him.

KINNOSUKE NAKAMURA. Son of the Kabuki actor Tokizo Nakamura and himself a former Kabuki apprentice, twenty-seven-year-old Kinnosuke Nakamura entered films in 1952, one year later receiving a contract from Toei, with whom he has been ever since. An enormously popular actor both in movies and radio, his appeal has nothing whatever to do with the Kabuki. Rather, he receives from his young devotees all the adulation which was once reserved for James Dean, though his appeal is much less sophisticated and his talent much less apparent.

Essentially, he reflects the world of childhood where a virtuous sword-wielding youngster can kill a dozen adult samurai and where, amid the squalor and relative values of real life, he is the shining symbol of complete purity and utter success. Thus, appearing in only one kind of film, the *chambara*—though the older he grows the more he will tend to specialize in the perennial period-hero rôles—his fan mail

is the largest of any star, except possibly Hibari Misora; his
frequent radio and television appearances are eagerly awaited by his predominantly teen-age female public; and his many films—about twenty a year—continue to pack the theaters.

NOBUKO OTOWA (see Plates 103, 105). Born in Osaka in 1924, Nobuko Otowa graduated from the Takarazuka Girls Opera School and in 1950 entered Daiei, where she was originally billed as "the girl with the million-dollar dimples" and cast in light and sentimental rôles to which she was completely unsuited. Not satisfied with the treatment she was receiving, she left to become a member of Kimisaburo Yoshimura's and Kaneto Shindo's new independent company, the Kindai Motion Picture Association, thus beginning her long affiliation with the two directors.

Since that time some of her best pictures have been directed by the two, for example, *The Beauty and the Dragon* and *Gutter*. She has also appeared in several of Gosho's films, one of her most memorable performances being that of the geisha in *An Inn at Osaka*.

Extremely serious about acting, she is a frequent writer and lecturer on the craft of film acting and has been called, by Japanese critics, a "nun" in her devotion to her art.

CHISHU RYU (see Plates 70, 80, 83, 93, 121). Though Chishu Ryu has worked under many directors, his name is usually associated with that of Yasujiro Ozu, who gave him his first big part in the 1935 *College Is a Nice Place* (Daigaku Yoi Toko). Some critics have even gone so far as to say that the celebrated Ozu atmosphere would be quite impossible without Ryu.

Born in 1906 in Kyushu, the son of a Buddhist priest, he entered the Shochiku Kamata studios as a bit player in 1925 and was kept busy in various minor rôles until Ozu "discovered" him. Now considered by many Japanese to be one of the most talented of actors, he is perhaps best remembered for his rôles in Ozu's *The Flavor of Green Tea and Rice* and *Tokyo Story*.

HIDEKO TAKAMINE (see Plates 68, 90, 95, 97, 110, 118, 128, 132, 133, 138). The Japanese have upon occasion called Hideko Takamine "the Mary Pickford of Japan" and the comparison is apt if only because Miss Takamine also began her career as a child actress and because, like Miss Pickford, she is an excellent businesswoman.

Born in Hokkaido in 1924, she entered the Shochiku To-
kyo studios as a child, where she was used in imitations of Shirley Temple pictures, later moving to Toho in 1937. Since the war she has appeared in many films, including several by Kinoshita, one of the directors who uses her talents to best advantage, as in her light comedy rôle in *Carmen Comes Home* and her part of the school teacher in *Twenty-four Eyes.*

An actress of great versatility, the rôle she most often takes is that of the average neurotic Japanese girl beset by the many difficulties which face the average neurotic Japanese girl. Sometimes as in *Where Chimneys Are Seen,* they are financial; sometimes, as in *Floating Clouds,* they are emotional. Given the proper script, as in Toyoda's *Wild Geese,* she creates a character of unusual strength.

Always, to the movie-going public, she is completely representative of both their problems and their hopes. When she was sent to the United States for the Second Japanese Film Week in 1958, the West was given its first opportunity to see not only one of Japan's most representative actresses but also one of its very best.

KINUYO TANAKA (see Plates 33, 75, 86, 89, 104, 128, 142). Born in 1910, Kinuyo Tanaka entered Shochiku in 1924 after serving as apprentice in a musical troupe and has remained active in the films ever since, both acting and directing. Among her earlier successes were Gosho's *The Neighbor's Wife and Mine,* Japan's first successful talkie, and a number of films directed by her former husband, Hiroshi Shimizu.

During the early 1930's she was the favorite female star of the Japanese. In 1953 she became Japan's first woman film director and since then has directed with considerable skill one picture every two years.

Since the war her most important acting work has been in the films of Mizoguchi, Gosho, and Naruse. The West will long remember her performance as the potter's wife in *Ugetsu,* but equally memorable were her rôles of the wife in *Where Chimneys Are Seen* and the maid in *Flowing.*

KEIJI SADA (see Plates 133, 138). Born in Kyoto in 1926, Keiji Sada came to Tokyo, where he graduated from Waseda University. His elder sister was a good friend of the wife of star Shuji Sano, who agreed to recommend the young student to Shochiku. There he met director Keisuke Kinoshita, who gave him the leading rôle in his 1947 film, *Phoenix* (Fujicho).

Since then he has made at least a dozen films a year and
has long established himself as one of the more popular
romantic leads. His particular talent lies in the half-comedy
rôle that James Stewart used to specialize in: the sincere
young man continually misunderstood by the cynical world.
There is little of the Stewart folksiness, however, and even
less of his rural humor.

Sada's best rôle is that of the rueful comic hero with a
romance. He may do stupid things, but always with the
audience's full approval and understanding, as in his early
films with Kinoshita, particularly *Here's to the Girls*. The
vestiges of this rôle may be seen in the later *Candle in the
Wind*, though his rôle in Kinoshita's *Times of Joy and
Sorrow*, called *The Lighthouse* in the United States, is by
now his most typical.

TAKASHI SHIMURA (see Plates 81, 91, 102). As Ryu is to
Ozu, Shimura is to Kurosawa: an actor always in perfect
accord with the director's intentions and appearing in almost
every one of the director's films.

Shimura, however, rarely takes the lead in a Kurosawa film,
his rôle in *Living* being an exception. Rather, he is perhaps
to Kurosawa what Ward Bond was to John Ford, and it is in
such character rôles that the West has seen him: the woodcutter in *Rashomon*, the leader of the samurai in *Seven Samurai*.

Born in Hyogo Prefecture in 1905, he appeared with several
Shingeki troupes, entered the second-rate Shinko in 1934, and
later went to Nikkatsu, where he specialized in *chambara*. In
1943 he joined Toho and soon after the war appeared in two
of Kurosawa's films, *Drunken Angel* and *Stray Dog*, both of
which established his talent and his popularity.

EITARO SHINDO (see Plates 54, 126). Although Shindo has
recently been playing mainly in the Toei period thrillers,
specializing in the-man-you-love-to-hate kind of rôle, he is
generally considered to be one of the best character actors
in Japan today.

Born in Kyushu in 1899, he was first a stage actor and in
the early 1920's joined a third-rate film company. Finding
this an insufficient challenge, he joined and became a star of
the Kansai Shimpa troupe. Later he reentered pictures in
Mizoguchi's *Osaka Elegy* and continued to appear in many
of that director's films, among them *The Princess Yang*, *A
Story from Chikamatsu*, and *Red Light District*, being perhaps

best remembered for his interpretation of the title rôle in Mizoguchi's *Sansho the Bailiff*.

JUKICHI UNO (see Plate 103). Born in Fukui in 1914, Jukichi Uno left college shortly after coming to Tokyo and in 1932 entered one of the main prewar Shingeki troupes as an apprentice. A year later he made his debut in the movies. Since the war he has appeared in a number of films: Kinoshita's *Broken Drum* as well as Kaneto Shindo's *Gutter* and *Children of the Atom Bomb*.

Politically extremely active, he has long interested himself in union matters and has taken an active part in organizing committees for political action. As an actor he is somewhat reminiscent of such socially conscious stars as William Holden and Gérard Philipe, but his charm on the screen is very much like that of Gary Cooper or James Stewart as directed by Frank Capra. Intensely serious about the art of acting, he is also a film and stage director and, despite his film success, is very active in stage work.

AYAKO WAKAO (see Plate 126). Perhaps most representative of those really talented young actresses caught in the snares of type-casting is Ayako Wakao, who has been condemned to an endless repetition of the rôle of the brainless young ingénue, the sweet-young-thing who goes through picture after picture meeting no difficulty more serious than an occasional coldness on the part of the male lead.

This is her kind of rôle in *The Phantom Horse* (Maboroshi no Uma), and this is precisely what her many young fans want. She was, in fact, made famous by the teen-agers who flocked to see her in Daiei's sex pictures for youth, and is now the most overwhelmingly popular of all the young non-singing actresses.

Born in Tokyo in 1933, she was selected by Nagata himself from his Daiei training school for young actors and especially groomed for stardom. It was not generally understood that she could act, however, until her appearance in Mizoguchi's *Gion Music*.

The director again cast her in *Red-Light District* where she distinguished herself in the rôle of the most ambitious whore in the whole whorehouse. Make-up completely gone, her usually sweet little mouth shutting with all the firmness of a steel trap, the rôle was as much of a personal triumph as it was a shock to her fans. One of the results was that she has since then been allowed more variety in her rôles.

Isuzu Yamada (see Plates 46, 50, 54, 87, 117, 125, 128, 130,
137, 139). Born in Osaka in 1917, Isuzu Yamada was trained as a samisen performer but at the age of fourteen entered the movies, one of the reasons being that her mother was a very great friend of the head of the Nikkatsu Kyoto studios.

As the perfect example of traditional Japanese beauty, she was soon famous as a period-drama heroine. In 1936 she entered Mizoguchi and Nagata's Dai-Ichi Company, where she appeared in two excellent Mizoguchi films, *Osaka Elegy* and *Sisters of the Gion*, both of which showed that she had more than a pretty face to offer.

Later, after the war, she entered Kazuo Hasegawa's Shin Engi-za troupe and, after it broke up, became an independent actress, appearing on radio and television in addition to making stage and screen appearances.

Though even one marriage is rare for Japan's spinster-prone actresses, Isuzu Yamada has had six husbands—among them director Teinosuke Kinugasa—and then gone on to become one of Japan's most honored actresses.

Completely talented, she is at home in any kind of rôle, playing parts as dissimilar as the spurned wife in *A Cat, Shozo and Two Women*, the aged prostitute in *Growing Up*, the tragic widow in *Downtown*, the fiendish landlady in *The Lower Depths*, and "Lady Macbeth" in Kurosawa's *The Castle of the Spider's Web*.

17 theaters and audiences. IN 1914 AN

impressed observer wrote: "A Japanese audience is usually silent, but the wonder-working movies created excitement that could not be suppressed. When the silent people gazed for the first time at their own kind jumping about in pictures after the manner of real life, and saw on the screen water dashing against a rockbound coast, just as they had often seen it do on their native shores, their speechless astonishment broke into a paroxysm of applause that still goes on." Now, forty-five years later, the applause continues, and in Japan, as in most countries, going to the movies is the most popular form of urban entertainment.

According to a 1958 survey conducted by the Ministry of Trade and Industry, the average Japanese goes to the films about twelve times a year. During the same period the average American goes ten times, and the average Englishman, eighteen. This survey also discovered, however, that the typical Tokyoite goes to films over twenty times a year.

Anyone entering a Tokyo theater and finding it packed to the rafters, people sitting in the aisles or standing in the lobby, unable to force their way in, would conclude that all Japan must be an exhibitor's paradise. The truth, however, is that the movies are essentially an urban affair. In the country—and Japan's population is forty percent rural—Saturday night shows in barns and public halls or at the local theater in the nearest small town are the only movies available. Still, the urban movie-going audience in Japan is both large and lively. Despite the fact that Tokyo now has more movie theaters than any other city in the world (well over six hundred by the end of 1958, which is two-and-a-half times more than New York, and many times more than London or Paris) there never seem to be enough to go around. By the beginning of 1959 there were 6,863 theaters in the country, with one or two new movie houses opening daily throughout the country.

This tremendous expansion in theater outlets is reflected by the fact the number of film prints released has enormously increased. Before the war only fifteen prints were made of the average feature, though a really big picture was distributed with up to twenty-five. Today, the average film is distributed with fifty prints. If it is a New Year's release or something of a special, seventy is the usual number. For extra-specials, one hundred prints are made. The industry believes that if there were only places to show them they could distribute double this number.

One of the reasons for the theater shortage is that until recently new theaters were thrown up with such haste that in only a few years many had to be torn down before they fell down. Despite the building boom, the houses themselves are so poorly maintained that what only several seasons before appeared as a glittering rival to the best theaters anywhere is soon run down, dumpy, and dangerous. There are numerous fires; the Japanese audience is quite destructive to seats and other theater furniture; there is almost no attempt made to repair or "beautify" a theatre once it is completed; and the Japanese custom of throwing water on the floor to "hold down the dust" contributes to give even the more expensive places their characteristically damp and moldy atmosphere.

In addition, by any international standard, Japanese theaters are extremely poorly managed. A trip to the neighborhood motion picture house is, in fact, the best way to become quickly disillusioned with the myth that "Japanese service is the best in the world." There are often no indications outside of a theater that there is standing-room only, and some cashiers are positively reluctant to tell anyone that there are no seats. The result is that the theaters are frequently dangerously packed. The aisles at the sides and down the middle are full of people. Some even sit on the edge of the stage while others stand outside the exit doors looking into the auditorium. Once you enter to discover these conditions —frequently so extreme that not even a piece of the screen is visible—you next find out that under no conditions whatever is any money ever refunded. In fact, the only time that any kind of sro sign is placed in front of the theater is when it is packed so solidly that literally not another person can be squeezed in. Then the manager cheerfully places large placards everywhere which proclaim: "Celebrating a Full House." There are, to be sure, laws designed to prevent such conditions, but in practice these laws are seldom enforced. The usual penalty is a temporary closing of the theater, but since 1948 the Fire Defense Agency, whose partial responsibility it is, has forced only ten theaters to close.

Though there are no-smoking signs prominently displayed, smoking anywhere in the house is not uncommon and there is no effort made by the management to control it. The attitude is that if a customer has finally squeezed himself in, he has paid his money and may now do what he likes.

After the feature has ended, the intermission usually stretches on and on, sometimes up to twenty minutes. During this time ice-cream vendors and candy butchers parade up and down the aisles, pushing through the crowds to sell their wares. The philosophy is obvious. The longer the intermission, the more they can sell. Yet, even after suffering through the intermission, the audience is not usually at once treated to the film they came to see. After the houselights dim there is another procession, advertising slides this time, which lasts from five to fifteen minutes. Usually they go on for a long time since this is one of Japan's most popular forms of advertising. As if this were not enough, some theaters showing double bills repeat the same ads before each film. This means that the audience must endure the same advertisements twice. Then the film finally begins.

Even then all is not well. Technically, film projection in Japan is not up to international standards. Reel changes are somewhat less than perfect and projector breakdowns are frequent. Also, little attention is paid to sound level. In one theater you will be deafened; in another the characters will seem to barely whisper. One would think that, since there are often as many as three projectionists in one booth, the show would be run smoothly but it is not—perhaps for the very reason that the booth is so crowded.

The one-man projection booth, so common elsewhere, is unknown in Japan. There are always two projectionists and usually a third man to do the rewinding. One reason all these people might be needed, however, is that, although the standard two-thousand-foot reel is not unknown, the Japanese standard until recently was the one-thousand-foot or ten-minute reel, which requires twice as many changeovers.

Also, since second and third runs in Japan are serviced with a relatively small number of prints, it is often necessary for theaters showing the same program to pool one print. This is accomplished by staggering the time schedules and bicycling the reels between theaters. Boys, especially trained in high-speed bicycling in heavy traffic, man racing bicycles and shuttle the prints between the theaters. Japanese city traffic being what it is, delays and collisions are common, and the interval between films grows longer and longer.

The majority of theaters show the films of only one company, a very old distribution policy in Japan which goes back to 1910 when there were theaters showing only Matsunosuke films. This "exclusive theater" policy is, in many ways, an economic necessity, which appears in other forms in other countries. Out of all the theaters in Japan today, the six production companies together own outright less than 350. Toho, owning over 100, has the largest chain. And there are no important independent chains. This means that the only way a company can guarantee that its pictures will have a ready-made market is to tie independent theaters to it with an exclusive or semi-exclusive distribution contract. This is the "exclusive theater" policy and most Japanese films are booked in this manner.

Foreign pictures are usually obtained on a free-booking basis, that is, separate contracts for each picture shown. Japanese films, however, are usually block-booked. Often these contracts confine a theater to one company's pictures for as long as a year. The theater knows nothing of the values of the coming productions and has no refusal rights. At times this Japanese form of block-booking means that to get even one desired film a theater owner must buy a package of 104 features—all unseen.

Competition between companies being severe, a like competition between theaters arises, with the double- or multiple-feature program always representing the way out for a hard-pressed company. During the very early 1920's, when Nikkatsu was having trouble, its usual program was a triple feature: a period-film on top, a contemporary-life film in the middle, and a foreign film at the bottom. A bit later, the financially distraught Taikatsu Company pushed quadruple features. Even today in the country and in the lower class urban theaters, triple-features are not uncommon. The most prevalent of double bills, however, has long been one period-film and one film about contemporary life.

Foreign films are handled in a manner completely different

from Japanese films. They are often given "prestige" open-
ings, play—at first—only in first-class theaters, are relatively
more expensive to see, and—usually—the spectator is given a
bit more for his money. He is given a choice of admission
prices, including reserved seats, and usually buys his ticket
in advance—just as in the legitimate theater. He arrives during
the interval so that he may see the film from the beginning,
and tends to treat seeing a first-run foreign film as an event
a bit out of the general run of movie-going. Though he must
still endure the lantern-slide advertisements, there is ample
evidence that the management has attempted to add "class"
to its services.

Anyone noticing the popularity of foreign films in the big
cities of Japan would perhaps guess that here is where the
real exhibition money is made, but he would be quite wrong.
Foreign pictures make money but not nearly so much as
Japanese pictures do. The market in recent years has remained much the same: twenty-five percent of the market belongs
to the foreign film, seventy-five percent to the Japanese. In
an average year there are about five hundred Japanese releases
and about two hundred foreign releases. Of the total number
of theaters, less than twenty percent play foreign pictures
regularly. This is in direct contradistinction to many other
countries. Italy, for example, only makes about 120 films a
year and imports around 300; France makes approximately
110 and imports over 340; England usually makes less than
100 and imports over twice that many. Japan, India, and
America are probably the only countries in the world whose
domestic production manages to outshow and outsell imported competition.

If the Japanese industry had a competitor it would be the
American industry. About half the foreign films shown in
Japan are American, and, by and large, all the popular for-
eign favorites in Japan tend to be among American films.
The biggest postwar grossers among foreign pictures have
all been American: first was *Gone With the Wind* with
$1,110,000, followed by *The Living Desert, Roman Holiday,
Shane,* and *The Robe,* in that order.

One of the main reasons for the popularity of foreign
films, American or whatever, has nothing to do with the
pictures themselves. It is the fact that only through films
can the Japanese see anything of the big wide world in which
they are so avidly, if so superficially interested, the big wide
world outside Japan. Thus the urban Japanese, knowingly or
not, tends to use the foreign films as a means toward instruc-

tion. He may sit back and uncritically enjoy a Japanese film, but he also seems to feel that a foreign film demands some kind of active participation. As has already been noted, even the distribution system itself seems to place the foreign product in a special category, and upon going to foreign films the Japanese seems to feel that something special is required of him. The film is something more important than entertainment, it becomes a kind of text which he studies. The result is that the really avid Japanese movie-goer has learned from the films not everything he knows but certainly everything he remembers about Western ways and manners.

At a foreign-film showing in one of the smarter theaters hardly anyone will enter the auditorium during the middle of the picture. They will go elsewhere or will wait in the refreshment-stocked lobby. While waiting they usually buy a program, much thicker than its European equivalent and containing information not only about the stars but about the director and cameraman as well. The story, in full detail, is also always included. Whether they read the story because they do not wish to be distracted by suspense, by finding out how-it's-going-to-end in advance, so that they may thus devote their attention to manners, mores, and languages, is problematical. Perhaps it is simply that the Japanese does not like to be surprised—even in a movie. For whatever the reasons, however, one can walk through the lobby and find nearly everyone immersed in the program, reading the full details of what they are going to witness in a few minutes.

In addition to buying the film's program, some will come armed with the complete dialogue script, usually published some time before the film opens and widely available. The original language is on one page with the Japanese translation facing it. These scripts are particularly popular with those studying English and it is not uncommon for students to sit through two or three showings, using the film as an English text.

Once the spectator is inside, having reserved a seat or found one recently vacated, a voice from the loudspeaker—that ubiquitous institution in Japan—will thank him for coming and ask him not to smoke, a request with which, in this palace of foreign culture, he sometimes complies. Then music will be played while the inevitable advertisements are flashed on the screen. These are usually followed by two newsreels—one Japanese, one English or American, both with Japanese commentary.

During the film itself the subtitles appear vertically on the right-hand side of the screen, though the widescreen processes often have them at the middle bottom. They are usually most complete and leave little to doubt or to chance. In some films, like Olivier's *Hamlet*, they may cover up a third of the screen, and a commonly heard complaint is that the titles are so full that by the time they are read the scene is already over. Occasionally too, no matter how full, the titles are quite misleading and/or inaccurate. *The Rose Tattoo* baffled its audiences by rendering "he's mixed up in the numbers racket" as "he plays Bingo."

The audience is usually very quiet during the showing of a first-run foreign film. There will be some rustling of candy-bar wrappers or the cellophane surrounding dried squid, but there is little conversation. Those who want to leave in the middle usually wait until the end of a sequence, rather than in the midst of a shot as is common in the West, and in many other ways the audience betrays the fact that going to foreign films is a very serious business indeed. Part of the seriousness is because first-run foreign films are expensive and the outlay of money is in all countries greeted with ceremonial gravity. Part, too, is the fact that the Japanese always respect their teachers.

It is perhaps for this reason that the majority of Japanese whom foreigners meet usually expressly declare their preference for foreign films. They feel, perhaps, that it would be impolite to prefer one's own films over those of a foreign guest's, but, more likely, they are quite sincere. The fact that they are speaking a foreign tongue with a foreigner practically insures their preferring foreign films.

Just what kinds of foreign films these Japanese like is easily discovered by noting which films are most revived. *Sous les Toits de Paris* and *Quatorze Juillet* are shown again and again; *Le Million* is never revived. *La Grande Illusion* is vastly preferred to *La Règle du Jeu*; *La Bandera* to *La Fin du Jour*; *Quai des Brumes* to *Les Enfants du Paradis*. Carol Reed is admired to distraction, particularly the final scene of *The Third Man*, but before *The Bridge on the River Kwai*, he was the only English director anyone knew anything about. De Sica is preferred to Rossellini. Luis Buñuel is unknown except for *Los Olvidados*, which is very seldom revived; Carl Dreyer has been utterly forgotten. *East of Eden* is liked better than *On the Waterfront*; *Stagecoach* is revived weekly, *The Informer*, never; *The Desperate Hours* is preferred to *The Little Foxes*; and *Shane* is liked much better than *A Place in the Sun*.

It is difficult to find any particular meaning in a handful of "best-loved" films, but one can be fairly certain that, in all countries, empathy accounts for popularity. Critic Foumy Saisho, writing of the postwar popularity of De Sica, says: "It was the postwar sense of social insecurity in a defeated country, not any abstract aesthetic appeal, that did it." She continues with: "The Japanese found a similar appeal in the fine British film, *The Third Man*....It was good that the scene of action was Vienna rather than Korea where the spectators might have found their own caricatures in even more acute form."

Interested to find out just what kind of foreign film is liked and why, C. Lee Colegrove, teaching a sophomore class at the Tokyo Women's College, asked his students to write down the name of the best movie they had ever seen. Only sixteen percent named a Japanese film and, of the remainder, fifty-eight percent were American. *East of Eden* and *Gone with the Wind* got seven votes apiece and others ranged all the way from *Hiroshima* to *Little Women*. The winner, however, with ten percent, was *Die Letze Brücke*. Though obviously limited, Mr. Colegrove's private poll indicates a very public situation. *Die Letze Brücke* had just opened, and novelty accounts for popularity in Japan. It also contained the enormously popular Maria Schell and, more, showed her in a rôle guaranteed to appeal to the "inferiority-conscious" Japanese female, particularly if the female was going to a progressive university and learning all about her rights. Then, like all of Japan's favorite foreign films, it was thoroughly sentimental.

Only a certain kind of sentimentality, however, is popular. Usually, it is the weepy variety. Clement's *Gervaise* had the same kind of vogue that Stella Dallas films had before the war and for much the same reasons. *Carnet de Bal* is weekly wept over by hundreds of high-school girls. The higher sentiment leaves the audience dry-eyed. *Jeux Interdits* is appreciated but no one carries on over it; *Le Ballon Rouge* lifted few Japanese hearts; and the stark tragedy of *Los Olvidados* left almost everyone unmoved. Counting on the Japanese feeling for sentiment, *Marty* was brought over. It utterly failed; the higher sentiment was not appreciated and one criticism often heard was that it was "too much like a Japanese film."

One of the reasons for the extreme sentimentality of the Japanese audience is its comparative youth. As in most countries, youngsters go to films more often than adults, and

in Japan there are over forty million who are under twenty.
In fact, more than eighty percent of those under twenty-four
go to the films. Only half of those between forty and seventy
go at all.

The over-all audience vastly prefers Japanese films, as has
already been indicated, but just what kind of Japanese film
this large general audience likes is a bit difficult to discover.
The *Kinema Jumpo* awards almost invariably show that the
critics' "best ten" were also among the better-than-average
money-makers of the year, but, on the other hand, the ten
biggest box-office hits of the year seldom grace the *Kinema
Jumpo* lists. The only really vocal segment of the audience
is the teen-agers, those between fifteen and nineteen. Recently a large group of them, from all over the nation, were
polled and it was found that from eighty-five to ninety percent disliked foreign films and never went; first, because they
could not understand the subtitles, second, because they
found the films uninteresting. Eighty percent also preferred
period to modern films.

This teen-age audience is very influential and extremely
decided in its preferences, as witness the Toei Company's
rise to power and fortune. And in it no single section is
noisier than the fans of Misora Hibari and Kinnosuke Nakamura. Both of these stars make dozens of pictures a year,
have one daily radio program and at least three extra weekly
programs, appear frequently on television, and are seen in
numerous "guest appearances." The former is a young lady
in her early twenties whose only serious rôle has been in
Gosho's *Growing Up;* the latter is a young man from a Kabuki family who specializes in dashing sword-drama rôles,
and who is particularly liked when he takes on occasional
female rôles, in the manner of the Kabuki *oyama.*

Kinnosuke's fans, ninety percent of whom are female, often
skip school the first hour in order to hear his morning radio
program; the Hibari fans, fifty percent of whom are male,
particularly like her when she appears as a boy. These fans
are separate from the other youngsters who are drawn to
young Western-popular-song singers such as Chiemi Eri or
Izumi Yukimura; they are also obviously quite separate from
The Third Man crowd, separate too from those succumbing
to the charms of such faddish idols as Yujiro Ishihara.

Of these young Kinnosuke-Hibari fans, only a minute
fraction does not read the magazine *Heibon*—which might
be translated as *Mediocrity*—a monthly publication devoted
to the interests of teen-agers, containing pictures of their

favorite actors and athletes and long descriptive articles about them. It contains very little gossip and no salacious material whatever; it is hence rather different from the Western fan magazine. *Heibon* is extremely popular but, it must be noted, it is apparently the extent of this teen-age group's reading.

When a nationwide poll was taken, these young people were asked to name the person "liked the most" and the person "respected the most." Most could not make the distinction, though the question was fully explained to them, and a number named the same person both times. Of the large number who said they most respected Hibari, the main reason was: "I respect Miss Hibari the most because she is so young but earns so much money." Others qualified the statement with: "I respect Miss Hibari because, though she is young and makes lots of money, she takes good care of her parents."

When asked in the same poll what to do about a love which parents opposed, forty-five percent answered that double suicide was the best and "most beautiful" way to solve the problem. When asked what country they would most like to live in, had they their choice, eighty percent chose Japan. Next in order were America, Switzerland, and "Kinnosuke's Japan"—or the feudal era of the Tokugawas.

Obviously, when these youngsters grow up, they change their views, but even in the slightly older group there are fans of a type which would make a Hollywood star envious. Ayako Wakao, one of the most popular of the young actresses, gets three thousand fan letters a month, and every year receives over sixty thousand New Year's greeting cards. She, and other popular female stars, also receive a number of requests, usually from girls. There are many who ask if they can serve as a maid. They want no salary, merely their board and keep, and they apparently do not envision this service as the road to anything in particular. It, in itself, is its highest reward. They want a chance to serve the star they love. Most of these fan letters seem to come from depressed farm areas, but almost as frequent is the letter which says: "Please consider me your younger [or as the case may be, older] sister." Others contain requests for money; requests for a free pass to see the star's pictures; and, from men, offers of marriage.

The majority of all fan letters come from girls. Hibari Misora's fan mail is full of notes from other females telling her how wonderful she is as a boy. Adolescence seems a particularly trying period for the Japanese girl and extreme crushes on female stage or screen stars are the rule rather than

the exception, a fact one may very easily verify by attending
the Takarazuka Opera, an all-girl troupe in which girls play
the parts of boys. These performances are extremely popular
and the theater is filled from first showing to last with a
struggling mass of barely nubile feminity, screaming, clawing,
and fainting dead away at the sight of their favorites. At the
last performance of the season, squads of police are often
called when the entire audience sweeps toward the stage and
throws candy, flowers, and teddy-bears at their favorites,
weeping, squealing, and groaning in an agony of ecstasy and
despair. But even these girls eventually grow up, get married,
have children, and continue to go to the movies.

A more reliable indication of audience preference is found
within the studio production programs, the way in which
the various studios have segmented their audience. One might
suspect that this audience segmentation is merely a product
of the lively imaginations of men in the publicity department, yet in Japan it is literally true that women tend to go
to Shochiku films, that the young salaried man in the city
patronizes Toho theaters, and that children adore the Daiei
and Toei period-films. Each company has its own audience
and, for the time being at any rate, the audiences seem
relatively loyal.

Despite occasional audience idiocies, one might say that on
the whole film-going is carried out in a more intelligent
manner in Japan than elsewhere. While the habit of running
down to the neighborhood theater no matter what is on is
common enough, many choose the pictures they see in a somewhat more intelligent manner. One of the indications of this
is the number of persons who read film reviews. Film news,
advertisements, and reviews are given much more space in
Japanese papers than in corresponding foreign publications.
In fact, the motion-picture companies are among Japan's
biggest buyers of advertising space and an individual film
company may be a newspaper's most important advertiser.
This is true not only of the national-circulation dailies but
also of school-papers, labor journals, and intra-company publications. Consequently, reviews appear daily and usually in
very full form. These reviews are read by about forty-eight
percent of all newspaper readers. An additional thirty-seven
percent reads them occasionally. Of this total, about fifteen
to twenty percent always compares the reviews of two or
more papers before going to a film, the incidence of multi-
newspaper readership being higher in Japan than in America
or Europe.

Hence the importance of good reviews to the motion-
picture industry. To this end the critics have worked out a universal classification system to help their readers. Having devised rigidly divided categories of excellence, each description has a place in a scale which directly relates to the other descriptions. In descending order of merit, films are classified as: *kessaku* (masterpiece), *shusaku* (excellent work), *kasaku* (fine work), *katsusaku* (powerful work), etc. This allows critics studying the work of a director to place each of his films in one of these categories (or lower ratings, not given here) and with the presentation of such a list indicate what, for the compiler at any rate, is an accurate evaluation of the director's work.

The level of Japanese film criticism in general is as abysmal as elsewhere. Ignorance and cinematic illiteracy reign supreme, further compounded by an addiction to critical jargon which is incomprehensible to the reader and leads to endless misunderstandings among the critics themselves. Particularly ludicrous are evaluations of foreign films. One of the more highly regarded critics read all sorts of dark meanings into *Baby Doll*. When Eli Wallach was making Carol Baker sign an acknowledgement of her husband's guilt while lying on the crumbling attic floor, the critic said that the scene was plainly allegorical in intention: Wallach was the late Senator Joseph McCarthy, and Baby Doll was signing an affidavit that she had never been a Communist. When *The Bridge on the River Kwai* opened, one of Tokyo's most influential critics dismissed it with "this film is about Japanese wartime atrocities."

Though this particular kind of idiocy is the exception rather than the rule, and though there are indeed a number of perspicacious film critics in Japan, the general level is so low, so corrupt, and so easily maneuvered by the major studios that one wonders the reading public bothers to even look at the reviews. That they do indicates, among other things, an attempt at a discriminating taste. As has been indicated, despite fan frenzy and over-commercialization, the Japanese take their films, both domestic and foreign, very seriously. Probably no other people lavishes such praise on a good film (public awards, prizes, compulsory attendance by school children, free performances, citations from the Education Ministry, etc.) and, likewise, no other public is louder in their condemnation of what they consider bad.

Because of this Japanese tendency to take films seriously, the foreign companies are particularly careful about what they show in Japan and, if necessary, will even cut their product before release. Danny Kaye's *Up in Arms* ended a bit abruptly in its Japanese showings since all of the scenes with "Japanese" soldiers had been taken out. *The Bridges of Toko-ri* had the scene of William Holden and Grace Kelly in a resort bath with a Japanese family removed because it was feared that this might offend the unduly sensitive.

Though this might seem overly particular, the truth is that when a film does offend, the Japanese are not only angry, they are scandalized. In 1955, Twentieth Century-Fox's *The House of Bamboo* used local color in the most meretricious and inaccurate manner and the Japanese press was instantly up in arms. The sensitivity extends even further. *The Blackboard Jungle*, which had no reference to Japan whatever, was almost universally vilified because, as the press took pains to point out, it "incited violence." When, sure enough, some schoolboy in Kyushu took a knife to a classmate and, coincidentally, happened to have seen the film, the press said: "There, what did we tell you?" The film was promptly banned by a number of local governments, and thus began an opposition to juvenile-delinquent films which the subsequent appearance of the *taiyozoku* pictures only accelerated.

It was due to public criticism of Japan's existing film-content overseer, the Motion Picture Ethics Regulation and Control Committee, usually called Eirin, an abbreviation of its Japanese name, that this body was completely reorganized and given considerably more power than it had when it was originally created as a self-regulating group within the industry in 1949 under the direction of SCAP. Originally, it was designed to replace the Occupation's official censorship organized under CI&E. After its establishment Eirin did relatively little until it was reorganized and revived in full force due to the threat of the 1957 "youth" films, particularly the *taiyozoku* pictures. As presently constituted, its reviewing committee is staffed by a chairman from the College of Law at Tokyo University, a cultural representative, an educational representative (once an Education Ministry official), a general representative (who is also a social critic), and a woman's representative (who is also a member of the Family Affairs Court). After the house-cleaning of 1957, these persons took the place of the previous committee, which had been composed entirely of people from within the industry itself.

Actually—even so—the reorganization of Eirin represented something of a triumph for the industry since, though the board was now no longer controlled from within the industry, neither was it controlled entirely by the government. In 1957 government censorship had been dangerously possible. Both the Diet and the Cabinet were busy discussing censorship laws during this period and the Education Ministry was proposing national laws to prevent minors from going to certain prohibited pictures. The Welfare Ministry and the Prime Minister's Office formed committees to study the problem and called hearings at which Eirin people testified. It soon became apparent that the politicians were not so much aroused by the *taiyozoku* films as they were willing to make use of the uproar as an excuse for civil censorship.

Very upset, the Japanese industry decided to reorganize Eirin and to this end approached the American motion-picture companies, asking them to join and thus present the government with a united front. The Americans' stand on Eirin had long been: "Our pictures have already passed our own rigid American production code so that ought to be sufficient for Japan." Despite an initial SCAP directive that all U.S. majors should join Eirin, and despite the fact that all the other foreign motion-picture companies had readily joined up, the Americans were still holding out. Their main reason was that they refused to submit their product to a body in which they had no representative. With the growing threat of governmental censorship, however, the U.S. majors finally began to show an interest, realizing that by helping reform Eirin they could also reinforce the industry's policy and do their bit in killing off official censorship. Still, they were more or less pressured into it. Just as SCAP had forced Eirin on the Japanese by saying "establish a self-regulatory body or face the continued prospect of Occupation censorship," now the Japanese said to the Americans: "Join Eirin or face the prospect of Japanese governmental censorship." The Americans joined, the reorganization was completed, and official censorship was, for the time being, averted.

The new Eirin is maintained by a fee on each foot of film reviewed. It then makes recommendations, not binding in any way, though no member has yet cared to defy them. Its jurisdiction now includes content, titles, and advertising; its regulations cover law and crime, education, national customs, sex, country and society, and religion. This last is most un-Japanese in concept and is plainly taken from the U.S. industry's Production Code.

In theory the Japanese code much resembles the American,

though it is much less concretely worded. In practice, however, interpretations vary. A typical Daiei film for young people, for example, ran into rather typical trouble. It was the 1957 *Springtime Too Long* (Nagasugita Haru), about a young couple engaged for two years. Though there were no sensational scenes, it did discuss sex. The film was approved by Eirin, but the committee objected to the main posters, which showed the couple in an embrace which was—by American or European standards—decent to the point of insipidity. Though Eirin objected to the "intimacy" of the still photography used, it apparently found nothing at all the matter with the main ad line, which was worded: "Should a couple have intercourse before marriage?"

Still, though Eirin is obviously not the ideal, it has made governmental interference impossible for the time being and is, in effect, a working body "protecting" the film audience. It is doubtful that any audience needs this kind of protection, but, if any audience does, it is the Japanese. Extremely impressionable, this audience takes the cinema so very seriously, using it as a method of instruction as well as a means of amusement, that it is regularly exploited by all of the major Japanese film companies, and always has been. Eirin's main function is that it controls this exploitation. It also has the accidental side-effect of postponing the execution of the goose which lays golden eggs at the box office.

Thanks to one of the world's most loyal audiences, the Japanese film industry is one of the most prosperous in the world today. All Japanese films are designed to recover their costs within the country itself. Hence the industry does not need worry about the balance of payments, international disturbances, or import permits, factors which so often make life miserable for companies producing for the world market.

Likewise, it faces foreign competition in its domestic market entirely on the merits of its own products. Thus, the industry needs no government support to keep it in business. The limitations on the number of foreign films coming into Japan—each foreign country being allowed a strict quota, with bonuses for good films—are based entirely on Japan's shortage of foreign currency and not on a desire to strengthen the local industry. Though the final effect is to restrict somewhat the foreign product, Japanese theaters (were there enough) could play every foreign film produced, and the Japanese movie industry itself would still show a very decided profit.

This remarkable audience, upon which depends the financial health of the Japanese film industry, has so far remained remarkably constant. Ever since the first days of cinema in Japan, it has continued to expand and the film business has expanded right along with it. As of 1959, however, there are signs that this state of affairs may not last too much longer. Television has already begun the damage it has carried to such extremes in other countries. Further, though there have been some tentative efforts by some film companies, the majority attitude within the industry is a touching if somewhat uncomprehending faith in the audience. No one really believes that this loyal and faithful body would ever desert the big wide films for the narrow little box, yet this is just what is going to happen.

There has already been some handwriting on the wall, though so small that no one within the industry has been able to decipher it. As of September, 1958, TV sets numbered about 1,290,000 units, which covers ten percent of the population. By 1962 some forty percent is expected to be covered. Thus, some observers are already looking forward to the beginning of the end and claim that in five years at least half of Japan's movie theaters will be closed. They see for the Japanese industry precisely the same blight that overtook the American industry.

The hopes for the future in other areas seem equally dim. The rationalization of the industry and the impetus toward mass production seem to indicate a decrease in the quality of production even though the financial aspects remain relatively healthy. The cost of the current prosperity within the industry is more than paid for by the growing lack of creativity. This was, in part, the plan for financial ruin which was adopted by the American motion-picture industry. It quite effectively alienated its audience, which turned to the waiting arms of television. The answer—if answer it was—lay in independent production and in films for television. In any event, the industry is dying a lingering and ignoble death.

Since, in the final analysis, the Japanese audience creates the Japanese film, one can only wait and see whether the recent growing intellectual and aesthetic poverty of the Japanese film product is a reflection of a more and more materialistic audience or whether, as in America, this materialism reflects only the industry itself. If the latter is true, then the Japanese companies will pay just as heavily as have the American. If, on the other hand, the reflection is accurate, and if this is indeed the portrait of the Japanese audience, then everyone will continue to make money and one of the most creative motion-picture industries in the world will have failed.

The Japanese industry—and the Japanese people—have reached yet another of those peaks of indecision, the like of which—as we have indicated—constitute the history of the Japanese film. Each drop from the summit has been met by a later rise, and every fallow period has been succeeded by one of full creative harvest. Today's peak, however, is the most dangerous. The industry was never healthier, never richer. Yet—because of this—the threat to genuine creative effort has never been stronger. As it now stands, the Japanese film industry is just about the last to survive as part of the world of big business. Compared with the American, and some European and Asian industries, it is something of an anomaly, something of a survival, something of a relic from the first half of this century. Whether it can continue to exist in its present form is doubtful. What is clear beyond any doubt whatever is that is has constituted one of the world's most vitally creative movie industries, and that it has created some of the most beautiful and truthful films ever made.

That this fact has never been fully recognized is, in part, the fault of the Japanese themselves. It will, however, become increasingly apparent that the Japanese industry has been responsible for many of those films which give cinema its claim as an art form, which move us to an acknowledgment of our real self, and which—all considerations of culture and nationality aside—allows us finally to comprehend the pattern of life itself.

145. *When a Woman Ascends the Stairs*, 1960, Mikio Naruse. The troubles of the working woman. Hideko Takamine.

146. *The River Fuefuki*, 1960, Keisuke Kinoshita. The anti-war period film.

147. *The Island*, 1960, Kaneto Shindo. The hard life and the farmer's lot.

148. *Bad Boys*, 1961, Susumu Hani. Juvenile delinquents and the documentary look.

149. *Yojimbo*, 1961, Akira Kurosawa. The period film as a human comedy. Toshiro Mifune, Seizaburo Kawazu, Susumu Fujita, Isuzu Yamada.

150. *An Autumn Afternoon*, 1962, Yasujiro Ozu. The last of the line. Chishu Ryu.

151. *Harakiri*,
1962, Masaki Ko-
bayashi. The pe-
riod film with a
conscience. Center,
Tatsuya Nakadai.

152. *The Insect
Woman*, 1963,
Shohei Imamura.
An honest look at
a woman's life.
Sachiko Hidari.

153. *An Actor's
Revenge*, 1963,
Kon Ichikawa.
The period spec-
tacular. Kazuo
Hasegawa.

154. *Assassination*, 1964, Masahiro Shinoda. A close look at Tokugawa politics.

155. *Sweet Sweat*, 1964, Shiro Toyoda. A woman's life—unidealized. Machiko Kyo.

156. *Intentions of Murder*, 1964, Shohei Imamura. Fictional actuality. Shigeru Tsuyuguchi, Masumi Harukawa.

157. *Woman in the Dunes*, 1964, Hiroshi Teshigahara. An existential allegory. Eiji Okada.

158. *The Hoodlum Soldier*, 1965, Yasuzo Masumura. Life in the Japanese army. Takahiro Tamura, Shintaro Katsu.

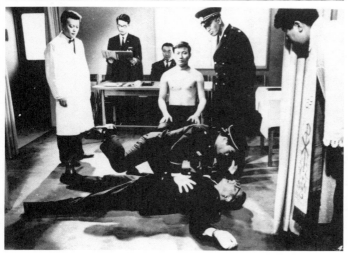

159. *Death by Hanging*, 1968, Nagisa Oshima. An allegory on justice. Mutsuhiro Tora, Masao Matsuda, Hosei Komatsu, Yundo Yun, Masao Adashi, Fumio Watanabe, Kei Sato, Toshiro Ishido.

160. *Double Suicide*, 1969, Masahiro Shinoda. Love, death, and the doll theatre. Kichiemon Nakamura, Shima Iwashita.

161. *Eros plus Massacre*, 1970, Yoshishige Yoshida. A political parable. Mariko Okada.

162. *The Family*, 1970, Yoji Yamada. The family system on the move. Hisashi Iigawa, Chieko Baisho, Chishu Ryu.

163. *Tsugaru Folksong*, 1973, Koichi Saito. The search for roots. Kyoko Enami, Tetsuo Iwashiro.

164. *The Assassination of Ryoma*, 1974, Kazuo Kuroki. Meiji period politics. Rie Nakagawa, Yoshio Harada.

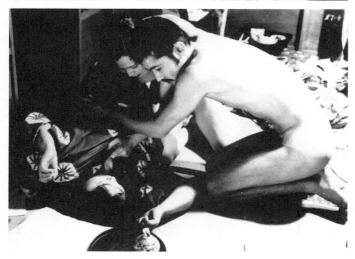

165. *The Realm of the Senses*, 1976, Nagisa Oshima. Love/sex and life/politics. Eiko Matsuda and Tatsuya Fuji.

166. *Love Suicide at Sonezaki*, 1978, Yasuzo Masumura. Chikamatsu seen as contemporary. Ryudo Uzaki, Meiko Kaji.

167. *Kagemusha*, 1980, Akira Kurosawa. The last of the samurai. Tatsuya Nakadai.

168. *Eijanaika*, 1981, Shohei Imamura. The vitality of the ordinary Japanese.

appendixes

by J. L. Anderson

In Praise of *Benshi*

Of course, there was no silent Japanese film. Obviously, no silence. But also no audience perception that film was an autonomous, totally new medium of entertainment.

Readers of film histories know by now that those old films without sound tracks were shown in their own time to the accompaniment of live music. Japan had the further complexity of the *benshi*—that person who sat to the left of the screen to "explain" and to perform narration and dialogue.

What Japanese audiences experienced in a movie theater was primarily an ephemeral performance that was an extension of native oral storyteller traditions.[1] The images projected on the screen provided a matrix for this live performance but they were only one part of a theater of mixed means. Regardless of later looks at the surviving mute film artifacts and regardless of the efforts of the anti-*benshi* reformists described in Chapter 2, film was a prop for what I shall call *benshi* cinema. Half a century ago, one heard "boring movie, great *benshi*" much more often than the other way around.

In *benshi* cinema, the combined film and *benshi*[2] elements were an unexceptional manifestation of the enactment/illustration mode joined with the narration/word mode that is found in Japanese theater, literature, and painting. Although such dual means are widely acknowledged in theater

[1] The situational aspects of viewing films have been long neglected elsewhere as well. Seeing American movies of the 1930s and 1940s outside their original continuous showing context obscures how they were perceived by their original audiences as narrative merry-go-rounds. These movies, with their widely comprehended genre conventions, functioned as circular narrative structures even though they were overlayed with linear plots. Audiences in the United States entered and left a first-run show at any point while it was underway. You didn't have to be there at the beginning. As I remember it, the most frequently heard phrases inside American movie theaters were "This is where we came in" and "Didn't we see this movie before?" Déjà vu, after all, is only a point on a circle. (In contrast, Japanese films have almost always been presented on a theatrical show-by-show basis with separate seatings for each show.)

[2] *Benshi* is not the only word used to designate the person or the art. *Katsuben, kojo katari, setsumeisha,* and *kaisetsusha* are alternative terms slightly different in meaning. *Benshi* on poetic occasions or after a few drinks liked to call each other "poets of the darkness."

as essential to No, Kabuki, and doll drama, there are also less
erary forms as *ezoshi, ekotoba*, and *kibyoshi* which integrate
picture and word.

Bunraku doll drama, with its silent dolls at center stage
and its *gidayu* chanters at the side (to the audience's right)
providing all of the vocal elements, exhibits an approximate
correspondence to *benshi* cinema but it was not the primary
model. Historically, doll drama plays were a minor source
of film stories. *Benshi* vocal performance was only secon-
darily derived from *gidayu* chanting.

The *benshi* vocal styles, eclectic in origin, grew out of the
wide range of solo performer storyteller traditions of Japan.
Rakugo and *Naniwa-bushi* contributed to *benshi* techniques.
The principal influence was classic *kodan*, which is a form
based on a declaiming and not on a chanting or singing voice.
Kodan played this primary role in the development of *benshi*
cinema largely because its repertory of tales, obsessed with
the bravery and loyalty of swordsmen, was a prime source
for the stories of many early period films. The oral means
usually associated with a story were ultimately inseparable
from narrative content.

Prior to 1920, many movies made directly from *Shimpa*
or Kabuki plays did not use solo *benshi*. Instead, they were
accompanied by a kind of live dubbing performed by a
group of actors or *benshi* who worked hidden behind the
screen or in sight beside it.[3] This voicing technique, called
moving-picture *kowairo*, was directly adopted from cen-
turies-old traditional *kowairo* in which one or two people
imitated the voices of famous actors in famous scenes from
famous plays. Like other oral storytellers, traditional *kowairo* performers usually worked in *yose* variety theaters.
The typical *yose* bill has always been a calculated assortment
of performers from different storytelling traditions mixed
with a few musical and novelty acts. Movies cut into *yose*
attendance much more quickly than they affected live
drama.

Further affirmation of the premise that the pre-talkie film
of Japan was not an independent visual medium but an element of live performance is found in the broad popularity of
chain drama (*rensa-geki*). In this mixed theatrical medium,

[3] Live vocal performance with movies, whether by a single narrator
or a troupe of dubbing actors, was apparently more widespread in
Europe and America before 1915 than the film history books suggest.
My sources are contemporary trade papers and actors' biographies.

live on-stage scenes alternated with filmed segments of exterior action of a play. Chain drama was easily the dominant form of Japanese theater during the 1910s. Rival chain drama companies collectively outdrew Kabuki, *Shimpa*, and all of the merging forms of modern drama. For a while, chain drama often outperformed *benshi* cinema at the box office. One-third of the acknowledged "major moving picture stars of 1915" were *Shimpa* or Kabuki actors who appeared only in chain drama. Many other aspects of the early movie experience in Japan reinforced its relationship with traditional dramatic and storytelling performances. For instance, movies brought back the mystical, essential darkness of the premodern Japanese theater that been burned away by gas and electric illumination imposed during the early 1890s.

The cosmopolitan reformers of the Japanese film who appeared after 1917 frequently sought to make films that could play independent of live performance. They absolutely failed to get their way in the movie theaters. No matter what the autonomous structure of a Japanese or foreign film, it could not escape *benshi* interpretation. In fact, the immediate effect of the new 1920s style Japanese films was to strengthen the institution of the solo *benshi* by driving out the alternative *kowairo* and chain drama forms. As the *benshi* emerged triumphant, separate *benshi* schools developed. *Jidai-geki*, *gendai-geki*, and foreign films each required distinctive literary and vocal styles. Not surprisingly, *jidai-geki* specialists tended toward the nasal and jugular voice techniques of *kodan* performers and Kabuki actors. Those *benshi* who interpreted foreign films were more conversational and sometimes more didactic in tone.

Benshi usually worked from a complete script which was a practice partially necessitated by the preperformance censorship regulations of the police. Master *benshi* prepared their own material although scripts also circulated with prints. Because the *benshi* ideal was to make film interpretation personal in both its literary and performance aspects, interpretation of any one film varied from *benshi* to *benshi*. Sometimes a theater alternated *benshi* for each showing. This gave audiences a choice of performer. It was also a common practice to switch *benshi* in the middle of a film. Such practices pitted one *benshi*'s skills against those of his (or in a few instances, her) peers in keeping with the eternal competitive spirit of Japan.[4] *Benshi* from all over were periodically rated

---

[4] During the 1920s, the average film show (often three features) lasted four and a half hours. Fatigue as well as performer rivalry encouraged the switching of *benshi*.

in a *banzuke*, which was a chart that displayed the relative
standing of all contenders in a field. The *banzuke* survives today only in sumo wrestling.

From the early 1920s, *benshi* performance theory mandated that *benshi* perform three simultaneous functions. They had to act out dialogue and recite narration; interpret and analyze the film (in a manner that prefigures Tzvetan Todorov's concept of reading a text); and intoxicate audiences with the virtuosity of their performance while leading everyone in a common emotional response.

As a multivalent narrative form, *benshi* cinema simultaneously exercised all four of Northrop Frye's separate "radicals of presentation." Here were 1) words acted in front of a spectator (the film actors through *benshi* dialogue along with the *benshi*'s own performance); 2) words spoken in front of a listener (the *benshi* narrative and commentary passages); 3) words sung or chanted (the *benshi* again);[5] and 4) words written for a reader (both the subtitles within the film and the printed program distributed by the theater).[6]

As early as 1913, Shoyo Tsubouchi, the major force in the cosmopolitization of Japanese literature and drama, investigated the literary potential of *benshi* interpretation and related *benshi* cinema to the picture-and-word narrative tradition of Japan. Later theorists explored the "three necessary stages of motion picture authorship: scriptwriter, director, and *benshi*." *Benshi* interpretations had three principal literary directions. The *joji* style emphasized detailed description of what was on the screen in a way that some said was derived from Balzac. *Jojo* was a lyrical style distinguished by its use of traditional poetic phrasing and imagery. In the *byosha* style, the *benshi* accented his personal impressions with overtones of first-person narrative viewpoint and ironic distance.

Benshi frequently performed without an accompanying

---

[5] Starting in the mid-1920s, many Japanese films had their own theme song which was sometimes sung live by a *benshi* or a singer. The recorded version of the song could also be played back on a phonograph in the theater. Cross-plugging a song and a movie was well established before the introduction of "sound films." Despite this practice, films were seldom distributed with full-length prepared scores.

[6] Movie theaters usually handed out elaborate printed programs to their audiences. Apart from the usual credits, star portraits, and gossip, programs had complete, ending-revealing synopses and commentaries.

film. Phonograph recordings of excerpts of *benshi* interpre-
tations were best sellers. Live *benshi* performances on radio not only provided the new broadcast medium with many of its most popular programs but also influenced the development of later radio narrative forms. *Benshi* vocal techniques were also fundamental to the development of standard radio announcer, newsreel commentator, and educational film narrator styles. *Benshi* themselves created *mandan*, a modern *yose* act of humorous topical commentary.

Even though most *benshi* lost their jobs as talking films spread, *benshi* cinema survived throughout the 1930s. Whether they had subtitles or not, quite a few foreign talkies played Japan with a live *benshi* backed by a low volume sound-on-film track. One of the most famous—and still surviving—of these interpretations was for von Sternberg's *The Blue Angel*. *Jidai-geki* talkies were sometimes shown silent with a *benshi* interpretation. Many low budget films of the late 1930s were shot silent and released with tracks of recorded *benshi* interpretation, music, and realistic sound effects.

During the Depression, hundreds of ex-*benshi* made a bare living as *kamishibai* ("paper play") performers who traveled about selling penny candy to children. They attracted their customers with *benshi*-like interpretations of exciting adventure stories accompanied by drawings that they displayed scene-by-scene in a small frame that suggested the borders of a movie screen. One could find this remnant of *benshi* cinema in many neighborhoods up to the coming of television.

Modern *kamishibai* not only imitated *benshi* cinema but also shared a common ancestor: *utsushie* ("projected pictures"). As is to be expected, *utsushie* was a syncretic picture and live narration form. Its picture mode, composed of handdrawn slides, required three to five magic lanterns. These were hand-held and individually manipulated to impart crude motion to composite parts of a scene projected on a screen. This entertainment originated in the early nineteenth century and reached its greatest popularity in *yose* theaters during the 1890s. *Utsushie* was wiped out by the higher technology of the Cinématographe and Vitascope.

Today, the great *benshi* like Musei Tokugawa, Rakuten Nishimura, Raiyu Ikoma, Shiko Kunii, and Shisei Umemura are gone. Their art survives in a few scattered public performances by second-generation professionals and by amateurs.[7] And not too long ago, I ran across a guy trying to keep *utsushie* alive.

444
appendixes

GLIMMERS OF A COSMOS

Looking back, it is clear that one of the distinguishing traits of the Japanese film is its extraordinary integration with other arts. That vast half of the Japanese film known as *jidai-geki* cannot be adequately comprehended if considered only as an isolated film form. For the past seven decades, modern popular novels, plays, and films about swordsmen have developed in closest symbiotic relationship. Together these three media share a cosmos of narrative materials that is the megagenre *jidai-geki*.[8]

While other national cinemas exhibit one-way borrowing and adaptation from other media, a *jidai-geki* story tends to move freely in any direction through novel, film, or play versions.[9] The process of film adaptation, which is a major concern of film theory and practice elsewhere—probably due to a compulsion to affirm the autonomy of film as an art—is not a matter of great interest in Japan. Indeed, many writers have moved as readily as their stories from one narrative medium to another.

The starting point for the modern *jidai-geki* megagenre goes back to 1913 when Kaizan Nakazato began serialized publication of his landmark novel, *Daibosatsu Pass* (Daibosatsu Toge), a story about a nihilistic swordsman.[10] This modern novel had been immediately preceded by widespread popularity of small books of stenographic transcriptions of *kodan* performers' narratives. Nakazato was in large part inspired by traditional *kodan* stories about swordsmen and sought to transform them for contemporary readers.

[7] I have been one of those amateurs for over ten years. There is not much call for a *benshi* in the United States these days even though he works in English.

[8] *Jidai-geki* is the term for film and drama. The equivalent for novels is *jidai-shosetsu* (period novel). *Jidai-geki* films have been inaccurately called "samurai films" abroad. Samurai, both those attached to fiefs as well those who are masterless (*ronin*) share the *jidai-geki* cosmos with many expert swordsmen who are nonsamurai commoners. These heroes from the lower classes are usually vagabond *yakuza*—gamblers and outlaws of the mid-nineteenth century.

[9] A Japanese art is often transmedia or multimedia in its "means" while its "subject" is seemingly constrained by a closely defined genre. This is the opposite of the post-Renaissance European tendency to attempt to push content beyond the restrictions of genre but to confine the work to a highly circumscribed, isolated medium.

[10] There have been many films based on this novel. Kenji Misumi's 1961 version, under the title of *Sword of Doom*, has been the one most widely shown outside Japan.

Following his lead, other *taishu bungaku* (popular literature)
writers such as Shin Hasegawa, Eiji Yoshikawa, Genzo Murakami, Kan Shimozawa, Jiro Osaragi, and Matsutaro Kawaguchi eventually broadened and "modernized" the world of Edo era (1600–1868) swordsmen.

In the same decade of the publication of *Daibosatsu Pass*, the Shinkokugeki troupe was organized with the goal of creating a modern form of popular theater. After several unsuccessful and excessively cosmopolitan experiments, this troupe began to concentrate on plays influenced by or adapted from the new swordsman novels of Nakazato and his followers. The exciting action of Shinkokugeki plays, especially their spectacular swordfighting scenes, helped establish the troupe as a commercial and artistic power in theater after 1919. In the early 1920s, a few screen versions of Shinkokugeki stage productions were the foundation for the new style of costume adventure movie that became the *jidai-geki* film.[11] Since then, novel, film, and drama have moved together in the evolution of the transmedia megagenre *jidai-geki*.

One of the defining characteristics of this megagenre is that it functions, in part, as if it were a preliterate oral epic tradition. Within such a tradition, the tellers of tales repeatedly transmit familiar stories of a widely known common heritage rather than create original, unique stories.[12] Similarly, the *jidai-geki* storytellers draw from a central narrative cosmos of established plots, themes, scenes, and characters to recreate—some might say reassemble—oft-told tales. The primary task of the teller is to tell the familiar story better than it has been told before.

[11] This development is discussed in Chapter 3. Apart from the principal Shinkokugeki influence, the spectacular swordfighting in Douglas Fairbanks's swashbuckling features and the solitary, avenging figure of William S. Hart in his pre-1920 Westerns suggested other useful choreographic and iconographic elements to the early makers of *jidai-geki* films.

[12] *Kodan* and other Japanese oral storyteller traditions that preceded the modern *jidai-geki* also exhibit some aspects of preliterate oral epics but are not, in themselves, such forms. Unlike the storytellers of oral literature, *kodan* performers do not reconstruct stories aloud and anew at each performance. They read from scripts or pretend to do so. As different performers tend to work from their individual proprietary fixed texts, the stories vary from performer to performer rather than from performance to performance. *Kodan* evolved out of fifteenth-century and earlier traditions of public *readers* of war chronicles and Buddhist sermons. The heroic, near legendary stories of *kodan* are not precisely epic according to conventional European definitions of epic. For a discussion of oral literature within the Western narrative tradition, see Robert Scholes and Robert Kellogg, *The Nature of Narrative* (London: Oxford University Press, 1966).

While researching films that present *The Forty-Seven*
Loyal Ronin (Chushingura) story or the many characters
and incidents related to it, I stopped counting at 220 features.
Films that touch on the Shinsengumi[13] must be at least this
numerous. These and other narratives within the *jidai-geki*
cosmos seem too extensive or too capable of sustaining interesting variations to be constrained and frozen in one definitive version. Thus, *jidai-geki*, although seemingly bound
by the limits of genre, is always open for innumerable per-
mutations of its narrative elements. With repetition as its aesthetic keystone, *jidai-geki* affirms both Freud's observation
that the reexperiencing of something identical is "in itself a
source of pleasure" and Jung's suggestion that reoccurrences
with slight variations produce unexpected insights of an order quite different from logically derived conclusions.

At all levels of making and witnessing *jidai-geki* there
seems to be an awareness of how the narrative elements were
handled before. This self-referential tendency manifests itself most obviously (as it does in other Japanese film genres)
in streams of remakes. Directors even remake their own
films. Here again is the Japanese fascination with competitive, gamelike artistic endeavor that allows opportunities to
directly test one's talents against those of others.

The typical *jidai-geki* narrative has an autonomy that
transcends individual interpretation by a writer, film director, or actor. The audience's familiarity with the story rein-
forces the supremacy of actors' performances over the
script itself—just as it has always done in Japanese theater.
The illusions of reality never completely mask the reality
of the film or play artifice. The actor does not become the
character, he performs the character. While an actor may
become known for his portrayal of a certain character, the
two seldom become one. On television today—whether *jidai-
geki* or *gendai-geki*—leading roles have been unhesitatingly
recast during the run of a series without any felt need to
write the character out. For thirty-five years, Kanjiro
Arashi played Kurama Tengu in forty *jidai-geki* films. During that time, at least eight other stars challenged Arashi's famous interpretation in forty other Kurama Tengu features.
None of the nine was Kurama Tengu. Most of the actors
were very good at playing Kurama Tengu. In Japan one

---

[13] A group of 1860s *ronin* mercenaries recruited by the faltering
Tokugawa Shogunate in its defense against the rising Imperial loyalists
of Kyoto.

can engage in serious, extended critical discourse about the
qualities of different interpretations of a character. In America only one or two eccentrics can talk discerningly about the varying qualities of the Wyatt Earps acted by Henry Fonda, Walter Houston, Johnny Mack Brown, Ronald Reagan, Joel McCrea, and James Garner.

This megagenre is a self-renewing activity. In each reworking of a *jidai-geki* story, the familiar elements and interpretations change with the times. Over a period of two decades, Hiroshi Inagaki made three versions of the story of Musashi Miyamoto and his archrival Kojiro Sasaki. Seen in tandem, each of these works beautifully projects the *Zeitgeist* of its making: early 1940s, Occupation, and post-Occupation eras.

Even as the genre elements of *jidai-geki* set apparent limits, these limits when approached give way to all kinds of innovation, for *jidai-geki* storytelling also embraces the modern impulse to create new, unique stories. Early on, novelist Nakazato invented a contemporary but costumed hero who was quite distinct from his *bushido*-ridden counterparts in feudal *kodan*. The *jidai-geki* cosmos readily absorbs new material from any source at any time. The essentials of *Les Misérables* were assimilated into *jidai-geki* half a century ago. During the early 1960s, the fundamental aesthetics for staging obligatory *chambara* swordfighting quickly transformed from a semirealistic, understated choreographic approach to a highly illusionistic, explicitly violent and bloody form that had been pioneered by Kurosawa in *Yojimbo* and *Sanjuro*.

The *jidai-geki* embodies yet another essential feature of the oral epic tradition. It treats historical personages, places, and events unrestrained by the limitations of history. Implicit in *jidai-geki* is that ancient invocation to the muse that Homer uttered to encourage his imagination. The empirical histories of the forty-seven *ronin*, the Shinsengumi, Musashi Miyamoto, Chuji Kunisada, Komon Mito, and Jirocho from Shimizu—all of whom really lived—have long been lost in the *jidai-geki* cosmos. There they mix freely with innumerable characters and events sprung out of authors' fancies. Fact and fable go hand in hand because the mythic impulse makes the imaginary and the historical equal.

While history as history gets lost, historical events and persons as well as specific geographic locations and precise temporal settings are essential. A *jidai-geki* sensibility maintains that artistic semblance of the historic is most important;

correspondence to fact is not. When Japan looked at the

American television series *Shogun* (in an abbreviated version), the author's disregard of broad historical fact was to
be expected. It was proper exercise of a storyteller's right to
fabulation. But along with the overall failure to capture the
feel of the early Shogun era, the author's use of fictitious
names for historical persons was perverse, even ridiculous.
The shogun of the title was Ieyasu. Ieyasu, as well as the
British hero Will Adams, once existed. The proper task was
to say whatever fascinating and imaginative things you
wanted to about Ieyasu and Adams but you had to get their
names and their milieu right.

A long time ago the shining prince Genji concluded—if I
read him correctly—that differentiation between fact and
fiction in a tale is of no consequence as long as the teller
evokes convincing pathos, records a sufficient number of accurate details, suggests imaginative truths, confronts the
duality of good and evil, and reveals the human soul.

TWO INFLUENCES AND THE JAPANESE FILM

Japanese film histories and autobiographies have come to
a consensus about an extraordinary American influence on
Japanese film. So strong have these been collective arguments over six decades that study of this seminal effect might
be a paradigm with which to test the very concept of influence.

Few American films played Japan until 1916, when Universal set up a Tokyo branch that became the first systematic importer of Hollywood product. Scattered among the
serials and action features were some items that Japanese
found different. These were hour-long program pictures
from one of the lesser Universal production units, Bluebird
Photoplays.[14]

Japanese welcomed the light melodramas of Bluebird as
an alternative to the usual foreign movie attractions of thrills,
slapstick, glamour, fantasy, spectacle, and sophistication.
Bluebird films revealed emotional and moral possibilities beyond the limits of feudally based *Kyuha* and *Shimpa* which,
up to that time, were the only narrative forms of the Japanese film. These Photoplays had "beautiful shots of nature,

[14] Of the 184 features made by the short-lived Bluebird Photoplay
unit of Universal between 1916 and 1919, approximately 120 were released in Japan. These Bluebird Photoplays are not to be confused
with features made by the independent Bluebird Company that was
active from 1916 to 1927.

downtrodden but determined young heroines, and an abundance of simple sentiment." The leads, especially the heroines played by Myrtle Gonzales and Louise Lovely, were
attractive young people. In the background there were suffering, iconized mothers. The settings in Bluebird films were
usually rural, although some took place in urban environments with stories about young working people new to city
ways.

One early Japanese film historian was certain that there
were only four major categories of American moving pictures: "farce-comedies, serials, action features, and artistic—
Bluebird." A critic wrote that "when you compare a Bluebird film with films that have come before, you get the sen-
sation of suddenly moving from the playwrights of the Edo
period to the literature of the Naturalists" (i.e., novelists
Toson Shimazaki, Katai Tayama, and Shusei Tokuda). The
most impressive pictures—or at least those best remembered
—were *Shoes, The Girl of Lost Lake, Southern Justice,
Mother of Mine, Desire of the Moth*, and *A Kentucky Cinderella*. The principal credits were scenarist-directors Lynn
F. Reynolds, Lois Weber, Rupert Julian, and Ida May Park.
The strong presence of women filmmakers (two in the
above list) at Bluebird is significant along with the emphasis
on heroines, mothers, and domestic situations. This canon
suggests uncommon feminine sentiment as well as unex-
plored, unrecognized feminine talent most likely descending
from the scribbling women of the American nineteenth century.

Bluebird films encouraged *benshi* to be less didactic about
the exotic and less pompous in their attitudes toward their
audiences. A *benshi* interpretation for the ending of *Southern Justice* in which two young lovers are at last united in
the hills of Kentucky is still quoted today as an exemplar.

> Stars scattered across a lavender sky
> Blossoms fallen like snow on the green earth
> Spring, ah, spring
> It is Spring and romance is in the South.
>   [Fade out. Over The End:]
> The title is *Southern Justice*.
> Complete in five reels.

The line "Spring, ah, Spring" became an epiclike formulaic
phrase. Innumerable *benshi* repeated it beside other young
lovers' closing embraces (or fond stares in Japanese films).

As far as I can determine, non-Japanese studies of the
American film ignore Bluebird Photoplays. Yet the importance of these obscure pictures to the Japanese has been continually reaffirmed even though no print or even a fragment is known to have survived. The search goes on, for the Bluebird Photoplay is the ur-film of post-1920 mainstream Japanese film. Meanwhile, the available evidence is in contemporary reviews and in old timers' reveries about distant shadows.[15] Such diverse, important early talents as Norimasa Kaeriyama, Kaoru Osanai, Shiro Kido, Teinosuke Kinugasa, Eizo Tanaka, Daisuke Ito, and Kiyohiko Ushihara acknowledged Bluebird inspiration.

The critical and popular success of Bluebird Photoplays spurred the 1917–1923 reformation of the Japanese film by the Motion Picture Art Association, the Pure Motion Picture movement, the Shochiku film studios, and others discussed in the original text of *The Japanese Film*. More important, Bluebird Photoplays were absorbed and transformed in Japan. Their scenic elements, their repose, their naturalistic veneer, their interplay of casual with causal incident resonated with Japanese narrative temperament. The Bluebird line survives in the oldest and most pervasive studio style in Japan: the Shochiku *gendai-geki* (contemporary-life film). Since the mid-1920s, Shochiku films within this megagenre have exhibited characteristics as a group that transcend or engross the personal styles of filmmakers. Critics designate this Shochiku studio style "Kamata flavor" or "Ofuna flavor" after the successive locations of the company's *gendai-geki* studios. Some prefer to call it "Kidoism" after Shiro Kido, who spent half a century at Shochiku as head of the *gendai-geki* studios and later as corporation president.

Under Kido's creative management, Shochiku became the primary force in shaping the two perennially dominant *gendai-geki* genres of melodrama (*merodorama*)[16] and *shoshimin-geki*.[17] Both genres were excellent vehicles for convey-

[15] Looking at U.S. Copyright Office synopses, the range of Bluebird Photoplay stories was broader than what the Japanese remember. The overall output was similar to that of several other contemporary American companies.

[16] As a genre term in Japanese, melodrama more precisely defines stories in which a young heroine faces obstacles—familial, physical, emotional, and chance-medley—to the consummation of her love for a young man.

[17] *Shoshimin-geki* has the approximate meaning of "drama about the petite bourgeoisie." The original text uses the broader term *shomin-geki* which means "drama about the common people."

ing Kido's philosophies about suffering and happiness, tears and laughter, ideals and realities. Kidoism makes the family the microcosm of the nation and of the world. (For more detailed definitions, trace the entries for "Kido, Shiro" in the original index.) *Shoshimin-geki* and its descendent genres, the mother film (*haha-mono*) and the wife film (*tsuma-mono*), have ended up as the home drama (*homu dorama*). Home drama is the genre that has overshadowed all other possibilities for stories about contemporary life. The collective work of the old Shochiku masters Shimazu, Gosho, Ozu, and Naruse represents the glories of early home drama. Their masterpieces, whether made at Shochiku or elsewhere, are built on quintessential Kidoism.

Kidoism has prevailed even as the mainstream Japanese film has faded. Today, the home drama, which is inescapable on television, exudes Kidoism. It is Kidoism modified, of course, to accommodate the new Japan: generational conflict is heightened, quiescence and pessimism are gone, a few social issues barely intrude. Basically, everything is all right. On a lesser but industrial note, desperate Shochiku survived in the theatrical film market during the 1970s almost entirely on earnings from the semiannual releases in Koji Yamada's home drama series, *It's Tough Being a Man* (Otoko wa Tsurai yo; known abroad as the Tora-san series). It is the highest grossing feature film series in Japanese history.

My candidate for the most influential person in the history of the Japanese film, art or industry, is Shiro Kido. As Shozo Makino already holds the title of father of the Japanese film, Shiro Kido must be called its mother. Was it both the past and the future that Yasujiro Ozu saw on his deathbed in 1964 when he called out to Kido, "Mr. President, it finally comes down to the home drama, doesn't it?"

On or Down the Tube

The Japanese Film ended as television in Japan began to take off. Early television was dominated by live, low budget, small studio dramas and by imported American Western and sit-com series. In the mid-1960s, as the new medium penetrated 60 percent of all Japanese homes, domestically produced television shows rapidly drove out most of the foreign product. The exception, then as now, was feature films from abroad.

By 1970, television sets were in 95 percent of all households. Japan became the world's largest producer of television programs in order to feed the nation's four and half commercial and two public television networks' appetites for made-in-Japan shows. The major film studios continued to seek some of this action. Most of them produced television programs, with varying success. Several acquired partial ownership of stations. But not one major theatrical film company was able to secure a continuing position of strength in the television market. Following scattered sales of their out-of-release product during the 1950s, the majors collectively withheld their features and prohibited their contract stars from appearing on television. Then, in 1961, Shintoho, the weakest of them all, sold its library to television in an unsuccessful attempt to hold off bankruptcy. Within three more years, television reduced movie attendance so severely that the five remaining majors were forced to raise cash by selling off their postwar product. Few prewar films ever appeared on television because the postwar masses found most of the few films that survived uninteresting.[18]

The mainstream *jidai-geki* film tradition, with its necessary *chambara* excitement, easily shifted into weekly television series formats. At first television drew heavily from the entire cosmos of period film narrative materials but eventually *torimono-cho* ("casebook") series came to dominate. This once minor genre about police detection in the Edo era was able to combine standard swordfight thrills with the attractions of law enforcement and combating evil so popular in both made-in-Japan and imported American television detective series.

Another *jidai-geki* genre, the historical film, which had limited success in the late 1930s, reappeared in a new television form as *taiga-geki* (saga drama). The fall of the Shogunate, the revenge of the forty-seven *ronin*, the rise of the Tokugawa Shogunate, the varying fortunes of the Heike and Genji clans, and similar near legendary historical events are the narrative substance of *taiga-geki*. The longest running *taiga-geki* series—it begins its thirtieth season in 1983—presents a forty-five minute episode weekly for a full twelve months with a new story beginning at the New Year. Most *taiga-geki* are either based on a novel or appear concurrently with a novelization. Invariably, these books become best sellers. Historical sites featured in a *taiga-geki* revive as tourist attractions during the run of a series and some attract over

[18] From 1920 to 1945, the Japanese made over 11,000 feature films. Prints of about 2 percent of this total production are now known to have survived. When research for the original text was done, prints of fewer than forty prewar features were available in Japan.

a million fans, thus destroying the notion that television is a
passive medium.

Afternoon television drama for the past decade and a half has been primarily *yoromeki merodorama* (infidelity melodrama). The essential difference between this and earlier film melodrama is that the heroine no longer suffers without satisfaction. She now suffers after satisfaction. These shows somewhat resemble—but are not influenced by—U.S. soap operas and Latin American television *novelas*. As with many other kinds of Japanese television narrative forms, these melodramas run for an extended but finite number of episodes. After they climax and end, the time period is filled with another melodrama series.

One unusual form of drama on Japanese television is the *chukei dorama* (remote broadcast drama). Plays performed in Tokyo or Osaka theaters are covered as ongoing events in the manner of concert or sports broadcasts. Similar to the early years of the Japanese film, there is no disguising of the fact that one is seeing the transmission of a theater performance.

Over the past two decades, no other narrative form has successfully challenged the dominance of the television *homu dorama* (home drama) which merged the separate radio and film strands of this basic *gendai-geki* genre. The home drama portrays intimate family life in series or single programs with approaches that range from serious drama to farce. Most television home drama scenes take place in the *chanoma*, which is the multifunctional living and dining room of a Japanese house. As the *chanoma* is also the place where most television viewing is done in Japan, home drama approaches the ultimate in doppelgänger drama. Middle-class families of the most middle-class nation in the world spend hours looking into the television mirror at middle-class life. Home drama and its *shoshimin-geki* antecedents, along with *jidai-geki*, dominated as well as defined the Japanese film for almost half a century. Even though television assimilated and changed both of these forms, continuity throughout change remains the way of life in Japan. In 1982, 27 percent of all prime time television dramatic series were *jidai-geki* and about 38 percent were home drama.

The year of the Tokyo Olympics, 1964, marked the watershed of Japanese film history. Television spread rapidly. The movie industry changed forever. That year the Toei company, seeing its *jidai-geki* features lose out to *jidai-geki* on television, switched to a new *chambara* genre set in pre-

war Japan and based on the swordfighting violence of gangsters and gamblers known as modern *yakuza*. The instant
popularity of the new *yakuza* film destroyed the *jidai-geki*
as the theatrical film's arena for *chambara* excitement. By
1969, this megagenre's share was down to less than 5 percent
while the *yakuza* film portion rose to 34 percent of total
feature production.

Between 1956 and 1972, annual production held to a
steady average of 450 features even though the product mix
changed in many ways, as did the economics of the industry.
Following international trends of the 1960s, Japanese film-
makers treated sexual themes and scenes with increasing directness. This expanding freedom, coupled with the drop
in movie attendance, encouraged the development of another new genre, the pink movie. These films are very low
budget, one-hour long, soft-core pornography and are usually made by nonmajor companies and talents. The sexual
explicitness of pink movies, particularly their sado-maso-
chism, has increased over the years, although censorship still
prohibits crossover into hard core. Since 1965, at least half
of all Japanese feature film production has been extremely
cheap pink movies.

Movie attendance continued to decline. In 1971, Daiei
went bankrupt. Its left-wing union seized the company's
production facilities and held on for four years. The object
of this occupation was not to establish a freer creative environment for filmmakers or even to make films with ideological commitment but rather to restore assembly-line production of movies for the whole family. It didn't work.

Nikkatsu halted regular feature production in 1971 and
in the same year the three remaining majors underwent extensive reorganization that ended a lot of employees' dreams
of lifelong employment. Nikkatsu soon resumed production
on a smaller scale after its management decided to specialize
in a new genre of their own making called *roman poruno*
(pornographic romances/novels). *Roman poruno* are films
that accent the sexual elements but occasionally exhibit artistic ambition and even genuine achievement. One example
of this is the work of director Tatsumi Kumashiro whose
erotic pictures have deservedly made it to several of the annual *Kinema Jumpo* Best Ten Films lists.

Throughout the 1970s, the remaining big three movie
companies—Shochiku, Toei, and Toho—sought alternatives
to assure their survival in the theatrical film market while
relying on their diversified interests in hotels, transportation,

recreation, and real estate for most of their net earnings.
One direction was the disaster spectacular. Despite a few
blockbusters like Shiro Moritani's *Japan Sinks* (Nihon Chim-
botsu) in 1973, the odds did not favor such expensive
gambles. The Japanese, unlike the Americans and Euro-
peans, could not significantly penetrate the international film
market to recover their spectacular investments. Other efforts to build life-saving cycles included film versions of
gekiga (adventure and sex comic books descended from
kamishibai) and adaptations of Japanese gothic mystery
novels.

While the majors were retrenching in the 1960s, independent feature production by both established and new directors expanded. Many of these independents exhibited
their films through the small ATG (Art Theater Guild)
circuit. This company offered a limited but fair alternative
to the "tied house" system under which most theaters contracted to exhibit product from only one—or at the most
two—majors to the exclusion of all others. ATG began to
coproduce low-cost features with independents in 1968. This
provided a viable base for much creative activity until ATG
ran out of operating capital several years later.

Many younger filmmakers sought a collective break from
the past. Some had been contract directors who wished to
be free from the restrictions of the majors. In 1958, director
Yasuzo Masumura called for the destruction of the mainstream Japanese film because it advocated suppression of the
individual personality. Mainstream films, he claimed, were
totally congruent with the literary tradition of Japan. Characters in all of these narratives invariably submitted to the
world around them and to a collective self. Those few films
made by the old left-wingers who were supposedly in opposition to the status quo always had heroes who deferred to
the will of the masses. Nagisa Oshima became the principal
polemicist and soon the leading filmmaker of this new cinema. In his critical writings, he demanded an end to lyricism,
to heaviness, to naturalism, to *mono no aware*, and to the
tradition that made the best Japanese films hymns to victimi-
zation. Passivity of every kind was to be rejected. This included submission to the omnipotent conventions of the international cinema of realism. For me, what followed was
the short but fourth Golden Age of the Japanese film whose
like we have not seen since.

In 1925, Japan's 813 movie theaters attracted 155 million
admissions. Ten years later, attendance had slowly expanded

to 202 million at 1,586 theaters. During the 1930s—the dec-

ade that saw the eventual supremacy of the talkies—domestic film production averaged 500 features a year. Then, after a severe wartime decline, the film industry came back quickly until the highest annual movie attendance in history was reached in 1958 at the 1,127 million level. Two years later the total number of theaters peaked at 7,457 and dropped off quickly. This was also the year feature production hit its postwar high: 547. By 1963, theater attendance was down to 511 million. Two years later it fell to 373 million. After 1975, the decline leveled out at 2,400 theaters and annual attendance of 170 million. Feature production stabilized at about 340 pictures a year in 1978. Of this total, 75 percent were pink movies, *roman poruno*, and other marginal sex exploitation pictures. Activity remained approximately on these levels in 1982.

The Japanese film achieved something in 1925 that few national cinemas ever achieve. That year, without official support or encouragement, home-produced films captured more than half of the domestic market. This Japanese share increased (with slight variations) until a rapid decline set in during the mid-1960s. By 1975, total receipts for Japanese feature films were well below those for imports and still falling. Meanwhile, made-in-Japan programs more than held their own on television. At the bottom line in 1982, the Japanese film industry, in contrast to so many other Japanese manufacturers, had no significant foreign markets and the worst prospects at home. It had become Japan's answer to Chrysler.

by Donald Richie

In the twenty-some years that have passed since this book was written, Japan has undergone a vast economic and social change. Put simply, for the first time in Japan's history, economic considerations became paramount. This small archipelago, lacking most natural resources, able to feed only two-thirds of its present population, embarked upon a continuing program of modernization based on the double principle of consumerism and foreign trade. This, in a phenomenally short time, raised the Japanese standard of living to a European level, gave the people their first taste of affluence and leisure, and occasioned a serious erosion of traditional values. It meant that Japan could no longer afford many things (kimono, tatami mats, traditional wooden architecture) that had formerly defined the country, and many qualities (love of nature, reverence for the old, filial attachment to family and ancestors) that had formerly distinguished it. Such tradition was no longer affordable in the new supermarket society.

Film was early affected. With the increasing prevalence of television and the resulting decline of a large film audience, the motion picture industry began to feel the need to rationalize. This meant, a complete restructuring of the motion-picture-making process. Those companies late in doing so (Daiei, Nikkatsu) collapsed. As it turned out, those continuing (Toho, Toei, Shochiku) were saved only by their wide landholdings and their diversified interests. Though the new product, now controlled by businessman producers and not film directors, cannot be said to have successfully won back the missing audience (and may be said to have further alienated a part of the remaining audience), motion picture investment was such that the entire operation could not be closed down, though the companies have had to add earnings from supermarket chains, bowling alleys, etc., in order to balance their books. Also remaining is the new system whereby the producer decides what picture is to be made, who is to write and direct it and, more important, how it is to be written and directed.

Though such an approach may produce more and better cars or digital watches, it cannot produce good films. It was for this reason that the majority of Japan's film directors left their various companies and attempted to set up independent production units. This story is told by Joseph Anderson in

his essay in this volume. I will content myself with chronicling first what happened to the directors mentioned in the original edition of this book, and then discussing those who came after and what filmmakers are doing today.

Among the first directors to suffer under the new business conditions were those of the older generation. Heinosuke Gosho, who had seen it coming, was unable to work with the new production methods. His *Firefly Light* (Hotarubi, 1958), a very flawed film, represented a concession to Shochiku production methods and was his last picture for some time. In 1965 he formed his own company to make *The Woman from Osorezan* (Osorezan no Onna, also known as *The Innocent Witch*), distributed by Shochiku, which took a large cut of its slender proceeds. Though an interesting study in demonic possession, in which organized religion received a thorough trouncing, it was not a success, despite the unveiled charms of Jutsuko Yoshimura. Gosho was to make only one further picture, a weak puppet-film, privately financed, before retiring. Loaded with honors from various motion picture boards, he turned to writing his autobiography.

In 1959 Yasujiro Ozu began a series of three films that could be seen as remakes of earlier pictures. The first was *Good Morning* (Ohayo, 1959), which owed much to his 1932 *I Was Born, But . . .* ; the second was *Floating Weeds* (Ukigusa, 1959), a new version of the 1934 *Story of Floating Weeds*; and the third was *Late Autumn* (Akibiyori, 1960) which, though not a remake, contained many elements of *Late Spring* (1949)—with Setsuko Hara, who had played the daughter in the earlier film, now playing the forsaken parent.

Having moved to Daiei to make *Floating Weeds*, Ozu now went to Toho to make *The End of Summer* (Koyagawake no Aki, 1961), one of his most beautiful and disturbing films. In the following year he returned to Shochiku to make what became his final picture, the serene and nostalgic *An Autumn Afternoon* (Samma no Aji, 1962). After that Ozu and his scenarist, Kogo Noda, began working on the next script, *Radishes and Carrots* (Daikon to Ninjin), eventually filmed by Minoru Shibuya in 1964. Ozu had died on his birthday, that same year.

In these five last films Ozu continued to perfect one of the most controlled and individual styles in cinema. Without compromise and with his customary combination of patience and integrity, he continued to describe the Japanese family and—his sole theme, one prophetic in retrospect—its dissolution. A remark often heard at the time of the director's demise was that he had died at just the right time. In the new world of Japanese cinema, Shochiku (and by extension all other Japanese film companies) could no longer afford to make Ozu-like pictures. Where there is no longer a *shomin* there can be no *shomin-geki*.

Shiro Toyoda continued on within the Toho studio system, and made one outstanding adaptation, Kafu Nagai's *A Tale from the Other Side of the River* (Bokuto Kidan, also known as *Twilight Story*, 1960). Later, in the very teeth of the new system, he made one of his finest pictures, the story of the rise and fall of an utterly commercial woman (Machiko Kyo) in *Sweet Sweat* (Amai Ase, 1964). Ruled completely by economic expediency, the heroine might be viewed as an emblem of the Toho producers. In the event, however, such unprofitable honesty was soon stopped. Toyoda made two or three undistinguished programmers and then died in 1973.

Mikio Naruse, a director who had always had his ups and downs, made several excellent pictures before a final decline occasioned in part by the worthless scripts he was given. He directed *When a Woman Ascends the Stairs* (Onna ga Kaidan o Agaru Toki, 1960), one of his finest delineations of a good woman (Hideko Takamine) trying (as a bar hostess) to preserve her integrity. After this the pictures became more and more undistinguished. Even so he managed to illuminate some bad scripts such as *Bride, Wife, Mother* (Musume, Tsuma, Haha, 1960), with an honesty that transcended the doctrinaire scenario. Several quite bad pictures followed, including one that had Hideko Takamine as a hit-and-run driver. Naruse died in 1969.

Keisuke Kinoshita had, as early as *The Lighthouse*, indicated that he was moving toward a more conservative and generally acceptable film. At the same time his style, never as personal as, for example, that of Kurosawa, became more and more Shochiku-like. The last film that showed an interest in stylistic experimentation was *The River Fuefuki* (Fuefukigawa, 1960), a picture about three generations in a feudal family. The experiments were mainly technical (the story was one of those antiwar *films à fleuves*): the backgrounds were colored, the actors left in black and white. Shochiku found the results financially disappointing and

after the initial release all further prints were plain black
and white.

Kinoshita's only other notable film was *The Scent of Incense* (Koge, 1964), a three-hour home drama, again about generations within a feudal family. After this the director turned to television (one of the first of the film directors to do so) and began making what was frankly soap opera. The earlier irony had long disappeared, along with the care and concern that kept even later films this side of sentimentality. Returning to the industry from time to time (Shochiku and Toho), Kinoshita will continue to make feature films until the companies decide that even soap opera no longer makes money. He now devotes himself almost entirely to television, where his product finds a more ready audience.

Akira Kurosawa, during the two years following the release of *The Hidden Fortress*, was working on *The Bad Sleep Well* (Warui Yatsu hodo Yoku Nemuru, 1969), one of his strongest statements on the collusion between the government and big business in Japan. This was followed by two films with the same theme, both laid in the early nineteenth century, *Yojimbo* (1961) and *Sanjuro* (Tsubaki Sanjuro, 1962), and both built around the same hero (beautifully played by Toshiro Mifune). These popular pictures were followed by the cops-and-kidnapper film *High and Low* (Tengoku to Jigoku, 1963) and the long, detailed, and very humanistic *Red Beard* (Akahige, 1965).

The year 1964, the year of the Olympics in Tokyo, is often given as the watershed year between "old" Japan and the new, economically motivated, transistorized country it has become. In any event, in the new world of company allocation and rationalized film budgets, Kurosawa was given no work. He involved himself in a series of projects that proved abortive, the most expensive being *Tora! Tora! Tora!*, accounts of which are still confused: 20th Century-Fox says Kurosawa was fired; the Kurosawa staff say that he quit. Finally he got enough money together to make the singularly optimistic *Dodes'ka-den* (1970).

One year later, the director attempted suicide, an act occasioned by a number of causes: ill-health, the Japanese reception of *Dodes'ka-den*, the inability to find further funds for future projects, and doubts about continued creative ability. It is true that, he was considered untouchable in budget-minded modern Japan. For this reason, when approached by Mosfilm, he agreed to go to Russia to make for them *Dersu Uzala* (1975). Though the completed film cannot be considered one of the director's best, all of the mistakes were (in contradistinction to those of *Tora! Tora! Tora!*) the director's own—including the last-minute scrapping of a very good script and the substitution of a very inferior one.

Again, the picture did not do well at the Japanese box office and no Japanese funding for his latest project, a period film, *Kagemusha*, was to be found. Had not two American directors, Francis Ford Coppola and George Lucas, shocked at the plight of this great film director, talked 20th Century-Fox into partially financing the picture (after which Toho reluctantly picked up the bill for the rest), it would probably not have been made at all.

Kagemusha (1980), a historical film about the extermination of a great ruling family, proved to be Kurosawa's most bleak and least hopeful film. Though filled with compassion, it entertains no expectations other than death and desolation. Its structure is as severe as its philosophy and the result is beautiful, expertly crafted, and chilling. As Kurosawa's first Japanese film in a decade, it has been seen as a commentary upon what he himself has gone through. The hero, excluded, desperately to the very end trying to belong, becomes the excluded Kurosawa himself. The carnage-filled battlefield of the final sequence is a metaphor for ravaged contemporary Japan.

Kimizaburo Yoshimura found himself, along with Ichikawa and Masumura, out of work when his studio, Daiei, went bankrupt. His last good film had been *The Naked Face of Night* (Yoru no Sugao, 1958), an excellent exposé of infighting in the world of Japanese classical dance. It also proved to be Yoshimura's last major picture.

After the collapse of Daiei, he worked for various other studios but none was interested in the kind of picture he could do best—the Mizoguchi-like study of women in business for themselves. Toho, for example, had him direct *The Heart of the Mountains* (Kokoro no Sammyaku, 1966), an earnest film about an inspirational woman schoolteacher who wins over a number of rural children—not, as one might expect, the kind of picture this director would do well. Shortly after completing this film Yoshimura fell ill and has now remained inactive for well over a decade.

Tadashi Imai (alone of these directors featured in the original edition of this book) continues on making the kind of picture he has always made. And, though he has moved among various companies (most recently Toei) he is the

single director who has managed to maintain something of
his former directorial power. Part of the reason for this is, of course, that Imai has long proved himself ready to make small concessions to various producers. The major reason, however, is that Imai's reputation (in contrast to, say, Kurosawa's) among Japan's critics remains of the highest. It is not so much that Japanese critics have any real power with the paying public (or that Japan really has any film critics worth the name, except for Tadao Sato), but that they control the various annual awards for "best" films. A leftist orientation, safely social-minded, is always popular in these quarters and Imai's air of making responsible "social" pictures (though his targets are always unexceptionable—the iniquity of the military, big business, prejudice) is such that it ensures a critical following.

This having been said, it must also be noted that, even so, the films themselves have long turned into company products that lack the concern and sincerity of the earlier pictures. *The Cruel Tales of Bushido* (Bushido Zankoku Monogatari, 1963) and *Revenge* (Adauchi, 1964) are both grandly conceived but actually toothless attacks on Japan's feudal mentality; the popular multipart *River Without a Bridge* (Hashi ga Nai Kawa, 1968–70), about a very real subject, the social prejudice encountered by members of Japan's hidden outcast group, treated it in a way so sentimental as to represent no criticism at all.

Imai's best post-1958 films have been atypical. *When the Cookie Crumbles* (Satogashi ga Kowareru Toki, 1967) is the story of a Japanese Marilyn-Monroe-type (Ayako Wakao) destroyed by "the system," and *Old Japanese Women* (Nippon no Obachan, 1962) is about the problems of the old, with the now deceased Kinuyo Tanaka playing her age. Both are outside Imai's political frame and might indicate a widening interest, but one that has not since been further enlarged. More typical are films such as *Special Navy Junior Corps* (Kaigun Tokubetsu Nenshohei, 1972) in which the strong antimilitarism of the immediate postwar films has so mellowed that, did one not know Imai's critical reputation, one might almost take it for an exercise in nostalgia.

Turning now to those directors not featured in the original edition of this book but already active in 1950s, the first, and one of the most promising, I will take up is Kon Ichikawa. His earlier works had been distinguished by a very personal directorial style: strong composition, unusually terse editing, extremely economical movement within the frame, authoritative control over actors, and a pervasive

essay

sense of incongruity. At the end of the decade he made a series of unusually good literary adaptations including Tanizaki's *The Key* (Kagi, also known, ludicrously, as *Odd Obsession*, 1959), Oka's *Fires on the Plain* (Nobi, 1959), and Toson Shimazaki's *The Sin* (Hakai, 1961). He also made his film most popular abroad, *An Actor's Revenge* (Yukinojo Henge, 1963), and the famous *Tokyo Olympiad* (Tokyo Orimpikku, 1965).

At that point his films changed. Though the visual style remained he never again made films as fine as these. One of the reasons—perhaps the main one—was that he lost his scenarist, his wife, Natto Wada. It was this combination of her scripts and his realization that had made his pictures extraordinary. Though he has since made some interesting films, notably Shuntaro Tanikawa's *The Wanderers* (Matatabi, 1973), it is indicative that the best in this later period are all documentaries: *Youth* (Seishun, 1968), the short he did for Olivetti, *Kyoto* (1969), and the Expo '70 multiscreen *Japan and the Japanese* (Nihon to Nihonjin, 1970).

Having left the bankrupt Daiei, Ichikawa became a freelance director, which meant that he had to take whatever was offered him. Through Toho, he became involved with a publisher named Haruki Kadokawa, who produced a number of inferior films that relied upon vast TV and press publicity to insure houses at least initially full. For this producer he did, between 1976 and 1978, a series of pot-boiling thrillers based on the novels of Seishi Yokomizo. It was not until 1980 that he was offered a somewhat better script, the remake of the Kawabata novel, *Koto*. Back in old Kyoto, scene of some of Ichikawa's best films, *Conflagration* and *The Key* among them, he turned out a competent programmer flawed by the many concessions (Momoe Yamaguchi, teenaged singing idol, in the lead—a double role) he made with his producers.

One cannot, however, call Ichikawa one of the industry's martyrs (a title that might be better reserved for Naruse or Yoshimura). Being able to work has been more important to Ichikawa than the calibre of the work itself. One of the consequences is that he has been constantly employed. Another is that the majority of these later films are not worth seeing.

Masaki Kobayashi went on to make the three parts of *The Human Condition* (Ningen no Joken, 1958–61) and then made one of the finest pictures of the period, *Harakiri* (Sep-

puku, 1962). Based on a script by Shinobu Hashimoto, it is
the story of a young samurai (Tatsuya Nakadai in his finest performance) who rebels against the feudal ethos. Filled with irony, it is a film in the direct tradition of Sadao Yamanaka, Mansaku Itami, and the young Daisuke Ito. Kobayashi later made another film on the same subject, *Rebellion* (Joiuchi, also known as *Samurai Rebellion*, 1967), again from a Hashimoto script. Both films are distinguished by a strong eclectic directorial style.

Kobayashi's eclecticism (as pronounced as that of his mentor, Keisuke Kinoshita) is perhaps best seen in his most popular film, *Kwaidan* (Kaidan, 1964), based on four Lafcadio Hearn stories about old Japan. Each segment is stylistically separate from the others, the direction indicating the qualities of the four fairy tales, creating, as it were, an illustrated edition.

Like many (indeed most) directors, Kobayashi's films are only as good as their scripts; or, only as good as the director's interest in his script. After the social interest of the earlier films, and the moral interest of the later ones, Kobayashi encountered great difficulty in being allowed to make the films that he wanted. Toho turned down one project after the other and so the director finally turned to television. For Fuji Television, he made an excellent thirteen-part series (the original written by the distinguished novelist Yasushi Inoue) about a Japanese executive who on a business trip to Europe learns that he is, perhaps, dying of cancer. Cut down to three hours, this became *Kaseki* (1975), Kobayashi's last good film to date.

Yasuzo Masumura, influenced by both Ito and Mizoguchi (and a director not discussed at all in the original edition of this book), studied at the Centro Sperimentale in Rome before coming back to Japan for a late start in films. He brought with him a very advanced editing technique that pushed his pictures along at a rate unusual in Japan. He was, perhaps consequently, particularly good at comedy, and his 1960 remake of the Yutaka Abe 1926 *The Woman Who Touched Legs* (Ashi ni Sawatta Onna), was quite successful, as was the fast, humorous modernity he brought his adaptations, among them Tanizaki's *Manji* (1964) and *Love for an Idiot* (Chijin no Ai, 1967). His most successful film, and probably his best, was the first in what turned out to be a profitable series, *The Hoodlum Soldier* (Heitai Yakuza, 1965), with Shintaro Katsu. Fast, funny, beautifully paced, nonsocial, nonpolitical, and resolutely nonsentimental, it also proved to be among the last films Masumura was allowed to make.

The reason was the collapse of Daiei. After a long hiatus, during which Masumura worked for television, in 1978 he made a surprising and quite interesting film, *The Love Death at Sonezaki* (Sonezaki Shinju), a very literal adaptation of a Chikamatsu *bunraku* play. In it he returned to the spirit, if not the methods, of Mizoguchi and even managed to turn his liabilities (a small budget, having to use a popular rock star in the male lead) into virtues. His method was that of Japanese traditional theater itself: frontal shots, few close-ups, frank artificiality, and tremendous pace. Though the picture was critically well received it was not a popular success. Audiences no longer want honest period films when the tube is crammed with colorfully dishonest spectaculars. In consequence, Masumura has to date made no more interesting films.

In following what happened to the older and middle generations of Japanese directors since 1958, it becomes apparent that the industry itself acerbated its own problems by allowing only the safest of products, giving its writers and directors no freedom, and refusing to take advantage of all of the directorial talent that was emerging. When the movies were still making big money, then the new projects of Mizoguchi or Ozu might be allowed, and the talents of Kurosawa or Kinoshita encouraged. With money tight only company hacks were trusted with new product—with the result that the remaining audience dwindled.

Change came from an unexpected direction. Shochiku, in many ways the most reactionary of the remaining film companies, had seen that in France the so-called *nouvelle vague* (young talent, small budgets) films had made money both at home and abroad. In Japan too the early films of Godard, Truffaut, and Malle had made money. The consequence was that Shiro Kido, now president of Shochiku, decided to allow new, young Japanese directors to make films. A result was that three young Shochiku low-ranking assistant directors were suddenly elevated. They were Oshima, Shinoda, and Yoshida.

Nagisa Oshima, at the time politically far to the left, was given very small budgets and less than complete freedom but managed to direct four original scripts for the company. All failed to make the great profits that Kido had envisioned and consequently the official *nouvelle vague japonais* was short-lived, from 1959 to about 1962. It did, however, give the

Japanese film a much-needed impetus and indicated a way
in which films could be made in Japan outside the industry
itself.

After having been dismissed (or having quit—the stories vary) Oshima left Shochiku and began independent production. His first film was *The Catch* (Shiiku, 1961), based on a Kenzaburo Oe story about a black airman captured during the war and eventually killed by Japanese villagers. A powerful picture, it was also a parable of modern Japan (a form that most of Oshima's best work takes), with its love-hate relationship with the West, and its tendency to revenge itself through foreign scapegoats. It was a thoughtful, critical film, a great rarity in the 1960s, and (having cost very little) it made money.

Oshima was thus able to finance a whole series of pictures. As his reputation grew, Shochiku, smelling success, agreed to undertake distribution. (The rest were distributed by the independent Art Theater Guild [ATG] that was responsible for some of the finest Japanese films of the 1960s and 70s.)

Among Oshima's better films are *Death by Hanging* (Koshikei, 1968), *Boy* (Shonen, 1969), *The Ceremony* (Gishiki, 1971) and—perhaps his best—*The Realm of the Senses* (Ai no Korida, 1976). Though Oshima's interests have remained political (expressed through parable and allegory), including a concern with minority groups in Japan, with big business taking a pseudo-military role, etc., he has also become more and more concerned with larger issues not specifically political, notably the ever-pressing problem of being Japanese: how the peculiarly conditioned character of his people survives (or fails to) in the modern world. The lovers in *The Realm of the Senses* (very like lovers in, say, the Kabuki) willingly sacrifice their *giri* (social obligations) to the fulfillment of their *ninjo* (personal aspirations). That this takes a completely sexual form makes even more clear their social abdication (as dramatized, for example, in the scene where the hero on his way home from another exhausting encounter passes a group of soldiers, society's servants, on their way to a future war); it also deepens the pathos of their very human situation. (And in this quite nonpornographic film, Oshima uses sexual scenes not to titillate but to show the naked human being in his pathetic nudity.) The statement of this quite traditional *giri/ninjo* theme is enough. The director is not concerned with the right or wrong of the situation. He is concerned only with the allegorization of the specifically Japanese character: the difference between Japanese personal and collective character, the ways in which monolithic Japanese society affects its individual members. These are also the concerns of an Ozu. Oshima's conclusions (when there are any) are different, but the concern is the same.

Masahiro Shinoda, another of the young Shochiku assistant directors suddenly elevated, made a number of juvenile-delinquency films (the subject that Shochiku, having seen *A Bout de souffle*, thought *nouvelle vague* films should be about). He made his first mature film in 1963. *Pale Flower* (Kawaita Hana) is a parable (or even an allegory) of contemporary Japan seen through the unusually original view of its *yakuza* criminals.

Shinoda, originally an assistant of Ozu (among other directors), was not interested (except in his very early films), in Japanese politics. An admirer of Mizoguchi, he is now much more concerned with the aesthetics of Japanese life and the overtones of emotions within Japanese settings, as his beautiful version of Kawabata's *With Beauty and Sorrow* (Utsukushisa to Kanashimi to, 1965), the famous *Double Suicide* (Shinju Ten no Amijima, 1969) based on a Chikamatsu *bunraku* play, and the raffish and Kabuki-like *Scandalous Adventures of Buraikan* (Buraikan), scripted by Shuji Terayama show. This concern led to his somewhat empty illustrated editions of the classics: *Himiko* (1974), *Banished Orin* (Hanare Gozen Orin), and the disastrous *Demon Pond* (Yashagaike, 1979).

In only one film, Shinoda's best, has his original political interest and this later aesthetic concern come together. *Assassination* (Ansatsu, 1964), is a convoluted, multi-flashback, and highly detailed picture about the events leading up to the Meiji Restoration of 1868. It is filmed (in black and white) with a consummate concern for composition, for shot-linkage, and for a tempo that precisely fits the intentions of the film. It does not have the look of a Mizoguchi film, but many of its methods are those of prewar Japanese film prevalence of long shots, in both focal length and duration, and a lively awareness of space outside the frame) and the result is beautifully arresting.

Yoshishige Yoshida, the third Shochiku assistant director suddenly elevated, has had the least satisfying career. If Oshima's major foreign influence was Godard, Yoshida's was Antonioni, an influence seen particularly in films such as *The Affair* (Joen, 1967). After leaving Shochiku, Yoshida made *Eros purasu Massacre* (Eros Plus Gyaksatsu, 1970), a

political love story about the activities of Japanese anarchists
in the 1920s that splintered time and dramatized 1970 problems, but that also (like *Zabriskie Point*) could be seen as a
conventional romance spiced with politics.

One of the reasons that Yoshida could make such elaborate
independent films was that he was by then married to Mariko Okada, at that time a major star, wealthy, and daughter
of a man well-entrenched in the Japanese film world. She
appeared in all of his films, thus ensuring an audience, and
her popularity also helped induce Shochiku and other companies to distribute these pictures. Whatever their other intentions, however, these are essentially women's films, the
like of which have long been a Shochiku staple. This is, so
far, the ironic conclusion of Yoshida's career. Like his
mentor, Antonioni, in *The Mysteries of Oberwald*, who
finds himself making women's films with Monica Vitti, Yoshida discovers no means to make films otherwise. Lately
he has turned to making documentaries for television.

By 1960 many of the young Japanese directors (connected with Shochiku or not) had seen that their only chance
was to become independent. There were many problems:
Japanese banks do not give loans to problematical projects
like movies; since there are no anticartel laws in Japan the
major film companies control most of the theaters and show
only their own products. Nonetheless, with the help of
their own companies, or with the assistance of the ATG,
more and more directors continued to make their own films.
It is these almost alone that created whatever was worthwhile during the 1960–1980 period.

One of the first was Susumu Hani. In 1961 he made his
best picture, the semidocumentary *Bad Boys* (Furyo Shonen), a picture made with honesty and compassion about the
incarceration and eventual release of a juvenile delinquent.
Shot in prisons and using nonactors, it was distinguished by
an absolute absence of the usual heavy-handed Japanese
moralism with its bromides about to build a better society.
Though the film was never an official part of the Japanese
New Wave, it perhaps best expressed the original intentions
of a director such as Truffaut, realized in a completely
Japanese milieu through an utterly Japanese sensibility.

Hani went on to make a number of good pictures. Among
them were *She and He* (Kanojo to Kare, 1963) and *The In-
ferno of First Love* (Hatsukoi Jigokuhen, 1968), both
marked, as were his other films during this period, with a
documentary directness (even when using stars, such as his

then wife, Sachiko Hidari), an absence of any overt moralism, and a complete lack of sentimentality. Later in his career he moved more and more toward the straight documentary, doing an excellent series of animal pictures for television. His mature style is a very interesting combination of the compassionate with the dispassionate, something he shares with such Japanese directors as Hiroshi Shimizu and his favorite film director, Jean Vigo.

Another early independent film director was Hiroshi Teshigahara. Among his first films was *Woman in the Dunes* (Suna no Onna, 1964), based on the well-known Kobo Abe novel. An existential parable about a man trapped in a sand pit with a recently widowed woman, it concluded with the man's refusal to escape, realizing that he had created his own boundaries and that he was happy. It was distinguished by Teshigahara's great technical skill (extreme depth of focus, immaculate detail, elaborately choreographed camera movement) and by a very strong sense of personal style—one that he shared with his father, Sofu Teshigahara, *iemoto* of one of Japan's most successful postwar *ikebana* schools.

Teshigahara went on to make a number of Abe novels into films, among the *The Face of Another* (Tanin no Kao, 1966) and *The Burned Map* (Moetsukita Chizu, 1968—also known as *The Man without a Map*), all of them on the theme of identity and the loss of it. His last film, *Summer Soldiers* (1972), based on a script by John Nathan, was a very interesting study of American Vietnam War deserters in Japan. Its timing was bad, however, and it was a financial and critical failure.

Turning from films, Teshigahara became a potter and achieved an entirely new artistic reputation. Upon the sudden deaths of both his father and his sister in 1979 and 1980, he was suddenly elevated to the position of *iemoto* in the Sogetsu *ikebana* school, a role so time-consuming that films were dropped permanently.

Among other independent directors was Kaneto Shindo, who achieved international fame with *The Island* (Hadaka no Shima, 1960) a film that won many international prizes before it was finally, years later, commercially released in Japan. The reason for this surprising neglect was that Shindo was known as a leftist independent director and though the leftist orientation appeals to intellectual Japanese critics it does not appeal to Japanese distribution managers and theater owners. Though *The Island* with its poor, hard-work-

ing island farmers seems singularly devoid of visible leftist
politics, the Japanese establishment (film or otherwise) is
quick to assume political intent in what may be (occasionally) disinterested humanity.

For whatever reason, Shindo shortly began making another kind of picture. *Onibaba* (1963) and *The Black Cat*
(Yabu no naka no Kuroncko, 1968) are both period pictures, filled with exoticism, whose aims seem much more
erotic than political. Like many leftist directors Shindo
eventually turned to the investigation of sex. (This movement is to be noticed in leftist directors in other countries as
well.) *Lost Sex* (Honno, 1966), *The Origin of Sex* (Sei no
Kigen, 1967), and *Naked Nineteen Year-Olds* (Hadaka no
Jukyusai, 1970) were the titles of some of the later pictures.
All were very serious, even solemn, and none were in the
slightest degree pornographic. All were high-minded, which
separated them at once from the soft-core product that has
dominated Japanese film production (accounting for half
of its yearly output) after 1965. (These so-called "pink"
films, though they commonly serve as incubator for young
directorial talent, will not be considered in the essay, for
reasons of their quality rather than for reasons of space.)
Though Shochiku was quick to distribute the Shindo sex-
pix, it stopped once soft-core porn had captured the market.
Shindo has been inactive for a number of years.

Another so-called leftist director, one who has fared
somewhat better than Imai and Shindo, is Satsuo Yamamoto.
Celebrating the little people in films such as the 1954 *Street
without Sun*, and condemning the militarists in pictures
like the 1952 *Vacuum Zone*, he took on the medical profession in *The Great White Tower* (Shiro Kyoto, 1966), and
the wartime government in the multipart *War and Men*
(Senso to Ningen, 1970–72). In *Kinkanshoku* (1975) he attacked government corruption itself. By 1979 he was back
with the exploited little people (girl silk-weavers during the
Meiji period in *Nomugi Pass* (Aa, Nomugi Toge, 1979). In
both *Nomugi Pass* and *Spare-part Street* (Asshiitachi no
Machi, 1981) he attacked company exploitation of workers, in the Meiji period in the first, and today in the second.
Though addicted to melodrama and using an axe when he
should use a scalpel, Yamamoto is still the only major director
to concern himself with social issues in any critical sense.
Like Imai, whom he resembles, Yamamoto is truly concerned about the various inequalities of his world; he is apparently the only director who can see what is wrong in

this new workaholic utopia. Part of Yamamoto's problem is the very excess of his championing. He is all theme and no style. Consequently, his pictures, all well-intentioned, have no focus. They are doctrinaire studio products about nondoctrinaire subjects.

More interesting and much less doctrinaire as a director is Kihachi Okamoto, who was stuck doing musicals and light comedies at Toho until he was allowed to make a highly popular series of action period films: *Samurai* (1965), *Blood and Sand* (Chi to Suna, 1965), and *Daibosatsu Pass* (Daibosatsu Toge, 1966). Though he originally worked under Naruse, the two directors who had the most influence upon him (and under whom he also worked) were Senkichi Taniguchi and Masahiro Makino, both specialists in action pictures. Toho allowed him to make such prestigious films as *Japan's Longest Day* (Nihon no Ichiban Nagai Hi, 1967), a meticulous reconstruction of the day Japan surrendered and thus ended the Pacific War, and then put him to work on the usual company product. *The Last Game* (Eireitachi no Oenka, 1979) is one such: rival baseball teams become kamikaze pilots and carry their baseball spirit through to the conclusions of their missions.

Okamoto, a very talented director though one who has yet to achieve a unique profile, has often fought to make the kind of film he wants. For his best picture *Human Bullets* (Nikudan, 1968) he left Toho for the independent ATG and made this sad and funny picture about a young soldier who does not realize that the war is over.

Another eclectic action director is Kei Kumai, who studied under many directors. His first big film was the immature but thoughtful *Japanese Archipelago* (Nippon Retto, 1965). Having made it, however, he turned around and for Nikkatsu made the large and empty *Kurobe Dam* (Kurobe no Taiyo, 1968), a picture that celebrated that engineering feat. And such has so far been his pattern. Kumai will make the deeply felt *Long Darkness* (Shinobugawa, 1972) and will also make empty pictures like *An Ocean to Cross* (Tempyo no Iraka, 1979) Japan's first picture filmed in mainland China. A director has to eat, of course, but when Mizoguchi, for example, had to do a company assignment like *The Princess Yang*, he made it his own and consequently made a picture direct, personal, and alive. This Kumai, and most other younger Japanese directors, have not done.

To be sure, as is already abundantly apparent, these past decades have not been the best of times for film directors in

Japan. There is no industrial support, no one is backed up
by the head office, and independent productions run into all sorts of troubles. Perhaps this accounts for a number of talented younger directors who have been able to make only a few films.

Masashige Narusawa made only one film, though it was a very nice one indeed—*The Body* (Ratai, 1962), based on a Kafu Nagai story and starring Michiko Saga, the daughter of Mizoguchi's favorite actress, Isuzu Yamada. Yoshitaro Nomura (son of a famous director) made *Tokyo Bay* (Tokyo Wan, 1963), a very superior thriller, and then turned house director for Shochiku. Koreyoshi Kurahara made *Black Sun* (Kuroi Taiyo, 1964), an intelligent film about the bond between a Japanese jazz-loving youth and an AWOL black GI. After that he did little and has only recently re-emerged as a director of animal documentaries. Akio Jissoji made *This Transient Life* (Mujo, 1970) a strongly atmospheric and very Japanese picture about incest, and made little else. Toshio Matsumoto made *Funeral of Roses* (Bara no Soretsu, 1969) about the male prostitutes and transvestites of Tokyo, and the interesting *Hell* (Shura, 1971) before turning to experimental films, in which he now interests himself exclusively.

Typical of what happens to a very talented young director in the new Japan is what happened to Kazuo Kuroki. He made the beautiful and mysterious *Silence Has No Wings* (Tobenai Chimoku, 1967) and had much difficulty getting it distributed. Then, with the help of ATG, he made *The Evil Spirits of Japan* (Nihon Akuryo, 1970), again interesting, if somewhat inconclusive. Finding no further work he made documentaries and then, through ATG, was able to make his finest picture, *The Assassination of Ryoma* (Ryoma Ansatsu, 1974), a beautiful and economically conceived film about the last days of the Tokugawa government and the coming of the West to Japan. He was also able to make a very interesting small-town picture, *Preparations for the Festival* (Matsuri no Jumbi, 1975). At least Kuroki is able from time to time to make a film. Others are not so fortunate. In 1973 Toichiro Narushima made one extraordinary picture, *Time Remembered* (Seigenki), about a man remembering his youth. He was never able to find funds to make another.

Just as often, however, young directorial talent in modern Japan manages to survive, though usually to the extent of only one film every two or three years. Koichi Saito in

1973 made *Tsugaru Jongarabushi,* a very interesting picture
about life in the far north of Japan. Since then, working with
various companies and various sponsors, he has averaged a
film a year. His latest is *The Ship of Happiness Sets Sail*
(Kofukugo Shuppan, 1980), a cynical slice of urban life
based on a Mishima novel. Yoichi Higashi made *The Gentle
Japanese* (Yasashii Nipponjin, 1971), and went on to direct
Third Base (Saado, 1978), based on a script by Shuji Terayama who himself also makes films, and recently the very interesting *No More Easy Going* (Mo Hohozu wa Tsukanai,
1979), about a very modern Japanese girl (Kaori Momoi)
who finds out that she cannot live off men (the traditional
Japanese way) but must make a life of her own. Kazuhiko
Hasegawa made his debut in 1976 with *Youth to Kill* (Seishun no Satsujinsha), a film designed to shock—Japanese
youth kills parents—and has found backing for most of his
projects since, including his latest, about another alienated
Japanese youth who makes an atom bomb, *The Man Who
Stole the Sun* (Taiyo o Nusunda Otoko, 1979).

Nor have all the older directors faded completely from
sight. Indeed, one has only now emerged into full view. This
is Seijun Suzuki, for many years a Nikkatsu house director.
During this time he made a series of quirky, eccentric films
about gangsters and delinquents, the best of which is *Elegy
to Violence* (Kenka Erejii, 1966). Fired just before the Nikkatsu collapse, Suzuki was as surprised as the Nikkatsu officials at the resultant outcry; there was even a street demonstration. The reason was that his films were very popular
among the young. This "martyrdom" was all that was needed to make him Japan's single cult director. In 1980 he returned with the very popular *Zigeunerweisen* (Tsuigoineru-
waizen, 1980), a gloriously noncommercial evocation of the
Twenties in Japan.

Among these many directors (and among the many I
have not mentioned) very few indeed have managed to continue to make films and at the same time retain control of
the kind of films they make. In times inimical to honest
cinema, a director who keeps his own integrity and yet at
the same time manages to find work is rare indeed. The results are, on one hand, new directors quickly seduced into
turning out products for theaters or the tube, and, on the
other, older directors who simply are not allowed to work.

One of the major tragedies of this period was what happened to Hiroshi Inagaki, born in 1905, and one of Japan's
best period-film directors. It was he who continued this

genre in its original form and he who, almost alone at the
end of his career, still retained the forms of the early Japanese cinema. His 1962 *Forty-Seven Ronin* (Chushingura) is arguably the best version of the very many that have been made, and his last major film, *Samurai Banners* (Furin Kazan, 1969—scripted by Shinobu Hashimoto) is one of the finest of period-pictures, as well as the last authentic example of that genre.

Despite its moderate success, Inagaki found himself unable to work after that. He was considered too old by the new producers, all of whom were much younger, and he had never cultivated a major philosophical overlook—as had Kurosawa—that could lend his *oeuvre* the density that invites critical and scholarly attention. In the face of this indifference, and with the help of Shunsei Matsuda, a professional *benshi*, a collector and distributor of period silent films, and perhaps the only man who has managed to keep this tradition alive, Inagaki made one final film. A remake of a 1938 picture of the same name, *The Worms of Hell* (Jigoku no Mushi, 1978) it is a silent (music but no dialogue), black and white, standard format picture, made on location with a very small budget and donated services—the hero is the well-known Takahiro Tamura, son of the great Tsumasaburo Bando, period-film star extraordinary and lead in many of Inagaki's early pictures, who worked for nothing. The picture, never theatrically released and viewed only in civic halls, ward offices, etc., is one of the Inagaki's most perfect. Though filled with nostalgia, it is also filled with an integrity, an unobtrusive rightness, a moral concern, that makes any comparison with period fare on the tube ludicrous. Two years later Inagaki, who had been drinking heavily and was once again unemployed, died of cirrhosis of the liver.

Though this sad story is all too typical, there have been at least several directors from the middle generation who have managed somehow to find work and at the same time kept their professional integrity. Among them are Yoji Yamada and—now the most important director in Japan—Shohei Inamura.

Yamada became famous in 1970 when his *Family* (Kazoku) won all the prizes and broke the box-office records. The story of the travels of a family from the southern island of Kyushu to the northern island of Hokkaido, it had emotional honesty, humor, and concern for ordinary feelings that many thought had deserted Japanese cinema forever.

His 1972 *Going Home* (Kokyo), the same kind of film, further cemented his reputation. In the meantime his enormously popular Tora-san series (Otoko wa Tsurai Yo, which might be translated as *It's Tough Being a Man*) may be credited with bolstering the finances of Shochiku. It has been said, perhaps rightly, that Yamada and Tora-san saved Shochiku from bankruptcy. The Tora-san character (now in nearly his thirtieth film and always beautifully played by Kiyoshi Atsumi) is a descendant of Ozu's Kihachi character (seen in such pictures as *Record of a Tenament Gentleman*) —excitable, not too bright, but the salt of the earth. Yamada, who both writes and directs his scripts, is able to perfectly balance his product: it is funny but never abrasive, filled with sentiment but rarely sentimental. In short it represents what is best in traditional Japanese postwar cinema. Shochiku maintains that the mantle of Ozu has now descended upon Yamada, but Yamada is not of Ozu's calibre nor does he pretend to be. It is true that he almost alone is keeping alive the values of the Ozu film.

Shohei Imamura, who studied under Ozu (he was assistant director on *Tokyo Story*), is in all ways different from Yamada. His films either ignore or subvert traditional values. They seem to question all the important assumptions of the traditional Japanese, and certainly reveal an amoral vitality, a will to survive, and a roistering, scrambling humanity extremely rare in Japanese cinema—so rare that it is seen mainly only in Imamura's other teacher, the late Yuzo Kawashima.

One of Imamura's contentions is that the real Japan is nothing like the one it officially presents. Japan is a technological tribe, a land filled with the latest gadgets but controlled by the most basic (and the most natural) of urges, compulsions, and superstitions. There is no doubt, however, that it is precisely this quality that he admires in the Japanese, just as much as he dislikes the pretentions of later Japanese civilization. It is this often denied and sometimes submerged raw humanity of the Japanese, in essence uncivilized, that his films are about.

Imamura first came to wide notice with *Pigs and Battleships* (Buta to Gunkan, 1961), about the lower classes and the U.S. Navy in Yokosuka, a film filled with wonderful seediness, humor, and splendid energy. He went on to make *The Insect Woman* (Nippon Konchuki, 1963), an extremely fine study of a lower-class Japanese woman (Sachiko Hidari) scrambling her way up. This was followed by *Inten-*

tions of Murder (Akai Satsui, 1964) and *The Pornographers* (Jinruigaku Nyumon), both distinguished by documentary realism and a completely iconoclastic attitude toward Japanese polite society. In 1967 he made his very experimental "documentary," *A Man Vanishes* (Ningen Johatsu), a picture that creates itself as it goes along and ends up by questioning even the basis upon which it was originally conceived. In 1968, Imamura made *The Profound Desire of the Gods* (Kamigami no Fukaku Yokubo, also known as *Kuragejima: Tales from a Southern Island*), a project he had long wanted to direct, in which primitive Japan directly confronts the contemporary country.

After this, Nikkatsu having collapsed, and able to find no further backing, Imamura turned to making documentaries for television, some of the most searing and most revealing that have ever been made in this country. It was not until 1979 that he was able (for Shochiku, of all companies) to make another feature film. This was *Vengeance Is Mine* (Fukushu Suru wa Ware ni Ari), a film about the modern, empty Japanese turned criminal. It won all the prizes and made Shochiku money. The consequence was that, for the first time, Imamura was given a very large budget and was able to make *Eijanaika* (1981), a superb picturization of low-life Japan during the last days of the Edo Shogunate in the mid-nineteenth century.

At the same time, during these two decades of filmmaking, Imamura was forging one of the most distinctive styles in Japanese cinema. He himself says that the most decisive influence upon his style was Ozu, a statement that might surprise, given the fast pace, swift cutting and highly personal framing of the Imamura picture. Yet there is a decided resemblance. Both use only straight cuts, both are as much concerned about what happens outside the frame as what happens inside of it, both are meticulous about just the proper take, and both are masters of the long-held shot.

Also, if one remembers the prewar Ozu films, in particular those about the lower classes, Imamura's concerns and those of the older director do not seem far distant. Certainly, it is Imamura alone who reflects (in inverted form) traditional values, questions them, concerns himself with them. It is he alone that, among all the younger directors, expresses himself through a strong and unmistakably personal cinematic style. He, like Ozu, is an artist.

Though much and many have been left out, this brings up to date an account of what has happened to Japanese film and Japanese directors during the decades since this book was first published. I do not want to suggest that Japanese film has regained its original qualities nor reachieved its preeminence—one Imamura does not make a renaissance.

Perhaps the preeminence of the Japanese film is lost forever. It was predicated, after all, upon an audience that was able to look at itself as it was and draw solace, instruction, and pleasure from the view. There is no longer any such audience. The Japanese now, like everyone else, only want to be shown themselves as they would want to be. That ability to honestly evaluate, recognize, and accept that so distinguished this audience (and hence the films) has quite vanished, along with much else of traditional Japan. The Japanese audience has been just as brutalized by the violent, the mindless, the wish-fulfilling, both on TV and the screen, as any other audience. The appeal of a Yamada film is frankly a nostalgic appeal.

The appeal of an Imamura film, however, is something else. It also shows the Japanese as they are. If they can accept something this raw, this unflattering, and this fundamentally honest, then it can be said that there is hope for Japanese cinema yet.

bibliographies

THERE HAS UNFORTUNATELY been little foreign translation of what Japanese have written about the Japanese film. Widely divergent as such writings are, they collectively present a critical context and essential information not found in non-Japanese works to date. This does not mean that foreign views are inconsequential or invalid but rather that audiences abroad remain ignorant of an intrinsic element of film activity in Japan.

This bibliography is a personal selection from among several hundred key titles. Many important books about Japanese film are omitted as well as all works related to but not primarily focused on the subject.

In the citations below, authors' names appear in Japanese order, surname first. Place of publication is Tokyo except as noted. (J. A.)

HISTORIES OF THE JAPANESE FILM

Fujita Motohiko. *Gendai eiga no kiten* (Starting Points for Contemporary Film). Kinokuniya Shinsho, 1965.

Hazumi Tsuneo. *Eiga gojūnen shi* (Fifty Year History of Film). Masu Shobō, 1942.

―――. *Shashin eiga hyakunen shi* (Hundred Year History of Film in Photographs). 5 vols. Masu Shobō, 1955–56.

Iijima Tadashi. *Nihon eiga shi* (A History of the Japanese Film). 2 vols: Hakusuisha, 1955.

Ishimaki Yoshio. *Ō-Bei oyobi Nihon no eiga shi* (A History of European, American, and Japanese Film). Ōsaka: Puratonsha, 1925.

Iwasaki Akira. *Eiga ni miru sengo sesō shi* (A History of Postwar Social Conditions as Seen in Film). Shinnihon Shuppansha, 1973.

Okada Susumu. *Nihon eiga no rekishi: sono kigyō gijutsu geijutsu* (A History of the Japanese Film: Its Commerce, Technology, and Art). Daviddosha, 1967.

Satō Tadao. *Nihon kiroku eizō shi* (A History of Japanese Documentary Images). Hyōronsha, 1977.

――― and Hani Susumu, eds. *Renzu kara miru Nihon gendai shi* (Modern Japanese History as Seen through the Lens). Gendai Shichōsha, 1959.

――― and Yoshida Chieo, eds. *Chambara eiga shi* (History of Swordfighting Films). Haga Shoten, 1972.

Sekai no eiga sakka (Film Makers of the World [series]). Vol. 31. *Nihon eiga shi* (History of the Japanese Film). Kinema Jumpō, 1976.

Takenaka Tsutomu. *Nihon eiga jūdan* (Traversing the Japanese Film). 3 vols. Shirakawa Shoin, 1974–76.

Tanaka Jun'ichirō. *Nihon eiga hattatsu shi* (History of the Development of the Japanese Film). 4 vols. Chūō Kōronsha, 1957, 1968.

Tsukada Yoshinobu. *Eiga shi shiryō hakkutsu* (Film Historical Materials Uncovered). 7 vols. Tsukada Yoshinobu, 1969– .

Yamada Kazuo. *Nihon eiga no hachijūnen* (Eighty Years of the Japanese Film). Isseisha, 1976.

Yoshida Chieo. *Mō hitotsu no eiga shi: katsuben no jidai* (One More Film History: The Age of the Film Interpreter [*Benshi*]). Jiji Tsūshinsha, 1978.

FILMMAKERS' AUTOBIOGRAPHIES, ESSAYS, CRITICISM

Inagaki Hiroshi. *Nihon eiga no wakaki hibi* (The Youthful Days of the Japanese Film). Mainichi Shimbun, 1978.

Itami Mansaku. *Itami Mansaku zenshū* (The Complete Works of Mansaku Itami). 3 vols. Chikuma Shobō, 1961.

Itō Daisuke. *Jidai-geki eiga no shi to shinjitsu* (The Poetry and Reality of Period Films). Kinema Jumpō, 1976.

Kido Shirō. *Nihon eiga den: eiga seisakusha no kiroku* (A Japanese Film Biography: Chronicle of a Film Producer). Bungei Shunjū, 1956.

Kinugasa Teinosuke. *Waga eiga no seishun* (My Youth in Films). Chūō Kōronsha, 1977.

Makino Masahiro. *Makino Masahiro jiden: eiga tōsei* (The Autobiography of Masahiro Makino: Earning a Living in Films). 2 vols. Heibonsha, 1977.

Okamoto Kihachi. *Heso no magarikado* (Contrary). Tōkyō Supōtsu Shimbunsha, 1977.

Ōshima Nagisa. *Dōjidai sakka no hakken* (Revelations about Contemporary Authors). San'ichi Shobō, 1978.

———. *Kaitai to funshutsu* (Dissolution and Eruption). Haga Shoten, 1970.

———. *Ma to zankoku no hassō* (Expressions of Evil and Cruelty). Haga Shoten, 1972.

———. *Taikenteki sengo eizō ron* (Personal Views of Postwar Images). Asahi Shimbunsha, 1975.

Tokugawa Musei. *Musei jiden* (Musei's Autobiography). Hayakawa Shobō, 1962.

Uchida Tomu. *Eiga kantoku gojūnen* (Fifty Years as a Film Director). San'ichi Shobō, 1968.

Ushihara Kyohiko. *Kyohiko eigafu gojūnen* (Fifty Years of the Kyohiko Film). Kyoho Shobō, 1968.

Yahiro Fuji. *Jidai eiga to gojūnen* (Fifty Years with the Period Film). Gakugei Shorin, 1974.

Yamada Yōji. *Eiga o tsukuru* (Making Films). Daigetsu Shoten, 1978.

Yamamoto Kajirō. *Katsudōya jitaden* (Memoirs of a Movie Man). Shōbunsha, 1972.

Yoshida Yoshishige. *Jiko hitei no ronri: sōzōryoku ni naru henshin* (The Logic of Self Denial: Transforming the Power of the Imagination). San'ichi Shobō, 1968.

Yoshimura Kōzaburō. *Eiga no inochi* (A Life in Film). Tamagawa Daigaku Shuppanbu, 1976.

BIOGRAPHIES AND STUDIES OF FILMMAKERS

Imamura Shōhei. *Sayonara dake ga jinsei da* (Life Is Only Goodbyes). Nōberu Shobō, 1969. About Yūzō Kawashima.

Kishi Matsuo. *Jimbutsu: Nihon eiga shi* (Personalities: A History of the Japanese Film). Daviddosha, 1970.

Kuwano Momoka, ed. *Nihon eiga no chichi, Makino Shōzō den* (The Father of the Japanese Film, the Biography of Shōzō Makino). Makino Shōzō Hakkō Jimusho, 1949.

Misono Kyōhei, ed. *Kaisō: Makino eiga* (Reminiscences: Makino Films). Makino Shōzō Sensei Kenshōkai, n.d.

Ōtsuka Yukikazu. *Nihon eiga kantoku ron* (Essays on Japanese Film Directors). Eiga Hyōronsha, 1937.

Ozu Yasujirō: hito to shigoto (Yasujirō Ozu: The Man and His Work). Ban'yūsha, 1972.

Satō Tadao. *Kurosawa Akira no sekai* (The World of Akira Kurosawa). San'ichi Shobō, 1969.

―――. *O-bake entotsu no sekai: eiga kantoku Gosho Heinosuke no hito to shigoto* (The World of Phantom Chimneys: Film Director Heinosuke Gosho, the Man and His Work). Nōberu Shobō, 1977.

―――. *Ōshima Nagisa no sekai* (The World of Nagisa Ōshima). Chikuma Shobō, 1973.

―――. *Ozu Yasujirō no geijutsu* (The Art of Yasujirō Ozu). Asahi Shimbunsha, 1971.

Sekai no eiga sakka (Film Makers of the World [series]). Kinema Jumpō.

Vol. 3. *Kurosawa Akira.* 1969.

Vol. 6. *Ōshima Nagisa.* 1970.

Vol. 8. *Imamura Shōhei. Urayama Kurirō.* 1971.

Vol. 10. *Shinoda Masahiro. Yoshida Yoshiage.* 1971.

Vol. 14. *Katō Tai. Yamada Yōji.* 1972.

Vol. 22. *Fukasaku Kinji. Kumai Kei.* 1974.

Vol. 27. *Saitō Kōichi. Kumashiro Tatsumi.* 1975.

Shindō Kaneto. *Aru eiga kantoku no shōgai: Mizoguchi Kenji no kiroku* (The Life of a Film Director: Records of Kenji Mizoguchi). Eijinsha, 1975.

Tsumura Hideo. *Mizoguchi Kenji to iu anoko* (That Person Called Kenji Mizoguchi). Haga Shoten, 1977.

Tsuzuki Masaki. *Kurosawa Akira*. 2 vols. Intanaru, 1976.

Yoda Yoshitaka. *Mizoguchi Kenji no hito to geijutsu* (Kenji Mizoguchi, the Man and His Art). Tabata Shoten, 1970.

Yokoda Tomiko, ed., *Imamura Shōhei no eiga* (The Films of Shōhei Imamura). Haga Shoten, 1971.

CRITICAL STUDIES OF THE JAPANESE FILM

Fujita Motohiko. *Saraba nagawakizashi: jidai eiga ron* (Farewell Long Sword: Essays on the Period Film). Tokyo Shobō, 1971.

Hazumi Tsuneo. *Eiga to minzoku* (Film and Ethos). Eiga Nihonsha, 1943.

Imamura Taihei. *Nihon geijutsu to eiga* (Japanese Art and Film). Suga Shoten, 1941.

Kaeriyama Norimasa. *Katsudō shashin geki no sōsaku to satsueihō* (The Principles of Moving Picture Playwrighting and Photography). Hikōsha, 1917.

Kamimura Ryūshi. *Gendai eiga no shisōteki kōan* (Ideological Schemes of Contemporary Films). Doyō Bijutsusha, 1974.

Kishi Matsuo. *Nihon eiga ron* (On the Japanese Film). Komatendō, 1935.

————. *Nihon eiga yōshiki kō* (A Treatise on the Style of Japanese Films). Kawade Shobō, 1937.

Nishiwaki Hideo. *Autorō no banka* (Elegy for Outlaws). Shirakawa Shoin, 1976.

Ogawa Tetsuo et al., eds. *Gendai nihon eiga ron taikei* (Comprehensive Collection of Contemporary Japanese Film Criticism). 6 vols. Fuyukisha, 1971–72.

Satō Tadao. *Gendai Nihon eiga* (Contemporary Japanese Films). 2 vols. Hyōronsha, 1969, 1974.

————. *Nihon eiga riron shi* (A History of Japanese Film Theory). Hyōronsha, 1975.

————. *Nihon eiga shisō shi* (A History of Ideas in the Japanese Film). San'ichi Shobō, 1970.

Sawamura Tsutomu. *Gendai eiga ron* (On Contemporary Films). Tōkei Shobō, 1941.

Tachibana Takahiro. *Kagee no kuni: kinema zuihitsushū* (The Land of Shadow Pictures: A Collection of Essays on the Cinema). Shuhōkaku, 1925.

Takeda Akira. *Eiga jūnikō* (Twelve Lectures on Film). Shirōtosha, 1925.

Tamaki Jun'ichirō. *Nihon eiga seisui ki* (A Record of the Vicissitudes of the Japanese Film). Manrikaku, 1938.

Terakawa Makoto. *Eiga oyobi eigageki* (Film and Film Drama). Ōsaka: Ōsaka Mainichi, 1925.

Watanabe Takenobu. *Hirō no yume to shi: eigateki kairaku no yukigata* (Dreams and Deaths of Heroes: Toward Filmic Pleasure). Shichōsha, 1972.

Yamada Kazuo. *Eizō bunka to sono shūhen* (Image Culture and Its Peripheries). Keiryūkaku, 1975.

——, ed. *Eiga ron kōza* (Lectures on Film Topics). 4 vols. Gōdō Shuppan, 1977.

Yamane Mikito. *Katsudō shashin no kenkyū* (Studies of Moving Pictures). Kōbunkan, 1923.

SCRIPT ANTHOLOGIES

Over six decades, scripts for more than 4,800 Japanese and foreign films have been published in Japan, primarily in film periodicals. (At least three or four times the number of American film scripts or shot-by-shot descriptions have appeared in Japanese translation than have been published in English.) Three of the series below are retrospective and contain scripts from as early as 1918.

Nihon eiga shinario koten zenshū (Comprehensive Collection of Classic Japanese Film Scripts). 6 vols. Kinema Jumpō, 1965–66.

Nihon shinario bungaku zenshū (Comprehensive Collection of Japanese Film Script Literature). 12 vols. Seibundō and Rironsha, 1956.

Shinario Sakka Kyōkai. *Nenkan daihyō shinario shū* (Yearly Collection of Representative Film Scripts). Mikasa Shobō, 1951–58 and Daviddosha, 1959– .

——. *Nihon shinario taikei* (The Japanese Film Script Compilation). 5 vols. Shinario Sakka Kyōkai, 1973–74.

REFERENCE WORKS

Eiga nenkan (Film Yearbook). Jiji Eiga Tsūshinsha, 1950–69, 1973– . Called *Eiga geinō nenkan* (Film and Entertainment Yearbook). 1947–49.

Hosoya Katsuo, ed. *Nihon eiga sakuin: gensakusha betsu* (Japanese Film Index: Classified According to Author of Original Literary Work). Hosoya Katsuo, 1966.

Imamura Miyo'o. *Nihon eiga bunken shi* (Chronological Bibliography of the Japanese Film). Kyōho Shobō, 1967.

Inomata Katsuhiko. *Nihon eiga meisaku zenshi* (Comprehensive History of Japanese Film Masterpieces). Shakai Shisōsha, 1974.

—— and Tayama Rikiya. *Nihon eiga sakka zenshū* (Compre-

Iwasaki Akira et al., eds. *Eiga hyakka jiten* (Film Encyclopedia).
Hakuyōsha, 1954.
Nambu Kyōichirō and Satō Tadao. *Nihon eiga hyakusen* (One
Hundred Selected Japanese Films). Akita Shoten, 1973.
Nihon eiga haiyū zenshū: dan'yū hen (Comprehensive Directory
of Japanese Film Actors: Male Actor Section). Kinema Jumpō, 1979.
Nihon eiga nenkan (Japan Film Yearbook). Tōkyō Asahi, 1925–30.
Nihon eiga sakuhin taikan (Comprehensive Directory of [Individual] Japanese Films [1896–1945]). 7 vols. Kinema Jumpō, 1960–61.
Nihon eiga taikan: eigajin hen (Comprehensive Guide to the
Japanese Film: Biography Section). Kinema Jumpō, 1955.
Okada Susumu et al., eds. *Gendai eiga jiten* (Contemporary Film
Encyclopedia). Bijutsu Shuppansha, 1967.
Shimaji Takamaro, ed. *Nihon eiga kantoku zenshū* (Comprehensive Directory of Japanese Film Directors). Kinema Jumpō, 1976.
————, ed. *Nihon eiga sakuhin zenshū* (Comprehensive Directory of Japanese Films). Kinema Jumpō, 1973.
Tayama Rikiya. *Nihon no eiga sakkatachi: sōsaku no himitsu*
(Japanese Filmmakers: Their Secrets of Creation). 2 vols.
Daviddosha, 1975.
————. *Nihon no shinario sakkatachi: sōsaku no himitsu* (Japanese Screen Writers: Their Secrets of Creation). Daviddosha, 1978.
Zenkoku ni okeru katsudō shashin jōkyō chōsa (A Nationwide
Survey of the Condition of Moving Pictures). Mombushō
Futsū Gakumukyoku, 1921.

PERIODICALS

Since 1909, there have been over 220 nationally distributed
fan, critical, and trade periodicals related to film. The three below are my long-term favorite critical journals. Collectively,
they offer the most comprehensive source of materials on the
Japanese film. Japanese periodicals in general often have an additional name in English even though they carry no English text.

Eiga hyōron (Film Criticism). Monthly. 1926–45, 1947–49, 1949–
75. English names: *The Film Crit.* and *The Magazine of Film
Review.*
Eiga shi kenkyū (Studies in Film History). Semiannual. 1973– .
English name: *The Study of the History of the Cinema.* An

English translation of a section from one of editor Tadao
Satō's film books appears in the back of each issue.
Kinema jumpō (Cinema Biweekly News). Semimonthly. 1919–40, 1946–50, 1950– . English name: *Motion Picture Times.* Called *Eiga jumpō* (Film Biweekly News), 1941–45.

IN PREPARING this bibliography, I am particularly grateful for the help given me by the British Film Institute, UniJapan Film and M. Max Tessier. (D.R.)

BOOKS, PAMPHLETS, AND SPECIAL ARTICLES ON JAPANESE CINEMA

Anderson, Joseph L. "Japanese Cinema." In *Encyclopedia of Japan*. Tokyo: Kodansha International, Ltd. In press.
The best current short survey of the Japanese cinema from its beginnings to the present day.
Bock, Audie. *Japanese Film Directors.* Tokyo: Kodansha International, Ltd., 1978.
Series of essays on ten Japanese directors including much new material from Japanese sources and full filmographies. Balanced accounts of each filmmaker and detailed descriptions of various films.
British Film Institute. *A Light in the Japanese Window.* London: B.F.I., 1959.
———. Orient: A Survey of Japanese Films. London: B.F.I., 1959.
Burch, Noël. *To the Distant Observer: Form and Meaning in the Japanese Cinema.* London: Scholar Press; Berkeley: University of California Press, 1979.
The first half of this work contains the most insightful account of Japanese cinema ever written. The latter half loses itself in value judgments and political considerations.
Cinéma [Paris] 55 (June-July, 1955). Issue on *Le cinéma japonsis*.
Cinema giapponese degli anni 60. Pesaro: Mostra Internazionale del Nuovo Cinema, 1972.
A three-volume work. The first contains material on Oshima, Wakamatsu, Ogawa, and Tsuchimoto. The second, Imamura, Hani, Teshigahara, Suzuki, Kato. The third is devoted to Nagisa Oshima alone. Much information, some of it presented in a manner both pretentious and inaccurate.
Cinémathèque française. *Initiation au cinéma japonais.* (*Chefs-d'oeuvres et panorama du cinéma japonais 1898–1961.*) Paris: Cinémathèque française, 1963.
Giuglaris, Marcel et Shinobu. *Le cinéma japonais.* Paris: Editions du Cerf, 1956.
The first book on Japanese film in a Western language. Still a reliable guide to the cinema of the first decade after the war.
Mellen, Joan. *Voices from the Japanese Cinema.* New York: Liveright, 1975.

A collection of interviews, some of them containing information found nowhere else. When the questions are germane
to the filmmaker the results are valuable; when germane mainly to the interviewer, they are not.

———. *The Waves at Genji's Door*. New York: Pantheon, 1976.
An attempt to explain Japan's social history through its film
and vice versa. The results are readable but simplistic.

Revue international du cinéma [Paris], no. 14: *Regards sur le
cinéma japonais*. Undated.

Richie, Donald. *Japanese Cinema: Film Style and National
Character*. New York: Doubleday Anchor Books; London:
Secker & Warburg, 1971.

———. *The Japanese Movie: An Illustrated History*. Tokyo:
Kodansha International, Ltd., 1966. Revised, expanded edition, 1981.

———. *Japanese Movies*. Tokyo: Japan Travel Bureau, 1961.

Svensson, Arne. *Japan: Screen Guide*. New York: A. S. Barnes,
1970.
Now over a decade out-of-date, this remains the only reference work in English to list the majority of Japanese directors, writers, photographers, actors. Even ten years ago, however, the majority of the filmographies were incomplete.

Tessier, Max, ed. *Cinéma d'aujourd-hui: Le cinéma japonais au
présent, 1959-1979* [Paris], no. 15 (Winter, 1979-80).
Interesting collection of essays concerning contemporary
Japanese cinema and the newer directors. Contains much information nowhere else available in a Western language.

———. *Images du Cinéma Japonais*. Paris: Henri Veyrier, 1981.
Excellent, up-to-date coverage of Japanese film from its beginnings. An illustrated history with an historical rather than
a theoretical concern.

Tucker, Richard N. *Japan: Film Image*. London: Studio Vista,
1973.
Originally complete account of its subject with interesting
new material on period film of the Twenties. Publisher, however, insisted upon drastically shortening ms., resulting in
many apparent omissions that seriously throw off balance
of book.

BOOKS, ARTICLES, AND MATERIALS ON INDIVIDUAL DIRECTORS

Kenji Mizoguchi
Il cinema di Kenji Mizoguchi. Venice: Mostra de Venezia,
1980.
The most complete catalogue so far of Mizoguchi's works.

Douchet, Jean. *Connaissance de Mizoguchi*. *Documentation
FFCC*, no. 2 (1965).

Dudley, Andrew. *Kenji Mizoguchi*. Boston: G. K. Hall. In press.
Iwasaki, Akira. *Mizoguchi. Anthologie du cinéma*, no. 29 (November, 1967).
McDonald, Keiko. *Kenji Mizoguchi*. Boston: Twayne. In press.
Mesnil, Michel. *Kenji Mizoguchi*. Paris: Seghers, 1965.
Mizoguchi, Kenji; Yoda, Yoshikata; and Fuji, Yahiro. *L'Intendant Sansho* (Sansho Dayu). Translated and edited by Max Tessier. *L'Avant-scène du cinéma*, no. 227 (May, 1979).
Mizoguchi, Kenji and Yoda, Yoshikata. *Les contes de la lune vague aprés la pluie (Ugetsu Monogatari)*. Translated and edited by Jean-Paul le Pappe. *L'Avant-scène du cinéma*, no. 179 (January, 1977).
Richie, Donald. "Kenji Mizoguchi." In *Cinema: A Critical Dictionary*, edited by Richard Roud. London: Secker & Warburg, 1980.
Tessier, Max. *Kenji Mizoguchi*. Dossiers du cinéma 2. Paris: Casterman, 1971.
Ve-ho. *Kenji Mizoguchi*. Paris: Editions Universitaires, 1963.

Yasujiro Ozu

Ozu, Yasujiro, and Noda, Kogo. *Tokyo Story*. Translated and edited by Donald Richie and Eric Klestadt. In *Contemporary Japanese Literature*, edited by Howard Hibbett. New York: Knopf, 1977.
————. *Le voyage à Tokyo*. Translated and edited by Jean-Paul le Pappe. *L'Avant-scène du cinéma*, no. 204 (March, 1978).
Richie, Donald. *Ozu*. Berkeley: University of California Press, 1972. As *Lettre du blanc*. Translated by Pierre Maillard. Geneva, 1980.
————. "Yasujiro Ozu." In *Cinema: A Critical Dictionary*, ed. Roud.
Schrader, Paul. *Transcendental Style in Film*. Berkeley: University of California Press, 1972.

Though only one section is devoted to Ozu, it is itself so fine that it becomes required reading. The author presents the filmmaking ethos of director in such an informed and persuasive manner that the neglect of this excellent book remains mysterious.

Tessier, Max. *Yasujiro Ozu. Anthologie du cinéma*, no. 64 (July-October, 1971).

Akira Kurosawa

Burch, Noël. "Akira Kurosawa." In *Cinema: A Critical Dictionary*, ed. Roud.
Erens, Patricia. *Akira Kurosawa: A Guide to References and Recourses*. Boston: G. K. Hall, 1979.
Ezratti, Sacha. *Kurosawa*. Classiques du Cinéma. Paris: Editions Universitaires, 1964.

Kurosawa, Akira. *The Complete Works*. Edited by Don Kenny.
Japanese/English edition. Tokyo: Kinema Jumpō-sha, 1971–72.
Only six of the proposed twelve volumes of this series ever
appeared—and so the work remain incomplete.

————, Hashimoto, Shinobu, and Oguni, Hideo. *Ikiru*. Edited
by Donald Richie. London: Lorrimer, 1969. New York: Simon and Schuster, 1970. Also in *Contemporary Japanese Literature*, edited by Howard Hibbet. New York: Knopf, 1977.

———— and Hashimoto, Shinobu. *Rashomon*. Edited by Donald
Richie. New York: Grove Press, 1969.

————, Hashimoto, Shinobu, and Oguni, Hideo. *Seven Samurai*.
Edited by Donald Richie. London: Lorrimer, 1971. New
York: Simon and Schuster, 1971. Also, as *Les Sept Samouraï*,
in *L'Avant-scène du cinéma* (April, 1971).

Mesnil, Michel. *Kurosawa*. Paris: Editions Segher, 1973.

Richie, Donald. *The Films of Akira Kurosawa*. Berkeley: University of California Press, 1965.

————. *Focus on Rashomon*. Englewood Cliffs, N.J.: Prentice-
Hall, 1972.

————. *Kurosawa: A Television Script*. Broadcast June 19, 1975,
Channel 7, NTV, Japan. Published, *The Thousand Eyes Magazine*, no. 10 (May, 1976).

Nagisa Oshima

Burch, Noël. "Nagisa Oshima and Japanese Cinema in the 60's."
In *Cinema: A Critical Dictionary*, ed. Roud.

Oshima, Nagisa. *La cérémonie*. (*Gishiki*.) *L'Avant-scène du
cinéma*, no. 1936 (May, 1973).

————. *Ecrits*—1956–1978. Translated by Jean-Paul le Pappe.
Collection Cahiers du Cinéma. Paris: Gallimard, 1980.

Others

Gillet, John. "Kon Ichikawa." In *Cinema: A Critical Dictionary*,
ed. Roud.

————. "Teinosuke Kinugasa." In *Cinema: A Critical Dictionary*, ed. Roud.

Richie, Donald. "Mikio Naruse." In *Cinema: A Critical Dictionary*, ed. Roud.

charts

CHART 1
DIRECTORS AS PUPILS AND TEACHERS

This chart outlines teacher-pupil relationships which traditionally lead to entrance into the ranks of feature film directors in Japan. Chapter 15 discusses this apprenticeship system.

Each director's name is located on the chart horizontally opposite the year he made his first feature and vertically under the person who was his principal mentor. A solid vertical line indicates that a director spent a significant part of his career as an assistant working under the director whose name appears over his.

A broken vertical line represents a tie to a senior director other than that of assistant director. These alternative relationships are usually labeled on the chart. In all instances, "writer" refers to scriptwriter.

A dotted vertical line which runs up from a name indicates that person became a director by means other than a dominant teacher-pupil relationship.

All vertical lines only connect names. Their respective lengths do not represent any time values.

For convenience in presentation, this chart appears in five sections. These segments should be viewed as forming a continuous, interlaced whole.

Although this chart does not list all of the more than 1,000 persons who have directed features, the intention is to include every important director in the history of the Japanese film. It contains the names of 229 men and four women.
(J. A.)

1A

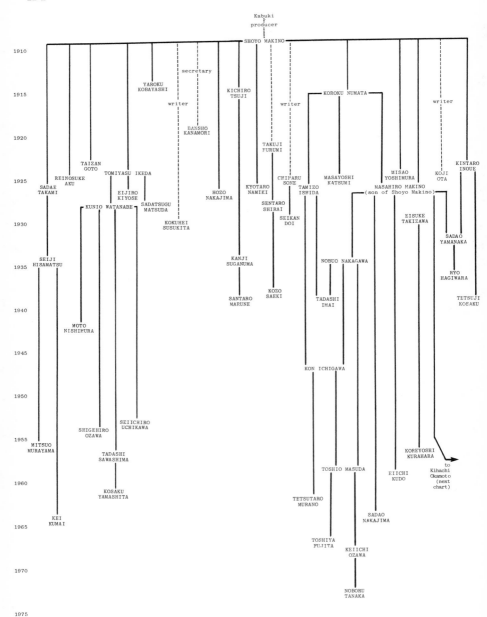

Kabuki
producer

SHOYO MAKINO

1910

YAROKU
KOBAYASHI

1915   secretary   KICHIRO
TSUJI   KOROKU NUMATA   writer

writer   writer

BANSHO
KANAMORI

1920   TAKUJI
FURUMI

TAIZAN
GOTO   KINTARO
INOUE

1925   REINOSUKE   TOMIYASU IKEDA   CHIFARU   MASAYOSHI   MISAO   KOJI
AKU   KYOTARO   SONE   KATSUMI   YOSHIMURA   OTA
SADAE   EIJIRO   NAMIKI   TAMIZO   MASAHIRO MAKINO
TAKAMI   KIYOSE   SADATSUGU   HOZO   ISHIDA   (son of Shoyo Makino)
KUNIO WATANABE   MATSUDA   NAKAJIMA   SENTARO
SHIRAI   EISUKE
TAKIZAWA

KOKUHEI   SEIKAN
SUSUKITA   DOI   SADAO
1930   YAMANAKA

SEIJI   KANJI   NOBUO NAKAGAWA   RYO
1935   HISAMATSU   SUGANUMA   HAGIWARA

SANTARO   KOZO   TADASHI   TETSUJI
MARUNE   SAEKI   IMAI   KOSAKU
1940

MOTO
NISHIMURA

1945

KON ICHIGAWA

1950

SEIICHIRO
UCHIKAWA

SHIGEHIRO
OZAWA   KOREYOSHI
1955   MITSUO   KURAHARA
MURAYAMA   TADASHI   to
SAWASHIMA   TOSHIO MASUDA   Kihachi
Okamoto
EIICHI   (next
KOSAKU   KUDO   chart)
1960   YAMASHITA
TETSUTARO   SADAO
MURANO   NAKAJIMA
KEI
KUMAI
1965   TOSHIYA
FUJITA   KEIICHI
OZAWA

1970

NOBORU
TANAKA
1975

1980

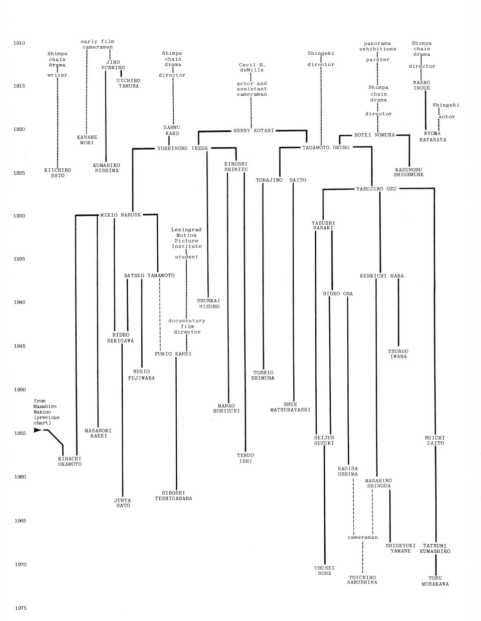

1C

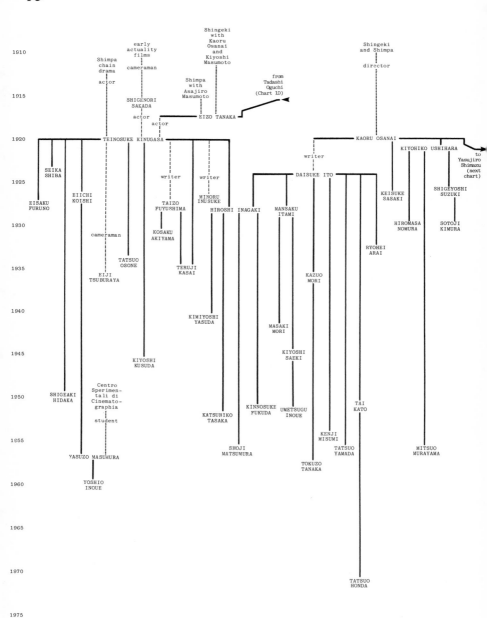

1D

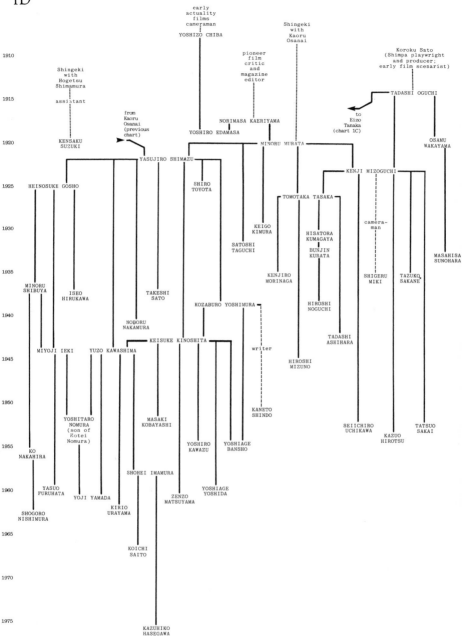

early
actuality
films
cameraman
⋮
YOSHIZO CHIBA

Shingeki
with
Kaoru
Osanai
⋮

1910

pioneer
film
critic
and
magazine
editor
⋮

Koroku Sato
(Shimpa playwright
and producer;
early film scenarist)

Shingeki
with
Hogetsu
Shimamura
⋮

TADASHI OGUCHI

1915

assistant

from
Kaoru
Osanai
(previous
chart)

NORIMASA KAERIYAMA

to
Eizo
Tanaka
(chart 1C)

OSAMU
WAKAYAMA

1920

KENSAKU
SUZUKI

YOSHIRO EDAMASA

MINORU MURATA

YASUJIRO SHIMAZU

KENJI MIZOGUCHI

1925

HEINOSUKE GOSHO

SHIRO
TOYOTA

TOMOTAKA TASAKA

1930

KEIGO
KIMURA

HISATORA
KUMAGAYA

camera-
man
⋮

SATOSHI
TAGUCHI

BUNJIN
KURATA

MASAHISA
SUNOHARA

1935

MINORU
SHIBUYA

ISEO
HIRUKAWA

TAKESHI
SATO

KENJIRO
MORINAGA

SHIGERU
MIKI

TAZUKO
SAKANE

KOZABURO YOSHIMURA

HIROSHI
NOGUCHI

1940

NOBORU
NAKAMURA

TADASHI
ASHIHARA

KEISUKE KINOSHITA

writer

MIYOJI IEKI

YUZO KAWASHIMA

HIROSHI
MIZUNO

1945

1950

KANETO
SHINDO

YOSHITARO
NOMURA
(son of
Hotei
Nomura)

MASAKI
KOBAYASHI

SEIICHIRO
UCHIKAWA

TATSUO
SAKAI

KO
NAKAHIRA

YOSHIRO
KAWAZU

YOSHIAGE
BANSHO

KAZUO
HIROTSU

1955

SHOHEI IMAMURA

1960

YASUO
FURUHATA

YOJI YAMADA

ZENZO
MATSUYAMA

YOSHIAGE
YOSHIDA

SHOGORO
NISHIMURA

KIRIO
URAYAMA

1965

KOICHI
SAITO

1970

1975

KAZUHIKO
HASEGAWA

1980

1E

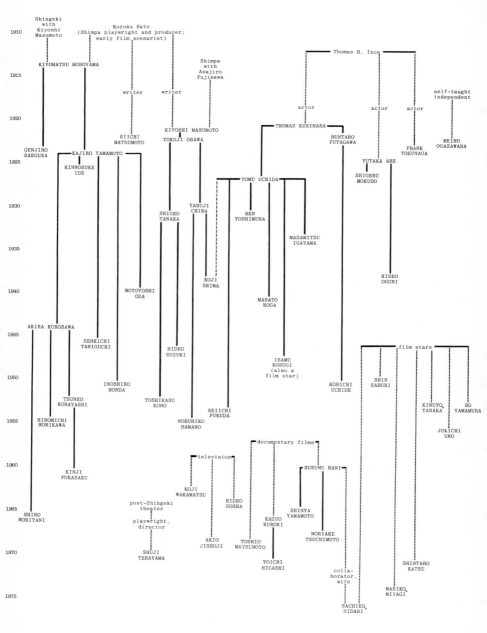

CHART 2
DEVELOPMENT OF FILM PRODUCTION COMPANIES

This chart traces the chronological development of all-important film production companies. A thick horizontal line designates a major company (which is defined here as one making more than 10 percent of total feature production during any year after 1912).

The length of a horizontal line represents the active production lifetime of a company. Dotted vertical lines which connect two or more companies show splits and mergers.

Data on prewar and immediate postwar companies comes primarily from a similar chart published by Tokutaro Osawa in 1948. (J. A.)

2A

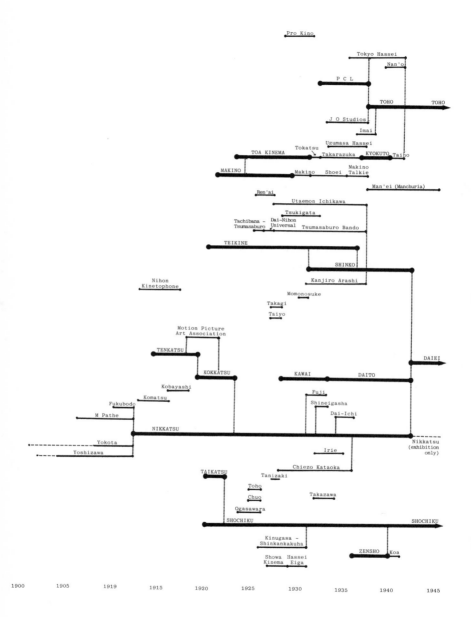

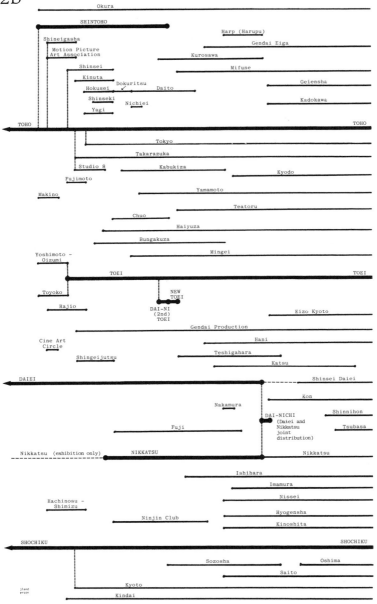

2B

index

index